Lecture Notes in Computer Science   8200

Commenced Publication in 1973
Founding and Former Series Editors:
Gerhard Goos, Juris Hartmanis, and Jan van Leeuwen

Marcin Grzegorzek   Christian Theobalt
Reinhard Koch   Andreas Kolb (Eds.)

Time-of-Flight and Depth Imaging

Sensors, Algorithms, and Applications

Dagstuhl 2012 Seminar on Time-of-Flight Imaging
and GCPR 2013 Workshop on Imaging New Modalities

 Springer

Volume Editors

Marcin Grzegorzek
University of Siegen, Pattern Recognition Group
Siegen, Germany
E-mail: marcin.grzegorzek@uni-siegen.de

Christian Theobalt
Max-Planck-Institute, Graphics, Vision & Video Group
Saarbrücken, Germany
E-mail: theobalt@mpi-inf.mpg.de

Reinhard Koch
University of Kiel, Multimedia Information Processing Group
Kiel, Germany
E-mail: rk@informatik.uni-kiel.de

Andreas Kolb
University of Siegen, Computer Graphics and Multimedia Systems Group
Siegen, Germany
E-mail: andreas.kolb@uni-siegen.de

ISSN 0302-9743   e-ISSN 1611-3349
ISBN 978-3-642-44963-5   e-ISBN 978-3-642-44964-2
DOI 10.1007/978-3-642-44964-2
Springer Heidelberg New York Dordrecht London

Library of Congress Control Number: 2013952935

CR Subject Classification (1998): I.4, I.5, I.2

LNCS Sublibrary: SL 6 – Image Processing, Computer Vision, Pattern Recognition,
and Graphics

Typesetting: Camera-ready by author, data conversion by Scientific Publishing Services, Chennai, India

Printed on acid-free paper

Springer is part of Springer Science+Business Media (www.springer.com)

Preface

Cameras for 3D depth imaging, using either time-of-flight (ToF) or structured light sensors, have received a lot of attention recently and have matured considerably over the last few years. Presently, these techniques make full-range 3D data available at video frame rates, and thus open the path toward a much broader application of 3D vision systems.

A series of workshops have closely followed the developments on ToF imaging over the years, like the Dynamic 3D Vision workshops in conjunction with the annual conference of the German Association of Pattern Recognition (DAGM) in 2007 and 2009, as well as the CVPR workshops Time-Flight Camera-Based Computer Vision (TOF-CV) in 2008 and later years. The advent of the Kinect depth sensor in 2010 as a versatile and inexpensive depth imaging device has further opened the field for depth-based algorithms. Today, depth imaging workshops can be found at every major computer vision conference.

As a consequence, a prominent selection of leading researchers in the field of ToF and depth imaging decided to initiate a seminar at Schloss Dagstuhl - Leibniz Center for Informatics, which was successfully held in October 2012. All aspects of ToF depth imaging, from sensors and basic foundations, over algorithms for low-level processing, to important applications that exploit depth imaging, were discussed. The results of this workshop are compiled in this state-of-the-art survey series on ToF imaging. Eleven chapters, with an average of 25 pages each and over 700 reference citations in total, convey an excellent overview over all aspects of ToF foundations, algorithms, and applications. The survey is divided into three parts. "Part I: Foundations of Depth Imaging", discusses in four contributions the basic working principle, sensor calibration, image enhancement, and the important issue of benchmarking ToF systems. "Part II: Depth Data Processing and Fusion", deals with advanced data fusion combining ToF, color and stereo sensors, the handling of mirror surfaces, and the tracking of deformable scenes. In "Part III: Human-Centered Depth Imaging", the important application area of human—machine interfaces using ToF images is surveyed. Human motion analysis from depth images, gesture interfaces, as well as full-body motion capture is analyzed. This section concludes with a survey on range imaging in health care.

As follow-up on recent activities in the field, a workshop on *Imaging New Modalities* was held at the German Conference on Pattern Recognition, GCPR 2013, in Saarbrücken, Germany. Part IV of this volume comprises the proceedings of this workshop. A state-of-the-art report on the Kinect sensor and its applications is followed by two reports on local and global ToF motion compensation, picking up a very current aspect closely related to Part I of the survey, and a novel depth capture system using a plenoptic multi-lens multi-focus camera sensor.

We would like to thank all the people who contributed to the workshops and the proceedings at hand. Special thanks go to the authors, the workshop co-organizers, the sponsors, the supporting organizations, and, last but not least, to the reviewers and members of the Program Committee.

August 2013

Marcin Grzegorzek
Christian Theobalt
Reinhard Koch
Andreas Kolb

Organization

Organizers of the Dagstuhl Seminar on Time-of-Flight Imaging: Algorithms, Sensors, and Applications

Christian Theobalt   Max Planck Institute, Saarbrücken, Germany
James Davis   University of California, Santa Cruz, USA
Bernd Jähne   University of Heidelberg, Germany
Andreas Kolb   University of Siegen, Germany
Ramesh Raskar   Media Lab, Massachusetts Institute of Technology, USA

Reviewers

Damien Lefloch   University of Siegen, Germany
Frank Lenzen   University of Heidelberg, Germany
Julien Thollot   SoftKinetic, Brussels, Belgium
Rahul Nair   University of Heidelberg, Germany
Ilya Reshetouski   Inria Bordeaux Sud-Ouest, Bordeaux, France
Andreas Jordt   University of Kiel, Germany
Mao Ye   University of Kentucky, Lexington, USA
Thomas Helten   Max Planck Institute, Saarbrücken, Germany
Foti Coleca   University of Lübeck, Germany
Sebastian Bauer   University of Erlangen-Nuremberg, Germany

Organizers of the Workshop on Imaging New Modalities

Reinhard Koch   University of Kiel, Germany
Andreas Kolb   University of Siegen, Germany
Ivo Ihrke   Max Planck Institute, Saarbrücken, Germany
Elli Angelopoulou   University of Erlangen-Nuremberg, Germany

Program Committee

Amit Agraval   MERL, USA
Oliver Bimber   University of Linz, Austria
Oliver Cossairt   North Western University, USA
Joachim Denzler   University of Jena, Germany
Jan-Michael Frahm   University of North Carolina, USA
Bastian Goldluecke   University of Heidelberg, Germany
François Goudail   Institute d'Optique, France
Oliver Grau   Intel Visual Computing Institute, Germany

Sponsoring Institutions

pmd technologies GmbH, Siegen, Germany
raytrix GmbH, Kiel, Germany
DFG Research Training Group 1564, University of Siegen, Germany
Deutsche AG Mustererkennung e.V.

Table of Contents

Part III: Human-Centered Depth Imaging

Part IV: Proceedings of the Workshop on Imaging New Modalities

Part I
Foundations of Depth Imaging

Technical Foundation and Calibration Methods for Time-of-Flight Cameras

Damien Lefloch[1], Rahul Nair[2,3], Frank Lenzen[2,3], Henrik Schäfer[2,3],
Lee Streeter[4], Michael J. Cree[4], Reinhard Koch[5], and Andreas Kolb[1]

[1] Computer Graphics Group, University of Siegen, Germany
[2] Heidelberg Collaboratory for Image Processing, University of Heidelberg, Germany
[3] Intel Visual Computing Institute, Saarland University, Germany
[4] University of Waikato, New Zealand
[5] Multimedia Information Processing, University of Kiel, Germany

Abstract. Current Time-of-Flight approaches mainly incorporate an continuous wave intensity modulation approach. The phase reconstruction is performed using multiple phase images with different phase shifts which is equivalent to sampling the inherent correlation function at different locations. This active imaging approach delivers a very specific set of influences, on the signal processing side as well as on the optical side, which all have an effect on the resulting depth quality. Applying ToF information in real application therefore requires to tackle these effects in terms of specific calibration approaches. This survey gives an overview over the current state of the art in ToF sensor calibration.

1 Technological Foundations

Time-of-Flight (ToF) cameras provide an elegant and efficient way to capture 3D geometric information of real environments in real-time. However, due to their operational principle, ToF cameras are subject to a large variety of measurement error sources. Over the last decade, an important number of investigations concerning these error sources were reported and have shown that they were caused by factors such as camera parameters and properties (sensor temperature, chip design, etc), environment configuration and the sensor hardware principle. Even the distances measured, the primary purpose of ToF cameras, have non linear error.

ToF sensors usually provide two measurement frames at the same time from data acquired by the same pixel array; the depth and amplitude images. The amplitude image corresponds to the amount of returning active light signal and is also considered a strong indicator of quality/reliability of measurements.

Camera calibration is one of the most important and essential step for Computer Vision and Computer Graphics applications and leads generally to a significant improvement of the global system output. In traditional greyscale imaging camera calibration is required for factors such as lens dependent barrel and pincushion distortion, also an issue in ToF imaging. In ToF cameras the on-board

M. Grzegorzek et al. (Eds.): Time-of-Flight and Depth Imaging, LNCS 8200, pp. 3–24, 2013.

technology is more complicated, and leads to different errors which strongly reduce the quality of the measurements. For example, non-linearities in distance which also require calibration and correction.

The work herein is a complete and up to date understanding of Time-of-Flight camera range imaging, incorporating all known sources of distance errors. The paper supplies an exhaustive list of the different measurement errors and a presentation of the most popular and state of art calibration techniques used in the current research field. We primarily focus on a specific ToF principle called Continuous Modulation Approach (see Sec. 1.1) that is widely used nowadays, because continuous wave technology dominates the hardware available on the market. However, many of the techniques described are also useful in other ToF measurement techniques.

The chapter is organized as follows: Sections 1.1 and 1.2 give an overview of the basic technological foundation of two different ToF camera principles. In Section 2, a presentation of all different measurement errors of ToF sensors will be given. Section 3 discusses camera calibration techniques and several issues that appear. To conclude, Section 4 will introduce current image processing techniques in order to overcome scene dependent error measurement which cannot be handled directly by calibration procedure.

1.1   Continuous Modulation Approach

Most of the ToF manufacturers built-in the following principle in their cameras such as pmdtechnologies[1], Mesa Imaging[2] or Soft Kinetic[3] (cf. Fig. 1). These cameras are able to retrieve $2.5D$ image at a frame rate of 30FPS; pmdtechnologies is currently working on faster device (such as the Camboard Nano) which operates at 90FPS. Note that common ToF cameras usually use high modulation frequency range that make them suitable for near or middle range applications.

Fig. 1. Different ToF phase based camera models available in the market. A PMD CamCube 2.0 (left), a swissranger SR 400 (middle) and a DepthSense DS325 (right).

---

[1] http://www.pmdtec.com/
[2] http://www.mesa-imaging.ch/
[3] http://www.softkinetic.com/

The continuous modulation principle, also known as a continuous wave intensity modulation (CWIM) [1], is based on the correlation of the emitted signal o_τ shifted by an offset phase τ and the incident signal r resulting from the reflection of the modulated active illumination (NIR light) by the observed scene. CWIM is used to estimate the distance between the target (i.e. observed objects) and the source of the active illumination (i.e. the camera). CWIM ToF sensors directly implement the correlation function on chip, composed of what is known in the literature as smart pixels [1].

The correlation function $c(t)$ at a specific phase offset sample $\tau = 0, \frac{\pi}{2}, \pi, \frac{3\pi}{2}$ is defined as

$$c_\tau(t) = r(t) \otimes o_\tau(t) = \lim_{T \to \infty} \int_{-T/2}^{T/2} r(t) \cdot o_\tau(t) \, dt. \tag{1}$$

Both emitted and incident signal can be expressed as a cosinusoidal function:

$$o_\tau(t) = \cos\left((\omega + f_m \tau) \cdot t\right), \qquad r(t) = I + A \cos\left(\omega t + \phi\right) \tag{2}$$

where $\omega = 2\pi f_m$ represents the angular frequency of f_m, I is the offset of the signal, A the amplitude of the reflected signal and ϕ is the phase shift directly relating to the object distance. Using trigonometric relations [1], one can simplified the correlation function as:

$$c_\tau = \frac{A}{2} \cos\left(\tau + \phi\right) + I. \tag{3}$$

There are three unknowns in Eq. 3 so at least three measurements are required in order to perform a single estimation of distance, amplitude and offset. Typically four samples of the correlation function c are sequentially acquired at specific discrete phase offsets $A_i = c_\tau, \tau = i \cdot \frac{\pi}{2}, i = 0, ..., 3$. More measurements improves the measurement precision but also incorporates additional errors due to the sequential sampling such as motion blur which will be discuss later on. The measured amplitude A, phase ϕ and intensity I are given by:

$$\phi = \arctan\left(\frac{A_3 - A_1}{A_0 - A_2}\right), \tag{4}$$

$$I = \frac{1}{4} \cdot \sum_{i=0}^{3} A_i, \tag{5}$$

$$A = \frac{1}{2} \cdot \sqrt{(A_3 - A_1)^2 + (A_0 - A_2)^2}. \tag{6}$$

Once the phase ϕ is reconstructed, the object distance d is easily computed using the speed of light in the dominated medium $c \approx 3 \cdot 10^8 m \cdot s^{-1}$ and the modulation frequency of the active illumination f_m:

$$d = \frac{c}{4\pi f_m} \phi. \tag{7}$$

Since the described principle is mainly based on phase shift calculation, only a range of distances within one unambiguous range $[0, 2\pi]$ can be retrieved. This range depends on the modulation frequency f_m used during the acquisition giving a maximum distance of $d_{max} = \frac{c}{2f_m}$ that can be computed. Note that the factor 2 here is due to the fact that the active illumination needs to travel back and forth between the observed object and the camera. It is understood that in this simple depth retrieval calculation from the phase shift, ϕ, simplifications are made which leads to possible measurement errors, e.g the assumption that the active illumination module and the ToF sensors are placed in the same position in space; which is physically impossible.

1.2   Pulse Based Approach

Conversely, pulse modulation is an alternative time-of-flight principle which generates pulse of light of known dimension coupled with a fast shutter observation. The 3DV System camera is using this class of technology also known as shuttered light-pulse (SLP) sensor in order to retrieve depth information. The basic concept lies on the fact that the camera projects a NIR pulse of light with known duration (i.e. known dimension) and discretized the front of the reflected illumination. This discretization is realized before the returning of the entire light pulse using a fast camera shutter. The portion of the reflected pulse signal actually describes the shape of the observed object. Conversely to the unambiguous range seen in continuous modulation approach, the depth of interest is directly linked to the duration of the light pulse and the duration of the shutter ($t_{\text{pulse}+\delta_s}$). This phenomenon is known as *light wall*. The intensity signal capture by the sensor during the shutter time is strongly correlated with the depth of the observed object. Since nearer object will appear brighter. This statement is not fully exact, since the intensity signal also depends of the observed object reflectivity property. As Davis stated [2], double pulse shuttering hardware provide a better depth measurement precision than the ones based on a single shutter.

Note that shuttered light-pulse cameras are also subject to similar errors introduced in Sec. 1. But due to the fact that this type of cameras are not easily available and that less calibration methods were specially designed for it, we will concentrate in the following sections on continuation modulation approach.

2   Error Sources

In this section, a full understanding of ToF camera error sources is developed (errors identification and explanation). Calibration approaches that tackle the intrinsic errors of the sensor to correct incorrect depth measurements are presented in Sec. 3. Errors based of extrinsic influences, such as multi-path reflection or motion can be corrected with methods presented in Sec. 4.

Beside integration time, that directly influences the signal-to-noise ratio (SNR) of the measurement and consequently the variance of the measured distance, the user can influenced the quality of the measurements made by setting the f_m value to fit the application. As stated by Lange [1], as f_m increases the depth resolution increases but the non ambiguity range decreases.

2.1 Systematic Distance Error

Systematic errors occur when the formulas used for the reconstruction do not model all aspects of the actual physical imager. In CWIM cameras a prominent such error is caused by differences between the actual modulation and correlation functions and the idealized versions used for calculations. In case of a sinusodial modulation Sec. 1.1 , higher order harmonics in the modulating light source (Fig. 2.1) induce deviations from a perfect sine function. Use of the correlation of the physical light source with the formulas 1.1 lead to a periodic "wiggling" error which causes the calculated depth to oscillate around the actual depth. The actual form of this oscillation depends on the strength and frequencies of the higher order harmonics. [1,3].

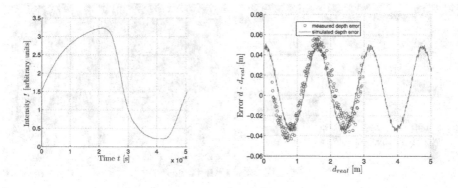

Fig. 2. Left:Measured modulation of the PMD light source: Right: Mean depth deviation as a function of the real distance. Images from [4].

There are two approaches for solving this problem. The first approach is to sample the correlation more phase shifts and extend the formulas to incorporate higher order harmonics[5]. With current 2-tap sensor this approach induces more errors when observing dynamic scenes. The second approach which we will further discuss in 3.2 is to keep the formulas as they are and estimate the residual error between true and calculated depth [6,7] . The residual can then be used in a calibration step to eliminate the error. Finally, [8] employ a phase modulation of the amplitude signal to attenuate the higher harmonics in the emitted amplitude.

2.2 Intensity-Related Distance Error

In addition to the wiggling systematic error, the measured distance is greatly altered by an error dependent of the total amount of incident light recieved by the sensor. Measured distance of lower reflectivity objects appear closer to the camera (up to 3cm drift for the darkest objects). Fig. 3 highlights this error effect using a simple black-and-white checkerboard pattern. The described error is usually known as Intensity-related distance error and its cause is not fully understood yet [9].

Nevertheless, recent investigation [10] shows that ToF sensor has a non-linear response during the conversion of photons to electrons. Lindner et al. [9] claims that the origin of the intensity-related error is assumed to be caused by non-linearities of the semi conductor hardware.

A different point of view would be to consider the effect of multiple returns caused by inter-reflections in the sensor itself (scattering between the chip and the lens). Since the signal strength of low reflectivity objects is considerably weak, they will be more affected by this behavior than for high signal strength given by brighter objects. For more information about multi-path problems on ToF cameras, referred to Sec. 2.5.

Fig. 3. Impact of the intensity-related distance error on the depth measurement: Left image shows the intensity image given by a ToF camera. Right image shows the surface rendering obtained by the depth map colored by its corresponding intensity map. Note that those images were acquired using a *PMD CamCube 2.0, PMDTechnologies GmbH*

2.3 Depth Inhomogeneity

An important type of errors in ToF imaging, the so-called *flying pixels*, occurs along depth inhomogeneities. To illustrate these errors, we consider a depth boundary with one foreground and one background object. In the case that the solid angle extent of a sensor pixel falls on the boundary of the foreground and the background, the recorded signal is a mixture of the light returns from both areas. Due to the non-linear dependency of the depth on the raw channels and the phase ambiguity, the resulting depth is not restricted to the range between foreground and background depth, but can attain any value of the camera's depth range. We will see in Section 4.1, that is important to distinguish between flying pixels *in* the range of the foreground and background depth and *outliers*. The fact that today' ToF sensors provide only a low resolution promotes the occurrence of flying pixels of both kinds.

We remark that the problem of depth inhomogeneities is related to the multiple return problem, since also here light from different paths is mixed in one sensor cell. In the case of flying pixels, however, local information from neighboring pixels can be used to approximately reconstruct the original depth. We refer to Section 4.1 for details.

2.4 Motion Artifacts

As stated in 1.1, CWIM ToF imagers need to sample the correlation between incident and reference signal at least using 3 different phase shifts. Ideally these raw images would be acquired simultaneously. Current two tap sensors only allow for two of these measurements to be made simultaneously such that at least one more measurement is needed. Usually, further raw images are acquired to counteract noise and compensate for different electronic charateristics of the individual taps. Since these (pairs) of additional exposures have to be made sequentially, dynamic scenes lead to erroneous distance values at depth and reflectivity boundaries.

Methods for compensating motion artifacts will be discussed in Section 4.2.

2.5 Multiple Returns

The standard AMCW model for range imaging is based on the assumption that the light return to each pixel of the sensor is from a single position in the scene. This assumption, unfortunately, is violated in most scenes of practical interest, thus multiple returns of light do arrive at a pixel and generally lead to erroneous reconstruction of range at that pixel. Multiple return sources can be categorised due to two primary problems. Firstly, the imaging pixel views a finite solid angle of the scene and range inhomogeneities of the scene in the viewed solid angle lead to multiple returns of light—the so-called *mixed pixed* effect which results in flying pixels (see Section 2.3 above). Secondly, the light can travel multiple paths to intersect the viewed part of the scene and the imaging pixel—the *multipath inteference* problem. Godbaz [11] provides a thorough treatment of the multiple return problem, including a review covering full field ToF and other ranging systems with relevant issues, such as point scanners.

In a ToF system light returning to the sensor is characterised by amplitude A and phase shift ϕ. The demodulated light return is modelled usefully as the complex phasor

$$\eta = Ae^{j\phi}, \tag{8}$$

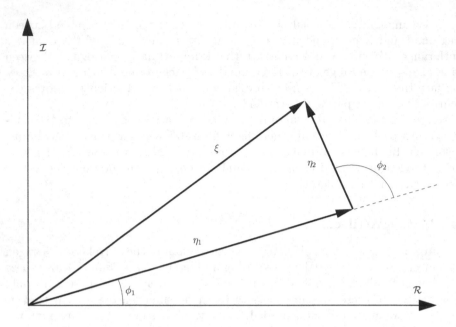

Fig. 4. Phasor diagram of the demodulated output in complex form. The primary return, η_1, is perturbed by a secondary return, η_2, resulting in the measured phasor, ξ.

where $j = \sqrt{-1}$ is the imaginary unit. When light returns to a pixel via N multiple paths then the individual return complex phasors add yielding a total measurement ξ given by

$$\xi = \sum_{n=1}^{N} \eta_n = \sum_{n=1}^{N} A_n e^{j\phi_n}. \tag{9}$$

One of the phasors is due to the primary return of light, namely that of the ideal path intended in the design of the imaging system. Note that the primary return is often the brightest return, though it need not be. Let us take η_1 as the primary return and every other return (η_2, η_3, etc.) as secondary returns arising from unwanted light paths. A diagram of the two return case is shown in Fig. 4. Note that when the phase of the second return ϕ_2 changes, the measured phasor ξ changes both in amplitude and phase.

It is useful to categorise multiple returns due to multipath interference as to those that are caused by scattering within the scene and those resulting from scattering within the camera. *Scene based multi-path interference* arises due to light reflecting or scattering off multiple points in the scene to arrive at the same pixel of the sensor, and is frequently the most obvious effect to see in a ToF range image. The following example illustrates a common situation. Consider a scene where there is a large region of shiny floor exhibiting specular reflection. When light diffusely reflects off some other surface, such as a wall or furniture, a portion of that light is diffusely reflected so that it travels down towards the floor. When the ToF camera is viewing the floor and wall a hole is reconstructed in the floor, where the position of the hole aligns with the light path from camera to wall, wall to floor, and then back to the camera. The distance into the hole is due to the phase of the total measured phasor and is determined by the relative amplitude and phase of the component returns, as per Eq. 9. Another example that exhibits strong multipath interference is the sharp inside corner junction between two walls [12]. The light bouncing from one wall to the other causes the camera to measure an erroneous curved corner.

Multipath interference can also occur intra-camera due to the light refraction and reflection of an imaging lens and aperture [13,14,15]. The aperture effect is due to diffraction which leads to localised blurring in the image formation process. Fine detail beyond the limits in angular resolution is greatly reduced, causing sharp edges to blur. Aberrations in the lens increase the loss in resolution. Reflections at the optical boundaries of the glass produce what is commonly referred to as lens flare [16], which causes non-local spreading of light across the scene. In ToF imaging the lens-flare effect is most prominent when a bright foreground scatterer is present. The foreground object does not need to be directly visible to the camera, as long as the light from the source is able to reach that object and reflect, at least in part, back to the lens [17]. Such light scattering leads to distorted reconstructed ranges throughout the scene with the greatest errors occurring for darker objects.

2.6   Other Error Sources

ToF camera sensors suffer from the same errors as standard camera sensors. The most important error source in the sensor is a result of the photon counting process in the sensor. Since photons are detected only by a certain probability, Poisson noise is introduced. We refer to Seitz [18] and the thesis by Schmidt [10, Sect. 3.1] for detailed studies on the Poisson noise. An experimental evaluation of noise characteristics of different ToF cameras has been performed in by Erz & Jähne [19]. Besides from that other kinds of noise, e.g. dark (fixed-pattern) noise and read-out noise, occur.

In ToF cameras, however, noise has a strong influence on the estimated scene depth, due to the following two issues

- The recorded light intensity in the raw channels is stemming from both active and background illumination. Isolating the active part of the signal reduces the SNR. Such a reduction could be compensated by increasing the integration time, which on the other hand increases the risk of an over-saturation of the sensor cells, leading to false depth estimation. As a consequence, a trade-off in the integration time has to be made, often leading to a low SNR in the raw data, which occurs especially in areas with extremely low reflectivity or objects far away from the sensor.
- Since the estimated scene depth depends non-linearly on the raw channels (cf. Eqs. 4 and 7), the noise is amplified in this process. This amplification is typically modeled ([1,20]) by assuming Gaussian noise in the raw data and

performing a sensitivity analysis. By this simplified approach, it turns out that the noise variance in the final depth estimates depend quadratically on the amplitude of the active illumination signal. In particular, the variance can change drastically within the different regions of the scene depending on the reflectivity and the distance of the objects.

Due to these short-comings current ToF cameras have a resolution smaller than half VGA, which is rather small in comparison to standard RGB or grayscale cameras.

We remark that the noise parameters of ToF cameras are part of the EMVA standard 1228[21], thus they are assumed to be provided in the data sheet, if the ToF camera conforms to the standard.

We finally consider a scenario, where several ToF cameras are used to retrieve depth maps of a scene from different viewpoints. As a consequence of the modulation of the active illumination, the emitted light of each camera can affect the recordings of the other cameras, leading to false depth estimates. Some camera manufacturers account for this issue by allowing to change the modulation in the camera settings. In case that the modulation frequency of one sensor does not match the frequency of the light from a different light source, the effect of interference can be reduced as long as the integration time for the raw channels is far larger than $\frac{1}{f_m}$.

3   Calibration Approaches

In this section, the approaches to handle individual error sources are explained in detail. First a foundation on standard camera calibration techniques is presented to be followed by ToF depth calibration and depth enhancement.

3.1   Standard Camera Calibration

Optical camera calibration is one of the basic requirements before precise measurements can be performed. The optical lens configuration and the camera assembly determine the optical path of the light rays reaching each pixel. One has to distinguish between the camera-specific parameters that determine the optical rays in camera-centered coordinates, termed *intrinsic calibration*, and the *extrinsic calibration* which determines the 3D position and 3D orientation (the pose) of the camera coordinate system in 3D world coordinates.

Typically, the intrinsic parameters are defined by the linear calibration matrix, K, which holds the camera focal length f, the pixel size s_x, s_y, and the optical image center c_x, c_y of the imaging chip. In addition, non-linear image distortion effects from the lens-aperture camera construction have to be included, which can be severe in cheap cameras and for wide-angle lenses. A polynomial radial and tangential distortion function is typically applied to approximate the distortion effects. Radial-symmetric and tangential coefficients for polynomials up to 3rd order are included in the intrinsic calibration.

Unfortunately, it is very difficult to determine the intrinsic parameters by inspecting the optical system directly. Instead, intrinsic and extrinsic parameters have to be estimated jointly. A known 3D reference, the *calibration object*, is needed for this task, since it allows to relate the light rays emitted from known 3D object points to the 2D pixel in the camera image plane. A non-planar 3D calibration object with very high geometric precision is preferred in high-quality photogrammetric calibration, but these 3D calibration objects are difficult to manufacture and handle, because they ideally should cover the complete 3D measurement range of the camera system. In addition, when calibrating not only optical cameras but also depth cameras, the design of such 3D pattern is often not possible due to the different imaging modalities of depth and color.

Therefore, a planar 2D calibration pattern is preferred which allows a much easier capture of the calibration data. A popular approach based on a 2D planar calibration pattern was proposed by Zhang[22]. The 2D calibration object determines the world coordinate system, with the x-y coordinates spanning the 2D calibration plane, and the z coordinate spanning the plane normal direction, defining the distance of the camera center from the plane. For 3D point identification, a black and white checkerboard pattern is utilized to define a regular spacing of known 3D coordinates. In this case, a single calibration image is not sufficient, but one has to take a series of different calibration images while moving and tilting the calibration plane to cover the 3D measurement range of the system. For each image, a different extrinsic camera pose has to be estimated, but all intrinsic parameters remain fixed and are estimated jointly from the image series. This is advantageous, since some of the calibration parameters are highly correlated and need disambiguation. For example, it is difficult to distinguish between the extrinsic camera distance, z, and the intrinsic focal length, f, because f is similar to a simple magnification and inversely proportional to z. However, if sufficiently many different camera distances are recorded in the calibration sequence, one can distinguish them from the constant focal length.

Another source of error during calibration is the optical opening angle of the camera, the field of view *fov*. Calibration of a camera with narrow fov leads to high correlation between extrinsic position and orientation, because moving the camera in the x-y plane and simultaneous rotating it to keep the camera focused on the same part of the calibration pattern is distinguishable only by the perspective distortions in the image plane due to out-of-plane rotation of the calibration object[23,7]. Hence it is advisable to employ wide-angle cameras, if possible, for stable extrinsic pose estimation. Brought to the extreme, one would like to use omnidirectional or fisheye cameras with extremely large fov for best possible extrinsic pose estimation. In this case, however, it is also advisable to increase the available image resolution as much as possible, since for large fov optics the angular resolution per pixel decreases. See [24] for a detailed analysis.

The focus of this contribution is to calibrate a tof depth camera from image data. Given the above discussion, it is clear that this will be a difficult problem. The cameras typically have a limited fov by construction, since its infrared lighting has to illuminate the observable object region with sufficient intensity.

Thus, wide fov illumination is not really an option, unless in very restricted situations. In addition, the image resolution is typically much lower than with modern optical cameras, and this will not change soon due to the large pixel size of the correlating elements. Finally, no clear optical image is captured but only the reflectance image can be utilized for calibration. Early results show that the quality of the calibration using the approaches as described above is poor[6,25].

However, there is also an advantage of using depth cameras, since the camera distance z can be estimated with high accuracy from the depth data, eliminating the f/z ambiguity. The calibration plane can be aligned with all depth measurements from the camera by plane fitting. Hence, all measurements are utilized simultaneously in a model-based approach that compares the estimated plane fit with the real calibration plane. More general, a virtual model of the calibration plane is built, including not only geometry but also surface color, and is synthesized for comparison with the observed data. This *model-driven analysis-by-synthesis approach* exploits all camera data simultaneously, and allows further on to combine the ToF camera with additional color cameras, which are rigidly coupled in a camera rig. The coupling of color cameras with depth cameras is the key to high-quality calibration, since it combines the advantages of color and depth data. High-resolution color cameras with large fov allow a stable and accurate pose estimation of the rig, while the depth data disambiguates z from f. The synthesis part is easily ported to GPU-Hardware, allowing for fast calibration even with many calibration images[4]. For details about this approach we refer to [26,7]. The approach allows further to include non-linear depth effects, like the wiggling error, and reflectance-dependent depth bias estimates into the calibration[27]. Depth calibration will be discussed next.

3.2 Depth Calibration

As described in 2, there are several reasons for a deviation of actual depth and depth measured by the ToF camera. To record accurate data, a thorough depth calibration has to be done. It should be noted here, that since the ToF camera measures the time of flight along the light path of course, error calibration should be done with respect to the radial distance as well, not in Cartesian coordinates.

One of the first contributions to this topic is [6] by Lindner and Kolb. They combined a pixelwise linear calibration with a global B-splines fit. In [7] Schiller et. al. used a polynomial to model the distance deviation.

Since a large share of the deviation is due to the non-sinusoidal illumination signal 2.1, an approach modelling this behavior is possible as well, as shown in [10]. But a completely model based behaviour would have to incorporate other error sources as well, like the intensity related distance error 2.2, which is not yet understood and hence, there is no model to fit to the data.

Lindner and Kolb used two separate B-spline functions to separate the distance and intensity related error in [28], even the integration time is considered

---

[4] Software is available at
http://www.mip.informatik.uni-kiel.de/tiki-index.php?page=Calibration

by linear interpolation of the control points. The drawback of this method is the large amount of data, necessary to determine all the parameters of the compensation functions.

Lindner et. al. reduce the amount of necessary data in [27]. They use a modified calibration pattern, a checkerboard with different greylevels and introduce a normalization for the intensity data of different depths, reducing the amount of necessary data considerably.

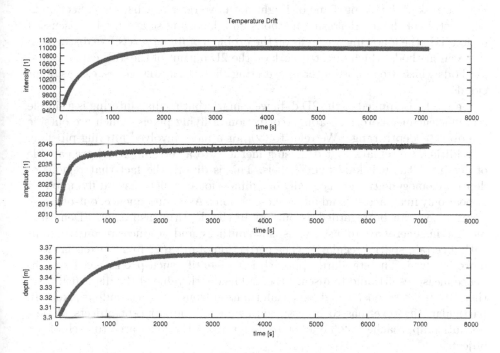

Fig. 5. Average intensity, amplitude and depth over time, showing an obvious temperature drift

However, the calibration is only valid for the camera temperature it was recorded at, since the behavior changes with the temperature ([29,10]). Fig. 5 shows the temperature drift of intensity, amplitude and depth measurement of a PMD CamCube 3, averaged over the whole image for two hours after power on.

For the temperature drift, there does not yet exist a proper investigation. Also the cameras usually lack a sensor to measure the current temperature.

4   Post-Processing Data Correction

The final part of the chapter will focus on depth correction that cannot be handled directly using calibration. Since those additional errors are usually scene dependent (as dynamic environment), a last processing needs to be applied after the depth correction via calibration in order to increase the reliability of ToF range measurements.

This section is divided into three subsections and will present state-of-the-art techniques to correct the remaining errors.

4.1 Depth Inhomogeneity and Denoising

For the task of denoising Time-of-Flight data, we refer to Chapter 2, Section 2, where state-of-the-art denoising methods and denoising strategies are discussed in detail. In the following, we focus on the problem of *flying pixels*. We distinguish between methods which directly work on the 2D output of the ToF cameras and methods which are applied after interpreting the data as 3D scenes, e.g. as point clouds.

On methods applied to the 2D data we remark that median filtering is a simple and efficient means to for a rough correction of flying pixels, which are outside the objects' depth range. We refer to [30] for a more involved filtering pipeline. In addition, we remark that denoising methods to a certain extend are capable of dealing with such kind flying pixels. This is due to the fact that regions of depth inhomogeneities are typically one dimensional structures and flying pixels appear only in a narrow band along these regions. As a consequence, out-of-range flying pixels can be regarded as outliers in the depth measurement. Denoising method in general are robust against such outliers, and produces reconstructions with a certain spatial regularity. The correction of in-range flying pixels is much more involved. The standard approach is to identify such pixels, e.g. by confidence measures [31] and to discard them. The depth value of the discarded pixel then has to be reconstructed using information from the surrounding pixels. In particular, the pixel has to be assigned to one of the adjacent objects. Super-resolution approaches [32,33] allow to assign parts the pixel area to each of the objects.

Also when considering 3D data (point clouds), geometrical information can be used to correct for flying pixels, for example by clustering the 3D data in order to determining the underlying object surface (e.g. [34,35]).

Finally, flying pixels can be dealt with when fusing point clouds [36,37] from *different* sources with sub-pixel accuracy. Here, it is substantial to reliably identify flying pixels, so that they can be removed before the actual fusion process. Missing depth data then is replaced by input from other sources. In order to identify flying pixels, confidence measures [31] for ToF data can be taken into account.

4.2 Motion Compensation

As stated in 2.4, motion artifacts occur in dynamic scenes at depth and reflectivity boundaries due to the sequential sampling of the correlation function. There are three (or arguably two) different approaches to reduce such artifacts. One way is by decreasing the number of frames obtained sequentially and needed to produce a valid depth reconstruction. As current two-tap sensors have different electronic characteristics for each tap, the raw values belonging to different taps cannot be combined without further calibration. In 4.2.1 a method proposed by Schmidt et al. [10] will be presented where each of these taps are dynamically calibrated, such that a valid measurement can be obtained with the bare minimum of 2 consecutive frames. Another approach commonly employed is composed of a detection step, where erroneous regions due to motion are found, followed by a correction step. The methods presented in 4.2.2 differ how these two steps are undertaken and in how much knowledge of the working principles is put in to the system. The final approach proposed by Lindner et al [38] is to directly estimate scene motion between sub-frames using optical flow. This approach can be seen as an extension of the detect and repair approach, but as the detection is not only binary and the correction not only local it will be presented separately in 4.2.3.

4.2.1   Framerate Enhancement
Current correlating pixels used in ToF cameras are capable of acquiring $Q = 2$ phase images simultaneously, shifted by 180 degrees. N of these simultaneous measurements are made sequentially to obtain a sufficient sampling of the correlation function.

Table 1. Illustration of raw frame $y_{phaseindex,tapindex}$ for $Q = 2$ taps and $N = 4$ acquisitions

time	t_0	t_1	t_2	t_3
tap 0	$y_{0,0}$	$y_{1,0}$	$y_{2,0}$	$y_{3,0}$
tap 1	$y_{3,1}$	$y_{2,1}$	$y_{1,1}$	$y_{0,1}$

As shown by Erz et al [19,39] these taps have different amplification characteristics, such that the raw values obtained from the taps cannot directly be used. Instead N has to be chosen as 4. and the A_i used in Eq. 3 calculated as

$$A_i = \sum_{k=0}^{Q} y_{i,k} \tag{10}$$

The relationship between the different taps is given implicitly per pixel by

$$y_{i,0} = r_{i,k}(y_{i,k}) \tag{11}$$

Schmidt [10] models these $r_{i,k}$ as a linear polynomial and proposes a dynamic calibration scheme to estimate them. For different intensity and depth static sequences are obtained and a linear model fitted between $y_{i,0}$ and $y_{i,k}$. The full model with further extensions such as interleaved calibration can be found in [10]. Note that this only reduces, but does not eliminate motion artifacts.

4.2.2   Detect and Repair Methods

Detect and repair approaches can be further categorized in methods that operate directly on the depth image [40,41] and the methods that harness the relation between the raw data channels [10,42,43].

Filter based methods
Gokturk et al. [40] applied morphological filters on a foreground/background segmented depth image to obtain motion artifact regions. These pixels are replaced by synthetic values using a spatial filtering process. Lottner et al. [41] proposed to employ data of an additional high resolution 2D sensor being monocularly combined with the 3D sensor, effectively suggesting a joint filtering approach which uses the edges of the 2d sensor to guide the filter.

Methods operating on raw data
Detection Schmidt [10] calculates the temporal derivatives of the individual raw frames. Motion artifacts occur if the first raw frame derivative is near 0 (no change) whereas one of the other raw frames has a large derivative. This means that movement occured between sub-frames. Lee et al. [43] operates on a similar principle. But evaluates the sums of two sub-frames.

Correction Finally once regions with artifacts are detected, they need to be repaired in some where. Here Schmidt uses the last pixel values with valid raw images whereas Lee uses the spatially nearest pixel with valid data.

Correction Finally once regions with artifacts are detected, they need to be repaired in some way. Here Schmidt uses the last pixel values with valid raw images whereas Lee uses the spatially nearest pixel with valid data.

4.2.3   Flow Based Motion Compensation

So far, the detection step gave a binary output whether or whether not motion was present in a pixel. Subsequently some heuristic was applied to inpaint the regions with detected motion. Lindner et al. [38] took a somewhat different approach by loosening the requirement that the 4 measurements used for reconstruction need to originate from the same pixel. Instead, the "detection" is done over the whole scene by estimating the optical flow between sub-frames. The application of optical flow to the raw data and the subsequent demodulation at different pixel positions require the following two points to be considered:

- Brightness constancy (corresponding surface points in subsequent sub-frames should have the same brightness to be able to match). This is not the case for the raw channels due to the internal phase shift between modulated and reference signal. Fortunately, in multi-tap sensors, the intensity (total amount of modulated light) can be obtained by adding up the measurements in different taps. Thus, the brightness constancy is given between the intensity of sub-frames:

$$I_i = \sum_{j=0}^{Q} u_{i,j} \tag{12}$$

– Pixel Homogeneity. The application of the demodulation at different pixel locations requires a homogeneous sensor behavior over all locations. Otherwise artifacts will be observed which usually cancel out by using the same pixel for all four measurements. Again, this is not the case for the raw channels due to pixel gain differences and a radial light attenuation toward the image border. To circumvent this, Lindner et al. [38] proposed a raw value calibration based on work by Stürmer et al. [44].

Once the flow is known, it can be used to correct the raw image before applying the standard reconstruction formulas. The strength and weakness of this method is strongly coupled with the flow method used. It is important to obtain the correct flow especially at occlusion boundaries, such that discontinuity preserving flow methods should be preserved. Lindner et al. [38] reported a rate of 10 frames per second using the GPU implemented version TV-L1 flow proposed by Zach et al. [45] on a 2009 machine. Lefloch et al. [46] has recently proposed an alternative solution, based on the previous work of Lindner et al., in order to improve the performance of the motion compensation by reducing the number of computed subsequent optical flows.

4.3   Multiple Return Correction

The determination of the multiple returns of multipath or mixed pixels essentially is the separation of complex phasors into two or more components. Given the complex measurement arising from the demodulation, Eq. 9, correction is the separation of the total phasor into its constituent returns. The problem of multiple return correction of a single range image is underdetermined as only one complex measurement is made but the signal at each pixel is the linear combination (in the complex plane) of more than one return. To separate out multiple returns more information is needed, either in the form of *a priori* assumptions or multiple measurements.

Iterative offline processing of range images has been used to demonstrate sucessful separation of multiple returns [47], however the algorithm is not suitable for realtime operation. Here we summarise the work of Godbaz [11], who provides a mathematical development that leads to a fast online algorithm. Godbaz employs multiple measurements with the assumption that two returns dominate the measurement process, thus requiring at least two measurements for return separation. Note that a fully closed form solution is possible for the overdetermined case of three or more measurements and two returns [11,48].

We begin by writing Eq. 9 for two returns with the implicit assumption that the measurement is taken at camera modulation frequency f_1, namely

$$\xi_1 = \eta_1 + \eta_2. \tag{13}$$

Now, consider measurement at a second frequency $f_r = rf_1$, where r is the *relative frequency* between f_r and f_1. A measurement at relative frequency r is

$$\xi_r = \frac{\eta_1^r}{|\eta_1|^{r-1}} + \frac{\eta_2^r}{|\eta_2|^{r-1}}. \tag{14}$$

Qualitatively, the action of making a new measurement at relative frequency r rotates each component return so that its phase is increased to r times its original while leaving the amplitude unchanged.[5] This phase rotation is the information that is exploited to separate the returns. It can be shown that the measurement made at relative frequency r factorises as

$$\xi_r = \frac{\eta_1^r}{|\eta_1|^{r-1}} \Lambda_r(b, \theta), \tag{15}$$

where

$$\Lambda_r(b, \theta) = 1 + be^{jr\theta} \tag{16}$$

with

$$b = \frac{|\eta_2|}{|\eta_1|}, \tag{17}$$

and

$$\theta = \phi_2 - \phi_1. \tag{18}$$

Here b and θ are the relative amplitude and phase and describe the perturbation of the primary return by the secondary return. From these we obtain the *characteristic measurement*, χ, defined by

$$\chi = \frac{\xi_r |\xi_1|^{r-1}}{\xi_1^r} \tag{19}$$

$$= \frac{\Lambda_r(b, \theta) |\Lambda_1(b, \theta)|^{r-1}}{\Lambda_1(b, \theta)^r}. \tag{20}$$

The computation of χ normalises for the primary return, yielding a number that is explicitly dependent on b and θ.

A look-up table of the inverse of Eq. 20 can be constructed using parametric curve fitting. Given indices $|\chi|$ and $\arg \chi$ into the table, b and θ are read from the look-up table, $\Lambda_1(b, \theta)$ is computed, and the estimate of the primary return is simply

$$\eta_1 = \frac{\xi_1}{\Lambda_1(b, \theta)}. \tag{21}$$

The relative frequency $r = 2$ is used in the implementation described by Godbaz [11], with the development and merit of other frequency ratios also considered. It is important to note that the characteristic measurement χ is multivalued thus multiple solutions arise in calculating its inverse. For the case $r = 2$ there are two solutions, but there is a symmetry in $\Lambda_r(b, \theta)$ that leads to a degeneracy. The two solutions are equivalent up to the fact that the second solution physically corresponds to solving for η_2 in Eq. 21.

The multiple return correction is demonstrated using the Mesa Imaging SR4000 camera with a frequency combination of 15:30 MHz. An amplitude and phase pair is shown in Fig. 6 of a scene of a hallway with a shiny floor and a

---

[5] The assumption of invariance of the component amplitude with respect to a change in modulation frequency is an ideal one. In practice factors arising due to the light and sensor modulation mean that a calibration of amplitude with respect to frequency is required.

Fig. 6. The amplitude (left) and phase (right) of a range image pair. The reflection of a bright white circular object manifests as multipath returns from the floor.

Fig. 7. The estimated primary (left) and secondary (right) returns

target object of a black board with a large round white circle. The board is 4.5 m from the camera. The effect of the reflection of the white circle is visible on the floor near the bottom of both the amplitude and phase images. The estimates of the primary and secondary returns are shown in Fig. 7. The appearance of the phase shift induced by the reflection of the white circle is greatly reduced in the primary return estimate. Godbaz [11] analysed the noise behaviour of multiple return correction and found an increase in noise, as is seen when comparing the primary return estimate with the distance measurement.

5 Conclusion

In this paper, we present state-of-the art techniques that improved significantly raw data given by ToF sensors. We have seen that ToF cameras are subject to a variety of errors caused by different sources. Some errors can be handled by *simple* calibration procedure, nevertheless other sources of errors are directly related to the observed scene configuration which thus require post processing techniques. Nevertheless, there are still some open issues that need to be further investigated. One concerns the intensity-related distance error which is, as stated previously, not fully yet understood. The second open issue lies on multi-path problem where separation of global and local illumination is required to provide a reliable correction. Finally, there are still some difficulties for researchers to evaluate their work since groundtruth generation is still an open issue.

References

1. Lange, R.: 3D Time-of-Flight Distance Measurement with Custom Solid-State Image Sensor in CMOS/CCD-Technology. PhD thesis (2000)
2. Davis, J., Gonzalez-Banos, H.: Enhanced shape recovery with shuttered pulses of light. In: Pulses of Light? IEEE Workshop on Projector-Camera Systems (2003)
3. Rapp, H.: Experimental and theoretical investigation of correlating tof-camera systems. Master's thesis (2007)
4. Schmidt, M., Jähne, B.: A physical model of time-of-flight 3D imaging systems, including suppression of ambient light. In: Kolb, A., Koch, R. (eds.) Dyn3D 2009. LNCS, vol. 5742, pp. 1–15. Springer, Heidelberg (2009)
5. Dorrington, A.A., Cree, M.J., Carnegie, D.A., Payne, A.D., Conroy, R.M., Godbaz, J.P., Jongenelen, A.P.: Video-rate or high-precision: A flexible range imaging camera. In: Electronic Imaging 2008, International Society for Optics and Photonics, pp. 681307–681307 (2008)
6. Lindner, M., Kolb, A.: Lateral and depth calibration of pmd-distance sensors. In: Bebis, G., Boyle, R., Parvin, B., Koracin, D., Remagnino, P., Nefian, A., Meenakshisundaram, G., Pascucci, V., Zara, J., Molineros, J., Theisel, H., Malzbender, T. (eds.) ISVC 2006. LNCS, vol. 4292, pp. 524–533. Springer, Heidelberg (2006)
7. Schiller, I., Beder, C., Koch, R.: Calibration of a pmd camera using a planar calibration object together with a multi-camera setup. In: The International Archives of the Photogrammetry, Remote Sensing and Spatial Information Sciences, Part B3a, Beijing, China, vol. XXXVII, pp. 297–302 XXI. ISPRS Congress (2008)
8. Payne, A.D., Dorrington, A.A., Cree, M.J., Carnegie, D.A.: Improved measurement linearity and precision for amcw time-of-flight range imaging cameras. Applied Optics 49(23), 4392–4403 (2010)
9. Lindner, M.: Calibration and Real-Time Processing of Time-of-Flight Range Data. PhD thesis, CG, Fachbereich Elektrotechnik und Informatik, Univ. Siegen (2010)
10. Schmidt, M.: Analysis, Modeling and Dynamic Optimization of 3D Time-of-Flight Imaging Systems. PhD thesis, IWR, Fakultät für Physik und Astronomie, Univ. Heidelberg (2011)
11. Godbaz, J.P.: Ameliorating systematic errors in full-field AMCW lidar. PhD thesis, School of Engineering, University of Waikato, Hamilton, New Zealand (2012)
12. A., G.S., Aanaes, H., Larsen, R.: Environmental effects on measurement uncertainties of time-of-flight cameras. In: Proceedings of International Symposium on Signals, Circuits and Systems 2007, ISSCS 2007 (2007)
13. Shack, R.V.: Characteristics of an image-forming system. Journal of Research of the National Bureau of Standards 56(5), 245–260 (1956)
14. Barakat, R.: Application of the sampling theorem to optical diffaction theory. Journal fo the Optical Society of America 54(7) (1964)
15. Saleh, B.E.A., Teich, M.C.: 10. In: Fundamentals of Photonics, pp. 368–372. John Wiley and Sons, New York (1991)

16. Matsuda, S., Nitoh, T.: Flare as applied to photographic lenses. Applied Optics 11(8), 1850–1856 (1972)
17. Godbaz, J., Cree, M., Dorrington, A.: Understanding and ameliorating non-linear phase and amplitude responses in amcw lidar. Remote Sensing 4(1) (2012)
18. Seitz, P.: Quantum-noise limited distance resolution of optical range imaging techniques. IEEE Transactions on Circuits and Systems I: Regular Papers 55(8), 2368–2377 (2008)
19. Erz, M., Jähne, B.: Radiometric and spectrometric calibrations, and distance noise measurement of toF cameras. In: Kolb, A., Koch, R. (eds.) Dyn3D 2009. LNCS, vol. 5742, pp. 28–41. Springer, Heidelberg (2009)
20. Frank, M., Plaue, M., Rapp, H., Köthe, U., Jähne, B., Hamprecht, F.A.: Theoretical and experimental error analysis of continuous-wave time-of-flight range cameras. Optical Engineering 48(1), 13602 (2009)
21. Emva standard 1288 -standard for measurement and presentation of specifications for machine vision sensors and cameras, Release 3.0 (2010)
22. Zhang, Z.: A flexible new technique for camera calibration. IEEE Trans. Pattern Anal. Mach. Intell. 22(11), 1330–1334 (2000)
23. Beder, C., Bartczak, B., Koch, R.: A comparison of PMD-cameras and stereo-vision for the task of surface reconstruction using patchlets. In: IEEE/ISPRS BenCOS Workshop 2007 (2007)
24. Streckel, B., Koch, R.: Lens model selection for visual tracking. In: Kropatsch, W.G., Sablatnig, R., Hanbury, A. (eds.) DAGM 2005. LNCS, vol. 3663, pp. 41–48. Springer, Heidelberg (2005)
25. Kahlmann, T., Remondino, F., Ingensand, H.: Calibration for increased accuracy of the range imaging camera swissrangertm. In: Proc. of IEVM (2006)
26. Beder, C., Koch, R.: Calibration of focal length and 3d pose based on the reflectance and depth image of a planar object. In: Proceedings of the DAGM Dyn3D Workshop, Heidelberg, Germany (2007)
27. Marvin, L., Ingo, S., Andreas, K., Reinhard, K.: Time-of-flight sensor calibration for accurate range sensing. Comput. Vis. Image Underst. 114(12), 1318–1328 (2010)
28. Lindner, M., Kolb, A.: Calibration of the intensity-related distance error of the pmd tof-camera. In: Proc. SPIE, Intelligent Robots and Computer Vision, vol. 6764, p. 67640W (2007)
29. Steiger, O., Felder, J., Weiss, S.: Calibration of time-of-flight range imaging cameras. In: 15th IEEE International Conference on Image Processing, ICIP 2008, pp. 1968–1971. IEEE (2008)
30. Swadzba, A., Beuter, N., Schmidt, J., Sagerer, G.: Tracking objects in 6d for reconstructing static scenes. In: IEEE Computer Society Conference on Computer Vision and Pattern Recognition Workshops, CVPRW 2008, pp. 1–7. IEEE (2008)
31. Reynolds, M., Dobos, J., Peel, L., Weyrich, T., Brostow, G.J.: Capturing time-of-flight data with confidence. In: 2011 IEEE Conference on Computer Vision and Pattern Recognition (CVPR), pp. 945–952. IEEE (2011)
32. Lindner, M., Lambers, M., Kolb, A.: Sub-pixel data fusion and edge-enhanced distance refinement for 2d / 3d images. International Journal of Intelligent Systems Technologies and Applications 5, 344–354 (2008)
33. Pathak, K., Birk, A., Poppinga, J.: Sub-pixel depth accuracy with a time of flight sensor using multimodal gaussian analysis. In: IEEE/RSJ International Conference on Intelligent Robots and Systems, IROS 2008, pp. 3519–3524 (2008)
34. Moser, B., Bauer, F., Elbau, P., Heise, B., Schöner, H.: Denoising techniques for raw 3D data of ToF cameras based on clustering and wavelets. In: Proc. SPIE, vol. 6805 (2008)

35. H., S., Moser, B., Dorrington, A.A., Payne, A., Cree, M.J., Heise, B., Bauer, F.: A clustering based denoising technique for range images of time of flight cameras. In: CIMCA/IAWTIC/ISE 2008, pp. 999–1004 (2008)
36. Schuon, S., Theobalt, C., Davis, J., Thrun, S.: Lidarboost: Depth superresolution for tof 3d shape scanning. In: IEEE Conference on Computer Vision and Pattern Recognition, CVPR 2009, pp. 343–350. IEEE (2009)
37. Cui, Y., Schuon, S., Chan, D., Thrun, S., Theobalt, C.: 3d shape scanning with a time-of-flight camera. In: 2010 IEEE Conference on Computer Vision and Pattern Recognition, CVPR, pp. 1173–1180. IEEE (2010)
38. Lindner, M., Kolb, A.: Compensation of motion artifacts for time-of-flight cameras. In: Kolb, A., Koch, R. (eds.) Dyn3D 2009. LNCS, vol. 5742, pp. 16–27. Springer, Heidelberg (2009)
39. Erz, M.: Charakterisierung von Laufzeit-Kamera-Systemen für Lumineszenz-Lebensdauer-Messungen. PhD thesis, IWR, Fakultät für Physik und Astronomie, Univ. Heidelberg (2011)
40. Gokturk, S.B., Yalcin, H., Bamji, C.: A time-of-flight depth sensor-system description, issues and solutions. In: Conference on Computer Vision and Pattern Recognition Workshop, CVPRW 2004, pp. 35–35. IEEE (2004)
41. Lottner, O., Sluiter, A., Hartmann, K., Weihs, W.: Movement artefacts in range images of time-of-flight cameras. In: International Symposium on Signals, Circuits and Systems, ISSCS 2007, vol. 1, pp. 1–4. IEEE (2007)
42. Hussmann, S., Hermanski, A., Edeler, T.: Real-time motion artifact suppression in tof camera systems. IEEE Transactions on Instrumentation and Measurement 60, 1682–1690 (2011)
43. Hansard, M., Lee, S., Choi, O., Horaud, R.P.: Time of Flight Cameras: Principles, Methods, and Applications. SpringerBriefs in Computer Science. Springer (2012)
44. Sturmer, M., Penne, J., Hornegger, J.: Standardization of intensity-values acquired by time-of-flight-cameras. In: IEEE Computer Society Conference on Computer Vision and Pattern Recognition Workshops, CVPRW 2008, pp. 1–6. IEEE (2008)
45. Zach, C., Pock, T., Bischof, H.: A duality based approach for realtime tv-l 1 optical flow. In: Hamprecht, F.A., Schnörr, C., Jähne, B. (eds.) DAGM 2007. LNCS, vol. 4713, pp. 214–223. Springer, Heidelberg (2007)
46. Lefloch, D., Hoegg, T., Kolb, A.: Real-time motion artifacts compensation of tof sensors data on gpu. In: Proc. SPIE, Three-Dimensional Imaging, Visualization, and Display, vol. 8738. SPIE (2013)
47. Dorrington, A.A., Godbaz, J.P., Cree, M.J., Payne, A.D., Streeter, L.V.: Separating true range measurements from multi-path and scattering interference in commercial range cameras (2011)
48. Godbaz, J.P., Cree, M.J., Dorrington, A.A.: Closed-form inverses for the mixed pixel/multipath interference problem in AMCW lidar (2012)

Denoising Strategies for Time-of-Flight Data

Frank Lenzen[1,2], Kwang In Kim[3], Henrik Schäfer[1,2], Rahul Nair[1,2],
Stephan Meister[1,2], Florian Becker[1], Christoph S. Garbe[1,2],
and Christian Theobalt[3,2]

[1] Heidelberg Collaboratory for Image Processing (HCI), Heidelberg University,
Speyerer Str. 6, 69115 Heidelberg, Germany
{Frank.Lenzen,Henrik.Schaefer,Rahul.Nair,Stephan.Meister}
@iwr.uni-heidelberg.de, becker@math.uni-heidelberg.de,
Christoph.Garbe@uni-heidelberg.de
[2] Intel Visual Computing Institute, Saarland University, Campus E2-1,
66123 Saarbrücken, Germany
[3] Max-Planck-Institut für Informatik, Saarland University, Campus E1-4,
66123 Saarbrücken, Germany
kkim@mpi-inf.mpg.de, theobalt@mpii.de

Abstract. When considering the task of denoising ToF data, two issues
arise concerning the optimal strategy. The first one is the choice of an appropriate denoising method and its adaptation to ToF data, the second
one is the issue of the optimal positioning of the denoising step within the
processing pipeline between acquisition of raw data of the sensor and the
final output of the depth map. Concerning the first issue, several denoising approaches specifically for ToF data have been proposed in literature,
and one contribution of this chapter is to provide an overview. To tackle
the second issue, we exemplarily focus on two state-of-the-art methods,
the *bilateral filtering* and *total variation (TV) denoising* and discuss several alternatives of positions in the pipeline, where these methods can
be applied. In our experiments, we compare and evaluate the results of
each combination of method and position both qualitatively and quanti-
tatively. It turns out, that for TV denoising the optimal position is at the
very end of the pipeline. For the bilateral filter, a quantitative comparison
shows that applying it to the raw data together with a subsequent median
filtering provides a low error to ground truth. Qualitatively, it competes
with applying the (cross-)bilateral filter to the depth data. In particular,
the optimal position in general depends on the considered method. As
a consequence, for any newly introduced denoising technique, finding its
optimal position within the pipeline is an open issue.

1 Introduction

Measurements from Time-of-Flight cameras suffer from severe noise. This noise
is introduced when the raw image data are recorded by the camera sensor. It is
non-linearly amplified in the subsequent post-processing, where the actual depth
data are derived. For a detailed discussion on the noise we refer the reader to
the first chapter of this book.

M. Grzegorzek et al. (Eds.): Time-of-Flight and Depth Imaging, LNCS 8200, pp. 25–45, 2013.
© Springer-Verlag Berlin Heidelberg 2013

Higher level computer vision algorithms are often sensitive to the noise level typically for ToF data and it is inevitable to denoise the data before applying these methods. Three major questions arise concerning the denoising task:

1. Which state-of-the-art method should be chosen for denoising the depth data?
2. At which stage of the data processing should the denoising method be applied? Two obvious alternatives are to denoise the raw data or the final depth data. Denoising of some intermediate data is also possible.
3. Which modifications can be applied to state-of-the-art methods to increase their performance with respect to ToF data?

We start this chapter with an overview over state-of-the-art denoising methods for standard gray or color images in Section 2.1, including the class of learning approaches, which are gaining importance in this field. Afterwards, we discuss approaches which are proposed in literature specifically for denoising ToF data, cf. Section 2.2.

The main focus of this chapter is the question of the optimal position of the denoising method within the data processing pipeline. Not much research has been done in this direction so far. Most of the related work solely considers denoising of the depth map provided by the camera. One reason for this might be the fact that for most cameras, the raw data is not accessible to the users. However, since having access to raw data is of interest for scientific applications of ToF cameras, in future more camera manufactures might consider to provide corresponding interfaces.

To answer the question of positioning, we exemplarily consider in Section 3 two denoising methods, which are commonly used for ToF data, the *bilateral filter* and *total variation-(TV)*-based denoising. We discuss several alternatives of how to apply these methods to the raw, intermediate and final data processed by the ToF camera. In addition, we discuss modifications to improve the restoration quality of the considered methods. These modifications consist in making the approaches *adaptive, anisotropic* and, in particular for the TV denoising approach, to consider *second-order* smoothing terms.

In the experimental part in Section 4 we evaluate the different approaches based on a test data set with ground truth. It turns out that for TV denoising the optimal position is at the end of the processing pipeline. For the bilateral filter, we found that applying it to the raw channels and performing a subsequent median filter provides the smallest quantitative error. Qualitatively, it competes with applying the bilateral and the cross-bilateral filter to the depth data.

2   State-of-the-Art Denoising Techniques

2.1   Denoising of Standard Images

The task of denoising faces the major problem of finding a trade-off between removing the noise and preserving the detailed structures of the original data.

For images, these details are mainly the edges and textures. Applying for example classical Gaussian convolution for images, one obtains a blurred images with unsharp edges and with textures removed.

Various approaches exist in literature, which tackle both edge and texture preservation. One edge preserving variant of Gaussian convolution is the *bilateral filter* [1,2,3]. Here, the filter kernel decreases with increasing spatial distance as well as with increasing distance in intensity. Another family of denoising methods are the *PDE-based* approaches. They built on the fact that Gaussian convolution provides a solution to the linear diffusion equation, but use modifications to guarantee edge preservation. The most prominent methods of this kind are the *nonlinear diffusion* proposed by Perona and Malik [4] and the *anisotropic diffusion* [5].

The bilateral filter as well as the mentioned PDE approaches provide solutions which are smooth in the mathematical sense. As a consequence, sharp jumps in intensity or color can only be modeled by steep but smooth slopes. There exists approaches which explicitly allow for piecewise constant solutions, where edges can be represented by sharp jumps. Among these are the *wavelet methods*, see e.g. [6]. In image processing the most commonly used wavelets are the Haar wavelets, which represent a discrete space of piecewise constant functions. Soft thresholding then is applied to the wavelet coefficients of the image to remove highly oscillating components.

In 1992 Rudin, Osher and Fatemi [7] proposed to consider a variational approach using *total variation (TV)* regularization. In particular, this approach allows for piecewise constant solutions and thus is able to restore image edges sharply. Due to the variational formulation with a data-fidelity and a regularization term, this ansatz easily extends to other applications in computer vision such as optical flow and stereo, cf. Chapter 6.The classical TV regularization faces the drawbacks of a loss of contrast and stair-casing artifacts (piecewise constant reconstruction of the data where a smooth slope would be expected). Various TV variants have been proposed to overcome these drawbacks, including *adaptive TV* [8,9], *anisotropic TV* [10,11] and *approaches of higher order TV* [12,13,14].

Another approach dealing with piecewise smooth functions has been proposed by *Mumford and Shah* [15,16].

The methods mentioned so far all share the problem that textures in the data are over-smoothed. Non-local approaches such as *non-local means* [17], *non-local TV* [7,18,19] and the *BM3D* methods (e.g. [20]) turned out to have better texture preserving qualities.

Besides image denoising techniques, which are driven by a single input image, we also discuss data-base driven methods, which are gaining importance in image processing.

The underlying idea of database-driven methods is to learn a map from low-quality (noisy) images to high-quality images based on example pairs of low- and high-quality images. Burger et al. [21] proposed denoising images using multi-layer Perceptrons (MLPs): A given noisy image is divided into an overlapping set of image patches (small sub-windows). For each noisy patch, the corresponding clean patch is predicted using an MLP that is trained based on a large collection of pairs of input noisy and the corresponding output clean image patches. Given the patch predictions, the final image-valued output is reconstructed by taking averages for overlapping windows. A similar approach has also been proposed by Jain and Seung [22] in which convolutional networks are adopted.

An important advantage of database-driven methods is that they relieve the user from the extremely difficult task of designing an analytical noise model. This is especially important when the underlying noise generation process is non-Gaussian or, in general, not well-studied or modeled. Accordingly, conventional analytic noise models cannot be straightforwardly applied. Database-driven approaches enable building a denoising system (and general image enhancement system) by preparing a set of example pairs of clean and noisy images and learning specific degradation models from such training data. This has been demonstrated by the success of database-driven approaches for the related problems of single-image super-resolution and artifacts removal in compressed images, in which no analytical noise models are available. The reported results in these domains were superior to the state-of-the-art algorithms [23,24,25,26]. Even for the extensively studied Gaussian noise case, the reported performances were comparable to state-of-the-art image denoising algorithms [22,21].

One major drawback is that these algorithms are 'black boxes': due to the non-parametric nature of modeling, the trained denoising algorithms do not assist understanding the underlying noise generation or image degradation processes. Another limitation that is especially relevant for ToF image denoising is that they require pairs of clean and noisy images. Please see the next section for a more detailed discussion.

2.2   Denoising Techniques for Time-of-Flight Data

We start this section with a discussions of the **challenges**, which arise with denoising ToF data compared to denoising standard images.

- As already discussed in Chapter 1, the noise in ToF data varies depending on the amplitude of the recorded signal. A Gaussian distribution with variance proportional to $A^{-2}(x)$, where $A(x)$ is the amplitude of the recorded signal at pixel x, provides a efficient approximation, cf. [27]. Standard denoising models, however, often assume identically distributed Gaussian noise and thus can only be applied after adapting to the locally varying noise variance.
- Due to their low spatial resolution, textures are not as dominant as in standard images and the issue of texture preservation is less relevant. As a consequence, the texture preserving properties of non-local methods are of less importance for denoising ToF data.
- To model depth data, it is common to assume piecewise smooth data with salient depth edges. Depending on the scene recorded, planar surfaces might dominate, which could be considered in the denoising approach, e.g. by regularization methods which favor piecewise affine reconstructions. However,

one has to keep in mind that the depth maps provided by ToF cameras are actually the radial distances of the objects to the camera center. We refer to this as *radial depth*. As a consequence, surfaces which are flat in 3D are represented by curved surfaces on the camera grid. Calculating for each pixel the scene depth parallel to the viewing direction (*z-depth*) without adapting the (x,y)-pixel positions reduces the projective distortion, but does not completely compensate it (cf. [28]). An alternative would be to generate a 3D point cloud from the depth map, project these points onto the image plane and associate each of these 2D sampling points with its z-depth. The drawback for such an approach is, that these sampling points in general are no longer equally distributed. However, in our experiments we experienced that when just using the z-depth stored on the original pixel grid, the projective distortion of planar surfaces can be neglected compared to other systematic errors of the ToF systems.

- Finally, we want to stress the fact that the quality of ToF data is evaluated different to natural images. While for natural images the visual impression often is used for evaluation, for ToF data their precision is the most important criterion. Denoising methods might reveal effects that do not significantly change the visual appearance of the outcome, for example a loss of contrast. On depth maps such effects instead might significantly falsify the data. Therefore, when selecting appropriate denoising methods for ToF data, care has to be taken to preserve the accuracy of the depth data.

Let us now give a short overview over the **methods** discussed in literature for denoising ToF data.

2.2.1 Image Driven Methods

In this subsection, we consider *image driven* methods, i.e. methods which as input require only the data, which are to be denoised. Opposed to these are the *database-driven* (or learning) methods, which require a training phase with additional input prior to their actual application.

Clustering approaches for ToF denoising have been proposed by Schöner, Moser et al. [29,30]. Frank et al. [31] have considered *adaptive weighted Gaussian* as well as *median filtering*. For these approaches, they consider different positions within the depth acquisition pipeline. They come to the conclusion that, among the alternatives considered, adaptive weighted Gaussian filtering on the final depth in general gives the best results. However, it is not clear if this statement can be generalized to other denoising methods. *Wavelet denoising* of ToF data has been considered by Moser [30] and by Edeler et al. [32,33]. A popular denoising method used for ToF data is the already mentioned *bilateral filter* (see e.g. [34]). A *joint- or cross-bilateral filter* on both the depth and intensity data shows good denoising capabilities. We give a short overview over the standard and the cross-bilateral filter below. Schöner et al. [35] recently applied *anisotropic diffusion* to ToF data. In [28] we considered *total variation* regularization for ToF denoising.

In order to deal with the low spatial resolution of ToF data, fusion of multiple data sets has been proposed. In principle, ToF data can be fused with data from any other imaging device. The most prominent variants are multiple ToF data [36,37,38], fusion of ToF with rgb data (*rgbd*) [39,40,41,42] and fusion of ToF with stereo data. For the latter, we refer to Chapter 6 for a detailed discussion.

In all these approaches, denoising of the data is also an issue. Denoising techniques considered within the fusion approaches are for example bilateral TV regularization [38], (cross-)bilateral filtering [41,39] and adaptations of non-local means [42,40].

2.2.2   Database-Driven Methods

Despite the success of database-driven approaches for image denoising and enhancement, their applications to ToF data have not been actively explored. This can partially be attributed to the difficulty in generating the training data: The performance of database-driven algorithms rely heavily on the availability of large-scale and high-quality data. However, unlike the images, generating the ground truth data is highly non-trivial, as it requires measuring the 3D geometry of the scene of interest. One way of generating example pairs is to scan the scene with a laser scanner as well as with the ToF camera. However, accurate registration between ToF and laser scan data is necessary [43].

Although this chapter does not evaluate this class of algorithms, recent work breaks the limits of ground truth generation in this respect. Mac Aodha et al. [44] proposed an algorithm for single-depth image super-resolution. Similar to existing approaches for image denoising and enhancement, they adopt a local patch-wise prediction combined with a global image prior where the patch prediction step takes account of the training data. Unlike typical example-based approaches, the training examples are generated from synthesized 3D geometries, i.e., an example pair is generated by capturing a view of a synthesized scene followed by the corresponding degradation which, in the context super-resolution, is the down-sampling. This approach can facilitate applying well-developed database-driven image enhancement algorithms to ToF data without having to set up a laser scanning studio or involve other expensive hardwares.

For denoising ToF data, this approach requires building the corresponding noise model which may invalidate an important advantage of database-driven approaches: There is no need to analyze the noise characteristics. Nevertheless, database-driven approaches have certain potential advantages over conventional approaches that we believe justify future investigation: 1) Sampling and adding noise to synthetic data is still easier than constructing an algorithm that explicitly inverts the noise generation process; 2) It is easy to reflect a certain type of a priori knowledge into database-driven approaches. For instance, if it is known that the scene of interest shows a specific class of objects (e.g., faces), one could train an algorithm on examples generated from this specific class. As exemplified in Fig. 1, this strategy can significantly improve the performance over using generic databases for the case of super-resolution [26] and may show promise for denoising. This type of a priori knowledge can not be straightforwardly exploited in conventional approaches.

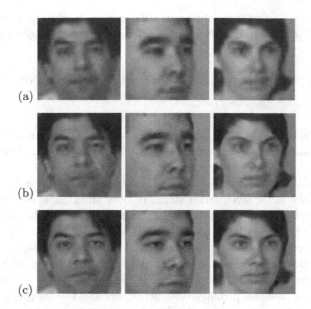

Fig. 1. The improvement made possible when training on a specific class of objects, here demonstrated for face image super-resolution (magnification factor 4). (a) bicubic resampling, (b) super-resolution results of Kim and Kwon's algorithm trained based on a generic image database [25], and (c) super-resolution results of Kim et al.'s algorithm trained based on a face database [26]. We expect a similar behavior for database driven *denoising* of ToF data.

3 Denoising Strategies

3.1 Methods under Consideration

The methods we consider here use as input some of the data provided by the ToF camera, which are the raw data, the amplitude, the intensity and/or the depth data. We exemplarily focus on the bilateral filter and total variation (TV) denoising approach and compare different modifications of both working on specific subsets of the available data. We start this section with a review of the standard versions of the bilateral filter and the TV denoising.

3.1.1 Bilateral Filter

The bilateral filter was first introduced by Aurich and Weule in [1] as edge preserving smoothing. Its actual name was conceived later by Tomasi and Manduchi [2] in 1998. The idea of the bilateral filter is to have a second domain, usually the intensity data, that weakens the smoothing of a standard Gaussian at intensity discontinuities. A Gaussian weighting in this second domain is commonly used. The bilateral filter, providing filtered data u from input v, is given as

$$u(\boldsymbol{x_0}, v) = \frac{1}{a_{Norm}} \int_{\Omega} v(\boldsymbol{x}) G_s(\|\boldsymbol{x_0} - \boldsymbol{x}\|) G_i(|v(\boldsymbol{x_0}) - v(\boldsymbol{x})|) d\boldsymbol{x}, \qquad (1)$$

where $\Omega \subset \mathbb{R}^2$ is the image domain, G_s and G_i are the Gaussian convolution kernels in spatial and intensity domain, respectively, and a_{Norm} is a normalization factor. Image coordinates are denoted by $\boldsymbol{x}$.

Regarding ToF-depth data, it is hard to find a suitable σ for the second domain, since the noise level varies strongly over the image, depending on the intensity or amplitude of different regions. The results are either smeared edges in bright parts or unsmoothed noise in darker areas. But the filter can be applied to the four different raw-images, which are basically intensity images.

Still, there are different ways to apply a bilateral filter to the depth data by incorporating other information as well. So called joint- or cross-bilateral filters [45] do not use the primary data to determine the weight in the second domain but calculate it from an additional image, which is less prone to noise (cf. [46,47]). In case of a ToF-camera, this second image could be the intensity or amplitude data. As mentioned already in Section 2.2, a different image with higher resolution can even be used to achieve super-resolution directly in the denoising step.

An alternative is to use both the intensity or amplitude image and the depth image for a combined bilateral filter, following [28]. This method especially preserves edges which are visible in both data sets. Applying the bilateral filter to the complex representation of the data has a similar effect. In the complex representation, the angle of each point towards the x-axis corresponds to the phase shift of the signal, while the distance to the origin is the amplitude. As a second weighting for the bilateral filter, the distance of points in the complex plane is used. We finally remark that the bilateral filter can be efficiently implemented on a GPU.

3.1.2   Denoising with Total Variation

Standard Total Variation denoising (the Rudin-Osher-Fatemi (ROF) model [7]) follows the classical form of a regularization approach, where the objective function to be minimized consists of a data-fidelity term combined with a regularization term. We describe the approach in a discrete framework. Let $\mathcal{N}$ denote the set of nodes of the pixel grid with grid size h. We denote image coordinates by $\boldsymbol{x} = (x, y)$. The optimization problem to be solved to obtain smoothed data u from noisy input f is given as

$$\min_u \left[\left(\sum_{\boldsymbol{x} \in \mathcal{N}} \tfrac{1}{2} w(\boldsymbol{x}) \left(u(\boldsymbol{x}) - f(\boldsymbol{x}) \right)^2 \right) + \lambda \mathcal{R}(u) \right]. \qquad (2)$$

We refer to the first term in (2) as the *data (fidelity) term* and to $\lambda\mathcal{R}(u)$ as the *regularization term*. For the ROF model, the latter is given as

$$
\begin{aligned}
\mathcal{R}(u) :&= \sum_{(x,y)} \|\nabla u(x,y)\| \\
&= \sum_{(x,y)} \sqrt{\left(u(x+h,y) - u(x,y)\right)^2 + \left(u(x,y+h) - u(x,y)\right)^2}.
\end{aligned}
\tag{3}
$$

The *regularization parameter* $\lambda > 0$ in (2) controls the amount of smoothing. $w(\boldsymbol{x})$ is a weighting term, which is used to account for the locally varying noise variance. For independent and identically distributed Gaussian noise with zero mean, one would use a constant weighting $w(\boldsymbol{x}) \propto \frac{1}{\sigma^2}$. After rescaling the parameter λ, $w(\boldsymbol{x}) = 1$ can be assumed. For ToF data, which show a locally varying noise variance proportional to $\frac{1}{A^2}$, we propose to use

$$
w(\boldsymbol{x}) = \tfrac{1}{c} \min(c, A^2(\boldsymbol{x})),
\tag{4}
$$

where we cut off the weighting function above some constant $c > 0$, and rescale it to $\max_{\boldsymbol{x}} w(\boldsymbol{x}) = 1$, so that the regularization parameter λ can be chosen in the same range as in the case of constant $w(x) = 1$.

In order to solve the optimization problem (2), we propose to use a primal-dual approach as for example described in [48]. Such a primal-dual approach is able to handle the non-differentiability of $\mathcal{R}(u)$ and thus leads to a better edge preservation (in terms of sharpness) than for example methods approximating $\mathcal{R}(u)$ by smooth functions. We remark that also primal-dual approaches can be efficiently implemented on GPUs.

3.2   Positioning within the Processing Pipeline

We start with a short review of depth acquisition process of a ToF camera as already discussed in detail in Chapter 1:

- Four individual raw images $A_j(\boldsymbol{x})$ at $\tau_j = \frac{\pi}{2}j, j = 0, \ldots, 3$, are recorded with the camera sensor. Here we denote with $\boldsymbol{x}$ the pixel position. Typically, the measurements are obtained using multiple taps. To deal with individual tap characteristics, recordings from corresponding taps are averaged [49, Sect. 5.2.]. We assume that $A_j(\boldsymbol{x})$ are already the averaged values.
- These raw data are related to the signal $\frac{A(\boldsymbol{x})}{2} \cos(\tau_j + \phi(\boldsymbol{x})) + I(\boldsymbol{x})$ amplitude $A(\boldsymbol{x})$, phase shift $\phi(\boldsymbol{x})$ and intensity $I(\boldsymbol{x})$. Optimal values for $A(\boldsymbol{x}), \phi(\boldsymbol{x})$ and $I(\boldsymbol{x})$ can be found by minimizing the least-squares error

$$
\sum_{j=0}^{3} \left(\tfrac{A(\boldsymbol{x})}{2} \cos(\tau_j + \phi(\boldsymbol{x})) + I(\boldsymbol{x}) - A_j(\boldsymbol{x}) \right)^2.
\tag{5}
$$

In particular, this optimization problem is independent in each pixel position. The standard approach is to transform it into a quadratic minimization problem by a change of variables. The analytic solution of the transformed problem is given as

$$I(\boldsymbol{x}) = \tfrac{1}{4} \sum_{j=0}^{3} A_j(\boldsymbol{x}),$$

$$A(\boldsymbol{x}) = \tfrac{1}{2} \sqrt{(A_0(\boldsymbol{x}) - A_2(\boldsymbol{x}))^2 + (A_3(\boldsymbol{x}) - A_1(\boldsymbol{x}))^2}, \tag{6}$$

$$\phi(\boldsymbol{x}) = \arctan\left(\frac{A_3(\boldsymbol{x}) - A_1(\boldsymbol{x})}{A_0(\boldsymbol{x}) - A_2(\boldsymbol{x})}\right)$$

(cf. Chapter 1 and [27]). We remark that ϕ is the phase of the complex-valued signal z with $Re(z) = A_0 - A_2$ and $Im(z) = A_3 - A_1$. One of the denoising strategies discussed below considers smoothing of this complex-valued signal z.

- The depth map is retrieved by

$$d(\boldsymbol{x}) = \frac{c}{4\pi f_m}\phi(\boldsymbol{x}), \tag{7}$$

where c is the speed of light and f_m is the modulation frequency.
- Depending on the respective ToF camera, post-processing for correcting systematic errors is applied.

Let us now turn to the optimal location of the denoising method within the processing pipeline. The various positions within the pipeline, where total variation denoising and bilateral filtering can be applied, are

Smoothing the Raw Data: We apply the ROF model given by (2) and (3) and the bilateral filter to each of the four raw images to obtain the filtered images. Denoting the individual results by $\tilde{A}_j$, we then proceed in the processing pipeline with $\tilde{A}_j$ instead of A_j.

Filtering the Complex Data: In this approach, we consider the vector valued data

$$z(\boldsymbol{x}) = \begin{pmatrix} z_1(\boldsymbol{x}) \\ z_2(\boldsymbol{x}) \end{pmatrix} = \begin{pmatrix} A_0(\boldsymbol{x}) - A_2(\boldsymbol{x}) \\ A_3(\boldsymbol{x}) - A_1(\boldsymbol{x}) \end{pmatrix}. \tag{8}$$

$z_1(\boldsymbol{x})$ and $z_2(\boldsymbol{x})$ can be interpreted as the real and imaginary part of a complex-valued signal $z(\boldsymbol{x})$. We have to keep in mind that the depth $d(\boldsymbol{x})$ we are actually interested in is related to the *phase* $\phi(\boldsymbol{x})$ of this complex signal $z(\boldsymbol{x}) = r(\boldsymbol{x})e^{i\phi(\boldsymbol{x})}$ by (7). For smoothing data $z(\boldsymbol{x})$, we consider again two alternatives, the bilateral filtering on vector-valued data and a TV-based approach consisting in the minimization of the objective function

$$\tfrac{1}{2}\left(\sum_{\boldsymbol{x}}(\|z_1(\boldsymbol{x}) - (A_0(\boldsymbol{x}) - A_2(\boldsymbol{x}))\|^2 + \|z_2(\boldsymbol{x}) - (A_3(\boldsymbol{x}) - A_1(\boldsymbol{x}))\|^2)\right) + \lambda\mathcal{R}(z), \tag{9}$$

with some regularization parameter $\lambda > 0$. As regularization term $\mathcal{R}(z)$ we choose isotropic total variation for vector valued data (see e.g. [50]). The term isotropic here refers to the fact that the filtering in the complex domain does not favor any direction. As an alternative one could consider a filtering which smooths the phase stronger than the amplitude of the image. We refer to such an approach as anisotropic.

Combining the Cosine Fit with Spatial Regularization: Here the approach is to find $A(x)$, $\phi(x)$ and $I(x)$ minimizing

$$\left(\sum_x \sum_{j=0}^{3} \left(\tfrac{A(x)}{2} \cos(\tau_j + \phi(x)) + I(x) - A_j(x) \right)^2 \right) + \mathcal{R}(A, \phi, I). \tag{10}$$

For the regularization term $\mathcal{R}$, we propose to consider the total variation of each of the unknowns independently, i.e.

$$\mathcal{R}(A, \phi, I) = \lambda_1 TV(A) + \lambda_2 TV(\phi) + \lambda_3 TV(I), \tag{11}$$

for some $\lambda_1, \lambda_2, \lambda_3 > 0$. Note that $\mathcal{R}(\cdot)$ couples the local optimization problems considered in (5). The optimization problem (10) has the advantage that the spatial regularity of the solution compensates for local distortions of the data A_j. The drawback of (10) is its non-convexity. The existence of a unique solution is not guaranteed and, even if, it is likely that the numerical optimization gets stuck in a local minimum. As a consequence, the retrieved numerical solution depends on the initialization and might not be the global minimum. The standard approach to cope with this non-convexity is to find a convex reformulation of the data term in (10) by applying a change of variables from (A, ϕ, I) to $(z, \bar{z}, I) = (\tfrac{A}{2} Z, \tfrac{A}{2}\overline{Z}, I)$, where $Z := e^{i\phi}$ (dependency on x omitted for simplicity). Then

$$\tfrac{A}{2} \cos(\tau_j + \phi) + I = \tfrac{1}{2}(e^{i\frac{\pi j}{2}} z + e^{-i\frac{\pi j}{2}} \bar{z}) + I, \qquad j = 0, \dots, 3. \tag{12}$$

Moreover, standard calculus shows that the data term in (10) locally can be split into terms depending only on either z or I:

$$\sum_{j=0}^{3} \left(\tfrac{A}{2} \cos(\tau_j + \phi) + I - A_j \right)^2 = T_1(z) + T_2(I) + T_3, \tag{13}$$

where

$$T_1(z) := 2(Re(z) - \tfrac{1}{2}(A_0 - A_2))^2 + 2(Im(z) - \tfrac{1}{2}(A_3 - A_1))^2, \tag{14}$$

$$T_2(I) := 4(I - \tfrac{1}{4} \sum_{j=0}^{3} A_j)^2, \tag{15}$$

$$T_3 := \tfrac{1}{4} \sum_{j=0}^{3} A_j^2 - \tfrac{1}{2}(A_0 A_1 - A_0 A_2 + A_0 A_3 + A_1 A_2 - A_1 A_3 + A_2 A_3). \tag{16}$$

In particular, (13) can be optimized with respect to z and I independently. We remark that we are mainly interested in z and $\phi = \arg(z)$. For z we retrieve the complex-valued data term already considered in (9). However, the regularization terms $\mathcal{R}(A, \phi, I)$ and $\mathcal{R}(z)$ differ. The strong advantage of (9) compared to (10) with respect to numerical treatment is the strong convexity of optimization problem. In particular, a unique solution is guaranteed.

Denoising the Depth Data: Finally, we consider the approach of filtering the depth data $d(\boldsymbol{x})$. This is the most commonly used strategy for denoising ToF data. Here we exemplarily consider total variation filtering, bilateral filtering and cross-bilateral filtering using both depth and intensity as input.

We remark that the approaches considered above differ in their numerical effort, which is approximately proportional on the number of channels (unknown variables) which have to be filtered. These are *four* in the case of filtering the raw data, *three* in the case of the cosine fit, *two* for filtering the complex data and *one* for smoothing the depth map. Thus, regarding numerical efficiency, the filtering of the depth map is preferable.

3.3   Restoration Quality

Since the basic aim of ToF cameras is to provide the depth of objects in the scene, the most important issue of filtering ToF data is to preserve the accuracy of the measured depth. This also concerns the location of depth edges, the depth difference at those edges and the optimal reconstruction of the slopes of surfaces.

Various techniques exist to improve given denoising schemes. We recall some particular, which concern the bilateral filter as well as the TV denoising approach. One important modification is to introduce *adaptivity* of the smoothing parameters. At edges, these parameters can be reduced to improve the edge preservation properties of the methods. This requires additional information about the edge location. For TV denoising, in particular, adaptivity of the regularization parameter significantly reduces the unfavorable loss of contrast.

Another way to improve denoising methods by local information is introduce directional dependency or *anisotropy* (also being a form of adaptivity). The basic idea goes back to the anisotropic diffusion approach presented in [5]. The aim is to provide a stronger smoothing parallel to edges than in normal direction. In the bilateral filter, the convolution mask can be made directionally depended. In the TV approaches, the regularization term can be made anisotropic, see e.g. [11]. In both cases, additional information on the location and orientation is required.

In particular, for TV approaches aiming at denoising depth data it has proven successful to include *second-order regularization* terms. Instead of piecewise constant data, these methods then favor piecewise planar structures.

We remark that with planar surfaces the following issue arises: As already mentioned above, ToF cameras provide the radial depth. After projection into 2D, planar 3D surfaces show up with a certain curvature. Using the z-depth reduces this projection effect. Thus, the model of piecewise planar, which second-order TV assumes, is fulfilled only approximately. The most accurate way to deal

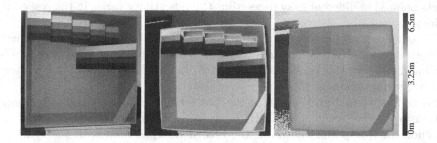

Fig. 2. The HCI box: recorded scene (left), ToF amplitude (middle) and ToF depth map (right) recorded wit a PMD Cam Cube 3

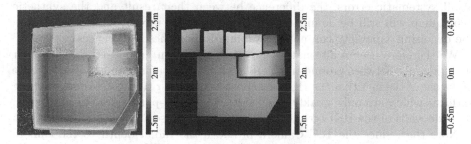

Fig. 3. Depth map with color bar clipped from 1.5 to 2.5 m, corresponding ground truth (dark blue areas are void) and difference image

with planar surfaces would be to directly work in 3D coordinates and consider the surface curvature of the objects, with the drawback that the numerical effort increases. However, the mentioned projection effect is relatively weak compared to systematic errors occurring in ToF data, such as the multi-path problem. Thus the dominant systematic errors should be tackled first before accounting for this effect.

For a detailed discussion on how edge information from both intensity/amplitude and depth data can be used to steer adaptivity, and for details on higher order TV denoising, we refer to [28].

4 Experiments and Evaluation

In this section we experimentally compare the methods presented in Section 3, applied at different positions in the processing pipeline.

As test data set, we use a recording of the *HCI box*[1] with a PMD Cam Cube 3, see Fig. 2. The box is made of medium-density fiberboard and shows different kinds of planar surfaces. Some of the surfaces are covered with paper

---

[1] http://hci.iwr.uni-heidelberg.de/Benchmarks/document/hcibox/

sheets painted in different gray tones, thus the reflectivity varies in the respective regions.

For our evaluation, we require ground truth to determine the error of each method considered. Therefore, we start with a discussion on appropriate ground truth and a description on how it is obtained. In addition, we refer to Chapter 4 for further discussion on this topic.

There is a virtual grid model of the box available, from which, after registration to the real scene, a synthetic depth map in view of the real camera can be rendered. Comparing, however, the recorded depth map with the synthetic one, the difference between both reveals not only the noise of the ToF camera but also all other kinds of systematic errors such as multi-path or an intensity dependent error. These systematic errors even dominate compared to the noise. Since the denoising methods considered above are not designed for the removal of all systematic errors, the difference between their result and the synthetic depth map will still be dominated by the systematic errors. As a consequence, the denoising capability can not be evaluated upon these differences.

We therefore use an alternative approach to obtain ground truth, such that the difference between ground truth and test data contains mainly noise. Here we make use of the fact that the HCI box consists of planar surfaces. We select those surfaces which are only weakly effected by the multi-path error. In particular, the side walls of the HCI box are left out for this reason.

Note that, since the ToF Camera provides the radial depth to the camera center, these surfaces appear curved in the 2D depth maps. After projecting the 2D data back into 3D, a linear regression can be applied to approximate the noise free 3D surfaces. In the linear regression, regions of high noise due to low amplitude are disregarded. The ideal planar surfaces then can be projected back to retrieve the radial depth of the scene. Fig. 3 shows the result for selected regions in the depth map. We use the resulting depth in these regions as ground truth.

In order to have a fair comparison of the individual methods, care should be taken to choose the optimal parameters for each method. For our experiments we retrieve approximately optimal parameters for each method by means of the ground truth, which in practical applications of course is not at hand: for each method we seek for optimal parameters on a adaptively refined grid, so that the mean squared error (MSE) to the ground truth is minimized.

The results of the individual methods applied with these parameters are depicted in Fig. 4. Close-ups of an inner part of the HCI box are provided in Fig. 5. In addition we provide the MSE to the ground truth in Table 1.

We observe that the methods act differently on the background regions with strong noise. The cosine fitting as well as the bilateral filter applied to the depth data do barely smooth these regions at all. In order to further reduce this noise, a stronger smoothing would be preferable. Moreover, since the parameters where chosen to optimally reconstruct the planar areas where ground truth is provided, the restoration of edge regions are not as good as expected. Again, increase of the smoothing parameters would improve the regularity of the edges.

We recall that our objective is to compare methods with respect to their position in the processing pipeline. We therefore consider TV denoising and bilateral filter separately. When comparing the errors of the TV-based methods in Table 1, the cosine fitting clearly represents an outlier. This seems to be due to the non-convexity of the considered objective function, so that the optimization process most likely got stuck in a local minimum. Besides from this outlier, the TV-based methods show a clear trend. The MSE decreases the more the method is shifted to the end of the pipeline. Also the reconstruction of edges becomes better, the later the denoising methods is applied. It turns out, that the optimal strategy is to apply TV denoising at there very end of the pipeline.

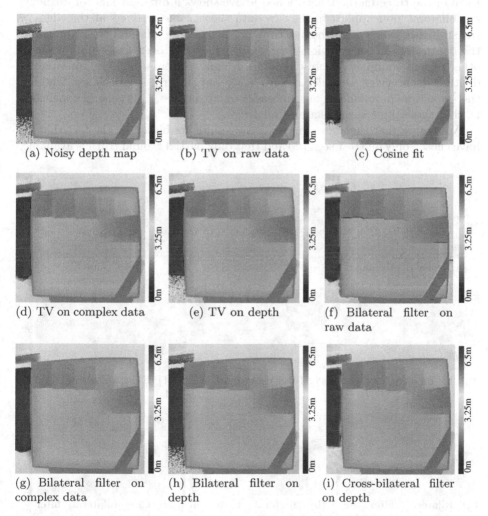

(a) Noisy depth map   (b) TV on raw data   (c) Cosine fit

(d) TV on complex data   (e) TV on depth   (f) Bilateral filter on raw data

(g) Bilateral filter on complex data   (h) Bilateral filter on depth   (i) Cross-bilateral filter on depth

Fig. 4. Applying the bilateral filter and TV denoising at different positions of the processing pipeline. Besides the accurate restoration of surfaces (cf. MSE in Table 1) the removal of heavy noise (left region of the data) and a sharp reconstruction of edges is of importance

Concerning bilateral filter, the smallest MSE is achieved by applying the bilateral filter to the four raw channels. The result, however, reveals some distorted pixels, see Figs. 4 and 5. These distorted pixels result from the phase ambiguity after evaluating $\arctan(\cdot)$. These distortions can be corrected by subsequently applying a median filter, which reduces the MSE further to $1.3524 \cdot 10^{-4}$. The second best result is provided by the bilateral filter applied to the depth data. Interestingly, the standard bilateral filter on the depth data slightly outperforms the cross-bilateral filter in terms of MSE.

Since the ground truth data only cover a part of the data set, it is inevitable to also compare the different variants in the remaining parts, especially at edges. Each of the three methods mentioned above shows a different kind of artifacts: the bilateral filter applied to the raw data shows some artifacts at the edges of the staircase, which might be due to flying pixels. The bilateral filter applied to the depth data in some regions (e.g. stairs) shows an over-smoothing, while in other regions (ramp) some noise remains. Finally, the cross-bilateral filter on the depth data provides a regular reconstruction of the true depth edges, while in the same time pronouncing false intensity-related edges. Our general conclusion is, that these three variants are competitive.

We remark that the above quantitative results are biased by the fact that we have chosen only one test scenario and that only partial ground truth is available.

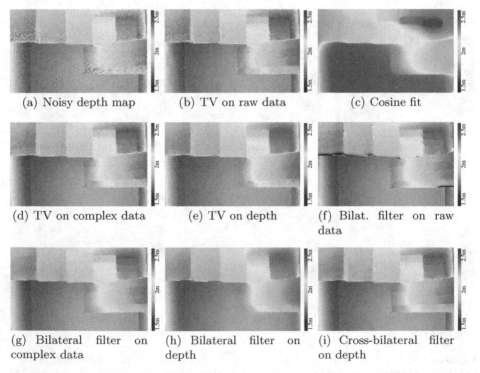

(a) Noisy depth map   (b) TV on raw data   (c) Cosine fit

(d) TV on complex data   (e) TV on depth   (f) Bilat. filter on raw
                                                             data

(g) Bilateral filter on   (h) Bilateral filter on   (i) Cross-bilateral filter
    complex data   depth   on depth

Fig. 5. Close-ups of the results in Fig. 4, where the bilateral filter and TV denoising are applied at different positions in the processing pipeline

Table 1. Mean squared error (MSE) to the ground truth (cf. Fig. 3) of the methods under consideration. The MSE strongly varies depending on the position within the processing pipeline. The bilateral filter on raw data with subsequent median filtering gives the smallest MSE.

Method	MSE $(\cdot 10^{-4})$
Bilateral filter on raw data $A_j(x)$	1.4871
Bilateral filter on raw data plus median filter	1.3524
Bilateral filter on complex data $z(x)$	1.5444
Bilateral filter on depth map $d(x)$	1.5391
Cross bilateral filter on depth map $d(x)$	1.5819
TV denoising on raw data $A_j(x)$	1.6699
Non-convex cosine fit	7.1208
TV denoising on complex data $z(x)$	1.6320
TV denoising on depth map $d(x)$	1.5862

This stresses the need for larger data sets with highly accurate ground truth as well as a good error measure for evaluating the restoration of edges.

As mentioned in Section 3.3, additional strategies can be applied to improve the standard methods considered so far. We exemplarily consider the total variation denoising of the depth data to illustrate the potential of improvement of the methods considered so far. For TV denoising, in order to reduce the loss of contrast and prevent stair-casing, *anisotropic* total variation of first- and second-order can be applied. We refer to our work [51] for details on this approach. The result of this method is shown in Fig. 6. It achieves an MSE of $1.5105 \cdot 10^{-4}$ compared to $1.5862 \cdot 10^{-4}$ for the standard TV approach. For the bilateral filter corresponding modifications can be considered.

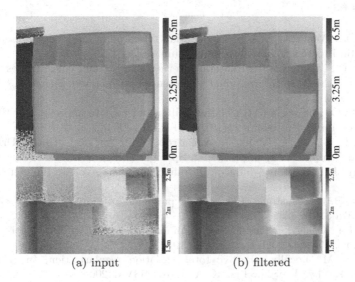

(a) input (b) filtered

Fig. 6. Applying adaptive first- and second-order TV on the depth map

5   Conclusion

This chapter started with an overview of state-of-the-art image denoising techniques as well as denoising algorithms especially designed for ToF data. Both image-driven and database-driven approaches were considered. As the central theme of this chapter, we discussed two alternatives for positioning the denoising algorithms in the data processing pipeline. Two well-established exemplary methods were considered and experimentally evaluated for this purpose: One is the *bilateral filtering* and the other is the *total variation-based denoising*. It turned out that for TV denoising the optimal position is at the end of the processing pipeline. For the bilateral filter, we found that applying it to the raw channels and performing a subsequent median filter provides the smallest quantitative error. Qualitatively, it competes with applying the bilateral and the cross-bilateral filter to the depth data. The general conclusion is, that the optimal position depends on the considered denoising method. As a consequence, for any newly introduced denoising technique, finding its optimal position within the pipeline is an issue which should be discussed along with the method.

Acknowledgements. This work is part of two research projects with the Intel Visual Computing Institute in Saarbrücken and with the Filmakademie Baden-Württemberg, Institute of Animation, respectively. It is co-funded by the Intel Visual Computing Institute and under grant 2-4225.16/380 of the Ministry of Economy Baden-Württemberg as well as the further partners Unexpected, Pixomondo, ScreenPlane, Bewegte Bilder and Tridelity. The content is under sole responsibility of the authors.

References

1. Aurich, V., Weule, J.: Non-linear Gaussian filters performing edge preserving diffusion. In: Proceed. 17. DAGM-Symposium (1995)
2. Tomasi, C., Manduchi, R.: Bilateral filtering for gray and color images. In: Proceedings of the Sixth International Conference on Computer Vision (ICCV 1998), p. 839 (1998)
3. Elad, M.: On the origin of the bilateral filter and ways to improve it. IEEE Transactions on Image Processing 11(10), 1141–1151 (2002)
4. Perona, P., Shiota, T., Malik, J.: Anisotropic diffusion. In: Geometry-Driven Diffusion in Computer Vision, pp. 73–92. Springer (1994)
5. Weickert, J.: Anisotropic diffusion in image processing, vol. 1. Teubner Stuttgart (1998)
6. Donoho, D.L., Johnstone, J.M.: Ideal spatial adaptation by wavelet shrinkage. Biometrika 81(3), 425–455 (1994)
7. Rudin, L.I., Osher, S., Fatemi, E.: Nonlinear total variation based noise removal algorithms. Phys. D 60(1-4), 259–268 (1992)
8. Grasmair, M.: Locally adaptive total variation regularization. In: Tai, X.-C., Mørken, K., Lysaker, M., Lie, K.-A. (eds.) SSVM 2009. LNCS, vol. 5567, pp. 331–342. Springer, Heidelberg (2009)

9. Dong, Y.: Multi-scale total variation with automated regularization parameter selection for color image restoration. In: Tai, X.-C., Mørken, K., Lysaker, M., Lie, K.-A. (eds.) SSVM 2009. LNCS, vol. 5567, pp. 271–281. Springer, Heidelberg (2009)
10. Steidl, G., Teuber, T.: Anisotropic smoothing using double orientations. In: Tai, X.-C., Mørken, K., Lysaker, M., Lie, K.-A. (eds.) SSVM 2009. LNCS, vol. 5567, pp. 477–489. Springer, Heidelberg (2009)
11. Lenzen, F., Becker, F., Lellmann, J., Petra, S., Schnörr, C.: A class of quasi-variational inequalities for adaptive image denoising and decomposition. Computational Optimization and Applications, 1–28 (2013)
12. Bredies, K., Kunisch, K., Pock, T.: Total Generalized Variation. SIAM J. Imaging Sciences 3(3), 492–526 (2010)
13. Setzer, S., Steidl, G., Teuber, T.: Infimal convolution regularizations with discrete l1-type functionals. Comm. Math. Sci. 9, 797–872 (2011)
14. Lenzen, F., Becker, F., Lellmann, J.: Adaptive second-order total variation: An approach aware of slope discontinuities. In: Pack, T. (ed.) SSVM 2013. LNCS, vol. 7893, pp. 61–73. Springer, Heidelberg (2013)
15. Mumford, D., Shah, J.: Optimal approximations by piecewise smooth functions and associated variational problems. Communications on Pure and Applied Mathematics 42(5), 577–685 (1989)
16. Pock, T., Cremers, D., Bischof, H., Chambolle, A.: An algorithm for minimizing the piecewise smooth mumford-shah functional. In: IEEE International Conference on Computer Vision (ICCV), Kyoto, Japan (2009)
17. Buades, A., Coll, B., Morel, J.: A review of image denoising algorithms, with a new one. Multiscale Model. Simul. 4(2), 490–530 (2005)
18. Gilboa, G., Osher, S.: Nonlocal operators with applications to image processing. Multiscale Model. Simul. 7(3), 1005–1028 (2008)
19. Kindermann, S., Osher, S., Jones, P.: Deblurring and denoising of images by nonlocal functionals. Multiscale Model. Simul. 4(4), 1091–1115 (2005) (electronic)
20. Dabov, K., Foi, A., Katkovnik, V., Egiazarian, K.: Image denoising by sparse 3-d transform-domain collaborative filtering. IEEE Transactions on Image Processing 16(8), 2080–2095 (2007)
21. Burger, H.C., Schuler, C.J., Harmeling, S.: Image denoising: Can plain neural networks compete with BM3D? In: IEEE Conference on Computer Vision and Pattern Recognition (CVPR 2012), pp. 2392–2399. IEEE (2012)
22. Jain, V., Seung, H.S.: Natural image denoising with convolutional networks. In: Advances in Neural Information Processing Systems, pp. 769–776 (2008)
23. Freeman, W.T., Jones, T.R., Pasztor, E.C.: Example-based super-resolution. IEEE Computer Graphics and Applications 22(2), 56–65 (2002)
24. Tappen, M.F., Russel, B.C., Freeman, W.T.: Exploiting the sparse derivative prior for super-resolution and image demosaicing. In: Proc. International Workshop on Statistical and Computational Theories of Vision (2003)
25. Kim, K.I., Kwon, Y.: Single-image super-resolution using sparse regression and natural image prior. IEEE Trans. Pattern Analysis and Machine Intelligence 32(6), 1127–1133 (2010)
26. Kim, K.I., Kwon, Y., Kim, J.H., Theobalt, C.: Efficient learning-based image enhancement: application to compression artifact removal and super-resolution. Technical Report MPI-I-2011-4-002, Max-Planck-Insitut für Informatik (February 2011)
27. Frank, M., Plaue, M., Rapp, K., Köthe, U., Jähne, B., Hamprecht, F.: Theoretical and experimental error analysis of continuous-wave time-of-flight range cameras. Optical Engineering 48(1), 13602 (2009)

28. Lenzen, F., Schäfer, H., Garbe, C.: Denoising time-of-flight data with adaptive total variation. In: Bebis, G. (ed.) ISVC 2011, Part I. LNCS, vol. 6938, pp. 337–346. Springer, Heidelberg (2011)

29. Schöner, H., Moser, B., Dorrington, A.A., Payne, A., Cree, M.J., Heise, B., Bauer, F.: A clustering based denoising technique for range images of time of flight cameras. In: CIMCA/IAWTIC/ISE 2008, pp. 999–1004 (2008)

30. Moser, B., Bauer, F., Elbau, P., Heise, B., Schöner, H.: Denoising techniques for raw 3D data of ToF cameras based on clustering and wavelets. In: Proc. SPIE, vol. 6805 (2008)

31. Frank, M., Plaue, M., Hamprecht, F.A.: Denoising of continuous-wave time-of-flight depth images using confidence measures. Optical Engineering 48 (2009)

32. Edeler, T.: Bildverbesserung von Time-Of-Flight-Tiefenkarten. Shaker Verlag (2011)

33. Edeler, T., Ohliger, K., Hussmann, S., Mertins, A.: Time-of-flight depth image denoising using prior noise information. In: Proceedings ICSP, pp. 119–122 (2010)

34. Seitel, A., dos Santos, T.R., Mersmann, S., Penne, J., Groch, A., Yung, K., Tetzlaff, R., Meinzer, H.P., Maier-Hein, L.: Adaptive bilateral filter for image denoising and its application to in-vitro time-of-flight data, 796423–796423–8 (2011)

35. Schöner, H., Bauer, F., Dorrington, A., Heise, B., Wieser, V., Payne, A., Cree, M.J., Moser, B.: Image processing for 3d-scans generated by time of flight range cameras. SPIE Journal of Electronic Imaging 2 (2012)

36. Schuon, S., Theobalt, C., Davis, J., Thrun, S.: Lidarboost: Depth superresolution for tof 3d shape scanning. In: IEEE Conference on Computer Vision and Pattern Recognition, CVPR 2009, pp. 343–350. IEEE (2009)

37. Mure-Dubois, J., Hügli, H., et al.: Fusion of time of flight camera point clouds. Workshop on Multi-camera and Multi-Modal Sensor Fusion Algorithms and Applications-M2SFA2 2008 (2008)

38. Edeler, T., Ohliger, K., Hussmann, S., Mertins, A.: Super resolution of time-of-flight depth images under consideration of spatially varying noise variance. In: 16th IEEE Int. Conf. on Image Processing (ICIP), Cairo, Egypt, pp. 1185–1188 (November 2009)

39. Chan, D., Buisman, H., Theobalt, C., Thrun, S., et al.: A noise-aware filter for real-time depth upsampling. In: Workshop on Multi-camera and Multi-modal Sensor Fusion Algorithms and Applications-M2SFA2 2008 (2008)

40. Huhle, B., Schairer, T., Jenke, P., Straßer, W.: Robust non-local denoising of colored depth data. In: IEEE Computer Society Conference on Computer Vision and Pattern Recognition Workshops, CVPRW 2008, pp. 1–7. IEEE (2008)

41. Yeo, D., Kim, J., Baig, M.W., Shin, H., et al.: Adaptive bilateral filtering for noise removal in depth upsampling. In: 2010 International SoC Design Conference (ISOCC), pp. 36–39. IEEE (2010)

42. Park, J., Kim, H., Tai, Y.W., Brown, M.S., Kweon, I.: High quality depth map upsampling for 3d-tof cameras. In: 2011 IEEE International Conference on Computer Vision (ICCV), pp. 1623–1630. IEEE (2011)

43. Reynolds, M., Doboš, J., Peel, L., Weyrich, T., Brostow, G.J.: Capturing time-of-flight data with confidence. In: IEEE Conference on Computer Vision and Pattern Recognition, CVPR 2011, pp. 945–952. IEEE (2011)

44. Mac Aodha, O., Campbell, N.D.F., Nair, A., Brostow, G.J.: Patch based synthesis for single depth image super-resolution. In: Fitzgibbon, A., Lazebnik, S., Perona, P., Sato, Y., Schmid, C. (eds.) ECCV 2012, Part III. LNCS, vol. 7574, pp. 71–84. Springer, Heidelberg (2012)

45. Kopf, J., Cohen, M.F., Lischinski, D., Uyttendaele, M.: Joint bilateral upsampling. In: ACM SIGGRAPH 2007 Papers. SIGGRAPH 2007. ACM, New York (2007)
46. Eisemann, E., Durand, F.: Flash photography enhancement via intrinsic relighting. ACM Transactions on Graphics (TOG) 23, 673–678 (2004)
47. Petschnigg, G., Szeliski, R., Agrawala, M., Cohen, M., Hoppe, H., Toyama, K.: Digital photography with flash and no-flash image pairs. ACM Transactions on Graphics (TOG) 23, 664–672 (2004)
48. Chambolle, A., Pock, T.: A first-order primal-dual algorithm for convex problems with applications to imaging. Journal of Mathematical Imaging and Vision 40(1), 120–145 (2011)
49. Schmidt, M.: Analysis, Modeling and Dynamic Optimization of 3D Time-of-Flight Imaging Systems. Dissertation, IWR, Fakultät f ür Physik und Astronomie, Univ. Heidelberg (2011)
50. Blomgren, P., Chan, T.F.: Color tv: Total variation methods for restoration of vector-valued images. IEEE Transactions on Image Processing 7(3), 304–309 (1998)
51. Schäfer, H., Lenzen, F., Garbe, C.S.: Depth and intensity based edge detection in time-of-flight images. In: Proceedings of 3DV. IEEE (in press, 2013)

Stabilization of 3D Position Measurement

Julien Thollot, Xavier Baele, and Ilse Ravyse

SoftKinetic, Boulevard de la Plaine 15, 1050 Brussels, Belgium
ira@softkinetic.com

Abstract. Within the particular context of ToF imaging we investigate a real-time cost-efficient filtering method for the stabilization of 3D data. The current limitation in frame rate, resolution and intrinsic depth measurement accuracy of range finding imaging systems, together with the reflective and motion properties of the objects in the scene, may lead to noisy or inaccurate depth map reconstruction. Still, in many applications such as gesture recognition or skeleton modeling and rendering, reliable and stable point location data has to be extracted from the depth map. To overcome the depth map limitations in the context of human-computer interaction, we propose a simple, fast and efficient stabilization method to filter the raw 3D data measurements or their derivatives. This filter maintains the reliability of the original measurements of an identified 3D point when smoothing the continuous change in its 3D position, avoids jerky movements without introducing noticeable latency nor impacting rapid motion.

1 Introduction

Time-of-flight cameras measure the distance of the imaged objects to the camera at each pixel, at an intrinsic noise rate. At the borders of the objects the pixels tend to be mixed when a single measurement includes closeby depths of a foreground object and far away depths of a background, or when multipath light effects happen. This effect has more impact for objects further away from the camera because they are measured in a lower resolution (pixels/meter). The combination of all those disturbing characteristics may lead to perturbations in the object depth measurement. In the domain of image processing, and especially in relation to video stabilization, several filtering methods have been developed to reduce the noise while tracking objects. They can be classified according to the constraint of computation cost, namely (i) low cost but latency sensitive methods based on conventional statistical models such as the median filter and (ii) higher cost based on predictive analysis models such as the Kalman filters. In this paper we propose a low cost stabilzation method with a better smoothing performance as a Kalman filter when the object is in nearly static condition and similarly performing for human dynamic motion conditions.

The remainder of the paper is organized as follows. Section 2 summarizes the context of 3D gesture tracking and section 3 formulates the stabilization method. Finally, in Section 4 experimental results are discussed and main conclusions are exposed in Section 5.

M. Grzegorzek et al. (Eds.): Time-of-Flight and Depth Imaging, LNCS 8200, pp. 46–51, 2013.

2 Human Motion Analysis Context

In many human computer interaction applications, including motion analysis, reliable data has to be extracted from depth maps. According to the defects observed, the representation in a virtual environment of an object may exhibit instability of its 3D position over time. In particular, the mentioned defects may break the spatio-temporal coherency of the representation of a captured object as a 3D points cloud or of one of its derivatives (e.g. a cluster, center of mass, or other associated data). This is a strong limitation for smart visual feedback of moving or static object based 3D interactions, for skeletal modeling, and especially for performing reliable analysis or gesture recognition in a human to computer interaction context, as shown for example in the tracking by iisu® middleware of a fingertip in close interaction mode [1] in Figure 1.

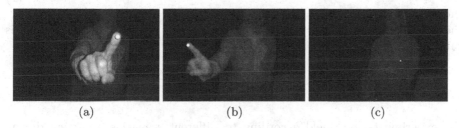

(a)   (b)   (c)

Fig. 1. Depth images of close interaction tracking of a fingertip at (a) $0.17m$ (b) $0.29m$ and (c) $0.43m$ away from the SoftKinetic DepthSense® ToF camera and iisu® [1]

3 Method of Stabilization

The sequential 3D positioning of a 3D point of interest in space is filtered on the fly using its current position, denoted $\mathbf{x}(t)$, and the previous position measurement, denoted $\mathbf{x}(t-1)$, as well as the position measurement before $\mathbf{x}(t-1)$, denoted $\mathbf{x}(t-2)$. To prevent from introducing a noticeable delay between the real position of the 3D point of interest and its measurement, the filter comprises a standard attenuation of the observed movement between $\mathbf{x}(t)$ and $\mathbf{x}(t-1)$, using an attenuation filter such as a power function based filter, only when this movement amplitude is below threshold T, as depicted in Figure 2a. The treshold T represents a distance in the 3D space that defines a limit under which the filtering is applied. Namely, at slow motion, when unstable or incoherent movement of the 3D point of interest may occur due to discretization errors, the 3D distance between $\mathbf{x}(t)$ and $\mathbf{x}(t-1)$ is stabilized and hence a distance threshold T must be chosen at least bigger than the errors that might occur. Note that, as mentioned before, these errors are function of the sensor resolution, acquisition frequency and speed of the 3D point of interest. At fast motion, the position of the 3D point of interest will not be stabilzed because the discussed discretization errors are less prominent. The power of the attenuation function (a power strength s in the experiments) is modified (divided by $r > 1$) in accordance with the filtering status of the previously observed movement between $\mathbf{x}(t-1)$ and $\mathbf{x}(t-2)$ to moderate the strength of the filtering and to enhance and smooth dynamically the behavior of the 3D point that requires filtering on each new frame. The power strenght s is dimmed by the attenuating factor r to ensure that stabilization will still occur and can decrease gradually when the previous position has been filtered. The value of r can be set emperically or as function of the number of previous considered measurements in the stabilization (in this work fixed at 2) and the average speed of the meaningful motion of the 3D point of interest. Hence, the filter is formulated as:

$$
\widehat{\mathbf{x}}_i(t) = \begin{cases} \widehat{\mathbf{x}}_i(t-1) + (\mathbf{A}_i(t)/T)^s * T & \text{if } d_i(\mathbf{A}(t)) \leq T, d_i(\mathbf{B}(t-1)) = 0 \\ \widehat{\mathbf{x}}_i(t-1) + (\mathbf{A}_i(t)/T)^{max(1,s/r)} * T & \text{if } d_i(\mathbf{A}(t)) \leq T, d_i(\mathbf{B}(t-1)) > 0 \\ \mathbf{x}_i(t) & \text{if } d_i(\mathbf{A}(t)) > T \end{cases}
$$

$$(1)$$

where $i = \{x, y, z\}$, $\mathbf{A}(t) = \mathbf{x}(t) - \widehat{\mathbf{x}}(t-1)$, $\mathbf{B}(t) = \mathbf{x}(t) - \widehat{\mathbf{x}}(t)$, $d_i(.) = |._i|$. The condition $d(\mathbf{B}(t)) > 0$ verifies if the movement between $\mathbf{x}_i(t)$ and $\widehat{\mathbf{x}}_i(t)$ is stabilized.

4   Experiments

The experiments were held according to different scenarios occurring during gesture based interactions between a human and a computer. More precisely, we have analyzed the behavior of a 3D point captured by a ToF camera that represents a part of a human body, namely a 3D position representing a fingertip of a hand. This data was recorded using a QVGA DepthSense® 325, using the gesture recognition software iisu® in close interaction at 30fps. Figure 2b shows the motion of the x-coordinate of the fingertip over a series of depth images depicted in Figure 1. The data is grouped per depth (z), and comprises periods of static, slow dynamic waving motion, and similar rapid motion. The x-coordinate was set to 0 when tracking was lost.

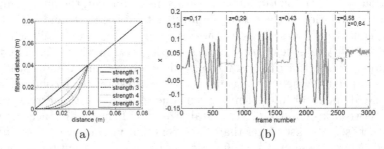

(a)   (b)

Fig. 2. (a) Stabilization function with $T = 0.04$m; (b) unstabilized tracked fingertip at (green) non , (blue) slow , (red) rapid horizontal motion in a plane perpendicular to the camera view direction

The proposed patented stabilization method was compared to the median filter as conventional low cost filtering method and to the Kalman predictive filter [2,3]. On the x-axis the data was stabilized with $T = 0.04$m, $s = 2.5$ and 3 and $r = 2$. Figure 3 zooms in the results on the static period at $z = 0.64$m distance from the camera, and Figure 4 on the rapid motions at 0.17m and 0.29m. Table 1 compares the standard deviation of the movement amplitude per period per filter.

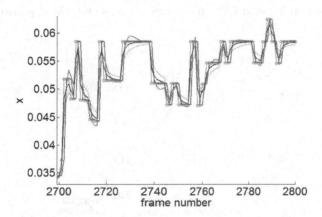

Fig. 3. Tracked fingertip at 0,64m ; in (grey) unstabilized, (blue) stabilized with $s = 2.5, T = 0.04$, (cyan) stabilized with $s = 3, T = 0.04$, (red) median filtered (green) kalman filtered

Table 1. Standard deviation of the movement amplitude $\sigma(|\mathbf{x}(t-1)_\mathbf{x} - \mathbf{x}(t)_\mathbf{x}|)$ in mm

period of	static					slow motion			rapid motion		
at z (in m) =	0.17	0.29	0.43	0.58	0.64	0.17	0.29	0.43	0.17	0.29	0.43
unstabilized	0.3	0.5	0.7	1.8	3.4	4.0	3.6	3.6	9.7	10.0	16.6
stabilized $s = 2.5$	0.05	0.1	0.3	0.7	1.5	3.7	2.2	2.3	9.0	8.7	16.0
stabilized $s = 3$	0.1	0.2	0.4	1.1	2.2	3.8	2.5	2.7	9.1	8.8	16.0
median	0.3	0.5	0.6	1.8	3.3	4.0	3.6	3.6	5.8	9.9	16.6
kalman	0.2	0.3	0.4	1.0	1.8	2.3	1.8	1.8	4.5	5.3	9.1

Figs. 3 and 4 reveals that both the proposed stabilization and the Kalman filter lead to smoothed estimations close to the measured position, wheras the median filter introduces a noticeable delay and skips lost tracking data of less than the filterwindow duration. The proposed filter cannot exceed one frame delay, which is an acceptable and not noticeable latency for graphical user interface based interactions as targeted by the hand analysis motion iisu software of SoftKinetic [1]. At the rapid motions the Kalman filter tends to overshoot when changing direction, while the proposed filter does not. This Kalman filter overshoot may cause problems of false path matching in dynamic gesture recognition and to collision with virtual objects of the virtual hands operated by a set of stabilized tracked points in an augmented reality context. Thus in this application context our proposed stabilization is more appropriate. Indeed, the closeness of the standard deviation of the movement amplitude of the stabilized data to the unstabilized data for dynamic movements, in Table 1, indicates that the distribution of the position measurement is preserved. Furthermore, with a similar amount of filtered values (2580 for $s = 2.5$, 2491 for Kalman, out of 2691 frames) and less computational load, by comparing the equations in [2] and eqn. 1, our stabilization methods is better suited for a real-time gesture-recognition implementation on low-end CPU platforms such as embedded platforms.

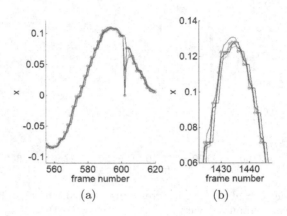

(a)   (b)

Fig. 4. Tracked fingertip at (a) 0.17m (b) 0.29m; in (grey) unstabilized, (blue) stabilized with $s = 2.5, T = 0.04$, (cyan) stabilized with $s = 3, T = 0.04$, (red) median filtered (green) kalman filtered

5   Conclusion

One of the advantages of this stabilization method is that it filters efficiently standard noise on static objects whilst still allowing smooth and slow variations in the series of measurements, whereas other conventional low cost methods introduce latency. On dynamic motion data the method is better suited for gesture recognition than a predictive Kalman filter. We suggest further global improvements specifically for human-computer interaction by using a 3D distance based formulation of this stabilization method and by automating the choice of s and T parameters contextually (e.g. according to z). Hence, in iisu [1] the method is applied in parallel for several points of interest. The experiments have shown that the stabilization of the 3D point positions keeps the fluidity of the movement of the analyzed person without introducing noticeable lag between the real performance and its representation in a virtual world. This low latency is critical when applying real time gesture recognition or articulated object modeling and rendering.

References

1. The interface is you, iisu® sdk, 3d gesture recognition softkinetic middleware, version 3.6 (2013), http://www.softkinetic.com
2. Kohler, M.: Using the kalman filter to track human interactive motion: Modelling and initialization of the kalman filter for translational motion (1997)
3. Murphy, K.P.: Kalman Filtering toolbox for Matlab (1998, 2004)

Ground Truth for Evaluating Time of Flight Imaging

Rahul Nair[1,2], Stephan Meister[1,2], Martin Lambers[3], Michael Balda[4],
Hannes Hofmann[4], Andreas Kolb[3], Daniel Kondermann[1,2], and Bernd Jähne[1]

[1] Heidelberg Collaboratory for Image Processing (HCI),
Heidelberg University, Germany
{firstname.lastname}@iwr.uni-heidelberg.de
http://hci.iwr.uni-heidelberg.de/
[2] Intel Visual Computing Institute, Saarland University, Germany
http://www.intel-vci.uni-saarland.de/
[3] Computer Graphics Group, University of Siegen, Germany,
{firstname.lastname}@uni-siegen.de
http://www.cg.informatik.uni-siegen.de/
[4] Metrilus GmbH, Erlangen, Germany
{firstname.lastname}@metrilus.de
http://www.metrilus.de/

Abstract. In this work, we systematically analyze how good ground truth (GT) datasets for evaluating methods based on Time-of-Flight (ToF) imaging data should look like. Starting from a high level characterization of the application domains and requirements they typically have, we characterize how good datasets should look like and discuss how algorithms can be evaluated using them. Furthermore, we discuss the two different ways of obtaining ground truth data: By measurement and by simulation.

1 Introduction

Time-of-Flight imaging is known to suffer from various random and systematic error sources such as multi path, depth wiggling and sensor noise (cf. Chapter 2). Their low resolution additionally restricts their suitability to tasks that do not require a high lateral accuracy. Many methods have been proposed in literature to over-come these problems. Many of them were also published together with ground truth data on which the algorithms were validated. As these works center on the methods themselves, usually less attention is given to the nature of the ground truth (GT) data, with the content chosen to be 'realistic' without further specification what 'realistic' actually means. Furthermore, the simultaneous optimization of the GT data and the method at hand runs in danger of over fitting the algorithm to the data or vice versa. Therefore, we believe that a more rigorous definition of ground truth for Time-of-Flight imaging is necessary, independent of a specific method at hand or a specific camera manufacturer. The goal of this paper is to better define many of these problems. Starting from

M. Grzegorzek et al. (Eds.): Time-of-Flight and Depth Imaging, LNCS 8200, pp. 52–74, 2013.

a problem domain analysis we will investigate and discuss requirements for good GT data in Section 2. Next, in Section 3, we will discuss different ways of creating GT data by measuring reference data or by simulation. Then we will explore existing datasets and discuss what characteristics good datasets have in Section 4 before discussing performance measures to evaluate algorithms in Section 5. Finally, we will conclude with a section on best practices and lessons we learned during ground truth acquisation in Section 6.

2 Application Domains and Requirements Engineering

It is unlikely that we can find one generic algorithm which optimally works under all circumstances: This is called the generalization-specialization-dilemma. It states that given an application, our algorithm might either be so specific that it is not able to deal with previously unobserved data (overfitting). On the other hand the algorithm might generalize well over many scenarios but yield mediocre results in each of them. Thus, in order to analyze the appropriateness of an ToF algorithm for a given application, we need to know the application.

On the other hand, there might be an infinite number of yet unknown applications for ToF algorithms. It seems unlikely that we can first enumerate all applications and then analyze the performance of each and every algorithm for each and every application. System engineers found a way around this problem by identifying a number of meaningful and intuitive properties for each system component (c.f. Table 1). These are measured and then listed in a specification sheet. These properties are selected by finding those which are, ideally, important for as many relevant applications as possible. In order to select the most indicative properties, all currently available applications are considered. Then, by experimentation, system properties are selected and tested for their usefulness.

For four example applications we have identified a set of requirements, and analyzed which ones are relevant for each application. Table 1 enumerates the importance of several requirements for the example applications. Based on these findings, ground truth data and appropriate test scenarios can be acquired / generated to evaluate the performance and suitability of depth imaging devices and algorithms with respect to the application requirements. In the following we will discuss the requirements of various application fields, except for multimedia, which is discussed in Chapter 6. As low-level pre-processing algorithms are used in all applications below, we will first summarize their requirements separately.

Low-Level Pre-processing Algorithms

Well-known issues (cf. Chapter 1) such as noise (cf. Chapter 2), multi-path or motion-induced artifacts often need to be reduced before high-level algorithms can try to understand the scene. Superresolution (SR) is regularly used to scale up depth images and thereby increase the detail of depth edges. Usually, this approach is coupled with denoising and sometimes with sensor-fusion (cf. Chapter 6) were other cameras are used to obtain hints on how to increase the detail.

Table 1. Requirements and their importance for selected example applications. A + indicates an important requirement, 0 is less important and - unimportant.

Requirements	Gesture Control	Room Supervision	Driver Assistance/ Robotics	Multimedia
Low Latency	+	-	+	+
Low Noise / High Precision	0	0	+	+
High Accuracy	-	-	+	-
High Frame Rage	+	0	+	+
Motion Robustness	+	0	+	+
Robustness Against Environmental Influences	0	0	+	+
Interference Robustness	-	+	0	0
Low Hardware Requirements	0	0	+	-
Graceful Degradation Self-Inspection	0	+	+	0
Depth Range	-	0	+	-
Lateral Resolution	+	0	-	+

Multi-path is a largely unsolved problem, whereas motion artifacts can already be handled to some degree. In terms of requirements, these algorithms have in common, that they should ideally be able to annotate their outcome with confidences so that higher-level methods are able to judge whether they want to use the data at all.

All of these algorithms address information-theoretic problems: given a subset of the information of the scene, how can we add believable detail from other sources? Information is added by prior knowledge as simple as interpolation kernels, regularization techniques or more complex cues such as e.g. temporal coherence or different modalities (such as RGB color).

Other algorithms on intermediate and higher levels of semantic understanding could be 3D reconstruction and camera/object tracking as well as object detection and scene understanding. All of the discussed requirements can play a more or less important role, such as depth accuracy is important for 3D reconstruction but not necessarily for scene understanding whereas speed and beauty can play a role depending on the application domain.

Gesture Control

Gesture Control is one of the major and most mature depth imaging applications. Most gesture interaction systems do not need an overly high depth accuracy and precision, as they use distinct gestures to trigger actions and the accuracy of interactions is primarily limited by ergonomic considerations. However, low latency and motion robustness are mandatory for a good and pleasant gesture control system.

Room Supervision

With the room supervision application in mind, we are interested in the number of people in a room. Therefore, we want to use multiple cameras that observe the room from different angles to ensure that no person is occluded. The use of multiple cameras requires that they are able to observe the same scene without interfering with each other. The processing power required for image processing is increased with each added camera.

Reliability is very important in this application, so the system should be able to detect when it is in an undefined state. Since exact localization of the persons is not required, other requirements can be relaxed. Latency, motion robustness, accuracy and noise are not a big issue.

Driver Assistance/Mobile Robotics

In driver assistance and autonomous mobile robotics, i.e realtime systems with limited computational resources and possible public safety issues, speed is not the only important criterion: Energy, memory and bandwidth consumption have to be taken into consideration, as many subsystems are competing for limited system resources. Accuracy is also relevant, as the desired behavior depends on the distance to a detected obstacle - e.g. start breaking or initiate an evasive ma- neuver. Finally, the algorithm should not only have self-inspection capabilities, but also degrade gracefully, as small irritations such as specular reflections on other cars or interference with other ToF-equipped vehicles can occur frequently.

In the following chapters, we will discuss different techniques to create datasets for benchmarking such applications and requirements.

3   Ground Truth Generation

There are two ways of generating ground truth data. By measurement or by simulation. Both these approaches assume that the reference data is dense and has an error which is an order of magnitude smaller than the expected ToF error[1]. In all cases, two datasets are created simultaneously: A scene captured using ToF along with reference data for comparison. If reference data is measured, the accuracy of the reference modality and alignment issues need to be considered (cf. Chapter 3.1). GT can also be obtained by simulation. Here, a scene with known geometry is used as a starting point and the ToF data simulated using various ToF models (cf. Chapter 3.2). Even though such models usually need to make simplifications to remain tractable, they offer the opportunity of white box testing. Hence, this shifts the problem to the question what a good simulation is. The reference data may be exact but the derived data can show subtle differences compared to a real sequence.

---

[1] In Section 5.2 on weak and sparse ground truth we will discuss what can be done if this requirement does not hold anymore.

3.1 By Measurement

We will introduce various methods which can be used for measuring ground truth before discussing alignment issues that are relevant to all these methods. These datasets can be used for general black-box testing. In the last part, we will also discuss various strategies for isolating specific aspects of Time-of-Flight imagers for white-box testing.

3.1.1 Methods

A. High Precision Scanning

High precision scanning techniques include Time-of-Flight and triangulation based laser scanners as well as structured light scanners. **Structured light scanners** and **triangulation based laser scanners** both infer depth by triangulating the position of some active illumination pattern. Figure 1 depicts two example scans using these modalities. These scanners typically have an accuracy of 1 - 100 microns and can safely be considered to be an order of magnitude more accurate than ToF imagers [1]. They usually have a limited working volume of a few liters and have a working range of up to 2 meters[]. As all optical measurement techniques they succumb to objects with specular surfaces. Therefore, for best results, often the object to be scanned has to be coated with a diffuse paint.

Fig. 1. Left: high density point cloud of statue scanned using structured light. Right: Point cloud of office space acquired using terrestrial laser scanning.

In recent times ToF based **terrestrial laser scanners (TLS)** commonly used for large scale terrain and building scanning have received more attention for creating ground truth datasets for applications such as stereo matching or optical flow [2] and most recently also for Time-of-Flight imaging [3]. Most ToF laser scanners claim to have an accuracy of a few millimeters over a wide range of distances (2 - 100 m), making them an ideal modality to create ground truth for static scenes. As with ToF imaging the accuracy can deteriorate depending on the actual sensor-scene setup[1], though the effects of such errors are certainly smaller than in ToF cameras. Still, a few aspects should be considered while creating TLS datasets. Depending on model and position of the scanner as well as the skill of the operator the error can reach multiple centimeters.

Mixed Pixels. As the pixels have a certain size, the laser beam also has a certain width and is subject to beam divergence which causes mixed pixel effects at object boundaries. Since the reconstruction formulas used in most ToF scanners are not as highly nonlinear as in the ToF imager 1, these points lie between the foreground and background depth. Depending on the distance of the near object this can still lead to a substantial broadening of the object. Current TLS systems employ lasers with starting beam diameters of 6mm and beam divergences in the range of ≈ 0.1 mrad. Although the most often used gaussian beam profile allows for a more exact localization of the beam center in orthogonal direction, mixed pixel effects will be observed in a region of the size of the same magnitude as the beam diameter. A rough calculation with a 40 degrees FOV and 200 pixels sensor resolution for the ToF imager, yields that a pixel accounts for around 6 mm at 2 m distance (Effects dependent on the point spread function not taken into consideration). That means that especially super resolution, flying pixel compensation and denoising algorithms should evaluate whether mixed pixel effects actually affect their evaluation at depth boundaries. An example scan with mixed pixels can be seen in Figure 2.

Fig. 2. LiDAR based point cloud with high amount of flying pixels

Material Based Offset. Similarly Clark et al[4] and Boehler et al[1] have reported a material/albedo (amplitude) based offset in the order of magnitude of a centimeter. Though they cite different intensity based offsets, this can be due to calibration/environmental effects or equipment degradation (see last point). Again a visual inspection of the laser scan data is advisable to ensure that such effects are not present or are compensated for [4].

Resolution/Sparsity. The resolution or point density of various scanners can often be adjusted in a certain range. This can alleviate problems caused by depth discontinuities making sure that the scene is sampled denser than by the ToF camera to evaluate. Keep in mind that this will not automatically compensate for mixed pixel effects. Scan density can also be reduced in favor of speed. Velodyne scanners for example have a very small vertical resolution of only 64 scanlines. The advantage is that scan times are significantly lower, reaching even the typical frame times of ToF cameras. This provides for some interesting evaluation scenarios as reference data can be both accurate and dynamic but is also sparse in at least one spatial direction.

Angle of Inclination. A small effect of surface inclination towards the laser beam was observed by [5]. This effect was accounted to be up to 2 mm such that it alone most probably will not affect scan quality.

Scanning Volume/Shadowing. TLSs are made for large scale scanning. Hence, using them in closed cluttered scenes will lead to a lot of shadowing which requires tedious additional scans (especially as these scanners are usually quite heavy).

Calibration/Environmental Effects. Boehler et al[1] reported that scan performance can deteriorate depending on handling and age of the scan equipment. Also as high precision mirrors are used, a drift in depth can be caused due to temperature variations. Many of these effects can be compensated for by appropriate calibration and we refer to the methods proposed in [6].

Scan Time. Scan Time for these devices is typically at least a few seconds, although real-time scanners with severely reduced lateral resolution exist. This limits their use to static ground truth scenes.

B. Kinect Fusion

Although depth cameras using different modalities may only offer comparable but not superior accuracy, their output can still be useful for evaluations. Examples would be the use of intelligent data fusion or temporal integration approaches. We will demonstrate this on the example of the KinectFusion pipeline [7,8].

The Kinect camera itself does not have a better lateral resolution than typical Time-of-Flight cameras and its depth accuracy is also only in the centimeter range [9]. Depth images acquired from the camera are therefore not directly suited for evaluation.

Nonetheless, an interesting approach to ground truth generation using the Kinect was presented by Meister et. al [10]. The Kinect Fusion algorithm presented by Newcombe, Izadi et al. [7,8] uses the input of a kinect camera to recreate a 3D representation of a scene. This is done by converting the

Fig. 3. Left: KinectFusion generated mesh of evaluation target. Middle: Euclidean error of mesh(red:15mm). Right: ToF depth image of the test target.

cameras depth data into a voxel based implicit surface representation [11]. Each new view and camera position is matched to the previous ones using an special variant of an iterative closest point algorithm and the voxel volume is then updated with new surface data.

This approach could be described as volumetric superresolution since the resulting 3D representation is more accurate and shows less noise than the individual depth frames. The polygon meshes created by applying marching cubes to the zero-level set of the surface are known to have a geometrical precision of 10 to 80 mm, depending on scene size. This does at least fulfill the requisites for weak ground truth (c.f Section 5.2). Advantageous is that this method works without complicated setup procedures and does not require expensive equipment. It should be noted though, that as Kinect Fusion relies on depth map registration, the quality will also depend on the the amount of "clutter" in the scene.

C. Self Made Targets

Up until now arbitrary scenes were measured with ToF and a reference modality for later comparison.

A different approach to creating real world test objects is to start off with a computer model and produce them using various manufacturing processes. This allows to create targets with specific characteristics such as known curvature or controllable reflection properties using different materials.

Hand Measurement/Construction. Though probably considered somewhat archaic, for simple geometries it is possible to create the test targets manually. Objects with accuracy of a few millimeters or lower can be created using standard materials like wood or metal. The test object in Figure 5 was created from fiberboard with an accuracy of ≈ 1mm.

Milling. On the other end of the accuracy spectrum, processes such as CNC milling have a precision of a couple of microns. The size of objects created this way is typically limited. An example object can be seen in Figure 4.

3D Printing. Automated 3D manufacturing even for private home use is becoming increasingly popular in the recent years. So called 3D printers which can produce arbitrary objects by depositing thermoplastics are available for a few hundred Euros. Although typically limited to objects as few dozen centimeters wide they also reach precisions of tenth of millimeters.

Fig. 4. Left: CNC milled object, Right: Photogrammetric Target

3.1.2   Alignment

Once the same Dataset has been acquired using different modalities, the ToF data needs to be aligned to the 3D data by estimating the relative rotation and translation between the camera and the reference coordinate system. The first decision that has to be made is whether this alignment is done using the point cloud data directly or by first estimating the ToF camera pose in the reference dataset and then back projecting the ToF points into space.

Manual Alignment. As a baseline it is possible to manually align the ToF with reference data. This can be a very tedious job as 6 DOF have to be optimized by hand. We suggest that instead users choose a set of correspondences between the ToF data and the Reference data, and then align them by means of standard pose estimation techniques [12].

Point based matching. This will work if the scene is cluttered enough, otherwise it may result in drifts. Also it should be noted that systematic errors in the scene will lead to a bias in matching. This can be circumvented to a certain extent by applying sparse point matching or robust versions of ICP [13] that also account for the anisotropic noise present in the ToF point clouds.

Using Targets. Photogrammetric targets can be used to semi-automatically align ToF with reference data. In case of RGBD reference data this amounts to finding and matching feature points of known properties. Typical examples are circles or checkerboard corners as they are easy and exact to locate (c.f. Figure 4).

Partial Alignment. In certain situations the geometric properties of specific areas of the image are known (e.g. a planar wall or table). It is therefore also possible to just fit the ToF pixels to these simple models.

3.1.3   Isolation of Effects

As many algorithms claim to target different specific aspects of ToF imaging, datasets should help assess how well they perform. In the following we propose various techniques to separate those specific aspects.

Temporal averaging. If the goal of the algorithm is to remove the statistical fluctuation of the depth map, a GT dataset can be simply created by temporal averaging of the input intensity images. The obtained dataset will still contain all systematic errors, but can still be used to assess the power of different regularizers (See Section 2).

Controlled Movements. Controlled Movements are interesting for algorithms that try to compensate for motion artifacts (Section 1). Basically two parameters can be optimized: *a*) How accurately the movement can be controlled and *b*) the accuracy with which the movement can be tracked. An example for a) was given by Schmidt et al. [14] who used a rotating target of known geometry with constant angular velocity to create ground truth for their experiments. Another possibility is to use a rail system to constraint the movement in one dimension. The movement can then either be estimated by tracking a target or by evaluating the optical flow.

Lighting. While the light is usually fixed to the camera, Schmidt et. al [14] separated the light from the sensor. This was done in order to decouple saturation effects from the wiggling error.

Materials. As different materials affect the ToF measurement, especially multi-path, the usage of specific materials can help making measurements with reduced multi-path effect.

- As specular surfaces tend to show more multi-path interference, the usage of highly lambertian surfaces such as spectralon could be used to isolate interreflection effects.
- Often white walls in rooms increase global multi-path effects. Hence, dark absorbing materials such as fleece should be used to reduce these effects.
- Another interesting idea is to use infrared retroreflecting spots or sprays while reducing the integration time such that the direct reflection outweighs the multi-path illumination. Combining this with dark materials in a scene can possibly be utilized to estimate intra-lens reflections.

3.2   By Simulation

Computer generated data is in many cases a suitable alternative to measured ground truth data for algorithm validation [15]. In the context of Time-of-Flight imaging, a sensor simulator can provide such data.

To be useful for Time-of-Flight imaging method evaluation, a sensor simulator must provide two kinds of data: ideal depth data without any noise or artefacts, and realistic sensor data with typical noise characteristics and relevant systematic errors. The latter may include intermediate results that a real sensor may provide to the user, such as phase images (c.f Chapter 1).

The problem of simulating Time-of-Flight sensor data encompasses two areas:

1. Modeling of scene geometry and materials, light source, and light propagation, and
2. Modeling of the sensor hardware and operating principle.

Ground truth data generation for imaging method evaluation requires simulation of sensor data that exhibits a clearly defined and identifiable challenge. Depending on this problem domain, a simulator can be based on models on different abstraction levels in both areas. Typically, some aspects of the complete system have to be simplified in order to maintain tractability. For example, to produce ground truth data for the evaluation of methods to reduce motion artefacts, a simulator might chose relatively straightforward optics and light propagation models in order to allow fast computation of multiple sensor data frames for dynamic data.

3.2.1 Light Propagation

The light propagation model determines the composition of light that reaches each sensor pixel in the sensor hardware model.

For that purpose, the light propagation model must encompass a modulated light source, a scene description consisting of geometry and material properties, a reflection model for each material, and a camera optics model.

Keller and Kolb [16] use a model based on the traditional computer graphics pipeline. The camera is a pinhole camera and the light source is a point light source located at the camera pinhole. All object surfaces in the scene are assumed to be Lambertian reflectors at the wave length of the sensor light source.

In this model, the light that reaches a sensor pixel traveled twice the distance d between camera / light source and a surface point. Thus, the phase shift of this incoming light relative to the light source is known. Furthermore, its amplitude can be computed from d, the direction from the light source to the surface point, and the surface normal.

Knowing phase shift and amplitude allows to compute the four phase images typically generated by Time-of-Flight sensors, and from these phase images the final depth map can be computed. See Sec. 3.2.2.

The advantage of this model is that a simulator can leverage the processing power of Graphics Processing Units (GPUs) to compute light propagation information for many sensor data frames, even for complex and dynamic scenes. Furthermore, existing modeling tools from the computer graphics domain can be used to create and animate test scenes.

Keller and Kolb use a spatial oversampling to simulate typical effects such as flying pixels. For each sensor pixel, the rasterization produces a block of subpixels with light source information for the cone covered by that sensor pixel. This allows to compute the incident light properties as a mixture of the responses of different surface points, which is important e.g. at object boundaries. Additionally, computing the four phase images at distinct points in time allows to simulate motion artefacts in dynamic scenes, with the limitation that the scene is still assumed to be static during the exposure time of each phase image.

The rasterization approach can be extended to support the simulation of more effects by using methods known from the Computer Graphics domain. This includes the approximation of area light sources with multiple point light sources, improved modeling of material and reflection properties, transparent materials, depth of field, and certain types of distortions caused by camera optics.

However, as known from Computer Graphics, rasterization has certain limitations that prohibits its use for more complex light propagation effects. In the context of Time-of-Flight imaging, multi-reflection (or multipath) artefacts are a particularly interesting example. To simulate such effects, global illumination methods such as Photon Mapping or Path Tracing have to be employed. These methods typically have significantly higher computational costs, to the point that they are impracticable for complex dynamic scenes. However, they can generate much more realistic light propagation information.

The main challenge in applying global illumination methods to Time-of-Flight sensor data simulation is that the composition of modulated light reaching a sensor pixel must be known, including phase shifts.

Calculating all possible or even only all physically relevant paths between (multiple) lightsources and the camera is practically impossible. So most GI algorithms try to infer the light distribution in a scene using intelligent sampling schemes and by making certain assumptions about the light contributions. Two of these assumptions namely that light propagation is instantaneous and that the lighting situation is in a steady state for a single frame do not hold for ToF imaging.

A possible approach to this problem is the simulation of individual phase raw-frames similar to the mentioned scanline renderers. The path length (and therefore the phase) of light which was reflected multiple times inside a scene can be tracked and then be used to modulate the individual light contributions when they hit a sensor pixel. These modifications could easily be added to most existing global illumination algorithms.

In most cases this image synthesis is a stochastic process and noise in rendered images is of a different nature than the sensor and photon noise present in real cameras. A physically correct simulation would therefore need to be sustained until the render noise has no more significant influence on the generated depth maps. Then correct sensor noise as shown in Section 3.2.2 could then be applied to the raw data. In practice, the minor differences in the noise characteristics of the various simulations seldom justify the massive increase in computation time this approach would necessitate.

A problem arises from the typically high-order parameter space of various global illumination methods. Apart from the possible settings of the render engine such as light sample sizes, recursion depth or sampling parameters, material parameters such as reflectivity, surface roughness or texture can be changed individually. The Time-of-Flight simulation may depend on any of these parameters and finding the correct ones can be a challenging task in itself. Experiences from computer graphics or image synthesis can only be applied partially as they may be focused on subjective expectations (Does it look good vs. does it look real) or e.g. be limited to the visual spectrum.

Light propagation effects that have not yet been addressed by simulators based on either rasterization or global illumination include advanced optics effects such as lens flare and scattering inside the camera casing. The properties for lenses used in Time-of-Flight imaging are generally quite different from those of regular lenses. For example, they need to be transparent for infrared wavelengths and suitable for intensities with high dynamic range. If a description of the lens is available, the lens effects can be computed using optical engineering software such as OSLO [17] or Zemax [18].

Fig. 5. Left: Ground truth geometry of test object. Middle: Geometry as seen by real ToF camera. Right: Simulation with method by Keller and Kolb.

3.2.2 Sensor Hardware

Given the composition of incoming light as computed by the light propagation model, a sensor hardware model can simulate the sensor pixel response. Again, such hardware models can have different abstraction models, depending on the problem domain.

Keller and Kolb [16] employ a phenomenological sensor model. Based on the light input for each of the four phase images of typical PMD sensors, their simulator computes the ideal theoretical phase image sensor response, as described in Chapter 1. To achieve a realistic simulation result (as opposed to a perfect result), Keller and Kolb apply additive and multiplicative Gaussian noise to these ideal phase images before computing the final depth map sensor response.

This phenomenological model focuses on computational efficiency for the handling of dynamic scenes: similar to their light propagation model, Keller and Kolb leverage the processing power of Graphics Processing Units (GPUs) to compute the sensor response for each pixel in parallel.

Schmidt and Jähne [19,20] employ a physical model of individual sensor pixel components, with the goal of simulating the cause of sensor data imperfections instead of applying noise effects after computation of the sensor response. This leads to better understanding of sensor data, more realistic simulation results, and more fine-grained control over simulator behavior.

In particular, their physical model accounts for real-world effects like non-sinusoidal light modulation, non-rectangular switching functions, non-linear photo response, and the influence of sensor-specific techniques such as the

Suppression of Background Illumination (SBI) method commonly found in PMD sensors. Consequently, their system can simulate various types of sensor noise realistically.

Both the phenomenological approach by Keller and Kolb and the physical modeling approach by Schmidt and Jähne originally used light propagation information generated by basic rasterization methods, but could also be combined with more sophisticated light propagation models.

In addition to these approaches on relatively high abstraction levels, sensor manufacturers can employ chip design evaluators that simulate chip behavior on a transistor level, based on chip descriptions in VLSI. Such simulators naturally require immense computational power even for small sensor resolutions, and are therefore typically impracticable for producing ground truth data targeted at the evaluation of imaging methods.

4   Content Selection and Available Datasets

4.1   Content Selection

An equally important question is which targets or scenes should be used for the ground truth sequences. Three important aspects of ground truth datasets are **interpretability, progression** and **realism**. Interpretability refers to the aspect that an algorithm failing or working on a certain dataset should not only tell us that it failed or worked but also give some insight that the algorithm fails due to certain conditions. As a baseline, isolated effects on simple planar geometries can be analyzed. In Section 5.2.1, simple geometries and measurement methods to obtain certain effects are discussed. In more complex scenes masks can be supplied that highlight only certain effects in the scene such as specular reflections, multi-path or transparency. The second aspect - progression - is concerned with avoiding a problem heavily used datasets have. As the optimization criterion is to minimize a certain error measure on this particular dataset researchers tend to overfit their algorithms to this specific dataset[21]. On the other hand, if the dataset is initially too challenging, it may not receive the needed traction in the research community.

Therefore we believe that a large database should include a progression of difficulty to accommodate for this. Progression can be obtained by combining different effects but also by more complex geometries that make simple regularizers etc. fail.

Finally, realism refers to the GT data being relevant to actual use cases. Obviously a dataset can not be exhaustive regarding all possible applications. But once an application domain is identified the goal should be to create ground truth data as close to the actual working conditions as possible.

4.2   Existing Datasets

So far the number of available datasets and scene compositions is limited. Here we present a short but representative selection of the available sets along a short description of the included data. Either the dataset name or the title of the corresponding publication is given.

Capturing Time-of-Flight Data with Confidence. To calculate confidence values for ToF imaging Reynolds et al. [3] provide a ground truth dataset based on laser scanner data. The set consists of four scenes of which two are augmented with ground truth data. ToF data includes depth maps as well as intensity and amplitude images and intrinsic calibration data. Alignment between the two modalities is enabled by the usage of reflecting calibration markers. The dataset is available at `http://visual.cs.ucl.ac.uk/pubs/tofconfidence/`.

Fig. 6. Left: ToF Intensity Image, Middle: ToF Z-Depth. Observe the 'halo' around object corners. Right: Ground Truth Z-Depth.

HCI LiDAR Dataset. A ToF dataset referenced with terrestrial laser scanner data is available at `http://hci.iwr.uni-heidelberg.de//Benchmarks/`.

It consists of images of a office scene taken with a PMD CamCube 3 ToF camera. Included are intensity images, depth images, sensor raw data as well as camera calibration data. The displayed room was also scanned using a RIEGL VZ-400 terrestrial laser scanner [2] with an stated accuracy of 5 mm and 3 mm precision. The scan was performed from 6 individual positions with approximately 5 Million points per scan.

Ground truth depth maps were created by manually selecting 2D-to-3D correspondences between the ToF intensity images and a delaunay triangulation of the scanned point clouds. Using these correspondences camera pose estimation was performed and the depth of the triangulated mesh was rendered.

It should be noted that the lidar based polygon mesh contains multiple errors or holes due to occlusions and flying pixels in the point cloud. See Section 3.1 for typical problems regarding laser scanner data. Figure 6 shows a ToF intensity image of the dataset as well as a depth map and corresponding

---

[2] `http://www.riegl.com`

ground truth map. The dataset does not adhere to all points mentioned in Section 6 but is still useful for many evaluation tasks.

HCIBOX Depth Evaluation Dataset. An additional dataset is available under the same url (http://hci.iwr.uni-heidelberg.de//Benchmarks/). The test object is a wooden box containing several simple geometric objects such as cylinders or spheres, see Figure 5 for an image. This set consists of ToF images of the same type as well as fully calibrated megapixel stereo images. Ground truth depth maps were again created using standard pose estimation techniques. For this set the 3D model was created by measuring the depicted test object by hand, reaching a general accuracy of ≈ 1 mm.

Locally Consistent ToF and Stereo Data Fusion. This dataset created by Mutto et al. [22] contains both rectified stereo camera data as well as data from a MESA SR4000 camera and is intended for use in sensor data fusion approaches (http://lttm.dei.unipd.it/downloads/tofstereo). The ToF data does include amplitude, depth and confidence images and is of particular interest as ground truth data for this camera model is rare. Three scenes containing household objects are contained in the set. Ground truth for was created using the Spacetime stereo method by Zhang et al. [23], relying on the stereo systems images itself to create the reference data. Although there are no indications about the accuracy of the used ground truth.

Additionally some rendered stereo images and ToF depth maps are also available from the same location. These depth maps are purely synthetic and lack typical ToF artifacts and errors.

5 Application of Ground Truth

5.1 Algorithm Performance Metrics

In this section we will give a short overview over the most often used error metrics and give advise on how or when they should be used.

The performance metric most commonly used for GT evaluation is the mean endpoint error/squared error. It is defined as the mean of the absolute distances between the ground truth and the measured depth. Though useful in many cases, the reduction of performance to a single scalar value may not be too meaningful. To name one example: Often a visually pleasing result that contains a bias is more preferable to a bias free solution with a high variance.

In general, performance metrics can be divided into different classes:

Local metrics are typically defined for every pixel of the depth map and independent of each other. Image processing and analysis has the advantage that these individual observations have a clear and descriptive meaning. Also the spatial structure of these observations has a meaning in itself so it is advantageous to use error metrics which preserve this spatial information. An example for a local metric would be the per pixel endpoint error.

Global metrics which includes the classical mean endpoint error are often derived from local metrics by statistical analysis. This could be standard deviation of the error, higher order momenta or more subjective metrics like the apparent smoothness (with smoothness deliberately left without a strict definition). If a local metric is used, there is practically no reason not to include some simple statistics for this property. Mean, standard deviation, median and quantiles are rather fast to compute and can give additional insights.

Another classification scheme would be the distinction between **direct metrics** which can be computed directly when the ground truth is given (or sometimes even independently of the GT), or **derived metrics** which need more or less extensive postprocessing before they can be applied. Examples would be the fit between polygon meshes which are based on the measured depth data. This is usually more application dependent and may be expressed in terms of the requirements presented in Section 2.

The following enumeration is in no way exhaustive as each application may define its own error metric. These metrics should be considered as a guideline for low-level examinations.

Endpoint error / Bias / Accuracy. The most basic error metric describes the absolute distance between a ToF pixel and the true depth. As ToF cameras are prone to systematic errors as well as high noise it can only give a rough estimate about the quality of a measurement.

Standard deviation / Variance / Precision. The expressiveness of this metric depends on whether it denotes the temporal or spatial deviation. Spatial variance is typically highly dependent on scene geometry and not very descriptive unless a flat will with uniform depth was imaged. Temporal variance can be of interest when the light situation and material of the underlying pixel is of interest.

(Root) Mean Squared Error ((R)MSE). The RMSE is equal to the sum of the standard deviation and the endpoint error (or bias). It is quite popular due to its statistic properties but is otherwise not very descriptive.

Local curvature/Slope. Due to the various effects of ToF cameras, otherwise planar or piecewise planar objects such as walls or room corners may appear curved or slanted. Differences between the actual and measured surfaces can give insight into the magnitude of those effects. Before this metric can be evaluated a appropriate surface reconstruction must be applied to the depth data.

Edges. Depth and texture edges are considered significant information for many low-level vision and image processing tasks, albeit they may lack a proper definition. ToF depth is known to vary depending on the observed intensity even if the true depth is constant. This can lead to false depth edges in regions where there is actually only a texture edge present. A yet to be defined metric for edge quality could help distinguish between true and false depth edges. This metric would be even more useful for ground truth with labeled depth as well as texture edges.

5.2   Weak Ground Truth

In Computer Vision, the finite accuracy of ground truth is often not taken into consideration. This is fine as long as the GT has an accuracy of over an order of magnitude more everywhere compared to the application at hand. Often there are methods that can create reliable GT data for only certain parts of the scene whereas other parts are erroneous. If those errors can be quantified and the regions clearly be localized such weak GT can still be feasible to use for a quick evaluation, as long as the analysis is mathematically/statistically sound.

5.2.1   Basic Example for Generation of Weak Ground Truth

A plane is a very basic example for ground truth that can be used to evaluate several kinds of distance errors like temperature drift, intensity related errors or distance offsets as well as noise characteristics. Given a carefully chosen setup, other influences such as multi-path or motion artifacts can be eliminated or reduced.

The weak ground truth for a plane can be generated by detecting and evaluating checkerboard corners in the amplitude image. From the detected points and the knowledge of the checkerboard geometry, the position of the checkerboard can be derived. For an ideally calibrated pin-hole camera, and a single corner distance measure in the center, the approximate distance error can be estimated using the intercept theorem:

$$e = \frac{2d_p e_d}{\hat{d}_p^2 - 2e_d \hat{d}_p} f. \tag{1}$$

with d_p being the corner distance, f is the focal length, distance between focal point and checkerboard t, $\hat{d}_p = \frac{d_p}{t} f$ is the according distance of the corners projected onto the sensor and e_d is the detection error with respect to distance on the chip (has to be divided by the pixel pitch to get the detection error in pixels).

For the technical specifications of a MESA SR 4000 camera, a typical corner detection error of a 10th of a pixel (for each corner) a checkerboard at $t = 1\,\text{m}$ distance and with a corner distance of $d_p = 85\,\text{mm}$, the maximum error in the estimated checkerboard distance is approx. $e = 0.73\,\text{mm}$. For a checkerboard with n corners the total estimation error decreases to $\frac{e}{\sqrt{n}}$ (assuming normally distributed error statistics). Given a sufficiently large number of corners in the checkerboard, the estimation error can be well below the typical ToF depth error which is in the centimeter range.

5.2.2   Weak Ground Truth of Another Modality

Even if the reference modality has an accuracy of the same order of magnitude as the ToF data, it can still be useful if a error distribution or a confidence score is known. An example would be, if somebody uses a Kinect Fusion scan to assess accuracy of a ToF denoising algorithm. If the reference modality has a error distribution that is known, The likelihood of the ToF Data given the probability distribution of the reference data can be easily computed. An increasing number of algorithms offer confidence measures [3,24] between 0 and 1 without any further probabilistic interpretation. As low confidence data points are not an error measure, low confidence data may still be interesting. We therefore propose to borrow from sparsification plots used for confidence measures [24]. Normal sparsification plots are concerned with the evaluation of confidence in presence of ground truth. The endpoint error is plotted as a function of removing points with a confidence lower than a certain threshold. In our case we plot the error metric between the ToF data and the reference weak ground truth as a function of the confidence of the reference data.

6   Best Practices

This last part is intended to be a tutorial section explaining how to create good ground truth data which can be comparable with other ground truth datasets. We will discuss various supplemental results that should be made available to facilitate such comparisons. Many points in this section may appear obvious but experience has shown that often data which is missing or was mislabeled during the measurement process is in fact crucial for any further research effort.

Generally speaking, it is advisable to capture as much data and metadata as possible. With data we designate individual frames from the camera, while metadata designates everything else, be it recorded automatically or by additional experiments or setup procedures.

Data and Metadata

The metadata for a ground truth set should at least include:

Temperature The depth output of a ToF camera can be highly temperature dependent. The camera should therefore have reached a steady state and temperature changes due to environmental conditions (sunlight etc.) should either be reduced or at least be recorded.

Light situation This does include the documentation of additional light sources apart from the cameras own as well as significant external changes (e.g. due to cloud movement etc.)

Camera parameters If possible, the camera should be calibrated and camera matrices as well as lens distortion parameters be provided. For lenses with fixed focus and aperture these values can be static over a long time but for otherwise the calibration should be considered invalid each time the lens is touched. If multiple cameras are used (e.g. in a stereo setup) the external calibration should be measured and treated in a similar manner. As ToF system are often used in image fusion approaches conjunction with other imaging systems this requirement is generally observed in existing datasets. This also includes all the presented example datasets in Section 4.2.

Materials What type of materials are visible in the scene? It should also be taken in to account, that the reflection and illumination behavior of certain materials may be radically different under infrared lighting. Glass for example may not be longer transparent while wood grain can appear much more distinct, etc.

Sensor settings This includes integration times, framerates, gain, etc. If it is adjustable it should be documented.

Software Which capture software and which version of it was used? If available the source code as well as any configuration files should be supplied. Data can be subtly different when seemingly unrelated program parameters or e.g. the capture drivers change.

A written scene description An image may say more than a thousand words but it may not always be as obvious as it seems. If many scenes with only slightly different parameters were captured, the motivation to do so could be included here.

Additional postprocessing or calibration data This may include the measured fixed pattern noise, data about sensor or light inhomogenities or calibration fits for depth calibrated cameras.

Regarding the images, raw data if available should always be saved alongside the derived depth maps. This is important as denoising or postprocessing on raw phase images is a ongoing field of study (See Section 2) and research will benefit from access to this data.

For static scenes it is advisable to capture multiple frames to allow investigation of e.g. temporal noise and to reduce the error by averaging. For dynamic scenes noting the approximate speed of the camera and scene objects allows for sanity checks.

Typical Errors

The following points are easily avoidable but may lead to inferior results or deteriorated data when not detected early:

Under/Overexposure. Depth data on overexposed pixels may be completely incorrect. Depth on pixels with a too low amplitude on the other hand may be more accurate but is prone to severely increased noise and should be considered unreliable.

Recording at different temperatures. The PMD CamCube camera for example needs to run for about 20 minutes before it reaches a temperature steady-state. During this warm-up-time the measured depths may change significantly.

Low-frequency light modulation. Often caused by fluorescent lamps. May not influence the measured depth but the intensities between adjacent frames.

Depth-of-field. Often neglected due to the rather low resolution of the most common ToF cameras and their use of fixed focus optics. Out-of-focus recordings may have increased artifacts based on flying pixels. Edge quality may also be effected.

Ignoring imaging modalities. Assumptions about material behavior (e.g. lambertian or specular reflectance) may not hold under infrared illumination. Black ink on regular paper for example may appear brighter than the surrounding white paper.

Incorrect interpretation of depth data. The depth maps produced by most ToF cameras represent radial depth, which is the distance of the point to the camera center. The depth from triangulation based methods (e.g. stereo) is generally given as z-depth, the orthogonal distance from the sensor plane. With known camera intrinsics both representations can be converted into each other to make them comparable.

Occlusion of depth maps. For ground truth acquired by means of measuring, the fields of view of the different sensors should overlap as much as possible. Small deviations in the scan positions can lead to occlusion in the depth maps, resulting in potentially sparse ground truth.

Multi path from unobserved walls. Often multi path effects from objects just outside the camera frustum can be observed, even though the object itself is not imaged by the camera.

7   Conclusion

While its creation is in no way easy we consider good ground truth to be a necessity for advancements in the field of ToF imaging. Both applicants as well as developers of ToF centric algorithms need ways to interpret their results. Starting with clear requirement definitions the performance of ToF systems and ToF based applications need to be evaluated. We have presented methods to create ground truth data, both *strong* and *weak* as well as metrics to compare and evaluate errors. We hope that with the help of these guidelines additional and more detailed ground truth datasets will soon be made available to the research community.

Acknowledgements. This work is part of a joint research project with the Filmakademie Baden-Württemberg, Institute of Animation. It is co-funded by the Intel Visual Computing Institute and under grant 2-4225.16/380 of the ministry of economy Baden-Württemberg as well as further partners Unexpected, Pixomondo, ScreenPlane, Bewegte Bilder and Tridelity . The content is under sole responsibility of the authors.

References

1. Boehler, W., Vicent, M.B., Marbs, A.: Investigating laser scanner accuracy. The International Archives of Photogrammetry, Remote Sensing and Spatial Information Sciences 34(Part 5), 696–701 (2003)
2. Geiger, A., Lenz, P., Urtasun, R.: Are we ready for autonomous driving? the kitti vision benchmark suite. In: Computer Vision and Pattern Recognition (CVPR), Providence, USA (June 2012)

3. Reynolds, M., Doboš, J., Peel, L., Weyrich, T., Brostow, G.J.: Capturing time-of-flight data with confidence. In: CVPR (2011)
4. Clark, J., Robson, S.: Accuracy of measurements made with a cyrax 2500 laser scanner against surfaces of known colour. Survey Review 37(294), 626–638 (2004)
5. Soudarissanane, S., Lindenbergh, R., Menenti, M., Teunissen, P.: Incidence angle influence on the quality of terrestrial laser scanning points. In: ISPRS Workshop Laserscanning (2009)
6. Lichti, D.D.: Error modelling, calibration and analysis of an am–cw terrestrial laser scanner system. ISPRS Journal of Photogrammetry and Remote Sensing 61(5), 307–324 (2007)
7. Newcombe, R.A., Izadi, S., Hilliges, O., Molyneaux, D., Kim, D., Davison, A.J., Kohli, P., Shotton, J., Hodges, S., Fitzgibbon, A.: KinectFusion: Real-time dense surface mapping and tracking. In: 2011 10th IEEE International Symposium on Mixed and Augmented Reality, vol. 7, pp. 127–136 (2011)
8. Izadi, S., Newcombe, R.A., Kim, D., Hilliges, O., Molyneaux, D., Hodges, S., Kohli, P., Shotton, J., Davison, A.J., Fitzgibbon, A.: KinectFusion: Real-time dynamic 3D surface reconstruction and interaction. In: ACM SIGGRAPH 2011 Talks, p. 23. ACM (2011)
9. Khoshelham, K.: Accuracy analysis of kinect depth data. In: ISPRS Workshop Laser Scanning, vol. 38, p. 1 (2011)
10. Meister, S., Izadi, S., Kohli, P., Hämmerle, M., Rother, C., Kondermann, D.: When can we use kinectfusion for ground truth acquisition? In: 2012 IEEE/RSJ International Conference on Intelligent Robots and Systems (IROS), Workshops & Tutorials (2012)
11. Besl, P.J., McKay, N.D.: Method for registration of 3-d shapes. In: Robotics-DL Tentative, International Society for Optics and Photonics, pp. 586–606 (1992)
12. Bradski, G.: The OpenCV Library. Dr. Dobb's Journal of Software Tools (2000)
13. Maier-Hein, L., Schmidt, M., Franz, A.M., dos Santos, T.R., Seitel, A., Jähne, B., Fitzpatrick, J.M., Meinzer, H.P.: Accounting for anisotropic noise in fine registration of time-of-flight range data with high-resolution surface data. In: Jiang, T., Navab, N., Pluim, J.P.W., Viergever, M.A. (eds.) MICCAI 2010, Part I. LNCS, vol. 6361, pp. 251–258. Springer, Heidelberg (2010)
14. Schmidt, M.: Analysis, Modeling and Dynamic Optimization of 3D Time-of-Flight Imaging Systems. PhD thesis, University of Heidelberg (20011)
15. Meister, S., Kondermann, D.: Real versus realistically rendered scenes for optical flow evaluation. In: Proceedings of 14th ITG Conference on Electronic Media Technology (2011)
16. Keller, M., Kolb, A.: Real-time simulation of time-of-flight sensors. J. Simulation Practice and Theory 17, 967–978 (2009)
17. Research, L.: Optics software for layout and optimization (oslo), http://www.lambdares.com
18. Zemax, R.: Zemax, optical design software, http://www.radiantzemax.com
19. Schmidt, M., Jähne, B.: A physical model of time-of-flight 3D imaging systems, including suppression of ambient light. In: Kolb, A., Koch, R. (eds.) Dyn3D 2009. LNCS, vol. 5742, pp. 1–15. Springer, Heidelberg (2009)
20. Schmidt, M.: Analysis, Modeling and Dynamic Optimization of 3D Time-of-Flight Imaging Systems. PhD thesis, University of Heidelberg (2011)
21. Geiger, A., Lenz, P., Urtasun, R.: Are we ready for autonomous driving? the kitti vision benchmark suite. In: Conference on Computer Vision and Pattern Recognition (CVPR) (2012)

22. Dal Mutto, C., Zanuttigh, P., Mattoccia, S., Cortelazzo, G.: Locally consistent toF and stereo data fusion. In: Fusiello, A., Murino, V., Cucchiara, R. (eds.) ECCV 2012 Ws/Demos, Part I. LNCS, vol. 7583, pp. 598–607. Springer, Heidelberg (2012)
23. Zhang, L., Curless, B., Seitz, S.M.: Spacetime stereo: Shape recovery for dynamic scenes. In: Proceedings of the 2003 IEEE Computer Society Conference on Computer Vision and Pattern Recognition, vol. 2, pp. II–367. IEEE (2003)
24. Haeusler, R., Nair, R., Kondermann, D.: (Ensemble learning for confidence measures in stereo vision)

Part II
Depth Data Processing and Fusion

Mirrors in Computer Graphics, Computer Vision and Time-of-Flight Imaging

Ilya Reshetouski and Ivo Ihrke

Inria Bordeaux Sud-Ouest
{ilya.reshetouski,ivo.ihrke}@inria.fr

Abstract. Mirroring is one of the fundamental light/surface interactions occurring in the real world. Surfaces often cause specular reflection, making it necessary to design robust geometry recovery algorithms for many practical situations. In these applications the specular nature of the surface is a challenge. On the other side, mirrors, with their unique reflective properties, can be used to improve our sensing modalities, enabling applications such as surround, stereo and light field imaging. In these scenarios the specular interactions are highly desirable. Both of these aspects, the utilization and circumvention of mirrors are present in a significant amount of publications in different scientific areas. These publications are covering a large number of different problem statements as well as many different approaches to solutions. In the chapter we will focus on a collection and classification of the work in this area.

1 Introduction

Apart from refraction and diffraction, mirroring is one of the fundamental means for shaping light distributions, either for imaging or for projection purposes. Whereas refractive, or *dioptric*, systems, mainly in the form of camera optics, are widely employed in the computer vision literature, *catoptric*, or mirror systems have mainly been used in the design of large scale optics where refractive elements are impractical, e.g. for telescopes. The combination of refractive and mirror elements in imaging and measurement systems is known as *catadioptric* imaging.

In this chapter, we review the design and application of mirror systems in computer graphics and computer vision, as well as the related problem of the determination of the geometry of a mirror or mirror system. While less obvious, we point out a connection between mirror calibration or mirror shape estimation and time-of-flight imaging.

Our methodology is based on a classification scheme for mirror systems, Fig. 1, that builds on the fundamental imaging properties of the employed mirror surfaces. We categorize existing systems into classes based on their mirroring properties and their use in active or passive imaging systems. The main categories for mirror systems are whether the mirrors are planar or curved, whether single or multiple mirrors are used and whether single-bounce or multi-bounce interaction is employed.

We first discuss the different classes with respect to their imaging properties, Sect. 2, and introduce the tool of ray unfolding for doing so. Next, we discuss

M. Grzegorzek et al. (Eds.): Time-of-Flight and Depth Imaging, LNCS 8200, pp. 77–104, 2013.

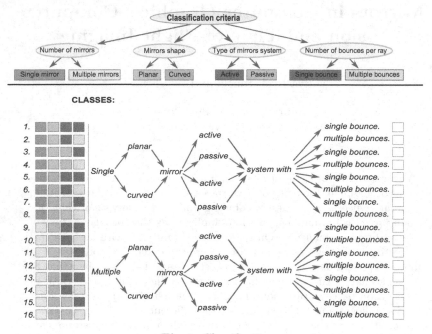

Fig. 1. Classification

passive imaging devices that utilize mirrors, Sect. 3. Passive systems have the property that light rays that cover a common scene point do not influence each other. On the other hand, if active illumination is introduced, light can superposition in a scene. We discuss active imaging systems in Sect. 4. All systems involving mirrors need to be calibrated, i.e. the geometry and position of the mirrors in the scene has to be determined. For this reason, we review computer vision methods that aim at determining the shape of specular reflective surfaces or the position of a camera with respect to a known mirror geometry in Sect. 5. The recovery of a mirror system's geometry from depth measurements is a special case of the calibration problem. However, this problem has its own literature and approaches in the field of time-of-flight imaging and acoustics. We therefore draw connections between the previously discussed techniques and the time-of-flight literature in Sect. 6. Finally, we summarize the article and formulate important open questions, that in our opinion, must be solved in order to achieve further progress in the area of mirror systems.

2 Classification Scheme and Mirror System Interpretation

Here we present our classification scheme, Fig. 1, in conjunction with a discussion of the main properties of the mirror systems involved. The two main classes are planar mirrors and curved mirrors. Planar mirrors preserve perspective views whereas curved ones only do so in very specific configurations. We will discuss planar mirrors first.

2.1   Planar Mirrors

2.1.1   Unfolding - A Convenient Way for Interpreting Image Formation in Planar Mirror Systems

Our discussion is based on the *ray unfolding* procedure which we will introduce and apply to different mirror systems. Ray unfolding has its origins in the optical literature on prism systems where the resulting plots are known as *tunnel diagrams* [1]. In this technique, every mirror interaction is applied to the world instead of the ray. The result is a straight ray that passes through a sequence of virtual copies of the world that is equivalent to the bouncing ray in the real world. This way, complex ray interactions can be visualized in an intuitive manner and a change of coordinate systems can easily be tracked.

2.1.2   Single-Mirror, Single-Bounce

Consider a single planar mirror and a camera observing an object via a single-bounce reflection, Fig. 2.

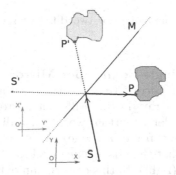

Fig. 2. Unfolding of a single reflection

When a ray of light is hitting the mirror it is mirrored from the plane according to the law of reflection. Instead of mirroring the ray, we can consider that the world is being reflected, creating a virtual world, or as we well call it, a virtual *chamber*. In this case, the ray appears to continue straight into the virtual mirror world. The mirror copy of the scene is an isometric transformation of the real world. The world coordinate system is transformed to the mirrored one by reflecting it in the mirror plane. Left-handed mirror system transform into right-handed ones and vice versa. The procedure of ray straightening just described is called *unfolding*. Because light paths are reversible, we can consider the ray straightening procedure from the point of view of a scene point or from the point of view of a camera or a projector. Consider a ray from camera S observing a scene point P through the reflection from the planar mirror M. Then from the point of view of the camera, we observe the virtual point P' which is the mirror copy of the real point P. But from the point of view of the point P we are observing the virtual camera S' which is the reflection of the real camera S.

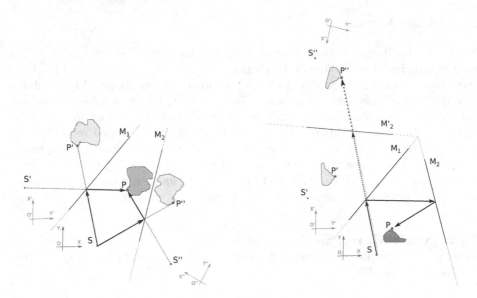

Fig. 3. Two planar mirrors: unfolding for two different rays (left) and unfolding for sequential reflection (right)

2.1.3 Multi-mirror, Single-Bounce per Mirror

If there are several planar mirrors that are arranged around a camera, as for example in Fig. 3 (left), for rays hitting different mirrors the ray straightening process will introduce a different virtual world (or a different virtual camera if we consider the point of view from the scene). A second possibility is to arrange the planar mirrors such, that there is a sequencial ray bouncing from mirror to mirror as shown in Fig. 3 (right). In this case the unfolding procedure is applied recursively. Thus, if an even number of reflections is involved, the resulting virtual world (virtual camera) coordinate system will not change its handness while it changes handedness if the reflection level is odd.

As long as the reflection sequence includes every mirror only once, the recursive unfolding procedure can be applied without ambiguity.

2.1.4 Multi-mirror, Multi-bounce

However, multiple bounces in systems with several planar mirrors could be such, that the same mirrors are participating in a reflection sequence multiple times. In a theoretical setting, this number could well be infinite.

The simplest such system is an angle constructed from two planar mirrors as in Fig. 4. There are several cases to consider that are instructive for the further discussion. If the angle $\angle ABC$ between the mirrors is $\frac{\pi}{k}$, where $k \in \mathbb{N}$, then the unfolding of all possible rays will introduce a partitioning of the space into continuous regions such that the space is divided into $2k$ different parts. These are the inner part of the original angle (base chamber) and the copies associated with different reflection levels (virtual chambers). The partitioning is, in this

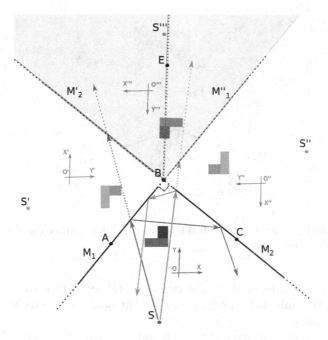

Fig. 4. Ray bouncing inside an angle with matching coordinate systems

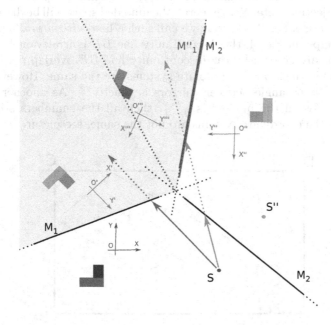

Fig. 5. Two different rays bouncing inside an angle where the chambers are matching but the coordinate systems do not

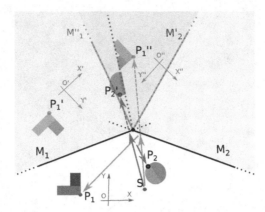

Fig. 6. Two different rays bouncing inside an angle where neither the coordinate systems nor the chambers match

case, independent of the origin of the ray. A useful result that can immediately be verified in the unfolded representation is that no ray can have a sequence of more than k bounces.

Note, that the ray can hit either of the mirrors first. Therefore, different reflection sequences will occur to the left or to the right of the half-line BE. This half-line cuts some of the virtual chambers and its position depends on the location of the projective center S. In general, the unfolded space will be discontinuous across this half-line. For this reason, we call such a lines *discontinuity lines* [2].

In the example in Fig. 4, the discontinuity line BE is irrelevant because the chambers that are crossed by the discontinuity line BE overlap perfectly and, moreover, their transformed coordinate systems are the same. However, this is only the case if the angle between mirrors is exactly $\frac{\pi}{k}$. As another example, if the angle between the mirrors is $\frac{2\pi}{2k+1}$, then all the chambers still overlap perfectly, but the coordinate systems are not the same, see picture Fig. 5. Even

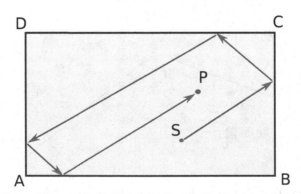

Fig. 7. Ray bouncing inside the rectangle ABCD. Light propagates from point S up to point P.

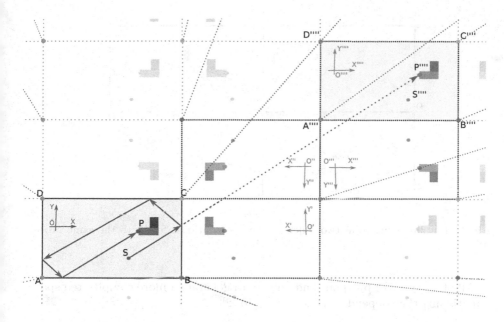

Fig. 8. Unfolding of the ray from Fig. 7 bouncing inside the rectangle

worse, if the angle between the mirrors is not an integer fraction of 2π, then the virtual chambers do not match properly and their coordinate systems do not align, Fig. 6.

A simple example involving several mirrors is a bouncing ray inside a rectangular room, see Fig. 7. This type of geometry is most often considered in multibounce time-of-flight image, Sect. 6. If we repeatedly unfold the ray while it is propagating in space, we obtain the result seen in Fig. 8. In every virtual rectangle (virtual chamber) we have a virtual world that is specific to the sequence of reflections. If we consider all possible ray directions from any possible inner point of the original rectangle, we obtain a partitioning of the space into virtual rectangles. Since the rectangle is a regular structure, unfolding via different reflection sequences yields the same virtual worlds (perfectly overlapping chambers and equal coordinate system), independent of the sequence of reflections we travel along the ray to reach the virtual rectangle from the real one (see Fig. 9).

Unfortunately, only few types of polygons produce this similarly perfect space partitioning schemes. In these cases, the partitioning is independent of the initial ray position. The polygons (or polyhedra in the $3D$ case) having this property are known as Coxeter polygons (polyhedra). A polygon is a Coxeter polygon iff all its angles are in the form of $\frac{\pi}{k}$, $k \in \mathbb{N}$. There are only 4 such polygons: rectangles, equilateral triangles, the isosceles right triangles, and right triangles with angles $\frac{\pi}{3}$ and $\frac{\pi}{6}$.

For polyhedra in $3D$, the condition to be a Coxeter polyhedron is that all the dihedral angles are of the form $\frac{\pi}{k}$, $k \in \mathbb{N}$. There are only 7 types of Coxeter polyhedra [3].

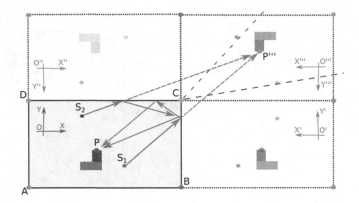

Fig. 9. Ray bouncing from two different camera locations, S_1, S_2 to the same object point P

All other types of polygons and polyhedra generate a more complicated space partitioning that depends on the ray origin [2].

2.2   Curved Mirrors

Curved mirrors are different from planar ones in the sense that they usually do not yield perspective views (except in special configurations) but rather transform the world according to their surface curvature. One can consider the curved mirror as a surface, that, at each point, has a corresponding planar mirror that is tangent to the surface. In order to use such mirrors in practice, their geometry and pose with respect to a recording camera or a projector has to be known very accurately. It is a difficult problem to estimate general mirror shapes precisely, Sect. 5. Therefore, in practice, only a limited number of mirror shapes are considered. The classes of mirrors utilized in practical settings, Sects. 3 and 4, are restricted to conic sections and to axially symmetric mirrors. In the following we classify these simple types of curved mirrors into the following groups

- General axial symmetric mirrors,
- Circular cone mirrors,
- Spherical mirrors,
- Elliptic mirrors,
- Parabolic mirrors,
- Hyperbolic mirrors, and
- Cylindrical mirrors,

and discuss their properties that are useful in imaging applications.

2.2.1   Single-Mirror, Single-Bounce

Since all of these mirror shapes are axially symmetric, we start with a discussion of the general properties of axially symmetric systems.

2.2.1.1 General Axial Symmetric Curved Mirrors

For any axially symmetric surface, an intersection with a plane orthogonal to the axis of symmetry is a circle. Therefore, if a projective center is placed on the axis of symmetry, rays through the projective center with the same angle towards the symmetry axis intersect the surface in the same circle. Moreover, the surface normal of the mirror at the intersection point is in the same plane as its symmetry axis and the propagation direction of the intersecting ray. The law of reflection implies that the reflected ray is contained in this same plane. Thus, the process of reflection can be described in terms of reflections from curved mirrors within this plane ($2D$). In addition, all planes containing the symmetry axis of the mirror yield the same $2D$ profile, or, in other words, the reduced description is independent of the initial ray direction. Ray propagation is rotationally invariant for the mirror's axis of symmetry.

Consider one of the rays with the origin S placed on the axis of symmetry l of an axially symmetric curved mirror and with propagation direction d, Fig. 10 (left). After reflection from the mirror surface, the ray changes its direction to d'. Let S' be the intersection of a line with its origin at the intersection point and slope in the new propagation direction d' with the symmetry axis of the mirror l (we exclude the case, when the direction d coincide with l). S' can be considered as a virtual origin of the reflected ray. Because the ray propagation is rotationally invariant with respect to the axis of rotation l, any ray leaving S at the same angle (w.r.t the symmetry axis) as d has the same virtual origin S after reflection. We call the point S' the virtual focus of the ray bundle with angle α. In general, different angles result in different virtual focii, except for some special cases discussed below. The situation is depicted in Fig. 10 (middle and right).

Another important property is related to convex curved axially symmetric mirrors (but it is also valid for an arbitrary convex mirror). If the surface of the mirror is convex, then the ray inclination angle at the virtual focus is larger,

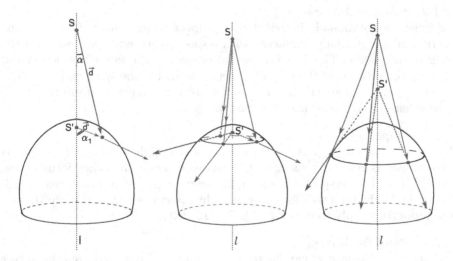

Fig. 10. Two different virtual foci together with a cones of rays propagation illustration

than the inclination angle at the real focus (see the angles α_1 and α on Fig. 10 (left)). In other words, convex mirrors widen the field of view.

This property is widely used in omnidirectional imaging devices, Sect. 3.2.1, and all subtypes of curved mirrors discussed below show this characteristic.

2.2.1.2 Circular Cone Mirrors
Circular cone mirrors are axially symmetric mirrors with a linear cross-section, see Fig. 11. Thus, propagation of rays inside such a mirror can be translated to the propagation of rays in the $2D$ angle that was previously described and to which the unfolding procedure can be applied.

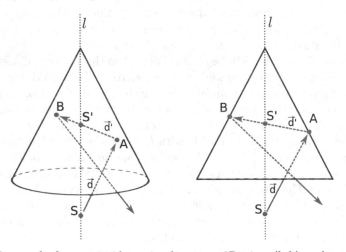

Fig. 11. Traversal of a ray inside a circular cone. 3D view (left) and corresponding plane projection (right).

2.2.1.3 Spherical Mirrors
The sphere is rotationally invariant with respect to its center. Therefore, the spherical mirror is axially symmetric with respect to any axis that intersects the center of the sphere. This is a very useful property as it solves the problem of adjusting the position of the projective center to match the symmetry axis. The second property of a spherical mirror is that all rays emanating from the center of the sphere are reflected back towards this point.

2.2.1.4 Elliptic Mirrors
The specific optical property of an ellipse is that light, exiting at one focus of the ellipse is reflecting such, that it passes through the other focus of the ellipse. Thus, if a perspective camera/projector is placed in one focus, it will observe/highlight the other focus for all light directions. Of course, in $3D$, the same properties apply to the ellipsoid, Fig. 12 (left).

2.2.1.5 Parabolic Mirrors
In a parabolic mirror, rays parallel to the main axis are reflected from the mirror surface to the mirror's focus and vice versa, Fig. 12 (middle).

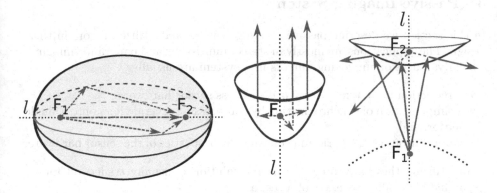

Fig. 12. Traversal of rays inside an ellipsoid (left), paraboloid (middle), and hyperboloid (right)

2.2.1.6 Hyperbolic Mirrors

The useful property of a hyperbola is that rays emanating from one of its focii have a common virtual origin in the second focus when reflecting from the surface, Fig. 12 (right).

2.2.1.7 Cylindrical Mirrors with Curved Cross Sections

The properties of a cylindrical mirror are dependent on its cross section (see Fig. 13). We will consider circular, elliptic, parabolic and hyperbolic types of a cylinder cross sections. Each of these types inherits the properties of the corresponding 2D surface in such a way that the focii are elongated along the axis of the cylinder. Therefore, the propagation of the ray inside such a figure can be decomposed into two independent motions - one in the plane perpendicular to the cylinder axis, and the other along the cylinder axis. The first motion can be completely described by the propagation of the ray inside the 2D curve (circle, ellipse, parabola or hyperbola), while the second motion is constant.

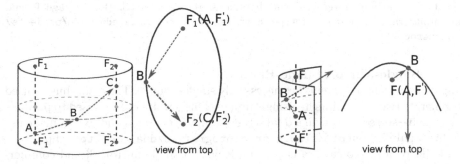

Fig. 13. Reflection of rays in cylindrical mirrors of elliptical cross section (left) and parabolic cross section (right)

3 Passive Imaging Systems

In this section we describe passive imaging devices that utilize mirrors in their design. The applications are mostly in stereo, multi-view and panoramic imaging. The advantages of employing mirrors in a system are usually

- a reduction in system cost by utilizing less sensor hardware,
- a simplification of synchronization by compressing several views onto a single sensor, and
- homogeneous radiometric and colorimetric properties of the sensor hardware.

In utilizing these advantages, sensor resolution is usually traded off for an expanded view point coverage of a scene.

3.1 Planar Mirrors

Planar mirrors are the simplest devices. As discussed in Sect. 2, single planar mirrors, and systems consisting of them have the advantage of preserving perspective projection properties at least in a subset of the pixels in an image.

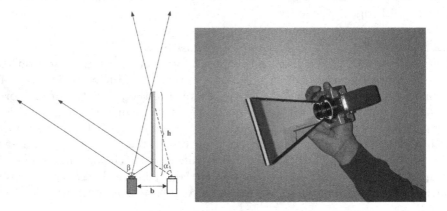

Fig. 14. Single mirror rectified catadioptric stereo camera [4]. (left) Image formation draft. (right) Camera prototype (http://www.cs.columbia.edu/CAVE/projects/cad_stereo/).

3.1.1 Single-Mirror, Single-Bounce

Single planar mirror systems are necessarily single-bounce. They can thus be used to generate two viewpoints in a single image. This feature is often used to produce inexpensive stereo viewers in a dual screen setup [5] and many hobbyists make use of this capability http://klub.stereofotograf.eu/dual_monitor.php.

Similarly, a stereo camera can be built with a single mirror [6] and commercial modifications of standard cameras are being offered http://hineslab.com/old/Mirror_Stereo.html. Depending on the mirror orientation with respect to the camera optical axes, the resulting epipolar geometry can be more or less suitable for stereo matching. Gluckman and Nayar [4,7] describe the conditions for epipolar lines to be parallel and along horizontal scan lines, a case that is particularly easy to handle in matching algorithms, see also Fig. 14.

In an early work, Mitsumoto et al. [8] describe object triangulation and geometric constraints for 3D reconstruction in case of a single plane mirror symmetry. They also time-sequentially move the mirror to different positions and merge the reconstructions to obtain a larger coverage of the object.

Moving planar mirrors are also used to inexpensively generate many viewpoints, e.g. for light field imaging [9] or 3D reconstruction [10,11].

Beamsplitters are often employed to distribute a single view of a scene onto several imaging sensors. These devices can be considered as a special case of a single mirroring operation for one of the sensors, whereas the beamsplitter appears transparent to the other.

3.1.2   Multi-mirror, Single-Bounce per Mirror

An increase in complexity and achievable imaging geometry is obtained when introducing several planar mirrors [4,7]. Restrictions that guarantee a single bounce per mirror are a) that inter-reflections between mirrors are avoided, or b) that all camera rays only encounter mirroring sequences where each of the mirrors participates at most once.

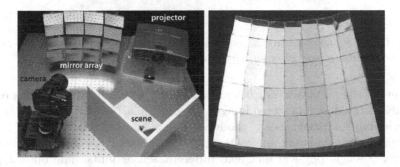

Fig. 15. A mirror array used for light field imaging [12] (left). A fabricated mirror array with an optimized facet distribution [13] (right).

3.1.2.1   No Inter-reflections

These arrangements are often employed for light field imaging with a single sensor [14,12,15,13], see also Fig. 15. Since light field views differ only slightly from one another, mirror arrangements like the ones shown in the Figure can be suitably employed without too strong requirements on the positioning of the mirrors to avoid inter-reflections. Since views are usually supposed to cover a common viewing area, the carrier surface is chosen in a concave manner. If manufactured on a very small scale, faceted mirrors can be used to mimic bidirectional reflection distribution functions (BRDFs) with pre-defined properties [16].

Another way to avoid inter-reflections is to position planar mirrors on a convex surface [17,18] and is realized using pyramidal or truncated pyramid structures.

This measure yields out-ward facing views for panoramic imaging [18], or a means of performing aperture splitting of a single image onto several sensors [17], an application that is heavily used in computational photography applications.

In optics, in the area of multi-spectral imaging, especially manufactured mirrors, so called "image slicers" are being used to differently deflect the scan-lines of an image such that vertical sensor space is freed up for sensing spectrally expanded versions of the scan-lines that are obtained by passing them through a diffraction grating [19,20,21].

3.1.2.2   Inter-reflections with a Single Reflection per Mirror

Several mirrors can also be arranged in a sequential sequence which yields a higher flexibility in generating virtual views and purely optical means of image manipulation. The most common commercial applications are probably erecting prisms in SLR view finders and other prism-based optical designs that are intended to flip or displace an image without distorting it otherwise [1].

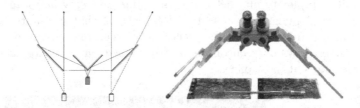

Fig. 16. Design for a four mirror stereo camera or viewing device [4] (left). The Sokkia MS27 commercial stereo viewer for aerial imagery (right).

However, several planar mirrors are also used to obtain a higher degree of flexibility in the design of stereo imaging systems [6,4,7] or in the production of stereo viewing equipment as e.g. produced by Sokkia, see also Fig. 16.

In computational photography settings, beamsplitter trees are often employed to deliver a single physical image to different sensor units. The optical path towards each of those sensor units can be modified such that optically differently filtered images are recorded. For an overview of this area the interested reader is referred to [22,23,24].

It should be mentioned that all applications discussed so far can be handled with the basic unfolding technique, Sect. 2.1.1.

3.1.3   Multi-mirror, Multi-bounce

Multi-bounce planar mirror systems are considerably more difficult to comprehend and to make use of. Early work in mirror-based single-image 3D reconstruction focused on setups consisting of two mirrors arranged such that their normals are in a common plane and that the angle between them is equal to $2\pi/N$. This has been a popular choice for three-dimensional imaging with a single camera with $N = 5$ views [26,27,25,28]. It should be mentioned that this geometry results in a non-Coxeter structure and therefore the camera position has to be

Fig. 17. The five-view case employing inter-reflections up to second order [25] – self-occlusion is clearly visible (left). In the case of many inter-reflections a pixel labeling procedure is necessary [2] that can resolve the view assignment to pixels – up to eight reflection levels have been employed (right).

suitably chosen to hide discontinuous views, see Sect. 2.1.4. The multiple view geometry of this setting has been explored in [29].

A common problem with this arrangement, and in fact with any multi-bounce system, is that the object position has to be chosen very carefully. The problem that occurs in the multi-bounce case is that an object might occlude its virtual counter parts, an effect that is easily observed when viewing one-self in a set of opened bathroom mirrors. A solution to this problem has been presented recently [2] and consists in a pixel labeling procedure that determines for every pixel of an image with multiple inter-reflections which virtual view it belongs to, see also Fig. 17. This assignment can be computed from a single image and for arbitrary calibrated planar mirror geometries. Because of the kaleidoscopic nature of the resulting images, these systems are referred to as kaleidoscopic imaging systems.

3.2 Curved Mirrors

Imaging systems employing curved mirrors commonly aim at achieving a larger field-of-view than is possible with refractive optics at a reasonable price and with acceptable distortions. In particular, wide-angle refractive elements often suffer from strong aberrations.

3.2.1 Single-Mirror, Single-Bounce

The most common use of single curved mirrors in conjunction with a camera device is omnidirectional or panoramic imaging. The applications of omnidirectional cameras are mainly in robotics for navigation purposes [30], omnidirectional stereo if multiple images are available [31], tele-conferencing [32] and panorama construction. Several companies such as Olympus and Canon have developed prototypes and other companies such as 0-360, GoPano, Neovision, RemoteReality, FullView Inc. and VersaCorp. are offering systems commercially. The technology has been employed in Microsoft's RoundTable.

Research efforts have been concentrated on determining adequate mirror shapes. While conic sections provide a single center of projection if the camera is placed in one of the focii for hyperbolic or ellipsoidal mirrors, see Sect. 2.2.1, a careful alignment of the camera and the mirror have to be performed. A more practical arrangement is the combination of an orthographic camera with a parabolic mirror [32]. This way, only the optical axis of the camera and the axis of the mirror have to align. The advantage of single center of projection systems is that proper projective views can be synthesized from the acquired imagery.

The design of non-center of projection systems has focused on achieving desirable properties of the observed projections. An inevitable feature of observations via curved mirrors are the distortions introduced by the curved surface. Some research has been performed on optimizing mirror shapes such as to achieve desirable projection properties such as a linear dependence between the incidence angle of world rays to radial image coordinates [33], the preservation of world space linearity in the images observed by the catadioptric system [34], the achievement of a pre-defined projection pattern [35], the capture of non-distorting wide-angle views [36], or the minimization of image space errors [37]. A common approach is the specification of derivative properties of the mirror surface, followed by solving a differential equation [33,34,37] or minimizing an error functional [35]. The concepts have been extended towards systems of catadioptric cameras [38].

When several cameras are available, catadioptric stereo matching can be performed [31] and depth maps can be computed. The associated research questions are related to the imaging geometry and therefore the calibration of such systems, Sect. 5.

An important aspect to be taken into account when using curved mirrors for imaging applications is their inherent property to refocus light rays. Studies concentrating on the effects of mirror-induced defocus characterization can be found in [39,40,41].

3.2.2   Single-Mirror, Multi-bounce

Curved mirrors are typically designed such that only a single reflection occurs for each camera ray. This is achieved by employing convex mirror shapes. However, it is possible to use multi-bounce mirror systems advantageously. In particular, conical mirrors with a specular interior can be seen as a kaleidoscopic imaging system that is continuous in one dimension, whereas offering discrete view points in the other. They have been used for omnidirectional texture acquisition and depth estimation [42]. Cross-sections of this type of mirror can be analyzed with the unfolding procedure, Sect. 2.1.1.

3.2.3   Multi-mirror, Single-Bounce

Systems utilizing multiple curved mirrors are designed such that inter-reflections are prevented, or the corresponding image regions are excluded from analysis. The most popular multi-mirror arrangement for curved mirrors consists of arrays of mirror spheres [43,44] or spherical caps [45,46], the reason being that the sphere is rotationally symmetric around its center, thus offering homogeneous viewing properties for a single perspective camera observing several of them. Applications include light field imaging and 3D reconstruction. An initial study of the latter utilized two spherical mirrors observed by a perspective camera and described the resulting epipolar geometry for stereo matching [47]. A linear array of mirroring spheres was used to calibrate the position of a point light source [48]. A study of two conic sections imaged by a single perspective camera and of the resulting epipolar geometry is found in [49].

Panoramic cameras can be made more compact if reflection of two or more mirrors is permitted. The camera is again arranged along the symmetry axis of the mirror system. In the case of conic sections, it was shown that multi-mirror systems of such shapes always have an equivalent single mirror interpretation [50]. In [51], a double mirror system of the shape previously discussed is designed such that a stereo pair is formed in a single panoramic 360° image.

Arrays of mirror spheres have primarily been employed for light field imaging and 3D reconstruction. In [43,44] the incident light field of scene illumination is acquired with an array of mirror spheres. The spatially and directionally varying illumination is then used to relight synthetic scenes [43] or to compute depth maps and perform refocusing operations [44]. Arrays of spherical caps reduce the unusable area at the sphere boundaries that suffer from inter-reflections. They have been used for light field imaging and 3D reconstruction [52,45,46].

4   Active Imaging Systems

Active imaging system employ a light source in addition to an imaging device. Nowadays, these light sources are typically digital projectors which enable a per-pixel control of the illumination. The use of combinations of cameras and projectors enables applications such as corrected projection onto curved surfaces, virtual large scale projection displays, 3D structured light scanning, reflectance scanning and more. An overview of the area of camera-projector systems is given in [53].

The combination of light sources with mirrors introduces additional problems in a measurement setting. Emitted light can super-position in a scene [54,55], defocus problems [39,40,41] are exaggerated since projectors typically employ large apertures for light efficiency. On the other hand, active light helps in coding a scene, as e.g. in structured light scanning, or enables the scanning of surface properties.

4.1   Planar Mirrors

Planar mirrors are most often used to multiply the number of physical projectors or to virtually position them in a physically impossible location.

4.1.1   Single-Mirror, Single-Bounce
The most common use of a single planar mirroring device is the use of a beamsplitter to bring a projector and a camera into a coaxial arrangement [56,41,57,58,59,60].

This configuration allows for illumination along the same rays that form the camera image and is often part of more complex active imaging systems.

In a different application, the use of a single planar mirror for range scanning inaccessible parts of an object has been reported [54]. To avoid the super-position of light, the operator has to manually ensure that the real and virtual laser lines are formed in distinct regions and that a distance heuristic can distinguish between the 3D points generated in the real space and in the virtual space, respectively.

4.1.2   Multi-mirror, Single-Bounce

In the active setting, systems of planar mirrors multiply a single projector into a set of virtual projectors, in effect realizing a large aperture projection system. These virtual large apertures have been employed in synthetic aperture confocal imaging techniques [14,15] where the superposition of light is a crucial part of the functioning of the device. Confocal imaging systems can slice a volumetric scene via very shallow depth-of-field imaging and illumination. The planar mirrors are arranged tangent to a concave base shape [14] which is ellipsoidal in the case of [15]. The mirror array is simultaneously used as a light field imaging unit, Sect. 3.1.2. The geometrical layout and interpretation are as discussed in Sect. 2.1.3.

Sequential folding of projection cones is often employed in rear-projection screens to reduce the size of the room that is required behind the screen. Typically, large-scale front-surface mirrors are employed for this purpose, http://www.screen-tech.eu.

4.1.3   Multi-mirror, Multi-bounce

As mentioned in Sect. 3.1.2, the main complication in utilizing multiple ray bounces in a mirror system is that self-occlusion between the object and its virtual counter-parts has to be avoided. The simplest solution to this problem is the imaging of flat objects [61,62]. In [61], a kaleidoscopic mirror system was introduced that was capable of scanning the bidirectional texture function (BTF), also known as spatially varying BRDF, of a surface without moving the acquisition apparatus or the sample. In this case it is possible to observe a surface light field with a single picture and the sample can be illuminated from different directions by using a digital projector that is only highlighting specific chambers. A sampling analysis of this type of system can be found in [62].

Kaleidoscopic reflectance scanning has been extended to take extended depth objects into account [55]. The solution is similar to the pixel labeling procedure [2], Fig. 17 (right), this time applied to the projector coordinate system. If only pixels that have a unique label are illuminated simultaneously, the virtual illumination is guaranteed to come from a single direction without causing illumination overlap in the scene. The authors combined reflectance scanning with omnidirectional laser-range scanning.

The superposition of light can also be arranged such that a projected pattern perfectly super-positions onto itself. This approach requires orthogonal illumination with a direction that is contained in the plane spanned by the mirror normals. The two-mirror/five-virtual view system mentioned in Sect. 3.1.2 has been used for this purpose [25,28].

4.2   Curved Mirrors

Curved mirrors are not widely used for projection purposes, most likely due to defocusing of the projected image. For this reason, apparently only small aperture "pocket projectors" use this technology.

4.2.1   Single-Mirror, Single-Bounce

An example for a curved mirror in a commercial projector is the RICOH PJ WX4130. It is used to achieve a very short focusing distance and a large field-of-view, http://www.ricoh.com/about/company/technology/tech/040.html. In research, curved mirrors have been investigated for achieving large fields of view [63] and optical undistortion when projecting onto tilted or curved walls [38].

In the area of reflection measurement, a combination of orthographic camera, collimated light source and a parabolic mirror section allows for convenient scanning of the BRDF of flat samples [64,65]. When the mirror is moved, the surface can be scanned and a spatially varying BRDF is measured. The directional scanning is performed angle-wise by using different projector pixels. A similar system can be built from elliptical mirrors and a perspective camera, putting the material sample in one focus and the projector-camera system in the other [66]. The latter reference also employs per-angle scanning, however, the system has been extended to multiplexed illumination [67].

4.2.2   Single-Mirror, Multi-bounce

Single curved mirror active multi-bounce systems have not been explored to our knowledge.

4.2.3   Multi-mirror, Single-Bounce

A combination of two curved mirrors and a coaxial camera/projector configuration has been used to perform BRDF measurements directly in some basis [58,59]. The basis is projected into the system and the observations consist of the integral between the incident illumination and the BRDF. This integral corresponds to a scalar product of the BRDF and the basis illumination and can therefore be used to measure a basis expansion of the BRDF signal, permitting to sample less coefficients if the reflectance is low frequency or the basis of the material is known.

4.2.4   Multi-mirror, Multi-bounce

Multiple curved mirror active multi-bounce systems have not been explored to our knowledge.

5   Mirror Calibration and Geometry Reconstruction of Specular Surfaces

In order to successfully use mirror systems, they have to be calibrated. Usually this involves the estimation of the mirror position and orientation, potentially its shape, and its radiometric properties [2,55].

5.1   Planar Mirrors

Planar mirrors are relatively simple to calibrate since they do not introduce additional distortions into the image. Instead, the image taken by a perspective camera shows different perspective sub-views in parts of the acquired image. It is therefore only necessary to determine the image regions that correspond to a particular view, a task that is often performed manually. Within these viewing regions, standard perspective camera calibration techniques can be employed [68]. In the case of single bounce observation, this calibration is usually sufficient.

5.1.1   Single Mirror, Single-Bounce

In case of a moving mirror, it is usually necessary to estimate the mirror pose with respect to the recording camera, since an offline calibration step cannot easily be employed. For this purpose, self-identifying markers that are attached to the mirror can be used [9]. Moving platforms are also often employed in the case of robotic applications. The case of a two-planar mirror setup with a moving camera mounted on a robotic platform has been analyzed in [69]. The authors derive a calibration procedure for computing the pose of the camera with respect to the mirrors as well as the mirrors' relative position and orientation.

5.1.2   Multiple Mirrors, Multi-bounce

In the case of multi-bounce observation, the mirror poses as well as the single real camera pose need to be estimated very accurately since the calibration error increases exponentially with the level of reflection. For this reason, special calibration procedures are necessary. In [70] a fixed (and known) mirror geometry is assumed and an algorithm for pose recovery of the real camera that is based on scene point correspondences (without knowing their reflection level) is derived.

For kaleidoscopic imaging systems, different procedures can be used. For systems that are only imaging flat samples, it is sufficient to determine the homographies mapping the acquired views to their rectified versions [61]. The geometry of the mirror system and the camera need not to be known. For kaleidoscopic systems that image extended objects, it is necessary to estimate the mirrors' positions and orientations with respect to the real camera. In [2,55] this is done by placing a checkerboard pattern at different heights into the system and manually identifying the direct view of the camera and the first order reflections. From this data, initial mirror parameters can be computed that are then used to predict higher order reflections. Incorporating this new information yields improved results. A global bundle adjustment step finishes the procedure.

The manual identification of reflection levels in a multi-bounce image is tedious and error prone. In [71], an automatic procedure is proposed that can recover the number of mirrors and their parameters without user intervention. Unfortunately, the method is restricted to $2\frac{1}{2}D$ settings.

5.2   Curved Mirrors

The calibration or geometry estimation of general curved mirrors or specular surfaces of general shape is a difficult subject. A recent review article covering the area can be found in [72]. When using curved mirrors in imaging systems, it is necessary to calibrate the shape parameters of the mirror as well as its pose with respect to the camera.

5.2.1   Single Mirror, Single-Bounce

The single-bounce case for parametric mirrors is the most investigated class of algorithms for mirror calibration. A good overview of imaging, pose estimation, and multiple view geometry that includes specific sections on catadioptric systems can be found in [73].

A prerequisite for investigating calibration problems is an understanding of the imaging geometry of such systems.

5.2.1.1   Imaging Geometry

An analysis and classification of distortions in multi-perspective images and a corresponding undistortion algorithm are discussed in [74]. The concept of general linear cameras has been introduced as a general piece-wise linear class of imaging models for multi-perspective images. Its application to reflection modeling and an overview of its applications are given in [75].

The class of conic section mirrors has received the widest attention. Viewpoint caustics of curved mirrors are intrinsically linked to their imaging properties and are discussed in [76]. The imaging geometry of central catadioptric systems, i.e. those featuring a single center of projection are discussed in [39,40,77,78]. Central systems require the camera to be in a specific point with its optical axis aligned with the mirror axis (except for the parabolic mirror/orthographic camera case). If the camera's optical axis is aligned but the camera is not in the correct location, the system is called non-central (because it does not have a single center of projection, see Sect. 2.2.1). For this case analytic forward projection models have been derived [79] that result in higher order polynomial formulations. The condition for the camera to be on axis has recently been lifted [80].

5.2.1.2   Shape Estimation

Imaging geometries as described above can be utilized to derive shape recovery algorithms. These usually aim at recovering the parameters of a conic section known as the intrinsic parameters of the mirror system as well as the effective focal length of the combined mirror-camera system. Shape estimation for central catadioptric systems has been analyzed from the apparent distortion of scene lines in an image [77]. The calibration of a parabolic mirror/orthographic camera system is discussed in [81,78]. The parameters of a conic section mirror can also be estimated from point correspondences between different frames of a moving camera [76].

Images of warped scene lines can also be used to compute the shape of more general shapes. In particular, near-flat specular surfaces can be recovered by locally fitting the general linear camera model [82,83]. More generally, specular surfaces can be scanned by establishing scene plane-to-image plane correspondences [84,85]. A naïve application of the principle results in a 1D ambiguity between the depth and the normal of the surface at one position. This ambiguity has recently been resolved [86].

5.2.1.3 Pose Estimation

An associated problem in calibration is the pose estimation problem: Given a known camera/mirror configuration that is moved to different positions, what is the relative pose of the two views ? An early analysis of the ego-motion problem with a central catadioptric is discussed in [30]. Here, optical flow in the recorded images is used to compute the trajectory of the camera. A similar problem based on sparse feature tracking was proposed in [87]. The epipolar geometry of central catadioptric cameras was investigated in [88,89]. It allows for pose estimation and simplified stereo matching.

5.2.2   Multiple Mirrors, Single-Bounce

Curved mirror arrays have mainly been used in the form of arrays of spheres, Sect. 3.2.3. Calibration methods use images of distorted checkerboards to infer the position and radii of the spheres with respect to the recording camera. A method for calibrating an array of spherical mirror caps positioned on a common ground plane is described in [45]. Recently, a method for calibrating several mirror spheres in general position has been developed [90].

5.2.3   Multiple Mirrors, Multi-bounce

The most general result so far on multiple specular surface interactions is that a maximum of two specular interactions of a ray with a general surface can be recovered, regardless of the number of measurements [91]. The article derives a theory of local specular surface interactions and derives tractable triangulation problems on a local per-ray basis. As input, the authors consider an arbitrary number of correspondences between several image planes and several world planes intersected by the ray in question.

6   Connection to Time-of-Flight Imaging and the Multi-bounce Problem

The time-of-flight problem, at first hand, appears to be disconnected from the problem settings considered so far and in fact, the literature is largely orthogonal. In time-of-flight imaging, a pulse is emitted at one spatial location and the time difference until the signal returns is measured by the sensor. The classical time-of-flight technique is RADAR, where radio waves are used as probes. SONAR uses sound waves and LIDAR is using light pulses, usually infrared, to determine the distance of objects. In pulse-based time-of-flight imaging, most commonly, a single reflection of the emitted pulse from the environment is assumed. This situation is equivalent to a single-mirroring operation. In practice, multiple echoes, or multi-bounce signals, can corrupt the detection. Most often, these echoes are considered to be undesirable noise and filtering procedures are developed to identify first time of arrivals, see [92,93] and the references therein.

Multi-bounce analysis in this area is investigating the forward modeling of reverberation and recovery of a room geometry from impulse responses of a room. The forward modeling frequently employs unfolding procedures, Sect. 2.1.1, for Coxeter geometries [94], or for arbitrary polyhedral models [95].

The recovery of room geometries from multi-bounce data often considers the special case of a rectangular Coxeter geometry [96] also known as the *shoebox* model, which allows for the interpretation as a perfectly sub-divided space. Only recently methods for general convex geometries have started to appear ([97] and the references therein). These methods usually assume the first-bounce, other reflection levels, or the number of walls of the room to be known. Two recent methods that do not use these assumptions are [98,71].

The computer vision literature on time-of-flight is presented elsewhere in this book. We would still like to point out recent developments that enable the recording of the temporal profile of light for every pixel [99]. While the initial *transient imaging* work used a very expensive femto-second laser setup, recently the use of a standard time-of-flight imager for the measurement of transient images has been proposed [100]. The information acquired with these devices can be used to reconstruct geometry from indirectly observed bounces, i.e. the geometry of hidden objects [101].

7   Conclusions

We have reviewed and classified the literature regarding the use of mirror systems in computer graphics and computer vision, and established some connections to the area of time-of-flight imaging. Some possible configurations of mirror systems have been identified as yet of unexplored, in particular, the use of multiple bounce curved mirrors in active imaging systems.

Another outcome of this review is that the design and optimization of mirror layouts is an area of study that has been only partially addressed so far. In particular, the global optimization of mirror system properties appears to be a promising, if challenging, research direction.

The analysis of multi-bounce reflection systems is more advanced in the computer graphics and computer vision literature than in time-of-flight imaging, where multi-bounce signals are predominantly considered as noise rather then a source of information.

Finally, we have discussed the, as of yet, little used tool of ray unfolding. It enables a simplified understanding of complex specular interactions and, in our opinion, can serve a useful role in exploring the area. It would be desirable to extend it such that more general classes of mirror shapes, especially non-central curved ones can be handled with similar ease as the planar multi-bounce case.

Acknowledgements. This work was supported by the German Research Foundation (DFG) through an Emmy-Noether Fellowship (IH 114/1-1).

References

1. Smith, W.J.: Modern Optical Engineering, 4th edn. McGraw Hill Professional (2008)
2. Reshetouski, I., Manakov, A., Seidel, H.P., Ihrke, I.: Three-Dimensional Kaleidoscopic Imaging. In: Proc. CVPR, pp. 353–360 (2011)
3. Sossinsky, A.B.: Geometries, vol. 64. American Mathematical Soc. (2012)
4. Gluckman, J., Nayar, S.K.: Rectified Catadioptric Stereo Sensors. In: Proc. CVPR, pp. 380–387 (2000)
5. Wu, H.H.P., Chang, S.H.: Design of Stereoscopic Viewing System Based on a Compact Mirror and Dual Monitor. Optical Engineering 49(2), 027401-1–027401-6 (2010)
6. Gluckman, J., Nayar, S.K.: A Real-Time Catadioptric Stereo System Using Planar Mirrors. In: Proc. of Image Understanding Workshop (1998)
7. Gluckman, J., Nayar, S.: Rectified Catadioptric Stereo Sensors. IEEE Trans. PAMI 24(2), 224–236 (2002)
8. Mitsumoto, H., Tamura, S., Okazaki, K., Kajimi, N., Fukui, Y.: 3-D Reconstruction Using Mirror Images Based on a Plane Symmetry Recovering Method. IEEE Trans. PAMI 14, 941–946 (1992)
9. Ihrke, I., Stich, T., Gottschlich, H., Magnor, M., Seidel, H.P.: Fast Incident Light Field Acquisition and Rendering. WSCG 16(1-3), 25–32 (2008)
10. Murray, D.W.: Recovering Range using Virtual Multi-Camera Stereo. CVIU 61(2), 285–291 (1995)
11. Hu, B., CRV: It's All Done with Mirrors: Calibration-and-Correspondence-Free 3D Reconstruction. In: Proc. CRV, pp. 148–154 (2009)
12. Sen, P., Chen, B., Garg, G., Marschner, S.R., Horowitz, M., Levoy, M., Lensch, H.P.A.: Dual photography. ACM TOG 24, 745–755 (2005)
13. Fuchs, M., Kächele, M., Rusinkiewicz, S.: Design and Fabrication of Faceted Mirror Arrays for Light Field Capture. In: Proc. VMV, pp. 1–8 (2012)
14. Levoy, M., Chen, B., Vaish, V., Horowitz, M., McDowall, I., Bolas, M.: Synthetic Aperture Confocal Imaging. ACM TOG 23, 825–834 (2004)
15. Mukaigawa, Y., Tagawa, S., Kim, J., Raskar, R., Matsushita, Y., Yagi, Y.: Hemispherical confocal imaging using turtleback reflector. In: Kimmel, R., Klette, R., Sugimoto, A. (eds.) ACCV 2010, Part I. LNCS, vol. 6492, pp. 336–349. Springer, Heidelberg (2011)
16. Weyrich, T., Peers, P., Matusik, W., Rusinkiewicz, S.: Fabricating Microgeometry for Custom Surface Reflectance. ACM TOG 28(3), 32:1–32:6 (2009)
17. Aggarwal, M., Ahuja, N.: Split aperture imaging for high dynamic range. In: Proc. ICCV, vol. 2, pp. 10–17 (2001)
18. Tan, K.H., Hua, H., Ahuja, N.: Multiview Panoramic Cameras Using Mirror Pyramids. IEEE Trans. PAMI 26(7), 941–946 (2004)

19. Harvey, A.R., Fletcher-Holmes, D.W., Gorman, A.: Spectral Imaging in a Snapshot. In: Proc. SPIE, vol. 5694, pp. 1–10 (2005)
20. Gao, L., Kester, R.T., Tkaczyk, T.S.: Compact Image Slicing Spectrometer (ISS) for Hyperspectral Fluorescence Microscopy. Optics Express 17(15), 12293–12308 (2009)
21. Gorman, A., Fletcher-Holmes, D.W., Harvey, A.R.: Generalization of the Lyot Filter and its Application to Snapshot Spectral Imaging. Optics Express 18(6), 5602–5608 (2010)
22. McGuire, M., Matusik, W., Pfister, H., Chen, B., Hughes, J.F., Nayar, S.K.: Optical Splitting Trees for High-Precision Monocular Imaging. IEEE Comput. Graph. & Appl. 27(2), 32–42 (2007)
23. Wetzstein, G., Ihrke, I., Lanman, D., Heidrich, W.: Computational plenoptic imaging. Computer Graphics Forum 30(8), 2397–2426 (2011)
24. Zhou, C., Nayar, S.: Computational Cameras: Convergence of Optics and Processing. IEEE Trans. IP 20(12), 3322–3340 (2011)
25. Lanman, D., Crispell, D., Taubin, G.: Surround Structured Lighting for Full Object Scanning. In: Proc. 3DIM, pp. 107–116 (2007)
26. Huang, P.H., Lai, S.H.: Contour-Based Structure from Reflection. In: Proc. CVPR, pp. 165–178 (2006)
27. Forbes, K., Nicolls, F., de Jager, G., Voigt, A.: Shape-from-Silhouette with Two Mirrors and an Uncalibrated Camera. In: Leonardis, A., Bischof, H., Pinz, A. (eds.) ECCV 2006. LNCS, vol. 3952, pp. 165–178. Springer, Heidelberg (2006)
28. Lanman, D., Crispell, D., Taubin, G.: Surround Structured Lighting: 3-D Scanning with Orthographic Illumination. CVIU (113), 1107–1117 (2009)
29. Ying, X., Peng, K., Ren, R., Zha, H.: Geometric Properties of Multiple Reflections in Catadioptric Camera with Two Planar Mirrors. In: Proc. CVPR, pp. 1–8 (2010)
30. Gluckman, J., Nayar, S.K.: Ego-Motion and Omnidirectional Cameras. In: Proc. ICCV, pp. 999–1005 (1998)
31. Gluckman, J., Nayar, S.K.: Real-Time Omnidirectional and Panoramic Stereo. In: Proc. of Image Understanding Workshop (1998)
32. Nayar, S.: Catadioptric Omnidirectional Camera. In: Proc. CVPR, pp. 482–488 (1997)
33. Chahl, J.S., Srinivasan, M.V.: Reflective Surfaces for Panoramic Imaging. Appl. Optics 36(31), 8275–8285 (1997)
34. Hicks, R.A., Bajcsy, R.: Catadioptric Sensors that Approximate Wide-angle Perspective Projections. In: Proc. CVPR, pp. 1–7 (2000)
35. Hicks, R.A.: Designing a Mirror to Realize a Given Projection. JOSA 22(2), 323–330 (2005)
36. Srinivasan, M.V.: A New Class of Mirrors for Wide-Angle Imaging. In: Proc. OMNIVIS, pp. 1–8 (2003)
37. Swaminathan, R., Grossberg, M.D., Nayar, S.K.: Designing Mirrors for Catadioptric Systems that Minimize Image Errors. In: Proc. OMNIVIS, pp. 1–8 (2004)
38. Swaminathan, R., Grossberg, M.D., Nayar, S.K.: Framework for Designing Catadioptric Projection and Imaging Systems. In: Proc. OMNIVIS, pp. 1–8 (2003)
39. Baker, S., Nayar, S.K.: A Theory of Catadioptric Image Formation. In: Proc. ICCV, pp. 35–42 (1998)
40. Baker, S., Nayar, S.K.: A Theory of Single-Viewpoint Catadioptric Image Formation. IJCV 35(2), 175–196 (1999)
41. Zhang, L., Nayar, S.K.: Projection Defocus Analysis for Scene Capture and Image Display. ACM TOG 25, 907–915 (2006)

42. Kuthirummal, S., Nayar, S.K.: Multiview Radial Catadioptric Imaging for Scene Capture. ACM TOG 25(3) (2006)
43. Unger, J., Wenger, A., Hawkins, T., Gardner, A., Debevec, P.: Capturing and Rendering with Incident Light Fields. In: Proc. EGWR, pp. 141–149 (2003)
44. Taguchi, Y., Agrawal, A., Veeraraghavan, A., Ramalingam, S., Raskar, R.: Axial-Cones: Modeling Spherical Catadioptric Cameras for Wide-Angle Light Field Rendering. ACM Trans. Graph. 29, 172:1–172:8 (2010)
45. Lanman, D., Crispell, D., Wachs, M., Taubin, G.: Spherical Catadioptric Arrays: Construction, Multi-View Geometry, and Calibration. In: Proc. 3DPVT, pp. 81–88 (2006)
46. Ding, Y., Yu, J., Sturm, P.: Multiperspective Stereo Matching and Volumetric Reconstruction. In: Proc. ICCV, pp. 1827–1834 (2009)
47. Nayar, S.K.: Sphereo: Determining Depth using Two Specular Spheres and a Single Camera. In: SPIE Optics, Illumination, and Image Sensing for Machine Vision III, vol. 1005, pp. 245–254 (1988)
48. Lensch, H.P.A., Kautz, J., Goesele, M., Heidrich, W., Seidel, H.P.: Image-based Reconstruction of Spatial Appearance and Geometric Detail. ACM TOG 22(2), 234–257 (2003)
49. Nene, S., Nayar, S.: Stereo with Mirrors. In: Proc. ICCV, pp. 1087–1094 (1998)
50. Nayar, S., Peri, V.: Folded Catadioptric Cameras. In: Proc. CVPR, vol. 2, pp. 217–223 (1999)
51. Jang, G., Kim, S., Kweon, I.: Single Camera Catadioptric Stereo System. In: Proc. OMNIVIS, pp. 1–8 (2005)
52. Lanman, D., Wachs, M., Taubin, G., Cukierman, F.: Reconstructing a 3D Line from a Single Catadioptric Image. In: Proc. 3DPVT, pp. 1–8 (2006)
53. Bimber, O., Iwai, D., Wetzstein, G., Grundhfer, A.: The Visual Computing of Projector-Camera Systems. CGF 27(8), 2219–2245 (2008)
54. Fasano, A., Callieri, M., Cignoni, P., Scopigno, R.: Exploiting mirrors for laser stripe 3d scanning. In: Proc. of 4th International Conference on 3D Digital Imaging and Modeling (3DIM 2003), Banff, Canada (2003)
55. Ihrke, I., Reshetouski, I., Manakov, A., Tevs, A., Wand, M., Seidel, H.P.: A Kaleidoscopic Approach to Surround Geometry and Reflectance Acquisition. In: Proceedings of IEEE International Workshop on Computational Cameras and Displays, pp. 29–36 (2012)
56. Fujii, K., Grossberg, M., Nayar, S.: A Projector-Camera System with Real-Time Photometric Adaptation for Dynamic Environments. In: Proc. CVPR, vol. 2, pp. 1180–1187 (2005)
57. Garg, G.G., Talvala, E.V., Levoy, M., Lensch, H.P.A.: Symmetric Photography: Exploiting Data-sparseness in Reflectance Fields. In: Proc. EGSR, pp. 251–262 (June 2006)
58. Ghosh, A., Achutha, S., Heidrich, W., O'Toole, M.: BRDF Acquisition with Basis Illumination. In: Proc. ICCV, pp. 183–197 (2007)
59. Ghosh, A., Heidrich, W., Achutha, S., O'Toole, M.: A Basis Illumination Approach to BRDF Measurement. IJCV 90(2), 183–197 (2010)
60. Holroyd, M., Lawrence, J., Zickler, T.: A Coaxial Optical Scanner for Synchronous Acquisition of 3D Geometry and Surface Reflectance. ACM TOG 29(4), article no. 99 (2010)
61. Han, J.Y., Perlin, K.: Measuring Bidirectional Texture Reflectance with a Kaleidoscope. In: Proc. SIGGRAPH, pp. 741–748 (2003)
62. Bangay, S., Radloff, J.D.: Kaleidoscope Configurations for Reflectance Measurement. In: Proc. AFRIGRAPH, pp. 161–170 (2004)

63. Ding, Y., Xiao, J., Tan, K.H., Yu, J.: Catadioptric Projectors. In: Proc. CVPR, pp. 2528–2535 (2009)
64. Dana, K.: BRDF/BTF Measurement Device. In: Proc. ICCV, pp. 460–466 (2001)
65. Dana, K.J., Wang, J.: Device for Convenient Measurement of Spatially Varying Bidirectional Reflectance. JOSA 21, 1–12 (2004)
66. Mukaigawa, Y., Sumino, K., Yagi, Y.: High-Speed Measurement of BDRF Using an Ellipsoidal Mirror and a Projector. In: Proc. CVPR, pp. 1–8 (2007)
67. Mukaigawa, Y., Sumino, K., Yagi, Y.: Multiplexed Illumination for Measuring BRDF Using an Ellipsoidal Mirror and a Projector. In: Yagi, Y., Kang, S.B., Kweon, I.S., Zha, H. (eds.) ACCV 2007, Part II. LNCS, vol. 4844, pp. 246–257. Springer, Heidelberg (2007)
68. Bouguet, J.Y.: Camera Calibration Toolbox for Matlab (2005)
69. Mariottini, G.L., Scheggi, S., Morbidi, F., Prattichizzo, D.: Planar Catadioptric Stereo: Single and Multi-View Geometry for Calibration and Localization. In: Proc. ICRA, pp. 2711–2716 (2009)
70. Ramalingam, S., Bouaziz, S., Sturm, P., Torr, P.H.: The Light-Path Less Traveled. In: Proc. CVPR, pp. 3145–3152 (2011)
71. Reshetouski, I., Manakov, A., Bandhari, A., Raskar, R., Seidel, H.P., Ihrke, I.: Discovering the Structure of a Planar Mirror System from Multiple Observations of a Single Point. In: Proc. CVPR, pp. 89–96 (2013)
72. Ihrke, I., Kutulakos, K.N., Lensch, H.P.A., Magnor, M., Heidrich, W.: Transparent and Specular Object Reconstruction. CGF 29(8), 2400–2426 (2010)
73. Sturm, P., Ramalingam, S., Tardif, J.P., Gasparini, S., Barreto, J.: Camera Models and Fundamental Concepts used in Geometric Computer Vision. In: Foundations and Trends in Computer Graphics and Vision, vol. 6, pp. 1–183. Now Publisher Inc. (2010)
74. Swaminathan, R., Grossberg, M.D., Nayar, S.K.: A Perspective on Distortions. In: Proc. CVPR, pp. 594–601 (2003)
75. Yu, J., McMillan, L., Sturnm, P.: Multi-Prespective Modelling, Rendering and Imaging. CGF 29(1), 227–246 (2010)
76. Swaminathan, R., Grossberg, M.D., Nayar, S.K.: Caustics of Catadioptric Cameras. In: Proc. ICCV, pp. 2–9 (2001)
77. Geyer, C., Danillidis, K.: Catadioptric Projective Geometry. IJCV 45(3), 223–243 (2001)
78. Geyer, C., Danillidis, K.: Paracatadioptric Camera Calibration. IEEE Trans. PAMI 24, 687–695 (2002)
79. Agrawal, A., Taguchi, Y., Ramalingam, S.: Analytical Forward Projection for Axial Non-Central Dioptric & Catadioptric Cameras. In: Daniilidis, K., Maragos, P., Paragios, N. (eds.) ECCV 2010, Part III. LNCS, vol. 6313, pp. 129–143. Springer, Heidelberg (2010)
80. Agrawal, A., Taguchi, Y., Ramalingam, S.: Beyond Alhazen's Problem: Analytical Projection Model for Non-Central Catadioptric Cameras with Quadric Mirrors. In: Proc. CVPR, pp. 2993–3000 (2011)
81. Geyer, C., Danillidis, K.: Catadioptric Camera Calibration. In: Proc. ICCV, vol. 1, pp. 398–404 (1999)
82. Ding, Y., Yu, J.: Recovering Shape Characteristics on Near-Flat Specular Surfaces. In: Proc. CVPR, pp. 1–8 (2008)
83. Ding, Y., Yu, J., Sturm, P.F.: Recovering Specular Surfaces using Curved Line Images. In: Proc. CVPR, pp. 2326–2333 (2009)
84. Tarini, M., Lensch, H.P.A., Goesele, M., Seidel, H.P.: 3D Acquisition of Mirroring Objects. Graphical Models 67(4), 233–259 (2005)

85. Bonfort, T., Sturm, P., Gargallo, P.: General Specular Surface Triangulation. In: Narayanan, P.J., Nayar, S.K., Shum, H.-Y. (eds.) ACCV 2006. LNCS, vol. 3852, pp. 872–881. Springer, Heidelberg (2006)
86. Liu, M., Hartley, R., Salzmann, M.: Mirror Surface Reconstruction from a Single Image. In: Proc. CVPR, pp. 129–136 (June 2013)
87. Kang, S.B.: Catadioptric Self-Calibration. In: Proc. CVPR, pp. 201–207 (2000)
88. Svoboda, T., Pajdla, T., Hlaváč, V.: Epipolar Geometry for Panoramic Cameras. In: Burkhardt, H.-J., Neumann, B. (eds.) ECCV 1998. LNCS, vol. 1406, pp. 218–231. Springer, Heidelberg (1998)
89. Svoboda, T., Pajdla, T.: Epipolar Geometry for Central Catadioptric Cameras. IJCV 49(1), 23–37 (2002)
90. Agrawal, A., Ramalingam, S.: Single Image Calibration of Multi-Axial Imaging Systems. In: Proc. CVPR, pp. 1399–1406 (2013)
91. Kutulakos, K.N., Steger, E.: A Theory of Refractive and Specular 3D Shape by Light-Path Triangulation. IJCV 76(1), 13–29 (2008)
92. Scheuing, J., Yang, B.: Disambiguation of tdoa estimates in multi-path multi-source environments (datemm). IEEE ICASSP 4, 837–840 (2006)
93. Ajdler, T., Sbaiz, L., Vetterli, M.: The Plenacoustic Function and its Sampling. IEEE Transactions on Signal Processing 54(10), 3790–3804 (2006)
94. Allen, J., Berkley, D.: Image method for efficiently simulating small-room acoustics. The Journal of the Acoustical Society of America 65(4), 943–950 (1979)
95. Borish, J.: Extension of the Image Model to Arbitrary Polyhedra. Journal of the Acoustic Society of America 75(6), 1827–1836 (1984)
96. Ribeiro, F., Florencio, D., Ba, D., Zhang, C.: Geometrically Constrained Room Modeling With Compact Microphone Arrays. IEEE Transactions on Audio, Speech, and Language Processing 20(5), 1449–1460 (2012)
97. Antonacci, F., Filos, J., Thomas, M.R.P., Habets, E., Sarti, A., Naylor, P.A., Tubaro, S.: Inference of room geometry from acoustic impulse responses. IEEE Trans. on Audio, Speech and Language Processing 20(10), 2683–2695 (2012)
98. Tervo, S., Tossavainen, T.: 3D Room Geometry Estimation from Measured Impulse Responses. In: Proc. ICASSP, pp. 513–516 (2012)
99. Kirmani, A., Hutchison, T., Davis, J., Raskar, R.: Looking around the Corner using Transient Imaging. In: Proc. ICCV, pp. 159–166 (2009)
100. Heide, F., Hullin, M., Gregson, J., Heidrich, W.: Low-Budget Transient Imaging using Photonic Mixer Devices. ACM TOG 32(4) (to appear, 2013)
101. Velten, A., Willwacher, T., Gupta, O., Veeraraghavan, A., Bawendi, M., Raskar, R.: Recovering Three-Dimensional Shape around a Corner using Ultrafast Time-of-Flight Imaging. Nat. Comm. 3, 745 (2012)

A Survey on Time-of-Flight Stereo Fusion

Rahul Nair[1,2], Kai Ruhl[3], Frank Lenzen[1,2], Stephan Meister[1,2],
Henrik Schäfer[1,2], Christoph S. Garbe[1,2], Martin Eisemann[3], Marcus Magnor[3],
and Daniel Kondermann[1,2]

[1] Heidelberg Collaboratory for Image Processing (HCI),
Heidelberg University, Germany
{rahul.nair,frank.lenzen,stephan.meister,
henrik.schaefer,daniel.kondermann}@iwr.uni-heidelberg.de,
christoph.garbe@uni-heidelberg.de
http://hci.iwr.uni-heidelberg.de
[2] Intel Visual Computing Institute, Saarland University, Germany
http://www.intel-vci.uni-saarland.de/
[3] Technische Universität Braunschweig, Germany
{ruhl,eisemann,magnor}@cg.cs.tu-bs.de
http://graphics.tu-bs.de

Abstract. Due to the demand for depth maps of higher quality than
possible with a single depth imaging technique today, there has been
an increasing interest in the combination of different depth sensors to
produce a "super-camera" that is more than the sum of the individual
parts. In this survey paper, we give an overview over methods for the
fusion of Time-of-Flight (ToF) and passive stereo data as well as applications of the resulting high quality depth maps. Additionally, we provide
a tutorial-based introduction to the principles behind ToF stereo fusion
and the evaluation criteria used to benchmark these methods.

1 Introduction

Will there ever be one depth sensor to rule them all? While this will hopefully
be true one day, all current depth sensing modalities fall short of obtaining
this title. Passive stereo works well on textured scenes and has a high lateral
resolution due to readily available mega pixel cameras. Conversely, there are
issues at occlusion boundaries and when the textures are ambiguous or when
no texture is present at all. Also, due to the number of pixels that have to
be compared, especially when global optimization techniques are used, stereo
matching algorithms are often computationally demanding. Time-of-Flight(ToF)
imaging on the other hand delivers images at high frame rates independent of
surface texture, but at the cost of a lower resolution and systematic errors. For
a more detailed description of Time-of-Flight cameras please refer to Chapter 1.
Finally, there is active stereo (e.g. Kinect), which triangulates correspondences
between a structured active illumination and a camera. While the effects at
occlusion boundaries (shadowing, edge fattening) remain, unstructured surfaces
are no longer a problem. This comes at a cost though, as the lateral resolution

M. Grzegorzek et al. (Eds.): Time-of-Flight and Depth Imaging, LNCS 8200, pp. 105–127, 2013.

is now limited by the resolution of the projection system. To summarize, the major drawback of all of these methods is that they usually only work in a limited domain and lack the robustness often required in various application domains. As these modalities often differ in the areas where they excel or fail, it appears natural to combine them to create a "super-sensor".

Depending on the camera systems used different methods ensue. With a single additional camera typically edge information from the high resolution intensity image is used to guide the upsampling of the depth image[1,2]. In [3], Castañeda et al. present a system using two Time-of-Flight cameras. In this survey paper we will focus on techniques to fuse of Time-of-Flight and passive stereo data.

The remainder of this paper is organized as follows. In Section 2 we shall further clarify, what we expect from such a fusion system and what use there actually is in having high resolution depth maps. Next, in Section 3 the basic fusion pipeline including common preprocessing steps will be introduced in a tutorial like fashion. As benchmarking such systems is as important as the innovation of new fusion systems we will dedicate Section 4 to common evaluation strategies. Finally, in Section 5 we will summarize the specifics of current fusion systems.

2   Requirements Engineering and Application Domains

2.1   Requirements

We have identified four basic requirements an application can have on a fusion system.

Speed up while retaining Quality. Current stereo algorithms are often quite time consuming. This is due to the vast search space that has to be analyzed. Given real time ToF imaging it may now be possible to reduce the search space and therefore make real-time implementations of the stereo methods possible.

Robustness/Self Awareness. Fusion methods should be able to be at least as good as the (locally) better of the two modalities and degrade gracefully in presence of small calibration/synchronization errors.

Increase in Quality. Other than identifying regions of erroneous values the system should also be able to use this information to produce depth maps that are better than either method alone.

Backward Compatibility. In many application areas it is easier to just add an additional camera to the working system than to completely alter the existing system.

It is clear that it is difficult to accommodate for all requirements simultaneously. A speed - quality trade off has always to be made depending on the application. For Human Computer Interaction and Robotic/Navigation applications a fast system that is able to detect and eliminate erroneous values [4,5] may suffice. More sophisticated multimedia application on the other hand require high quality depth maps partly with speed constraints imposed on the

Fig. 1. From left to right: Stereo-ToF rig on set, example image, high resolution disparity map

system (e.g. in 3DTV, Augmented Reality). As other application domains for depth data have been discussed in Chapter 4, Section 2, we will focus on the application of high quality depth maps in multimedia systems.

2.2 High Quality Depth Maps for Multimedia Application

In movie and film productions many post-production steps are commonly conducted including color corrections,(green-screen) matting, integration of computer generated imagery, compositing and many more. High-resolution depth or disparity maps can help to ease many of these steps. As edges in the depth maps depict object boundaries in general, they can be used to guide local color corrections, in the spirit of cross-bilateral filters [6,7]. Integration of virtual objects is possible with correctly handled occlusion [8]. For stereoscopic movie productions the aforementioned tasks become even more important due to additional challenges including color matching between the stereoscopic views, vertical alignment, disparity compensation, 3D compositing and image interpolation. To faithfully deal with these tasks, correspondences between the left and right image in the form of disparity or depth maps build the foundations of all these algorithms. Depth maps as a form of 2.5D scene representation ease the integration of computer generated imagery or video footage with depth information [9]. Precise depth maps also allow for image interpolation [10] which in turn can be used for disparity compensation [11]. To prevent a flickering appearance in stereoscopic video footage, appropriate local color corrections are necessary that consistently correct for color mismatches in both views [12]. The problem is even more difficult for specularities, here the solution is usually to replace the specular parts in the image by information from the other view [13] or to synthesize a consistent specularity for both views [14].

Not only post-production but also display and transmission of stereoscopic content requires high-resolution and high quality depth. In depth-image-based rendering the video stream consists of the typical RGB images plus an additional depth channel [15]. From this information the stereoscopic views are recreated by warping of the RGB image based on the depth and desired ocular distance.

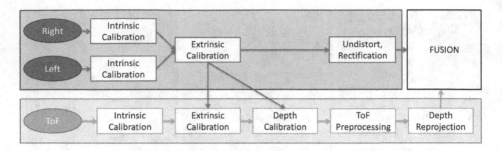

Fig. 2. Basic Fusion Pipeline

As most modern production settings already employ several cameras (cf. Figure 1), the idea of using an additional ToF camera lends itself to assist the depth map generation. It should be noted though that algorithms intended to work in such a setting require a higher amount of robustness as compared to the lab setting. At any given time many different people are (to a certain extent) independently monitoring several different aspects of the scene such as lighting, camera movement, focus of camera or the stereo baseline, often changing parameters frequently to accommodate for the requirements of the director. Also the time plan is quite strict, such that any additional in-between calibration steps need to be avoided. So if the ToF-Stereo setup is to be attached to the principal camera it will be more difficult to obtain high precision measurements and alignment than what is common for a lab setting. Therefore, robustness of the algorithms, especially towards slightly misaligned cameras, is extremely important. On the other hand, often post-production crews acquire their own footage of the scene separately beforehand, so that they can start working on set reconstructions etc. before receiving the main plates. In Section 5.3 two methods will be discussed in detail that cater to these different settings.

3 Setting Up Fusion Systems

In the following we describe the general aspects of ToF stereo fusion systems. These include the general pipeline (Section 3.1), possible camera setups (Section 3.2), calibration (Section 3.3) and data preprocessing (Section 3.4).

3.1 Pipeline

Most fusion systems differ mainly in how the data is merged, once it has been brought into the same reference frame. Figure 2 illustrates the basic pipeline employed. After choosing a specific camera setup the standard camera intrinsics have to be estimated for all three cameras, i.e. focal length, principal point as well as radial and tangential distortion coefficients. Next the spatial relationship(Roto-Translation) between the three cameras have to be found by means of pairwise or joint stereo calibration methods.

For the ToF camera, additionally a depth calibration has to be undertaken due to the systematic errors described in Chapter 1, Section 2. This can either be done after the intrinsic calibration with methods proposed in Chapter 1, Section 3 or by jointly using the additional stereo information. After applying preprocessing steps to clean up the ToF data (i.e. to reduce effects by noise pixels), the images must be brought into the same coordinate frame by means of rectification and reprojection. Finally, the fusion step involves a combination of the following:

- The ToF depth and the output of a Stereo algorithm are computed individually and then fused.
- The ToF data is used as an initial guess and/or to reduce the search space for subsequent stereo refinements
- The depth reconstruction algorithm uses both stereo and ToF costs as data terms.

Additionally various regularizers have been applied to obtain depth maps of sufficient smoothness despite noise. In the following we will describe the steps commonly employed by the methods presented in Section 5 before the data is fused in detail.

3.1.1 Choice of Depth Cues

In essence a ToF stereo fusion system corresponds to a trifocal camera system, with the third camera sensor having a lower spatial resolution, but a high temporal sampling. Therefore, there exist many different sources of dense or sparse depth information that may be exploited in a fusion system. In the following we would like to discuss these depth cues in detail. Though some of the cues are rarely used or not used at all, we believe that future algorithms may additionally use these modalities.

ToF depth from demodulation. This is the standard output of the Time-of-Flight sensor that is used in all fusion systems. The advantages of these modalities as opposed to stereo is that the depth estimation a) works on textureless surfaces, b) has a arguably simpler behavior at depth discontinuities (unlike edge fattening in stereo) c) is real-time capable out of the box. Major downsides are the limited lateral resolution and the various strong error sources such as noise, multi path, flying pixels, wiggling and to a certain extent susceptibility to background illumination.

A detailed description of these errors and methods to compensate for them is given in Chapter 1.

Photo consistency/Stereo. Depth from stereo is a well studied field of research [16]. In stereo depth estimation, dense correspondences between left and right view are found and the depth is inferred via triangulation. Unlike ToF cameras, the lateral resolution of this modality can be very high. Depth from stereo will fail in areas with little texture or in presence of highly repetitive patterns due to ambiguous matching. While this imposes a problem for fast local-evidence based stereo methods, global methods use regularization techniques to utilize prior knowledge about "normal" scenes such as temporal coherence. It should also be noted that with the large (Full HD, 4K) images commonly used for multimedia applications such global techniques often reach their limit in terms of computational cost without any search space reduction.

Cross-modal Stereo. While all current systems only use the photo consistency constraints between the stereo heads, additional information is available via the intensity image of the ToF camera. Unfortunately, due to the difference in resolution and wavelength sensitivity traditional photo consistency can not be used here. A promising line of research is cross-modal stereo [17], also known as IR/Thermal image-RGB registration [18,19,20], which tries to find correlations between the near or far IR with RGB/Intensity image to either infer depth as in the former case or find a warp as in the later case.

Structure from Motion. If the fusion system is moving and the scene mostly static, it is possible to use structure from motion (SFM) techniques [21,22] to additionally infer depth at some locations. Here, it has to be ensured that the synchronization is sufficiently accurate or that the fusion system is capable of handling slight misalignments robustly.

Monoscopic Cues. Lighting, Shading and Silhouettes are mostly used in monoscopic depth estimation [23,24]. Shape from Shading with unconstrained lighting is yet a difficult problem. But for the ToF camera, as the primary light source is around the camera, this could still be feasible and should be investigated. Indeed, Stürmer et al. [25] observed that the amplitude image in observed an inverse square falloff with distance. Finally, silhouettes constrain the direction of normals of the depth map to be perpendicular to the pixel ray.

Current fusion systems typically only use the ToF as a black box depth imager and the photo consistency constraint between the stereo heads. A notable exception is the method by Kim et al. [26] that uses additional silhouette constraints and the technique by Zhu et al. [27] that uses an optical flow based temporal smoothing (though no SFM information is used here).

3.2   Camera Setup

The camera setup employed should suit the requirements of the application and additionally aim to reduce the effects of visible errors due to alignment issues. Figure 3 illustrates various common camera configurations, though naturally many more are possible.

Symmetric Side-by-Side. This is the approach most commonly employed by most fusion systems with the stereo heads symmetrically placed left and right of the ToF camera. Though this approach seems to be the best on first instance, it depends on whether the paralax between the ToF camera and the stereo heads is actually being used to additionally infer depth. If the ToF data is going to be reprojected on to one of the stereo frames then more information is lost than in the assymmetric setup.

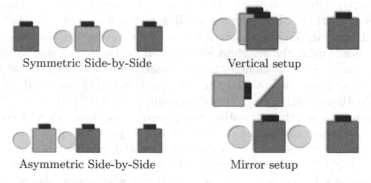

Fig. 3. Different possible camera setups. Green: ToF Camera, Red: RGB Camera, Yellow: ToF Lights.

Asymmetric Side-by-Side. This approach tries to compensate such parallax effects between the ToF and Stereo heads by placing the ToF camera closer to the primary camera. Depending on whether the ToF imager or one of the stereo heads is the primary camera, also different setups may make sense. In the latter case the ToF camera may additionally be placed on the other side of the primary camera to ensure available depth information, otherwise not obtainable due to occlusion between the stereo heads.

Vertical Setup. The vertical setup mostly corresponds to the asymmetric side-by-side setup. It is employed for the same reasons as above in situations, where placing the camera next to the primary camera is not feasible, such as in stereo-production rigs (cf. Section 1) which are often huge in size and would induce a bigger parallax in a side-by-side setup.

Mirror Rig. Ideally - if only ToF and passive stereo are used, there shouldn't be any parallax between the primary and ToF camera. This is achievable using a beam-splitting mirror/prism (commonly known as hot or cold mirrors) and sharing the same optical axis. The center for sensor systems (ZESS) in Siegen has produced such a prototype system[28]. The Arri group, manufacturers of production grade film cameras, have recently introduced another RGB-Z camera that works on the same principal. It should be noted though that such a setup still requires manual alignment of the mirror and cameras to actually achieve zero-parallax and in practice this may be difficult to achieve.

3.3 Calibration

Intrinsics and Extrinsics. Once the hardware is set up the system needs to be calibrated intrinsically for focus, principal point and distortion coefficients and the ToF camera additionally for depth. The extrinsic calibration is concerned with finding the Roto-Translation between the three cameras. Both procedures are straight forward for the stereo heads and can be done using standard libraries [29,30]. In our experience, the same methods often work on the intensity image (with parameter tweaking) for ToF imagers with higher resolutions. More details on calibration can be found in Chapter 1.

Joint Calibration The extrinsic calibration between the ToF camera and the stereo heads using the standard method will be less precice due to the lower resolution of the ToF camera. Some fusion techniques account for this by simply adjusting uncertainties that they utilize during fusion [31,32]. If the ToF depth calibration has already been obtained, DalMutto et al. [33] suggest using the depth information and planar calibration targets to obtain a precise extrinsic calibration. Schiller et al.[34] jointly do the intrinsic ToF calibration with the extrinsic calibration, as the depth estimates delivered by the ToF and stereo will not only be consistent but the ToF calibration can also be achieved more precisely. Similar methods were also proposed in [35,36] and can be summarized as follows:

1. Obtain pictures of planar calibration targets via a (calibrated) stereo setup and the ToF image.
2. Fit a Plane into this target via the triangulated target points in the stereo setup. To obtain dense stereo "ground truth points".
3. If the extrinsic calibration has not been estimated yet, use Horn's method [37] to find the transform between the stereo plane and ToF plane.
4. Finally, store the residuals between ToF depth and the plane for the ToF depth correction. This can be done in form of a 4D look-up table or by fitting a polynomial spline per pixel.

Finally, Guan et al. [38] use spherical targets that are detected in the RGB and ToF imagers.

3.4   Preprocessing

Stereo Rectification. Stereo rectification [39] reduces the search space to a line search along one image dimension by finding two homographies such that the epipolar lines between the two stereo heads become parallel.

Depth Reprojection. ToF delivers radial depth which has to be converted into z-depth before comparing with the stereo depth. Given the focal length f and centralized pixel coordinates p_x, p_y (i.e. principal point in $(0,0)$) and radial depth d the coordinates (X, Y, Z) can be computed via:

$$(X, Y, Z)^T = (p_x, p_y, f)^T \cdot \frac{d}{(f^2 + p_x^2 + p_y^2)}. \tag{1}$$

These points can then be rotated and translated into the reference coordinate frame. If a dense ToF depth map is required the values for reference frame pixels without a corresponding ToF pixel have to be interpolated. Finally, the z-depth z can be converted into disparities $disp$ using the baseline b:

$$disp = \frac{b \cdot f}{z}. \tag{2}$$

Depth Preprocessing. The depth data may be additionally filtered before reprojection to avoid false occlusions due to noise. This ranges from simple median filtering to remove flying pixels to more complex denoising techniques as presented in Chapter 2.

4 Evaluation of Fusion Methods

In this section we will discuss various evaluation datasets and performance metrics to benchmark fusion algorithms. Additionally, based on the requirements discussed in Section 2 we will propose some new experiments and performance measures that we believe will help in a better understanding of the fusion system.

4.1 Datasets

4.1.1 Available Stereo-ToF Datasets[1]
Currently, very few ground truth datasets for ToF stereo fusion are actually available. Nair et al. [32] used the HCI Box[2] for quantitative evaluations. The target consists of a box with various geometric primivitives that was hand measured to 1mm accuracy and aligned to PMD[Tec] CamCube 3 data. It contains little texture and shows strong multi-path effects on the box sides. The Padua[3] datasets introduced by Dal Mutto et al.[33,40] contain simple synthetic scenes as well as measured tabletop scenes containing a varied amount of textured objects. The reference data was obtained using space time stereo[41] and aligned with ToF data from a MESA SR4000.

4.1.2 Semi-synthetic GT
Since ToF stereo fusion ground truth datasets are not as readily available as datasets for assessing ToF or stereo alone, authors often resort to use existing datasets, by simulating the missing modality.

Synthesizing the ToF Image. Often the Middlebury ground truth dataset [16] is used [40,42] and the ToF view is synthesized from the ground truth data. Though an interesting way to compare the results, the naive implementation currently used is to just downsample the GT depth and add some noise to the obtained depth map.

This approach does not account for a) the different camera positions and b) the complex noise behavior of ToF cameras. We therefore believe that it can be improved in two important aspects.

- **Alignment.** The effects due to the ToF and the reference camera not sharing the same optical axis are completely ignored in this simple approach. This is fine as a baseline evaluation to isolate alignment effects

---

[1] Up to date list:
  http://hci.iwr.uni-heidelberg.de/Benchmarks/document/tofstereo
[2] http://hci.iwr.uni-heidelberg.de/Benchmarks/document/hcibox/
[3] http://freia.dei.unipd.it/nuovo/research/ToF.html

from the fusion part or if a mirror rig is used. Otherwise, the depth map should be first synthesized in the ToF view before warping the data back, possibly adding alignment noise.

- **Simulation.** Also some care should be taken into properly simulating the ToF sensor. Evaluation using the GT without any noise can only be used as a proof of concept. We suggest to use one of the simulators stated in Section 3.2 on page 61.

Synthesizing Stereo. Similarly, if a ToF GT dataset is available where the reference data has been obtained including RGB/Intensity information such as the datasets in [43] and the HCI- Laser scanning dataset (Section 4.2 on page 65), this can be used to synthesize additional views. If only a GT depth map is available occlusion effects need to be handled consistently.

4.2   Performance Measures

As ToF stereo fusion aims at finding high quality 3D reconstructions, the same evaluation criteria that are discussed in Chapter 4, Section 5 can be employed. Here, we will give an overview of the performance criteria reported in the ToF-Stereo fusion literature and propose some performance criteria specifically for ToF stereo fusion we deem useful.

4.2.1   Used Measures

Accuracy and precision. Conventional depth measuring approaches such as laser scanning always state precision (variance of measurement) and accuracy (systematic bias between GT and measurement). Assuming independently and identically Gaussian distributed errors in each pixel, then mean and standard deviation of the signed error would correspond to these measures. As many real life distributions often have heavy tails, skewing or more than one mode, robust statistics such as median and interquartile range should be used. Finally, as there often is a strong correlation between error and external factors such as viewing angle or texturedness, such scalar error metrics may not give the complete insight into the behavior. Therefore, wherever possible we suggest to additionally supply either the complete (1D) error distribution, or even the error images [32].

Mean squared error, median absolute error. In fusion literature [44,40] often the mean squared error is reported instead of accuracy and precision. For real valued functions this corresponds to the sum of variance and squared bias. Again, due to the inherent quadratic weighting of large errors a better metric would be the median absolute error instead. The same arguments against the scalarization of the error as above apply here as well.

Application specific evaluation. For   many   applications   geometry reconstruction is not the final goal but just a intermediate step. Song et al. [45] evaluate the edge quality by comparing the obtained depth edges with pre-labeled silhouette boundaries in a plant phenotyping application (cf. Chapter 4, Section 5.2 on page 69). This is not only interesting for plant phenotyping, where the leaf silhouettes have to be extracted reliably, but also in multimedia applications where the location and shape of silhouettes are of vital importance. Zhu et al.[35,44] analyze the deviation between a box model fitted into the depth data and the GT box by analyzing the angular deviation of the three observed box sides from 90 degrees. Finally, for view synthesis, the quality criteria is the credibility of the synthesized view. This evaluation could be achieved having an additional camera capturing the scene and comparing a synthesized view with the real view.

Eyeballing. The evaluation of ToF stereo fusion methods is still largely qualitative in nature due to the lack of sufficient ground truth datasets. For certain applications (e.g. visual effects) the users can often judge best, how useful the algorithm results are to them. This process, also called eyeballing, requires many different scenes to be visually inspected by one or more independent expert users. While all proposed methods show qualitative results, a proper user study has yet to be undertaken.

4.2.2 Proposed Measures/Experiments

Graceful degradation - Alignment. As spatial and temporal alignment (i.e. extrinsic calibration and synchronous triggering) is a big issue one possible quality criterion is the robustness towards misalignments. We propose the following experiments to assess this. First a calibrated dataset using the standard setup is captured. Fusion results for a spatially misaligned setup are then generated by artificially varying the calibration between ToF and the stereo setup. Temporal alignment can either be evaluated by capturing the stereo data in a higher framerate than the ToF images or by interpolating in between frames.

Speed vs. Quality. One claim that all Fusion papers make is that using ToF data speeds up computation considerably compared to a baseline and many authors also state the running times of their algorithms. Additionally, an assessment of execution time (number of iterations, change of search range, etc.) vs. quality improvement could be made. While it is clear that the speed of algorithm execution depends heavily on the implementation platform, hardware and implementation details, we think that a speed over quality assessment of the algorithms is still necessary. Quality can mean any quality criteria from endpoint error to precision of edges.

Effect of Fusion. The final claim that many fusion algorithms make is that the depth maps obtained is better than either depth map alone. The question that remains is how much better is the algorithm? And how does the scene composition affect this performance. A fusion algorithm should at least be as good as the better of the two modalities irrelevant of scene composition.

5   Overview of Fusion Methods

Following [16] we will group the fusion methods based on the optimization strategy that is employed. *Local methods* [4,46,47,48,49,42,32,50] tend to be faster

Table 1. General notation used

i, j	pixel location
$i \in \Omega$	pixel i in image domain Ω
$j \in N_i$	pixels j in neighborhood of i
$\{x_i\} = \mathbf{x}$	Value x at pixel i collectively referred to as $\mathbf{x}$
ste, ToF	stereo, ToF
L, R	Left/Right image
$\hat{\mathbf{x}}, \hat{x}_i$	Final estimate for $\mathbf{x}, x_i$
$\mathbf{d}^{\mathrm{ToF}}, \mathbf{z}^{\mathrm{ToF}}$	Disparity, Z-depth from ToF (as converted using Sec. 3.4)
$\mathbf{d}^{\mathrm{ste}}, \mathbf{z}^{\mathrm{ste}}$	Disparity, Z-depth from stereo
$\mathbf{A}^{\mathrm{ToF}}, \mathbf{I}^{\mathrm{ToF}}$	Amplitude, Intensity
$\mathbf{I}^{\mathrm{L}}, \mathbf{I}^{\mathrm{R}}$	Intensity in Left/Right image
$E(x), E_i(x)$	Objective energy to be minimized (at location i)
$R(x)$	Regularizer
c	Confidence / Weights
$\mathbf{1}_{ToF}(z), \mathbf{1}_{ste}(z)$	Range indicator functions for ToF/stereo
$\chi_{ToF}(x), \chi_{ste}(x)$	Spatial indicator functions for valid/trusted ToF/stereo
$\gamma_1, \gamma_2 \dots$	User Parameters

and parallelizable but cannot cope with locally erroneous data. They are often based on a line search that is guided by the ToF data. *Global methods*, [5,31,35,27,44,26,32,51,52,40,45] add the ToF information as an additional data term in a global energy functional is then jointly optimized. While the depth maps obtained are smoother due to the usage of prior information/regularizers, this is at the cost of additional computational resources. In this overview, we will further group the global techniques depending the framework that was chosen for optimization. While [31,35,27,44,45] employ different *graphical models* for inference, [51,32] formulate the problem in a *variational* framework. The last sub-group of the global methods[5,26,52,40] contains those which use *other non-local* optimization strategies.

After a discussion of commonalities in each group, we will proceed to describe each method in detail. The description will start from the point we left in Section 3 – that is after all data have been brought to the same reference frame and after all preprocessing has occurred – except for some special kinds of preprocessing not already mentioned in Section 3. The notation used in the following is summarized in Table 5. Please note that some algorithms work in the disparity (d) space while others operate in the depth (z) space. This doesn't impose any additional contraint as one representation can be converted into the other using the extrinsic calibration and Eq. 2.

5.1 Local Methods

The methods presented here have in common that the basic optimization employed only takes a local sets of pixel values are taken into account. Note, that the aggregation over support windows, whenever applied, make implicit assumptions (e.g. piecewise planar, fronto parallel patches) on surface regularity.

Kuhnert et al. 2006 [4]. Kuhnert and Stommel proposed the first ToF stereo fusion algorithm in 2006. Unlike many methods that incorporate the ToF data into the stereo matching, this methods first independently computes depth maps and uncertainties for ToF and for stereo and then fuses both data sources (see also [40]). The stereo algorithm (Winner Takes All [16]) is only applied to confident regions, using a thresholded Sobel operator response to obtain a binary confidence map. Then, for each data source per pixel ranges are estimated for ToF by adding and subtracting 2 sigma of the previously measured noise. Using indicator functions 1_{ToF} and 1_{ste} for the depth ranges, the fused depth is then given as.

$$\hat{z}_i = \int_0^\infty z_i 1_{ToF}(z_i) 1_{ste}(z_i) dz_i. \tag{3}$$

This amounts to choosing the mid point of the depth range where the two ranges from ToF and stereo overlap. Otherwise the depth is set to 0 (invalid).

Beder et al. 2007 [50]. Beder et al. derive a closed form solution to estimating patch orientation based on ToF and Stereo data. The patchlet is initialized with the ToF depth data. Next, by deriving analytical formulas for the gradient direction the patch orientation is optimized using stereo and ToF data. Beder et al. also give a thorough analysis on planar wall scenes as ground truth.

Gudmundsson et al. 2008 [46] applies a hierarchical stereo matching algorithm directly on the remapped ToF depth data. The reprojected depth is input into the 4th coursest level of a hierarchical stereo matching algorithm by van Meerbergen et al. [53] (see also [51]).

Hahne et al. 2009 [48]. First, a binary confidence map is obtained by thresholding the amplitude image. The depth data in unconfident areas are discarded and the holes filled via linear scan line interpolation. Next, only the unconfident regions are then further refined via correlation based block matching. The support window shape that is used guided by a watershed segmentation of the color image. The segmentation is seeded using an eroded version of the confident and unconfident regions.

$$\hat{d}_i = \begin{cases} \underset{d_i}{\text{argmin}} E_{ste}(d_i) & \text{if } A_i^{ToF} < \gamma \\ d_i^{ToF} & \text{otherwise} \end{cases}. \tag{4}$$

DalMutto et al. 2010 [49]. The technique is build around a confidence-based matching in a probabilistic framework. It computes pixel wise probabilities of ToF and probability of stereo in a cost volume. The ToF probability is assumed to be a Gaussian centered around the ToF depth. The stereo probability is given by the truncated absolute difference. The energy resembles the one used in Eq. 8 without the regularizing terms.

Bartczak et al. 2009 [47]. Bartczak et al. propose an iterative line search based fusion scheme. After each iteration of the algorithm the obtained depth map is fed back into the matching score in order to enforce local minima.

The local matching cost after the nth iteration is given by

$$E^n(d_i) = \frac{\sum\limits_{j \in N_i} w_j(d) \left(E_{PC}(d_i) + \sum\limits_{k<n} E_D(d_i|\mathbf{d}^k) \right) / (N+1)}{\sum\limits_{j \in N_i} w_{i,j}(d_i)} \tag{5}$$

with $\mathbf{d}^0 = \mathbf{d}^{ToF}, \mathbf{d}^k = \underset{\mathbf{d}}{\mathrm{argmin}} \left(\mathbf{E}^k(\mathbf{d}) \right)$. In Eq. 5 E_{PC} is the photo consistency cost based on truncated L_1 cost weighted and offset by a confidence in the cost given by the min max range of the cost function. The pixel-wise depth contribution E_D is a truncated L_2 cost. Finally, the weights used for aggregation are given as the product of normal distributions centered around center pixel a) color b) location and c) photo consistency.

Yang et al. 2010 [42]. The approach by Yang et al. is based on plane-sweeping stereo [54]. As a preprocessing the technique employs a fast RGB-assisted bilateral filter. The energy being minimized is

$$E(z_i) = cE_{ToF}(z_i|z_i^{ToF}) + (1-c)E_{ste}(z). \tag{6}$$

with E_{ToF} being modeled as a truncated quadratic loss between the depth and the ToF depth. E_{Stereo} corresponds to the plane sweeping cost based on the sum of square (SSD) distance per pixel costs. The confidence c used for matching is given as

$$c = \frac{(1-c_{ste})c_{ToF}}{((1-c_{ste})c_{ToF}) + (1-c_{ToF})c_{ste})}. \tag{7}$$

Here, c_{ste} is the stereo confidence given as the likelihood of the current matching assuming a Gaussian distribution of matching costs in the aggregation window centered around the center pixel cost and c_{ToF} is the ToF confidence, a Gaussian with the amplitude image used as standard deviation.

5.2   Graphical Models

Graphical models have frequently been used in the past to solve the stereo matching problem[55,56,57]. Here the problem of correspondence estimation is treated as a labeling problem, where each discrete label corresponds to a disparity value. The energy is interpreted as the negative logarithm of a joint probability distribution defined on a graph, where each node corresponds to an observed (data term) or latent (depth) random variables the probabilities are defined on cliques of these graphs. Though continuous extensions of graphical models do exist[58] the methods presented here still operate on a discrete domain and differ in how the graph is defined as well as the optimization method used for inference.

Zhu et al. 2008, 2010, 2011 [35,27,44]. In a series of publications starting with [35] Zhu formulates the problem in a Maximum a priori-MRF framework. In [44] the adaptive weight terms are added and finally in [27] a temporal smoothing term is added. The graph structure represented by the energy functional is given by a temporally layered graph. Each layer represents a normally 4 connected pixel neighborhood graph. The connections between layers are given by an optical flow estimate

$$
\begin{aligned}
E(d) = c_{stereo}E_{stereo} \\
+ c_{ToF}E_{ToF}(d|d_{ToF}) \\
+ R_{smooth} \\
+ R_{temp}
\end{aligned}
\tag{8}
$$

with $E_{ToF}(d|d_{ToF})$ being a function of the truncated L_1 distance between the estimated disparity and ToF disparity and $E_{stereo}(d)$ based on the Birchfield and Tomasi matching cost [59]. The spatial smoothness term R_{smooth} is a truncated quadratic penalization. Finally, the temporal regularization R_{temp} is given by the complete cost without the temporal term for the previous and next frame. The weights are set according to the confidence in each point. Stereo confidence is the peak to peak ratio of the cost function. ToF reliability is given by a normal distribution (cf. [49]). Optimization is done using Loopy Belief Propagation.

Hahne et al. 2008 [31]. The approach by Hahne et al. is based on Graph Cuts and regularizes the first order Total Variation (TV) of the reconstructed surface. The graph is defined on the cost volume with the optimal cut between foreground and background nodes being the desired surface. Each voxel is associated with an consistency edge in z direction. Additionally, smoothing edges connect the nodes in x and y direction. The nodes themselves reside in between voxels. The energy considered is

$$
E(z) = \sum_i (E_{fused}(z) + c_{fused,x}\partial_x z + c_{fused,y}\partial_y z)
\tag{9}
$$

where E_{fused} is a linear combination of photo consistency and truncated quadratic cost for the ToF and the smoothing weights c_{fused} determined by a linear combination of the color difference in the primary stereo image and the difference of median depth of the ToF output. Note that the variable z corresponds to the edges in z direction that are chosen in the cut.

Song et al. 2011 [45]. Song et al. use a the standard graph cut stereo approach [56]. Unlike the previous approach the graph is defined over the image grid using multiple labels. Inference is done using alpha expansion. The Time of Flight data is used to reduce the label space in each graph node.

5.3   Variational Fusion

Different to fusion approaches based graphical models as considered in the previous section, *variational* fusion approaches consider both a continuous image domain $\Omega \subset \mathbb{R}^2$ and continuous variables (functions), indicated by a dependency on the image coordinates $x \in \mathbb{R}^2$.

We start with a brief overview of a general variational framework, before discussing in detail two recently proposed ToF stereo fusions approaches [32,51],

Fig. 4. Nair et al. – comparison of ToF only, stereo with semi global matching (SGM) [60], local and variational fusion. We observe that the local approach gives a rough estimate of the disparity, which still compares favorably with SGM. The variational fusion approach provides the most regular result.

which are based on this framework. Since one of these approaches assumes unsynchronized data, the restriction to solely horizontal correspondences between the (rectified) stereo images I^L and I can not be applied. We therefore describe this correspondence in terms of an optical flow field $u = (u_x, u_y)^\top : \Omega \to \Omega$, also referred to as displacement field.

We recall the general form of an variational approach given as

$$E(u) := E_{data}(u) + \lambda R(u), \tag{10}$$

to be minimized w.r.t. u, where $E_{data}(u)$ is the data term, $R(u)$ is a regularization term and $\lambda > 0$ is a regularization parameter. A standard data term for optical flow based on the linearized brightness constancy assumption [61,62] is

$$E_{data}(u) := \|\rho(u)\|_{L^1} := \int_\Omega \rho(u(x)) \, dx, \tag{11}$$

where

$$\rho(u(x)) := \left| \mathbf{I^L}(x + u_0(x)) + \langle \nabla \mathbf{I^L}(x + u_0(x)), u(x) - u_0(x) \rangle - \mathbf{I^R}(x) \right| \tag{12}$$

with some approximation u_0 of u. The above framwork is typically used in combination with a coarse-to-fine multi-scale approach (image pyramid), see e.g. [62], where u_0 is updated on each scale. The two fusion approaches considered below differ to this standard form in the way how additional information on the image correspondence from a different modality is introduced into this framework and how the initial approximation u_0 is obtained.

Nair et al. 2012 [32]. Nair et al. consider a synchronized camera setup which allows rectification of the stereo images. As a consequence the displacement field can be assumed to be horizontal ($u_x = d$ with disparity d, $u_y = 0$).

The proposed approach consist of two stages, which both make use of confidence measures to determine regions where the ToF or the stereo data might be corrupted. These confidence measures cover problems with low signal intensity and flying pixels for the ToF data, and regions with weak textures and occlusions in the stereo data. A detailed review of the exact

(a)   (b)   (c)

Fig. 5. Ruhl et al. – input data example: approximate depth data from multiple unsynchronized Kinects to be used as uncertain prior to image correspondence estimation. (a) HD camera image, (b) VGA depth map (invalid depth data marked in red), (c) depth points projected into world space.

definition of these measures is out of the scope of this section; instead we refer the reader to [32].

The first stage of the proposed approach consists in a local fusion using block matching combined with these fidelity measures. Later on, in the second stage, the result of the local method is used as initialization. Alternatively, the local fusion approach can serve as a stand-alone method with low numerical costs.

To improve the result of the local fusion approach in a second stage, a modification of the variational framework in Eq. 10 is considered, where the standard data term is replaced by

$$E_{data}(u) := \int_{\Omega} \chi_{ToF}(x)\rho_{ToF}(u(x)) + \chi_{ste}(x)\rho_{ste}(u(x)) \, dx \qquad (13)$$

with two local terms $\rho_{ToF}(u)$ and $\rho_{ste}(u)$ penalizing the deviation from the ToF and stereo data, respectively. (We refer the reader to [32] for the exact definition of these two terms.) The aforementioned confidence measures are used to determine locally which of the two data modalities is preferable to the other by defining the indicator functions χ_{ToF} and χ_{ste} in Eq. 13. Thus, the individual data terms are active only in the corresponding image regions. As regularization term an adaptive approach based on first- and second-order total variation is used.

We refer to Fig. 4 for a comparison of the results from both stages.

Ruhl et al. 2012 [51]. The authors consider a fusion system, which focuses on settings with unsynchronized cameras. Such a setting complicates reconstruction as typical algorithms require input data captured at the same time instance. In particular, here, the images correspondences do not only depend on the camera geometry, but also on a change of the scene between the individual image recordings. As a consequence, the correspondences in general can not be assumed to be horizontal. The approach makes use of a given depth proxy to guide an image correspondence algorithm that establishes

(a)   (b)

Fig. 6. Ruhl et al. – stage 1 vs. 2: Approximate prior vs. estimation guided by approximate prior. (a) source image warped directly by approximate prior (b) source image warped after dense image correspondence estimation guided by the approximate prior. The large-displacement, occlusion and low-texture matching properties have been preserved while detail errors are much less present.

the necessary connections between the input RGB images. The proposed method is not restricted to ToF, as the depth data can be obtained with any available method, but it can be used directly in a ToF stereo fusion setting.

The two stage approach can be briefly summarized as follows:

First stage: Different alternatives are considered to obtain a prior for the stereo correspondence. One alternative is to use depth sensors such as ToF or Kinect (cf. Fig. 5). The second one is to use very coarse, manually modeled geometric proxies, which are e.g. a common byproduct of visual media productions. In both cases, the core idea is, after assuming fully calibrated camera systems, to project the 3D world coordinates from the scene into image planes of the stereo cameras to obtain (possibly sparse) correspondences that ideally map to a disparity field $u(x)$, but may also deviate from epipolar geometry to some extent.

Second stage: The variational framework introduced in Eq. 10 is used with the data term defined as in Eq. 11 and using total variation regularization. The correspondence prior $\tilde{u}(x)$ from the first stage enters the approach in the interpolation phase, when the initialization u_0 for the next finer step of the image pyramid is set up. Values of $u_0(x)$ from the coarser level are replaced by the values of prior $\tilde{u}(x)$, if the employed confidence measure allows it.

We refer to Fig. 6 for an example comparing direct application of a depth-based prior $\tilde{u}$ against the results of a dense image correspondence estimation merely guided by $\tilde{u}$ using a confidence measure.

5.4   Other Methods

Kim et al. 2009 [26]. Kim et al. propose a volumetric approach. The initial surface is given by the ToF depth. This is further refined by optimizing an energy function including ToF, stereo, silhouette terms and a Laplacian prior. Optimization is done with the L-BFGS optimizer [63].

Fischer et al. 2011 [5]. Fischer et al. extended Semi-Global Matching Stereo by the approach of Hirschmüller [64] to account for ToF-Stereo data. The algorithm works in disparity space. The energy being minimized is given as

$$E(d) = \sum_i C_{data}(d_i) + \sum_{j \in N_i} \gamma_1 \chi_{\{|d_i - d_j| = 1\}} + \sum_{j \in N_i} \gamma_2 \chi_{\{\{|d_i - d_j| > 1\}}, \quad (14)$$

where d is the disparity, χ_A is 1 when the condition A is true and 0 otherwise and $0 < \gamma_1 < \gamma_2$ are the user specified parameters. The data term in Eq. 14 is defined via

$$C_{data}(d) := \begin{cases} C_{ToF}(d) & \text{if the ToF data is valid,} \\ C_{BT}(d) & \text{otherwise,} \end{cases} \quad (15)$$

where C_{ToF} is a truncated reverse Gaussian centered around the ToF disparity estimate. Note that *either* ToF *or* stereo data are used but not both at the same time. The ToF data is invalidated, if the photo consistency score for the ToF disparity is below a certain threshold. The regularizer does not penalize small spatial variations in disparity. As no additional term is added to the functional the optimization step remains the same as in [64] and is done in 16 different 1D directions. As a preprocessing step outliers in the ToF depth image are removed via wavefront propagation.

DalMutto et al. 2012 [40]. Based on locally consistent stereo [65] the technique uses a segmentation of the RGB image to guide a bilateral filter for ToF data upsampling. The algorithm takes two depth hypothesis from a stereo algorithm (semi global matching) and ToF respectively which are calculated independently. Each pixel then propagates both depth hypothesis independently according to [65] to surrounding pixel based on color similarity, spatial proximity and photo consistency. Every pixel then has a number of 'votes' casted by neighboring pixels. From these hypothesis the one with the highest plausibility is finally chosen.

Gandhi et al. 2012 [52]. The basic idea here is to combine the reprojection and interpolation step of the ToF depth map on the reference frame with a stereo matching procedure. The proposed technique is based on [66], with the difference that , reprojected ToF pixels are used as input instead of sparsely matched feature points. The reprojected ToF points are used as initial seeds for a region growing stereo algorithm. The seeds are first put in a priority queue based on their photo consistency score. Next, the seed with the highest priority is removed from the queue and the corresponding disparity drawn into a final disparity map. The neighbors of the pixel that has just been finalized are then added to the priority queue using the depth estimate with the best stereo score, found by searching around the interpolated ToF depth estimate. This process is repeated until all pixels in the final depth map are drawn, thus implicitly discarding ToF measurements with a bad photo consistency score.

6   Conclusion

We presented an overview over current ToF stereo fusion techniques as well as a guide to setting up such a system. Furthermore, we discussed the importance of high quality depth maps in multimedia applications due to the requirements that applications such as matting, view synthesis or CG effects impose on depth map quality. Still, more effort has to be put into assessing the actual benefits of the ToF stereo fusion over either method alone in a more systematic fashion. We considered various approaches to evaluate these methods and proposed new experiments that should be included in a future evaluation. Finally, we note that currently not all possible depth modalities available from such a system are actually being made use of for fusion purposes. Systems in the future may use the additional modalities to achieve a better accuracy.

Acknowledgements. This work is part of a joint research project with the Filmakademie Baden-Württemberg, Institute of Animation. It is co-funded by the Intel Visual Computing Institute and under grant 2-4225.16/380 of the ministry of economy Baden-Württemberg as well as further partners Unexpected, Pixomondo, ScreenPlane, Bewegte Bilder and Tridelity . The content is under sole responsibility of the authors. The research leading to these results has received funding from the European Union's Seventh Framework Programme FP7/2007-2013 under grant agreement no. 256941, Reality CG.

References

1. Park, J., Kim, H., Tai, Y., Brown, M., Kweon, I.: High quality depth map upsampling for 3d-tof cameras. In: IEEE Proc. ICCV (2011)
2. Huhle, B., Fleck, S., Schilling, A.: Integrating 3d time-of-flight camera data and high resolution images for 3dtv applications. In: Proc. 3DTV Conf. IEEE (2007)
3. Castaneda, V., Mateus, D., Navab, N.: Stereo time-of-flight. In: 2011 IEEE International Conference on Computer Vision (ICCV), pp. 1684–1691. IEEE (2011)
4. Kuhnert, K., Stommel, M.: Fusion of stereo-camera and pmd-camera data for realtime suited precise 3d environment reconstruction. In: Int. Conf. on Intelligent Robots and Systems, pp. 4780–4785. IEEE (2006)
5. Fischer, J., Arbeiter, G., Verl, A.: Combination of time-of-flight depth and stereo using semiglobal optimization. In: Int. Conf. on Robotics and Automation (ICRA), pp. 3548–3553. IEEE (2011)
6. Eisemann, E., Durand, F.: Flash photography enhancement via intrinsic relighting. ACM Transactions on Graphics (Proc. of SIGGRAPH) 23 (2004)
7. Petschnigg, G., Szeliski, R., Agrawala, M., Cohen, M., Hoppe, H., Toyama, K.: Digital photography with flash and no-flash image pairs. ACM Trans. Graph. 23(3), 664–672 (2004)
8. Chen, J., Paris, S., Wang, J., Matusik, W., Cohen, M., Durand, F.: The video mesh: A data structure for image-based three-dimensional video editing. In: Proc. of the International Conference on Computional Photography (ICCP) (2011)
9. Lo, W.Y., van Baar, J., Knaus, C., Zwicker, M., Gross, M.: Stereoscopic 3d copy & paste. ACM Trans. Graph. 29(6), 147:1–147:10 (2010)

10. Zitnick, C.L., Kang, S.B., Uyttendaele, M., Winder, S.A.J., Szeliski, R.: High-quality video view interpolation using a layered representation. ACM Trans. Graph. 23(3), 600–608 (2004)
11. Devernay, F., Beardsley, P.: Stereoscopic Cinema. In: Ronfard, R., Taubin, G. (eds.) Image and Geometry Processing for 3-D Cinematography. Geometry and Computing, vol. 5, pp. 11–51. Springer, Heidelberg (2010)
12. Fei, Y., Yu, M., Shao, F., Jiang, G.: A color correction algorithm of multi-view video based on depth segmentation. In: International Symposium on Computer Science and Computational Technology (ISCSCT 2008), vol. 2, pp. 206–209 (2008)
13. Wilkes, L.: The role of ocula in stereo post production. The Foundry. Whitepaper (2009)
14. Templin, K., Didyk, P., Ritschel, T., Myszkowski, K., Seidel, H.P.: Highlight microdisparity for improved gloss depiction. ACM Transactions on Graphics (Proc. SIGGRAPH) 31(4) (2012)
15. Mcmillan, L., Gortler, S.: Image-based rendering: A new interface between computer vision and computer graphics. SIGGRAPH Comput. Graph. 33, 61–64 (2000)
16. Scharstein, D., Szeliski, R.: A taxonomy and evaluation of dense two-frame stereo correspondence algorithms. IJCV 47(1), 7–42 (2002)
17. Chiu, W.C., Blanke, U., Fritz, M.: Improving the kinect by cross-modal stereo. In: British Machine Vision Conf. BMVA, pp. 116–1 (2011)
18. Hrkać, T., Kalafatić, Z., Krapac, J.: Infrared-visual image registration based on corners and hausdorff distance. In: Ersbøll, B.K., Pedersen, K.S. (eds.) SCIA 2007. LNCS, vol. 4522, pp. 383–392. Springer, Heidelberg (2007)
19. Bilodeau, G., Torabi, A., Morin, F.: Visible and infrared image registration using trajectories and composite foreground images. Image and Vision Computing 29(1), 41–50 (2011)
20. Toet, A., Van Ruyven, L.J., Valeton, J.M.: Merging thermal and visual images by a contrast pyramid. Optical Engineering 28(7), 287789–287789 (1989)
21. Wu, C.: Visualsfm: A visual structure from motion system (2011)
22. Newcombe, R.A., Lovegrove, S.J., Davison, A.J.: Dtam: Dense tracking and mapping in real-time. In: 2011 IEEE International Conference on Computer Vision (ICCV), pp. 2320–2327. IEEE (2011)
23. Horn, B.K., Brooks, M.J.: Shape from shading. MIT Press (1989)
24. Barron, J.T., Malik, J.: Shape, albedo, and illumination from a single image of an unknown object. In: 2012 IEEE Conference on Computer Vision and Pattern Recognition (CVPR), pp. 334–341. IEEE (2012)
25. Sturmer, M., Penne, J., Hornegger, J.: Standardization of intensity-values acquired by time-of-flight-cameras. In: IEEE Computer Society Conference on Computer Vision and Pattern Recognition Workshops (CVPRW 2008), pp. 1–6. IEEE (2008)
26. Kim, Y., Theobalt, C., Diebel, J., Kosecka, J., Miscusik, B., Thrun, S.: Multi-view image and tof sensor fusion for dense 3d reconstruction. In: ICCV Workshops, pp. 1542–1549. IEEE (2009)
27. Zhu, J., Wang, L., Gao, J., Yang, R.: Spatial-temporal fusion for high accuracy depth maps using dynamic mrfs. IEEE Transactions on Pattern Analysis and Machine Intelligence 32(5), 899–909 (2010)
28. Ghobadi, S.E., Loepprich, O.E., Lottnera, O., Ahmadov, F., Hartmann, K., Weihs, W., Loffeld, O.: Analysis of the personnel safety in a man-machine-cooperation using 2d/3d images. In: Proceedings of the EURON/IARP International Workshop on Robotics for Risky Interventions and Surveillance of the Environment, Benicassim, Spain (January 2008)

29. Bradski, G.: The OpenCV Library. Dr. Dobb's Journal of Software Tools (2000)
30. Bouguet, J.Y.: Camera calibration toolbox for matlab (2004)
31. Hahne, U., Alexa, M.: Combining time-of-flight depth and stereo images without accurate extrinsic calibration. IJISTA 5(3), 325–333 (2008)
32. Nair, R., Lenzen, F., Meister, S., Schäfer, H., Garbe, C., Kondermann, D.: High accuracy TOF and stereo sensor fusion at interactive rates. In: Fusiello, A., Murino, V., Cucchiara, R. (eds.) ECCV 2012 Ws/Demos, Part II. LNCS, vol. 7584, pp. 1–11. Springer, Heidelberg (2012)
33. Dal Mutto, C., Zanuttigh, P., Cortelazzo, G.M.: A probabilistic approach to tof and stereo data fusion. In: 3DPVT, Paris, France, vol. 2 (2010)
34. Schiller, I., Beder, C., Koch, R.: Calibration of a pmd-camera using a planar calibration pattern together with a multi-camera setup. The International Archives of the Photogrammetry, Remote Sensing and Spatial Information Sciences 37, 297–302 (2008)
35. Zhu, J., Wang, L., Yang, R., Davis, J.: Fusion of time-of-flight depth and stereo for high accuracy depth maps. In: Proc. CVPR, pp. 1–8. IEEE (2008)
36. Kim, Y.M., Chan, D., Theobalt, C., Thrun, S.: Design and calibration of a multi-view tof sensor fusion system. In: IEEE Computer Society Conference on Computer Vision and Pattern Recognition Workshops (CVPRW 2008), pp. 1–7. IEEE (2008)
37. Horn, B.K.: Closed-form solution of absolute orientation using unit quaternions. JOSA A 4(4), 629–642 (1987)
38. Guan, L., Pollefeys, M., et al.: A unified approach to calibrate a network of camcorders and tof cameras. In: Workshop on Multi-Camera and Multi-Modal Sensor Fusion Algorithms and Applications (M2SFA2 2008) (2008)
39. Hartley, R.I., Zisserman, A.: Multiple View Geometry in Computer Vision, 2nd edn. Cambridge University Press (2004)
40. Dal Mutto, C., Zanuttigh, P., Mattoccia, S., Cortelazzo, G.: Locally consistent toF and stereo data fusion. In: Fusiello, A., Murino, V., Cucchiara, R. (eds.) ECCV 2012 Ws/Demos, Part I. LNCS, vol. 7583, pp. 598–607. Springer, Heidelberg (2012)
41. Zhang, L., Curless, B., Seitz, S.M.: Spacetime stereo: Shape recovery for dynamic scenes. In: Proceedings of the 2003 IEEE Computer Society Conference on Computer Vision and Pattern Recognition, vol. 2, pp. II–367. IEEE (2003)
42. Yang, Q., Tan, K.H., Culbertson, B., Apostolopoulos, J.: Fusion of active and passive sensors for fast 3d capture. In: MMSP (2010)
43. Reynolds, M., Dobos, J., Peel, L., Weyrich, T., Brostow, G.J.: Capturing time-of-flight data with confidence. In: 2011 IEEE Conference on Computer Vision and Pattern Recognition (CVPR), pp. 945–952. IEEE (2011)
44. Zhu, J., Wang, L., Yang, R., Davis, J., et al.: Reliability fusion of time-of-flight depth and stereo for high quality depth maps. TPAMI (99), 1 (2011)
45. Song, Y., Glasbey, C.A., van der Heijden, G.W.A.M., Polder, G., Dieleman, J.A.: Combining stereo and time-of-flight images with application to automatic plant phenotyping. In: Heyden, A., Kahl, F. (eds.) SCIA 2011. LNCS, vol. 6688, pp. 467–478. Springer, Heidelberg (2011)
46. Gudmundsson, S., Aanaes, H., Larsen, R.: Fusion of stereo vision and time-of-flight imaging for improved 3d estimation. IJISTA 5(3), 425–433 (2008)
47. Bartczak, B., Koch, R.: Dense depth maps from low resolution time-of-flight depth and high resolution color views. In: Bebis, G., Boyle, R., Parvin, B., Koracin, D., Kuno, Y., Wang, J., Pajarola, R., Lindstrom, P., Hinkenjann, A., Encarnação, M.L., Silva, C.T., Coming, D. (eds.) ISVC 2009, Part II. LNCS, vol. 5876, pp. 228–239. Springer, Heidelberg (2009)

48. Hahne, U., Alexa, M.: Depth imaging by combining time-of-flight and on-demand stereo. In: Kolb, A., Koch, R. (eds.) Dyn3D 2009. LNCS, vol. 5742, pp. 70–83. Springer, Heidelberg (2009)
49. Dal Mutto, C., Zanuttigh, P., Cortelazzo, G.M.: A probabilistic approach to tof and stereo data fusion. In: 3DPVT, Paris, France (May 2010)
50. Beder, C., Bartczak, B., Koch, R.: A combined approach for estimating patchlets from PMD depth images and stereo intensity images. In: Hamprecht, F.A., Schnörr, C., Jähne, B. (eds.) DAGM 2007. LNCS, vol. 4713, pp. 11–20. Springer, Heidelberg (2007)
51. Ruhl, K., Klose, F., Lipski, C., Magnor, M.: Integrating approximate depth data into dense image correspondence estimation. In: Proc. European Conference on Visual Media Production (CVMP) (August 2012)
52. Gandhi, V., Cech, J., Horaud, R.: High-resolution depth maps based on tof-stereo fusion. In: 2012 IEEE International Conference on Robotics and Automation (ICRA), pp. 4742–4749. IEEE (2012)
53. Van Meerbergen, G., Vergauwen, M., Pollefeys, M., Van Gool, L.: A hierarchical symmetric stereo algorithm using dynamic programming. International Journal of Computer Vision 47(1-3), 275–285 (2002)
54. Gallup, D., Frahm, J.M., Mordohai, P., Yang, Q., Pollefeys, M.: Real-time plane-sweeping stereo with multiple sweeping directions. In: IEEE Conference on Computer Vision and Pattern Recognition (CVPR 2007), pp. 1–8. IEEE (2007)
55. Kolmogorov, V., Zabih, R.: Computing visual correspondence with occlusions using graph cuts. In: Proceedings of the Eighth IEEE International Conference on Computer Vision (ICCV 2001), vol. 2, pp. 508–515. IEEE (2001)
56. Boykov, Y., Veksler, O., Zabih, R.: Fast approximate energy minimization via graph cuts. IEEE Transactions on Pattern Analysis and Machine Intelligence 23(11), 1222–1239 (2001)
57. Sun, J., Zheng, N.N., Shum, H.Y.: Stereo matching using belief propagation. IEEE Transactions on Pattern Analysis and Machine Intelligence 25(7), 787–800 (2003)
58. Ihler, A.T., Mcallester, D.A.: Particle belief propagation. In: International Conference on Artificial Intelligence and Statistics, pp. 256–263 (2009)
59. Birchfield, S., Tomasi, C.: A pixel dissimilarity measure that is insensitive to image sampling. IEEE Transactions on Pattern Analysis and Machine Intelligence 20(4), 401–406 (1998)
60. Hirschmüller, H., Scharstein, D.: Evaluation of cost functions for stereo matching. In: Proc. CVPR, pp. 1–8. IEEE (2007)
61. Brox, T., Bruhn, A., Papenberg, N., Weickert, J.: High accuracy optical flow estimation based on a theory for warping. In: Pajdla, T., Matas, J(G.) (eds.) ECCV 2004. LNCS, vol. 3024, pp. 25–36. Springer, Heidelberg (2004)
62. Zach, C., Pock, T., Bischof, H.: A duality based approach for realtime TV-L1 optical flow. In: Pattern Recognition: 29th DAGM Symposium, vol. 29, pp. 214–223 (2007)
63. Nocedal, J.: Updating quasi-newton matrices with limited storage. Mathematics of Computation 25, 773–782 (1980)
64. Hirschmüller, H.: Stereo processing by semiglobal matching and mutual information. TPAMI 30(2), 328–341 (2008)
65. Mattoccia, S.: A locally global approach to stereo correspondence. In: 2009 IEEE 12th International Conference on Computer Vision Workshops (ICCV Workshops), pp. 1763–1770. IEEE (2009)
66. Cech, J., Sara, R.: Efficient sampling of disparity space for fast and accurate matching. In: IEEE Conference on Computer Vision and Pattern Recognition (CVPR 2007), pp. 1–8. IEEE (2007)

Reconstruction of Deformation from Depth and Color Video with Explicit Noise Models

Andreas Jordt and Reinhard Koch

Multimedia Information Processing Group, University of Kiel,
Hermann-Rodewald-Str. 3, D-24118 Kiel/Germany
{jordt,rk}@mip.informatik.uni-kiel.de

Abstract. Depth sensors like ToF cameras and structured light devices provide valuable scene information, but do not provide a stable base for optical flow or feature movement calculation because the lack of texture information makes depth image registration very challenging. Approaches associating depth values with optical flow or feature movement from color images try to circumvent this problem, but suffer from the fact that color features are often generated at edges and depth discontinuities, areas in which depth sensors inherently deliver unstable data. Using deformation tracking as an application, this article will discuss the benefits of Analysis by Synthesis (AbS) while approaching the tracking problem and how it can be used to:

- exploit the complete image information of depth and color images in the tracking process,
- avoid feature calculation and, hence, the need for outlier handling,
- regard every measurement with respect to its accuracy and expected deviation.

In addition to an introduction to AbS based tracking, a novel approach to handle noise and inaccuracy is proposed, regarding every input measurement according to its accuracy and noise characteristics. The method is especially useful for time of flight cameras since it allows to take the correlation between pixel noise and the measured amplitude into account. A set of generic and specialized deformation models is discussed as well as an efficient way to synthesize and to optimize high dimensional models. The resulting applications range from real-time deformation reconstruction methods to very accurate deformation retrieval using models of 100 dimensions and more.

1 Introduction

Depth sensing in computer vision has come a long way since the beginning of stereo vision [1] and the introduction of 2D and 3D range imaging. Today, many reliable algorithms for computing dense depth maps from stereo data exist, but the continuing demand for alternative depth sensing technologies such as time of flight (ToF) cameras and structured light systems, e.g. the Microsoft Kinect, shows that stereo imaging still has its weaknesses. When using color camera

M. Grzegorzek et al. (Eds.): Time-of-Flight and Depth Imaging, LNCS 8200, pp. 128–146, 2013.

data, image registration and tracking have always been rigidly connected to the 3D estimation process, since registration, e.g. corresponding features [2,3] or correlation [4] are prerequisites to retrieve information about the third dimension as well as for object tracking.

Depth images however, as produced by ToF cameras and structured light systems, often lack significant structure that can be exploited in a similar fashion. Hence, the image registration that comes for free with stereo generated depth images can be difficult to retrieve if only the depth data is available. There are algorithms to generate points of interest [5] and even depth image features that are invariant to view point changes [6] but these require articulated surface information, limiting their field of application. Furthermore, descriptors as well as significant point retrieval fail when the objects at hand deform, because the (local) shape is the only invariant feature a depth image can provide.

Hence, the first works on aligning depth data did not refer to significant points and correspondences, but performed registration directly using the complete image. In 1992, Besl [7] published a method iteratively enhancing an unknown pose estimate between two given depth images by reducing the distance between the closest 3D points of each measurement, the iterative closest point (ICP) algorithm. This direct approach became a standard method for registering point clouds and depth data. It is for example used in the Kinect Fusion method [8] for real-time 3D reconstruction based on Kinect depth images.

Another direct method was introduced early on by Horn and Harris[9]. Laser range finder data was aligned for navigation purposes by iteratively generating sensor results for each pose hypothesis, which could be evaluated by directly comparing it to the actual sensor input. The class of such optimization methods that synthesize input data in order to evaluate hypothesis is called analysis by synthesis (AbS). In most cases, AbS methods optimize all parameters simultaneously, since a synthesis of the input data usually requires an estimate of the complete solution. Hence, AbS methods require a solution space that is parametrized with a limited number of dimensions, e.g. a pose [9], rag-doll parameters [10] or specialized deformation models [11,12]. Global search algorithms are usually slow compared to local optimization methods, and high dimensional optimization via synthesis of one or multiple input images is hardly capable of processing in real time. Nevertheless, real-time tracking can be achieved by combining a fast global optimization scheme, *covariance matrix adaptation - evolution strategy* (CMA-ES)[13] with sparse synthesis [14], as used in [15] and [11].

In this article, sparse synthesis and CMA-ES optimization are discussed and the approach in [14] is extended by explicit noise handling. Regarding noise explicitly not only leads to more accurate tracking results for known noise models, it also makes weighting heuristics for input data from different domains (color, ToF, structured light) obsolete, providing a solution to the data fusion problem that is much more sound and physically reasonable.

The remainder of this article is organized as follows: section 2 discusses the parametrization of the search domain and shows various examples from different applications. In section 3, the process of generating artificial input data is explained along with the sparse synthesis that allows for fast estimation evaluation. The explicit noise model is introduced in section 4 and the global optimization scheme CMA-ES is discussed. Section 5 provides example applications and evaluation results, reviewing the capability and limits of AbS and the benefits of explicit noise handling. Figure 1 depicts a schematic overview over the method.

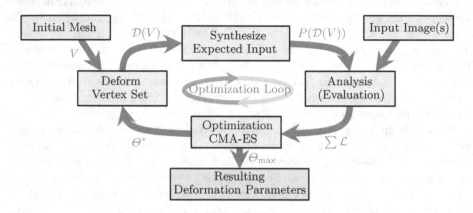

Fig. 1. An overview showing the components and the data processing of the AbS systems discussed in this article. The variable names are introduced in the corresponding sections in which the components are explained in detail.

2   Scene Parametrization

The primary difference between reconstruction methods like (Non-rigid) structure from motion (SfM) and AbS is the explicit model of the search space that is required by AbS methods. Hence, AbS methods are not suitable for e.g. 3D reconstruction from color data only, due to the lack of a generic parameter space describing arbitrary 3D scenes. But if depth cameras are involved, a 3D mesh is already provided for every frame, allowing to reduce the reconstruction problem to a tracking problem. For the rigid case, the direct reconstruction is already solved very well [8] and will not be discussed in this article. In the non-rigid case, the algorithms for tracking still leave room for improvement. One of the main reasons for this is the lack of a generic deformation model; unconstrained deformation in the real world cannot be described by a parameter space with a finite number of dimensions.

Therefore, the first step in setting up a tracking method for deformable scenes is the design of a deformation space. In this deformation (parameter-) space, the trade-off between versatility and ease of optimization is defined. In the following, three examples of deformation function classes are given. The initial triangle mesh is always given as a set V of vertices v, and $\mathcal{D}$ will denote the deformation function parametrized by the vector Θ, i.e.

$$\mathcal{D}_\Theta : V \to \mathbb{R}^3. \tag{1}$$

In the generic case of deforming surfaces, the co-domain of non-uniform rational B-splines (NURBS) [16] has proven to be a suitable parameter space for single objects [14]. This section will first introduce NURBS-based deformation and afterwards discuss specialized deformation functions for dedicated purposes.

2.1   Non-uniform Rational B-Splines

In the last decades, NURBS have become one of the standard tools in CAD applications to design arbitrary surfaces. Not only are 3D NURBS surfaces intuitively manipulated via 3D control points, the ability to match any given surface with arbitrary accuracy can easily be deduced from the mathematical definition [16]. It is justified to say that the co-domain of a NURBS surface function is a suitable parameter space to describe deformations. As discussed in [14], the common definition of a NURBS surface is given by

$$\mathcal{N}((u,w),C) := \sum_{p \in C} R_p(u,w)p. \tag{2}$$

$R_p(u,w)$ is the weighting function for each control point p for the parameters (u,w) where $\sum_{p \in P} R_p(u,w) = 1$ for all $(u,w) \in [0,1]^2$. Each control point p has a position in 3D space, i.e. $p \in \mathbb{R}^3$ and is associated with a spline function R_p, describing the influence of p at the parameter (u,w). Figure 2 shows a 2D example of a NURBS function. The points of maximum influence η, which are also the points at which the weighting functions "fade out", are arranged in a grid-like fashion in the parameter space, which allows to index the weighting functions R_p by their position i in the first and j in the second parameter space dimension. Using this definition of i and j, R_p can be defined as

$$R_p(u,w) := \frac{n_{i,d}(u)n_{j,d}(w)}{\sum_{k=0}^{m}\sum_{l=0}^{m} n_{k,d}(u)n_{l,d}(w)}. \tag{3}$$

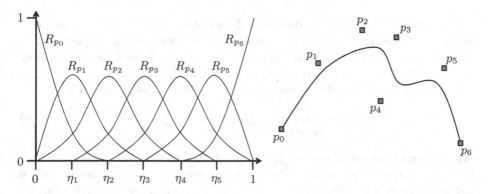

Fig. 2. Left: the weighting functions R_p defining the influence of each control point position in the parameter domain. Right: the NURBS function $\mathcal{N}$ together with its control points in the co-domain of the NURBS function, the world coordinate system.

The function n is the one-dimensional base spline of polynomial degree d for the indices i and j. The actual placement of the spline in each dimension of the parameter space is defined by an ordered set of knots $\{\eta_0, ..., \eta_m\} \in [0, 1]^{m+1}$, describing the "fade-out points" of the base splines (see Fig. 2). Given these parameters, the base splines are defined recursively by

$$n_{i,0}(u) := \begin{cases} 1 & \text{for } \eta_i \leq u < \eta_{i+1} \\ 0 & \text{otherwise} \end{cases} \tag{4}$$

and for $d > 0$ by

$$n_{i,d}(u) := \frac{u - \eta_i}{\eta_{i+d} - \eta_i} n_{i,d-1}(u) + \frac{\eta_{i+d+1} - u}{\eta_{i+d+1} - \eta_{i+1}} n_{i+1,d-1}(u). \tag{5}$$

The algorithms discussed in this article assume the knots $\eta_0, ..., \eta_m$ to be distributed equidistantly in each dimension [14].

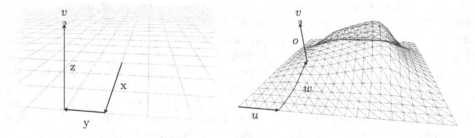

Fig. 3. Left: a vertex v as it is defined in world coordinates x,y,z. Right: the same vertex addressed by the parameters u and w describing the closest surface point and the orthogonal offset o.

In order to use a NURBS surface as a deformation function for a given mesh, the mesh vertices have to be associated with the surface function. As introduced in [15], a surface dependent coordinate system can be defined that allows any given mesh to follow the deforming movements of the NURBS function:
for each vertex v, the closest point on the NURBS surface is given by

$$(u, w) = \operatorname*{argmin}_{(u', w') \in [0,1]^2} \|\mathcal{N}((u', w'), \Theta^*) - v\|_2 \tag{6}$$

with Θ^* being the set of control points at the initial position. Assuming that the closest surface point is not at the edge of the surface, the surface normal of that point directly intersects with the vertex. Let $\hat{\mathcal{N}}(u, w)$ describe this surface normal, then there is an scaling factor $o \in \mathbb{R}$, such that

$$v = \mathcal{N}((u, w), \Theta^*) + \hat{\mathcal{N}}((u, w), \Theta^*)o. \tag{7}$$

Hence, every vertex position can be reconstructed from a function parameter (u, w) and an offset parameter o (see Fig. 3). If u,v and o are stored for each vertex in the initial surface shape, any further deformation of the NURBS function is also performed by the triangle mesh, if the positions are calculated by (7), i.e.

$$\mathcal{D}_\Theta(v) = \mathcal{N}((u, w), \Theta) + \hat{\mathcal{N}}((u, w), \Theta)o. \tag{8}$$

with Θ being the vector containing the current set of control points.

2.2 Specialized Deformation Functions

As the NURBS based deformation is very generic, its deformation space is often higher dimensional than necessary. In order to keep the optimization process efficient, it is useful to choose the deformation space to be as low-dimensional as possible. This does not only speed up the optimization, it also causes the resulting tracking to be more robust towards degenerative parameter constellations.

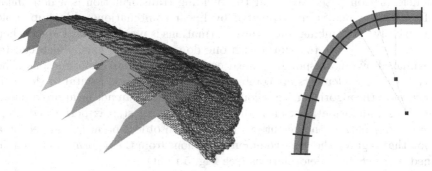

Fig. 4. Left: an object sliced into a set of segments, each assumed to have a constant deformation. Right: a schematic of a deformed object: each segment is modeled with constant curvature.

2.2.1 Deformation under Gravity

In [12], Fugl et al. describe an AbS approach to deformation tracking dedicated to the handling of flexible objects with a robot gripper. The basic principle is to adapt the angles of a set of curvatures within the object (see fig. 4) to synthesize the deformation of an object under the influence of gravity. For an angle α and an object of size x_{size}, a vertex v is deformed using the function

$$\mathcal{D}_\Theta : \begin{pmatrix} x \\ y \\ z \end{pmatrix} \mapsto \begin{pmatrix} x \cos(\alpha) - (z - r) \sin(\alpha) \\ y \\ (z - r) \cos(\alpha) + x \sin(\alpha) + r \end{pmatrix}, \alpha = \frac{x}{2\pi(r - z)}, r = \frac{x_{size}}{\beta} \tag{9}$$

with $\Theta = \{\beta\}$, if the object is made from a single curvature element. For multiple segments, (9) has to be applied subsequently to the mesh points with Θ containing the set of angles respectively (see [12] for details).

The limitation to one dimension in the main deformation allows to produce very robust and accurate results, up to the ability to determine the object material properties based on their physical plausibility. The fact that one end of the object is rigidly connected to the robot gripper adds to the robustness as this constraint can directly be used for the synthesis.

2.2.2   Paper and Virtual Display Deformation

Steimle et al. [11] introduced an AbS system for real-time tracking of virtual display surfaces, i.e. sheets of paper or foam onto which display content is projected by a video beamer. A key aspect of this method is the ability to track the position and deformation of the object with very low latency. To achieve high reconstruction precision and high frame rates, a dedicated deformation model was created that reduced the generic deformation to the ones plausible for sheets of paper or foam:

Four main deformation directions, intersecting at the center of the sheet, each with two independent curvature values for each side (see Fig. 5 left) form the linear deformation base. Note that the bending transformation is a non-linear transformation which is approximated by linear combinations of lookup table entries, merely the combination of the deformations is purely linear. Paper, when bend, has the property to deform with one dominant curve axis, which can be approximated by a corresponding linear combination of base deformations. The fact, that the base elements are combined in a linear fashion is vital to the real-time aspect of the algorithm. To account for effects that can not be approximated by the 8 base deformations, an additional z-mapping step is performed after the main deformation: the height (z-value) of each object point is mapped by a function that regards the most common deviations from the deformation domain spanned by the 8 base deformations (see Fig. 5 right).

In comparison, a NURBS function to model such a class of deformations would have required 4x4 control points, creating a 48 dimensional parameter space, this deformation only requires 8+1 deformation parameters and 6 pose parameters, that add up to a 15 dimensional parameter space for Θ. The low dimensionality

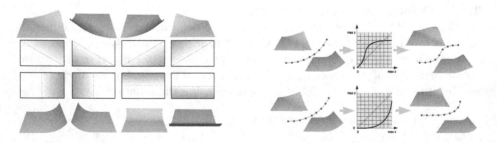

Fig. 5. Left: the four main bending directions, each with a separate curvature value for each side, are the deformation base for the FlexPad deformation function. Right: a post processing deformation executes a mapping of the high values of the deformed object points to regard non-constant curvature aspects.

leads to a faster and more robust deformation function at the cost of a lower generality.

3   Synthesis

A precondition to a correct synthesis is to have reliable calibration data of all sensors involved. For the results displayed in section 5, the calibration method from Schiller et al. [17] was deployed to all input sensors. Hence, for any image I_s from a sensor s, there is a corresponding projection function $P_s : \mathbb{R}^3 \to \mathbb{R}^2$ function given, yielding image coordinates for any 3D point and sensor s. Let $c_s \in \mathbb{R}^3$ be the camera center of s and $R \in \mathbb{R}^{3 \times 3}$ the rotation matrix for the sensor orientation. Let $K_s \in \mathbb{R}^{3 \times 3}$ be the camera matrix of s and $D_s : \mathbb{R}^2 \to \mathbb{R}^2$ the lens distortion function, then P_s can be written as

$$P_s(v) = D_s \left(K_s \cdot (R \cdot (v - c)) \cdot \frac{1}{(R \cdot (v - c_s))_z} \right). \tag{10}$$

with $\cdot_z$ denoting the z component of a vector.

In the general case, the synthesis (as e.g. performed in [12]) can easily be done by rendering the object at hand on a graphics card for each sensor s, using the set of deformed vertices $\mathcal{D}(V)$. The resulting RGB image can be used as a color sensor synthesis for a sensor while the z-Buffer of the rendered image can be used as a depth image. Lens distortion effects of the sensors can either be synthesized in a second render step (distortion rendering) or the inverse distortion function is applied to the input images.

The advantage of forward distortion, e.g. distortion rendering, is that values can be compared directly in the input domain, without relying on interpolated values generated by the undistortion of the input data, making it the right option if a high precision reconstruction is to be achieved.

In case of backward distortion on the other hand, images are undistorted prior to any processing, leading to a gain in processing speed because the input image is processed once for every frame, whereas several thousands of syntheses may be generated for one input frame. Backward distortion should be used when results have to be calculated in real time.

3.1   Sparse Synthesis

A more efficient way to synthesize the projections of a mesh is a sparse synthesis, first introduced in [15]: instead of rendering the complete mesh into an image buffer, only the significant parts of the mesh are evaluated. The surface of a triangle mesh can be understood as linear interpolation between vertices, i.e. the main information of an object is given by its set of vertices, not by the interpolating triangles. Hence, sparse synthesis does not generate a synthesized image, but only one image value for each position a vertex v is projected to in the sensor s with projection P_s. The color image synthesis for each sensor s at the image coordinates $P_s(\mathcal{D}(v))$ is a simple lookup of the vertex color of v.

For each depth sensor, the synthesized depth value is given by the Euclidean distance value

$$d = \|c_s - \mathcal{D}(v)\|_2 \tag{11}$$

for the image coordinates $P_s(\mathcal{D}(v))$ for all depth sensors.

3.2   Input Warping

If a 3D point v is already given in camera coordinates and if the corresponding projection P_s does not have to compensate lens distortion, (10) can be simplified to

$$P_s(v) = K_s \cdot \frac{v}{v_z}, \tag{12}$$

greatly reducing the amount of calculations that need to be performed per vertex and per synthesis. For a single sensor setup, this requirement is easily met by solving the problem directly in the camera coordinate system. If multiple sensors are used, such a simplification requires a warping step applied to the input images, changing the viewpoints of the input data into a common projection (see [18] for an introduction to warping). Although such a preprocessing step can greatly increase the overall performance of the algorithm, one has to be aware of the fact that the warping results are subject to artifacts caused by occlusion, quantization and noise in the depth input data. Warping helps to perform AbS in real time [14], but reduces the accuracy of the result.

4   Analysis and Optimization

With the ability to synthesize the input for a given parameter set, the parameter space can be searched for the parameter set most suitable for a given input image set, i.e. for the parameters whose synthesized output is as close to the real input as possible. In most cases [14,15,11,12] the objective function is modeled as a simple pixel-wise least squares error function augmented by heuristics to keep the target function from introducing singularities or optima at degenerative parameter constellations. Least squares errors are a suitable tool as long as the values compared are within the same domain, but require manual weighting or heuristics when used to compare values in different domains, e.g. depth differences and color differences.

In the area of sensor fusion, statistical modeling is common because it allows to define a global likelihood based on the expected distribution of each sensor input. This means if a noise model is present for every input, the global likelihood over an arbitrarily large set of different inputs from different domains is still well defined. A likelihood based AbS method is able to combine the input of different types of depth cameras (Kinect and ToF) along with color information and even binary information like light barrier feedback, regarding sensor specific shortcomings.

4.1 Direct Bayer Pattern Analysis

When formulating the idea of a direct method like analysis by synthesis, one of the main motivations is drawn from the argument of a most direct feedback because each solution is evaluated directly on the sensor input. A minor detail that is most often disregarded is the fact, that a color image is already an interpretation of the sensor values, as Bayer pattern cameras [19] only provide one color channel per pixel. The effect seen most often in RGB images generated by simple de-bayering methods are wrong color values at discontinuities and contrasting textures. There are very powerful demosaicing strategies [20], but in practice, these methods are only used in situations where the need for complex demosaicing is required, since they require GPU usage to run in real time on larger images. Figure 6 shows the large differences between different demosaicing algorithms. The results are sorted from left to right in the order of complexity of the reconstruction. It visualizes that even the most renown demosaicing method "Adaptive Homogeneity-Directed Demosaicing" (AHD) [21] has problems at reconstructing fine details and edges correctly.

Fig. 6. Left: the Bayer pattern as it is used in the Microsoft Kinect camera. Center left: a Kinect color image converted to RGB with a fast demosaicing method as it is used in the Open NI driver. Center right: demosaicing result by a simple bilinear demosaicing method. Right: demosaicing result by the AHD method as it is implemented in the DC1394 library.

Using analysis by synthesis, the de-bayering step is not required anymore, since it is possible to synthesize the Bayer pattern image directly, by masking the RGB synthesis accordingly. It even allows to simulate defocus, crosstalk, and insufficient color filters (as e.g. described in [20]), and even in cases where it is impossible to reconstruct the real RGB projection from the input image. AbS allows to process the data efficiently without the need for e.g. convolutions, by simply applying a kernel filter to the synthesized image to simulate the effects. This way, the problem of demosaicing and debluring is completely circumvented in an elegant and efficient way.

4.2 Likelihood

Modeling the noise of a sensor is not straight forward. Especially for more complex capturing systems like time-of-flight cameras, the problem of finding a suitable model is tedious and not sufficiently solved yet. The problem is that errors may depend on various environmental influences, correlated background noise within and from outside the camera housing, overexposure, and geometrical constellations that introduce multi-path effects as well es material properties (see chapter 1). Some of these effects can be modeled well, though a direct compensation is not always possible or only with reduction of image information as discussed in section 3.

The very advantage of AbS methods proposed in this article is that there is no need for any explicit compensation as long as the noise model can be given, i.e. the probability density can be calculated.

Let P be the probability density function for a distance measurement event x_{d_m} given the real distance x_{d_r}, i.e.

$$P(x_{d_m}|x_{d_r}), \tag{13}$$

providing the relative likelihood of x_{d_r} when the measurement event x_{d_m} is present

$$\mathcal{L}(x_{d_r}|x_{d_m}). \tag{14}$$

There has been the common observation, that the amplitude of the ToF signal can provide a hint on the accuracy of a measurement(see chapter 2.2 or [22,23]). Let this be regarded by the likelihood function as well. Given the additional amplitude measurement event x_a, the likelihood

$$\mathcal{L}(x_{d_r}|x_{d_m},x_a). \tag{15}$$

is augmented by the additional conditional x_a, regarding the amplitude measurement. The slight inaccuracy of regarding the amplitude measurement instead of the actual amplitude helps to create a system free of hidden random variables, since the amplitude is not rendered by the synthesis step. It can be assumed that the effect of exchanging the actual amplitude by its measurement is neglectable.

For a color sensor the likelihood can be denoted in a similar fassion, by calculating the propabilty of the color of a vertex projected onto sensor given the measured color at this point in the image.

The overall goal can now be formulated as finding the deformation parameters $\Theta_{\max}$ causing the solution with the highest likelihood over all measurements over all sensors

$$\Theta_{\max} = \operatorname*{argmax}_{\Theta} \sum_{v \in V} \sum_{s \in S} \log\left(\mathcal{L}_{v,s}\right) \tag{16}$$

where $\mathcal{L}_{v,s}$ denotes the likelihood function for the pixel in which $\mathcal{D}_\Theta(v)$ would be projected in sensor s, evaluated using the given synthesized distance ($\|\mathcal{D}_\Theta(v) - c\|_2$) (or vertex color) and the measured distance and amplitude (or color) of the pixel at image coordinate $P(\mathcal{D}_\Theta(v))$.

An example likelihood function can be found in section 5.

4.3   Optimization

The overall tracking goal can now be defined by finding $\Theta_{\max}$ which maximizes $\sum \log \mathcal{L}$ as formulated in (16). If e.g. approximated by Gaussian distributions, a

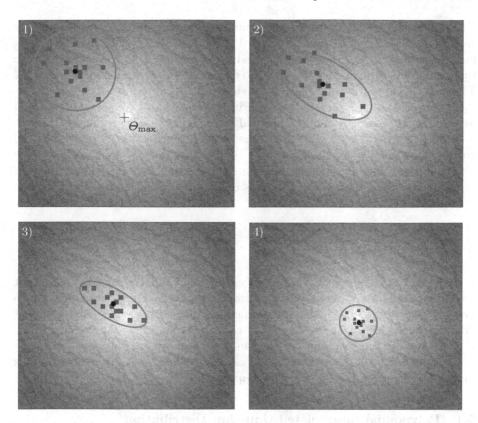

Fig. 7. A 2D visualization of CMA-ES distributions (circles) around the current mean (black dots) in the parameter space. Bright background color denotes high likelihood, darker color a smaller likelihood. The optimum Θ_{max} is located in the center. The evaluation points of each CMA-ES iteration are chosen according to the distribution (grey squares). 1) The initial distribution. 2) The distribution stretches towards the area of higher likelihood. 3/4) The distribution is narrowed down to the area of high likelihood.

problem that is formulated as maximizing the likelihood of a parameter can usually be optimized by local optimization methods for maximum likelihood estimation such as expectation maximization [24]. But the distributions do not regard the assignment of 3D points to 2D image coordinates performed by P_s, which prevents the convexity properties in a Gaussian distribution of the likelihood to be valid. In most cases this convexity is obviously not given, especially if repeating textures or structures are a part of the scene. Therefore, the global optimization algorithm Covariance Matrix Adaptation - Evolution Strategy (CMA-ES) [13] is used as proposed in [14,15] to maximize the given likelihood function.

CMA-ES is a global optimization method based on a Gaussian sample distribution that is iteratively updated in the optimization process. An initial distribution in the parameter space (Fig. 7,1) is evaluated by probing the likelihood function at discrete sample points, randomly chosen by the given distribution.

The evaluation results are then used to update the distribution, i.e. to adapt the covariance matrix and the mean such that it increases the likelihood of distributing the samples at positions of higher values of the fitniss function, in this case the likelihood (16), which is then used to distribute the samples again (Fig. 7,2). The iterative application of these steps shifts the distribution towards the optimum (Fig. 73). At a given stopping criteria, the best evaluation result is returned as the best approximation of the optimal parameter Θ_{max}. For a detailed introduction to CMA-ES, see [13]. If a dense sequence of images is processed, the current movement and side constraints that shape the likelihood space can be assumed to have similarities, i.e. the search path within the likelihood function of two consecutive input image sets are similar. In [14], this is exploited to speed up the optimization.

5   Application

In order to test the explicit noise handling of the likelihood-based system, a set of synthetic and real tests have been performed. The goal of these tests is not to evaluate a certain noise model, but to demonstrate that explicit noise handling does work in AbS methods and that it can greatly improve the fitting results. For this reason, a rather simple Gaussian-distribution-based approach has been implemented for the test cases, which can be replaced by any, more complex model based e.g. on [23,25] (see also chapter 2).

5.1   Polynomial Interpolated Gaussian Distribution

The implemented distribution, approximates the ToF measurement noise by a Gaussian distribution per pixel in respect to depth and amplitude image. Mean value and deviation are calculated based on distance and amplitude measurements. Let μ_p be the function to describe the average offset of the measurement for a pixel p, and let σ_p describe the average deviation of a measurement. Then the probability density of the approximating Gaussian distribution is given by

$$\phi(x)_p = \frac{1}{\sqrt{2\pi\sigma_p^2}}e^{-\frac{1}{2\sigma_p^2}(x-\mu_p^2)} . \tag{17}$$

for one measurement of pixel p.

The precision and the noise levels of ToF measurements depend on a rather large number of variables, including the integration time, the modulation frequency, sensor and illumination properties, the observed material and the surface normal, the scene geometry and the distance of each measurement. For a ToF camera with a fixed integration time setting and sensor properties, the most influential variable aspects remain the amount of reflected light and the distance to the measurements target. Both aspects can be estimated by the actual measurement, as the distance measurement of each pixels obviously correlates with the actual camera-object-distance and the amplitude image of the ToF measurement provides a hint on the amount of light reflected by the object for the measurement at hand subject to the distance.

To account for the influence of distance and amplitude on the measurement, 15 static ToF camera sequences have been acquired using 5 different distances to a large reference object and 3 different object materials each to change the reflectivity of the measured surface. The measurements have been performed using a Mesa Imaging SR4000. The ground truth for all meassurements is known. For each pixel and each combination of amplitude and distance, the mean measurement and the deviation of the measurements (over time) is available. Figure 8 depicts the measurments for a central pixel of the ToF camera to demonstrate the relation between distance, amplitude and noise. Note that the amplitude values of the SR4000 are preprocessed with a distance related factor.

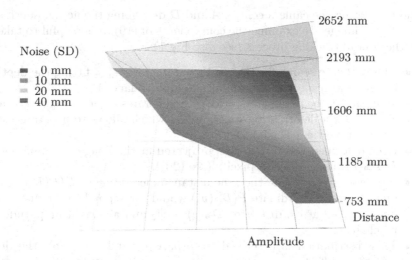

Fig. 8. Plot of the average noise (standard deviation in mm) as it was measured by a central pixel for various distances (ground truth) and amplitude values as returned by an SR4000 (distance compensated). The height is depicting the noise levels. For visualization purposes, the measurements have been connected to a 3D surface.

In order to apply the measured distribution to the analysis step, the likelihood function of each measurement is rendered based on the deviation σ_p and the mean μ_p which interpolate the measured mean and deviation values for the synthesized depth measurement and the amplitude measurement of the pixel p. Hence, σ_p and μ_p become functions depending on the actual distance x and the measured amplitude a, so (17) becomes

$$\phi(x)_{p,a} = \frac{1}{\sqrt{2\pi\sigma_p(x,a)^2}} e^{-\frac{1(x-\mu_p(x,a))^2}{2\sigma_p(x,a)^2}}. \tag{18}$$

The functions μ_p and σ_p interpolate the actual deviation and mean values of the measurements made by pixel p with available ground truth based on the synthesized distance x and the amplitude a, i.e. μ_p and σ_p are polynomial functions interpolating the discrete measurements retrieved by the real experiments with available ground truth. In a way, this error modelling follows the spirit of the reflectivity calibration by Lindner et al. [26] (see also chapter 2.2). If p is written as a function providing the actual pixel to an image coordinate, then the optimization goal is to find a Θ which maximizes the likelihood over all pixels given by

$$\Theta_{\max} = \operatorname*{argmax}_{\Theta} \sum_{v \in V} \log(\phi_{p,A(p)}(\|\mathcal{D}_\Theta(v) - c\|_2 - D(p))) \tag{19}$$

with

$$p = \lfloor P(\mathcal{D}_\Theta(v)) + \begin{pmatrix} 0.5 \\ 0.5 \end{pmatrix} \rfloor \tag{20}$$

and c denoting the camera center, A and D describing the actual depth and the amplitude image. To examine the components of (19), it is helpful to take a look at the overall tracking process (see also Fig.1):

- The goal is to search for the model parameters $\Theta_{\max}$ fitting the depth input image D in respect to the amplitude input image A.
- To optimize the parameters, CMA-ES generates a guess Θ that is evaluated.
- Θ provides a deformation function $\mathcal{D}_\Theta$ which allows to generate the set of deformed vertices $\mathcal{D}_\Theta(V)$.
- Each deformed vertex $\mathcal{D}_\Theta(v)$ is projected at the image coordinate given by $P(\mathcal{D}_\Theta(v))$ and visible in pixel p (see (20)).
- If Θ is a correct guess, then the distance measurement $D(P(\mathcal{D}_\Theta(v)))$ of the pixel at image coordinate $P(\mathcal{D}_\Theta(v))$ would correspond to the distribution of pixel p given a real distance $\|\mathcal{D}_\Theta(v) - c\|_2$ and a current amplitude of that pixel $A(p)$.
- This distribution is described by $\mu(p, A(p))$ and $\sigma(p, A(p)$, the deviation and mean offset retrieved by interpolating the sample measurements with available ground truth.
- Summing up the log-Likelihood over all vertices v yields how well Θ matches input images D and A
- This value is returned to CMA-ES as evaluation of Θ (equation 19)

Equation 19 can easily be extended to multiple depth and color sensors, by summing up all likelihood functions as suggested in (16). Let S be a set of sensors s and let D_s and A_s be the depth and amplitude image of a sensor s, then

$$\Theta_{\max} = \operatorname*{argmax}_{\Theta} \sum_{s \in S} \sum_{v \in V} \log(\phi_{p,A_s(p)}(\|\mathcal{D}_\Theta(v) - c_s\|_2 - D_s(p))) \tag{21}$$

with

$$p = \lfloor P_s(\mathcal{D}_\Theta(v)) + \begin{pmatrix} 0.5 \\ 0.5 \end{pmatrix} \rfloor \tag{22}$$

provides the likelihood of a solution Θ regarding all sensors, with c_s denoting the camera center of each sensor and P_s the corresponding projection. For color cameras, the likelihood can be computed analogously using the vertex color instead of the camera-to-vertex distance.

5.2   Test on Synthetic Data

To evaluate the distribution based approach to AbS for ToF cameras, an artificial deformation scene was generated (see Fig. 9) using the noise model as introduced in 5.1. Two sets of experiments have been conducted, one using the NURBS deformation model as described in section 2.1, and one using the Flex-Pad deformation described in 2.2.2. Each of these tests was performed using the fitness function as published in the original articles [14] and [11] and were compared to the new likelihood based fitness. Note that these tests are not suitable to validate the noise model itself, but how the algorithm performs if the noise model is known.

Fig. 9. Left: a 3D representation of an artificial deformation sequence showing the virtual camera and the deforming object. Center: the depth image of the artificial rendering using projection parameters of a Mesa Imaging SR4000. Right: the depth image augmented with noise simulating input data of an Mesa Imaging SR4000.

It shows that the distribution based AbS system outperforms the Euclidean based AbS approach for known noise levels. The ratio between the two systems can be driven arbitrarily high just by choosing the noise model accordingly, as the Euclidean error function has no possibility to compensate for any mean offset in the data set, e.g. shifting the complete measurements by 10cm results in an error of the Euclidean AbS raised by 10cm whereas the distribution based AbS compensates for the shift in the mean function μ.

To test the influence of applied knowledge about deviation in an isolated way, a synthetic sequence was generated applying artificial noise based on the pixel wise deviation measured in a real ToF camera. Using 10 different geometries, each tracked over a sequence of 500 frames, the deviation of the NURBS control points from the actual ground truth data was in average 1.92 times (SD 0.35) as high using the Euclidean based AbS as it was using the distribution based AbS. This shows that even without known mean offset, the tracking can profit from the knowledge of the deviation as the likelihood based AbS outperforms the Euclidean AbS.

5.3 Test on Real Data

The evaluation of deformation tracking algorithms on real data is always a difficult task. The reason is the lack of available ground truth for real scenes containing deforming objects and the missing generic model covering all possible deformations. An algorithm producing low reproduction errors does not necessarily yield true results, as e.g. optical flow can be used for efficient image compression but does not always describe the real motion in the scene since it does not use an underlying model to constrain itself to plausible movements.

To be able to offer comparable results nevertheless, the tests on real data in this article were performed using the NURBS deformation model as well as the FlexPad deformation model, which already proved the ability to model certain deformation scenes in a simulated setup (section 5.2) as well as in real tests using a structured light system [14,11]. To offer ground truth, the physical objects were not deformed, so any tracked deformation can be evaluated as deviation from ground truth. It is important to note that neither of the models encourages the optimizer to yield undeformed results by e.g. penalizing large deformations.

Fig. 10. The two test objects used in the real data tests. Left: The checker board has equally distributed areas of high and low reflection, Right: The black area in the center of the tracking object provides a special challenge for the tracking algorithm since the black area will cause an offset in the depth image.

The tests were performed using two objects with known geometry, a checker board and a stiff white object with a black center, especially designed to show how well the noise model can handle systematic errors caused by varying reflection properties in the time of flight measurements. Figure 10 depicts the tracking targets.

A sequence of 500 images was recorded of each object while changing the object position and orientation. This sequences were used as input data for the tracking algorithm. Table 1 shows the average error over all sequence images. The error in column 2 and 3 was calculated by measuring the average deviation of the NURBS control points from a planar alignment, i.e. the average distance in mm over all control points from the plane that minimizes the distance to the control points. A NURBS function of degree 2 with 4×4 control points was used, optimized with 1000 CMA-ES iterations using 32 individuals.

In contrast to the NURBS based tracking, the Flexpad tracking delivers pose estimation and deformation values separately. To evaluate the tracking results, the bending parameter containing the maximum absolute value was considered in every frame. Bending parameters range from -2 (full bending away from the

Table 1. Test results comparing the Euclidean fitness function to the likelihood fitness. The cells contain the average error and the standard deviation put in parenthesis. The rows contain results for the tests runs using the checker board (Fig. 10 left) and the stripe board (Fig. 10 right) as tracking target. Column 2 and 3 contain the average deviation in mm using the NURBS deformation model, column 4 and 5 contain the average maximum bending parameter using the FlexPad deformation model.

Parameter	NURBS		FlexPad	
Fitness	Euclidean	Likelihood	Euclidean	Likelihood
checker board	12.83 (5.31)	10.21 (5.49)	0.16 (0.11)	0.12 (0.09)
stripe board	35.71 (18.35)	17.08 (7.76)	0.92 (0.23)	0.24 (0.17)

camera) to $+2$ (full bending towards the camera). Table 1 contains the average maximum bending parameter for the two test sequences. The tracking used 400 CMA-ES iterations with 16 individuals for each frame.

6 Conclusion

Analysis by synthesis is a powerful tool to perform tracking tasks in situations in which, due to missing features, incomplete input data or the use of featureless depth data, feature based approaches may not yield good results. This article shows that explicit noise handling can be integrated into existing AbS methods by reformulating the fitness function as a likelihood function. This does not only lead to more accurate results for noisy input data and known noise models, but also allows a sound combination of several sensors as the weighting of error terms is implicitly handled by the noise models of the sensors. The noise model applied in this article is rather simple but still leads to an increased accuracy when applied to existing methods. The application of more sophisticated and complex noise models for depth sensors may, hence, lead to even higher accuracies.

References

1. Ballard, D.H., Brown, C.M.: Computer Vision. Prentice-Hall, Englewood Cliffs (1982)
2. Tomasi, C., Kanade, T.: Detection and tracking of point features. Technical report, International Journal of Computer Vision (1991)
3. Lowe, D.G.: Distinctive image features from scale-invariant keypoints. Int. J. Comput. Vision 60(2), 91–110 (2004)
4. Lucas, B.D., Kanade, T.: An iterative image registration technique with an application to stereo vision (ijcai). In: Proceedings of the 7th International Joint Conference on Artificial Intelligence (IJCAI 1981), pp. 674–679 (April 1981)
5. Li, X., Guskov, I.: 3d object recognition from range images using pyramid matching. In: International Conference on Computer Vision (ICCV), pp. 1–6 (2007)
6. Johnson, A.: Spin-Images: A Representation for 3-D Surface Matching. PhD thesis, Robotics Institute, Carnegie Mellon University, Pittsburgh, PA (August 1997)
7. Besl, P.J., McKay, N.D.: A method for registration of 3-d shapes. IEEE Trans. Pattern Anal. Mach. Intell. 14(2), 239–256 (1992)

8. Izadi, S., Kim, D., Hilliges, O., Molyneaux, D., Newcombe, R., Kohli, P., Shotton, J., Hodges, S., Freeman, D., Davison, A., Fitzgibbon, A.: Kinectfusion: real-time 3d reconstruction and interaction using a moving depth camera. In: Proceedings of the 24th Annual ACM Symposium on User Interface Software and Technology (UIST 2011), pp. 559–568. ACM, New York (2011)

9. Horn, B.K.P., Harris, J.G.: Rigid body motion from range image sequences. CVGIP: Image Understanding 53, 1–13 (1991)

10. Koch, R.: Dynamic 3-d scene analysis through synthesis feedback control. IEEE Trans. Pattern Anal. Mach. Intell. 15(6), 556–568 (1993)

11. Steimle, J., Jordt, A., Maes, P.: Flexpad: Highly flexible bending interactions for projected handheld displays. In: Brewster, S., Bødker, S., Baudisch, P., Beaudouin-Lafon, M. (eds.) Proceedings of the 2013 Annual Conference on Human Factors in Computing Systems (CHI 2013). ACM, Paris (2013)

12. Fugl, A.R., Jordt, A., Petersen, H.G., Willatzen, M., Koch, R.: Simultaneous estimation of material properties and pose for deformable objects from depth and color images. In: Pinz, A., Pock, T., Bischof, H., Leberl, F. (eds.) DAGM and OAGM 2012. LNCS, vol. 7476, pp. 165–174. Springer, Heidelberg (2012)

13. Hansen, N.: The CMA evolution strategy: A comparing review. In: Lozano, J.A., Larrañaga, P., Inza, I., Bengoetxea, E. (eds.) Towards a new evolutionary computation. STUDFUZZ, vol. 192, pp. 75–102. Springer, Heidelberg (2006)

14. Jordt, A., Koch, R.: Direct model-based tracking of 3d object deformations in depth and color video. International Journal of Computer Vision 102, 239–255 (2013)

15. Jordt, A., Koch, R.: Fast tracking of deformable objects in depth and colour video. In: Proceedings of the British Machine Vision Conference (BMVC 2011). British Machine Vision Association (2011)

16. Piegl, L., Tiller, W.: The NURBS Book, 2nd edn. Springer, Berlin (1997)

17. Schiller, I., Beder, C., Koch, R.: Calibration of a pmd camera using a planar calibration object together with a multi-camera setup. In: The International Archives of the Photogrammetry, Remote Sensing and Spatial Information Sciences, Part B3a, Beijing, China, vol. XXXVII, pp. 297–302 XXI. ISPRS Congress (2008)

18. Hartley, R.I., Zisserman, A.: Multiple View Geometry in Computer Vision, 2nd edn. Cambridge University Press (2004) ISBN: 0521540518

19. Bayer, B.: Color imaging array (July 1976)

20. Menon, D., Andriani, S., Calvagno, G.: Demosaicing with directional filtering and a posteriory decision. IEEE Trans. Image Process. 16, 132–141 (2007)

21. Hirakawa, K., Member, S., Parks, T.W.: Adaptive homogeneity-directed demosaicing algorithm. IEEE Trans. Image Processing 14, 360–369 (2005)

22. Stürmer, M., Becker, G., Hornegger, J.: Assessment of time-of-flight cameras for short camera-object distances. In: Proceedings of the Vision, Modeling, and Visualization Workshop 2011, pp. 231–238 (2011)

23. Reynolds, M., Doboš, J., Peel, L., Weyrich, T., Brostow, G.J.: Capturing time-of-flight data with confidence. In: CVPR (2011)

24. Dempster, A.P., Laird, N.M., Rubin, D.B.: Maximum likelihood from incomplete data via the em algorithm. Journal of the Royal Statistical Society. Series B (Methodological) 39(1), 1–38 (1977)

25. Falie, D.: Noise characteristics of 3d time-of-flight cameras. In: International Symposium on Signals Circuits and Systems (ISSCS 2007), vol. 1, pp. 1–4 (2007)

26. Lindner, M., Schiller, I., Kolb, A., Koch, R.: Time-of-flight sensor calibration for accurate range sensing. Computer Vision and Image Understanding 114(12), 1318–1328 (2010)

Part III
Human-Centered Depth Imaging

A Survey on Human Motion Analysis
from Depth Data

Mao Ye[1], Qing Zhang[1], Liang Wang[2], Jiejie Zhu[3],
Ruigang Yang[1], and Juergen Gall[4]

[1] University of Kentucky, 329 Rose St., Lexington, KY, 40508, U.S.A.
{mao.ye,qing.zhang}@uky.edu, ryang@cs.uky.edu
[2] Microsoft, One Microsoft Way, Redmond, WA, 98052, U.S.A.
liangwan@microsoft.com
[3] SRI International Sarnoff, 201 Washington Rd, Princeton, NJ, 08540, U.S.A.
jiejie.zhu@sri.com
[4] University of Bonn, Roemerstrasse 164, 53117 Bonn, Germany
gall@iai.uni-bonn.de

Abstract. Human pose estimation has been actively studied for
decades. While traditional approaches rely on 2d data like images or
videos, the development of Time-of-Flight cameras and other depth sensors created new opportunities to advance the field. We give an overview
of recent approaches that perform human motion analysis which includes
depth-based and skeleton-based activity recognition, head pose estimation, facial feature detection, facial performance capture, hand pose estimation and hand gesture recognition. While the focus is on approaches
using depth data, we also discuss traditional image based methods to
provide a broad overview of recent developments in these areas.

1 Introduction

Human motion analysis has been a major topic from the early beginning of computer vision [1,2] due to its relevance to a large variety of applications. With the
development of new depth sensors and algorithms for pose estimation [3], new
opportunities have emerged in this field. Human motion analysis is, however,
more than extracting skeleton pose parameters. In order to understand the be-
haviors of humans, a higher level of understanding is required, which we generally
refer to as activity recognition. A review of recent work of the lower level task
of human pose estimation is provided in the chapter *Full-Body Human Motion
Capture from Monocular Depth Images*. Here we consider the higher level activity recognition task in Section 2. In addition, the motion of body parts like the
head or the hands are other important cues, which are discussed in Section 3 and
Section 4. In each section, we give an overview of recent developments in human
motion analysis from depth data, but we also put the approaches in context of
traditional image based methods.

M. Grzegorzek et al. (Eds.): Time-of-Flight and Depth Imaging, LNCS 8200, pp. 149–187, 2013.

2   Activity Recognition

A large amount of research has been conducted to achieve the high level understanding of human activities. The task can be generally described as: given a sequence of motion data, identify the actions performed by the subjects present in the data. Depending on the complexity, they can be conceptually categorized as gestures, actions and activities with interactions. Gestures are normally regarded as the atomic element of human movements, such as "turning head to the left", "raising left leg" and "crouching". Actions usually refer to a single human motion that consists of one or more gestures, for example "walking", "throwing", etc. In the most complex scenario, the subject could interact with objects or other subjects, for instance, "playing with a dog", "two persons fighting" and "people playing football".

Though it is easy for human being to identify each class of these activities, currently no intelligent computer systems can robustly and efficiently perform such task. The difficulties of action recognition come from several aspects. Firstly, human motions span a very high dimensional space and interactions further complicate searching in this space. Secondly, instantiations of conceptually similar or even identical activities by different subjects exhibit substantial variations. Thirdly, visual data from traditional video cameras can only capture projective information of the real world, and are sensitive to lighting conditions.

However, due to the wide applications of activities recognition, researchers have been actively studying this topic and have achieved promising results. Most of these techniques are developed to operate on regular visual data, i.e. color images or videos. There have been excellent surveys on this line of research [4,5,6,7]. By contrast, in this section, we review the state-of-the-art techniques that investigate the applicability and benefit of depth sensors for action recognition, due to both its emerging trend and lack of such a survey. The major advantage of depth data is alleviation of the third difficulty mentioned above. Consequently, most of the methods that operate on depth data achieve view invariance or scale invariance or both.

Though researchers have conducted extensive studies on the three categories of human motions mentioned above based on visual data, current depth based methods mainly focus on the first two categories, i.e. gestures and actions. Only few of them can deal with interactions with small objects like cups. Group activities that involve multiple subjects have not been studied in this regard. One of the reason is the limited capability of current low cost depth sensors in capturing large scale scenes. We therefore will focus on the first two groups as well as those that involve interactions with objects. In particular, only full-body motions will be considered in this section, while body part gestures will be discussed in Section 3 and Section 4.

The pipeline of activity recognition approaches generally involve three steps: *features extraction*, *quantization/dimension reduction* and *classification*. Our review partly follows the taxonomy used in [4]. Basically we categorize existing methods based on the features used. However, due to the special characteristics of depth sensor data, we feel it necessary to differentiate methods that rely directly on depth

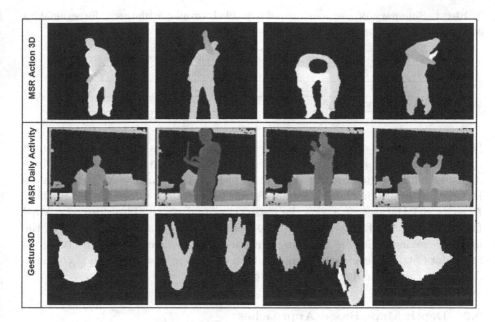

Fig. 1. Examples from the three datasets: MSR Action 3D Dataset [8], MSR Daily Activity Dataset [9] and Gesture3D Dataset [10] ©2013 IEEE

maps or features therein, and methods that take skeleton (or equivalently joints) as inputs. Therefore, the reviewed methods are separated into *depth map-based* and *skeleton-based*. Following [4], each category is further divided into *space time approaches* and *sequential approaches*. The space time approaches usually extract local or global (holistic) features from the space-time volume, without explicit modeling of temporal dynamics. Discriminative classifiers, such as SVM, are then usually used for recognition. By contrast, sequential approaches normally extract local features from data of each time instance and use generative statistical model, such as HMM, to model the dynamics explicitly.

We discuss the *depth map-based* methods in Section 2.2 and the *skeleton-based* methods in Section 2.3. Some methods that utilize both information are also considered in Section 2.3. Before the detailed discussions of the existing methods, we would like to first briefly introduce several publicly available datasets, as well as the mostly adopted evaluation metric in Section 2.1.

2.1   Evaluation Metric and Datasets

The performance of the methods for activity recognition are evaluated mainly based on *accuracy*, that is the percentage of correctly recognized actions. There are several publicly available dataset collected by various authors for evaluation purpose. Here we explicitly list three of them that are most popular, namely the MSR Action 3D Dataset [8], MSR Daily Activity Dataset [9] and Gesture3D

Table 1. Summary of the most popular publicly available datasets for evaluating activity recognition performance

Datasets	#Subjects	#Types of activities	#Data sequences
MSR Action 3D [8]	10	20	567
Gesture3D [10]	10	12	336
MSR Daily Activity 3D [9]	10	16	960

Dataset [10]. Each of the datasets include various types of actions performed by different subjects multiple times. Table 1 provides a summary of these three datasets, while Figure 1 shows some examples. Notice that the MSR Action 3D Dataset [8] is pre-processed to remove the background, while the MSR Daily Activity 3D Dataset [9] keeps the entire captured scene. Therefore, the MSR Daily Activity 3D Dataset can be considered as more challenging. Most of the methods reviewed in the following sections were evaluated on some or all of these datasets, while some of them conducted experiments on their self-collected dataset, for example due to mismatch of focus.

2.2   Depth Maps-Based Approaches

The depth map-based methods rely mainly on features, either local or global, extracted from the space time volume. Compared to visual data, depth maps provide metric, instead of projective, measurements of the geometry that are invariant to lighting. However, designing both effective and efficient depth sequence representations for action recognition is a challenging task. First of all, depth sequences may contain serious occlusions, which makes the global features unstable. In addition, the depth maps do not have as much texture as color images do, and they are usually too noisy (both spatially and temporally) to apply local differential operators such as gradients on. It has been noticed that directly applying popular feature descriptors designed for color images does not provide satisfactory results in this case [11]. These challenges motivate researchers to develop features that are semi-local, highly discriminative and robust to occlusion. The majority of depth maps based methods rely on space time volume features; therefore we discuss this sub-category first, followed by the sequential methods.

2.2.1   Depth Map-Based Space Time Volume Approaches

Li et al. [8] present a study on recognizing human actions from sequences of depth maps. The authors employed the concept of bag-of-points in the expandable graphical model framework to construct the action graph [12] to encode the actions. Each node of the action graph which represents a salient posture is described by a small set of representative 3d points sampled from the depth maps (example depth maps are shown in Figure 2. The key idea is to use a small number of 3d points to characterize the 3d shape of each salient posture and to use a Gaussian Mixture Model to effectively capture the statistical distribution of the points. In terms of 3d points sampling, the paper proposed a simple yet

(a) *Draw tick*   (b) *Tennis serve*

Fig. 2. Examples of the sequences of depth maps for actions in [8]: (a) Draw tick and (b) Tennis serve ©2010 IEEE

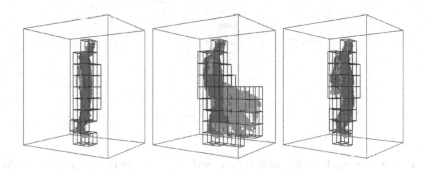

Fig. 3. Examples of the space-time cells of a depth sequence of the action Forward Kick used in [13] ©2010 Springer

effective projection based sampling scheme for sparse sampling from depth maps. Experiments were conducted on the dataset collected by the authors, which is later known as the MSR Action3D Dataset [8]. The results have shown that over 90% recognition accuracy is achieved by only sampling 1% of the 3d points from the depth maps.

One limitation of the approach in [8] is the loss of spatial context information between interest points. Also, due to noise and occlusions in the depth maps, the silhouettes viewed from the side and from the top may not be reliable. This makes it very difficult to robustly sample the interest points given the geometry and motion variations across different persons. To address these issues, Vieira et al. [13] presented a novel feature descriptor, named Space-Time Occupancy Pattens (STOP). The depth sequence is represented in a 4d space-time grid. A saturation scheme is then used to enhance the roles of the sparse cells which typically consist of points on the silhouettes or moving parts of the body. Figure 3 illustrates the space-time cells from a depth sequence of the action Forward Kick. The sequence is divided into three time segments, and each segment contains of about 20 frames. Only the non-empty cells are drawn. The red points are those in the cells that have more than a certain number of points. The accuracy of the STOP features for action classification was shown to be higher in a comparison with [8] on the MSR Action3D Dataset [8].

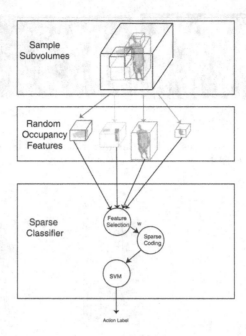

Fig. 4. The framework of the method proposed by [14]. Note that only 3d sub-volumes are shown for illustration. In the real implementation, 4d sub-volumes are used. ©2012 Springer.

Wang et al. [14] also studied the problem of action recognition from depth sequences captured by a single commodity depth camera. In order to address the noise and occlusion issues, the authors treated a three-dimensional action sequence as a 4d shape and proposed Random Occupancy Pattern (ROP) features, which were extracted from randomly sampled 4d sub-volumes with different sizes and at different locations. Since the ROP features are extracted at a larger scale, they are robust to noise. In the meantime, they are less sensitive to occlusion because they encode information from the regions that are most discriminative for the given action. The paper also proposed a weighted random sampling scheme to efficiently explore the large dense sampling space. Sparse coding is employed to further improve the robustness of the proposed method. The general framework of the method proposed in [14] is shown in Figure 4. The authors compared their results against those obtained from [8] and [13] using the MSR Action3D Dataset [8]. Experimental results conclude that [14] outperforms [8] by a large margin ($> 10\%$) and is slightly superior to [13].

Yang et al. [15] developed the so-called Depth Motion Maps (DMM) to capture the aggregated temporal motion energies. More specifically, the depth map is projected onto three pre-defined orthogonal Cartesian planes and then normalized. For each projected map, a binary map is generated by computing and thresholding the difference of two consecutive frames. The binary maps are then summed up to obtain the DMM for each projective view. Histogram of Oriented

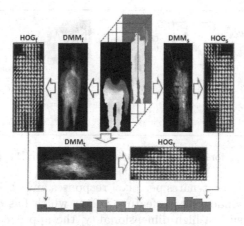

Fig. 5. The framework of the method proposed by [15] ©2012 ACM

Gradients (HOG) is then applied to each view to extract features, and features from three views are concatenated together to form the DMM-HOG descriptors. An SVM classifier is trained on such descriptors for recognition. Compared to many other methods in this category, the computational cost of this approach is relatively low, since HOG is only applied to the final DMM. Evaluations based on the MSR Action3D Dataset [8] showed high recognition rates. However, the hand-crafted projection planes might raise problems related to view-dependency. Their high recognition rate is partly due to the fact that subjects in the MSR-Action3D Dataset mostly face towards the camera. An interesting exploration they performed is to characterize the number of frames required to generate satisfactory recognition results. The conclusion they reached is that only short sub-sequence of roughly 35 frames is sufficient. Nonetheless, the number is in fact largely dependent on the complexity of the actions.

More recently, Oreifej and Liu [11] presented a new descriptor for depth maps. The authors describe the depth video sequence using a histogram capturing the distribution of the surface normal orientation in the 4d volume of time, depth and spatial coordinates. As the depth sequence represents a depth function of space and time, they proposed to capture the observed changing structure using a histogram of oriented 4d surface normals (HON4D). To construct HON4D, the 4d space is initially quantized using the vertices of a regular polychoron. Afterwards, the quantization is refined using a novel discriminative density measure such that additional projectors are induced in the directions where the 4d normals are denser and more discriminative. Figure 6 summarizes the various steps involved in computing the HON4D descriptor. Experimental results from the standard benchmark MSR Action3D Dataset [8] showed that using the proposed HON4D descriptors achieved the state of the art in recognition accuracy.

Rather than using depth maps only, Zhang et al. [16] proposed 4d local spatio-temporal features as the representation of human activities. This 4d feature is a weighted linear combination of a visual component and a geometric component.

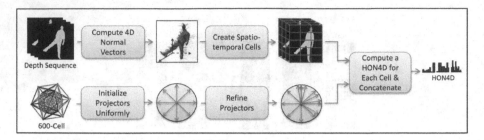

Fig. 6. The steps for computing HON4D descriptor in [11] ©2013 IEEE

This approach then concatenates per-pixel responses and their gradients within a spatial-temporal window into a feature vector which has over 10^5 elements. In order to reduce such a high dimensionality, the approach applies K-means clustering on all feature vectors collected from a training dataset and forms a codebook with 600 vocabularies which is used to code six activity categories: lift, remove, wave, push, walk and signal. In order to predict activities from input videos, the approach formulates this problem as a Latent Dirichlet Allocation (LDA) model where six activity categories are regarded as topics, and codes calculated from 4d features are regarded as words. Gibbs sampling [17] is then adopted for approximate estimation and inference for this high-dimensional model, due to its efficiency. They demonstrated their approach on a self-collected dataset with 198 short video clips, each lasting from 2 to 5 seconds, including 6 activities. Each activity has 33 video clips. The combined features (85.5%) using LDA outperforms features based on intensity (77.67%), demonstrating that depth is an important cue to improve activity recognition accuracy.

Lei et al. [18] also combine depth and color cues, while targeting at recognizing fine-grained kitchen activities. Different from the methods above that are mainly limited to single subject motions, this work demonstrated a successful prototype that tracks the interaction between a human hand and objects in the kitchen, such as mixing flour with water and chopping vegetables. It is shown that the recognition of objects and their state changes through actions is helpful in recognizing very fine-grained kitchen activity from few training samples. The reported system uses object tracking results to study both object and action recognition. For object recognition, the system uses SIFT-like feature from both color and depth data. These features are fed into an SVM to train a classifier. For action recognition, the authors combine a global feature and a local feature. The global feature is defined by PCA on the gradients of 3d hand trajectories since a hand can be tracked using human skin characteristics. The local feature is defined as bag-of-words of snippets of trajectory gradients. The training dataset includes 35 object instances and 28 action instances. Each action instance has only 3 samples compared with 33 in [16]. The reported overall action recognition accuracy is around 82% by combining trajectory-based action recognition with object recognition. This shows that by combining hand-object tracking and object-action recognition, systems like this are capable of identifying and recognizing objects and actions in a real-world kitchen environment with only a

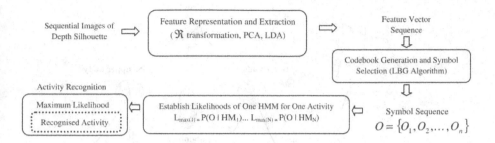

Fig. 7. The flow of the method proposed by Jalal et al. [19] ©2013 SAGE

small dataset. This work is only a proof of concept. Deploying such a system in a real environment requires a larger set of objects and actions, along with variations across people and physical environments that present many challenges not revealed in their work. Nevertheless, there are many possibilities to enhance their system, such as combining multiple sensors including wearable cameras and infrastructure sensors to robustify RGBD cameras in a real world environment.

2.2.2   Depth Maps-Based Sequential Approaches

As mentioned before, local differential operators are not suitable for extracting features from depth maps, resulting in difficulties in extracting reliable temporal correspondences. Therefore only few approaches have explored the possibility of explicitly modeling temporal dynamics from depth maps. This line of research lies in between pure depth map-based methods and skeleton-based methods. They try to design features from which reliable temporal motion can be extracted, while skeletons are one of the most natural features that embed such information.

Inspired by the great success of silhouette based methods developed for visual data, Jalal et al. [19] extract depth silhouettes to construct feature vectors. Figure 7 shows the overall flow of their proposed pipeline. The key idea is to apply $\mathcal{R}$ transform [20] on the depth silhouette to obtain compact shape representation reflecting time-sequential profiles of the activities. PCA is then used for dimension reduction and Linear Discriminant Analysis is adopted to extract most discriminant vectors as in [21]. Similar to most sequential methods for visual data, HMM is utilized for recognition. Experiments were performed on 10 daily home activities collected by the authors, each with 15 video clips. Upon this dataset, a recognition rate of 96.55% was achieved.

Together with the skeleton-based methods that will be studied in Section 2.3, the depth map-based approaches are summarized in Table 2 and Table 3.

2.3   Skeleton-Based Approaches

The study of skeleton-based activity recognition dates back to the early work by Johansson [23], which demonstrated that a large set of actions can be recog-

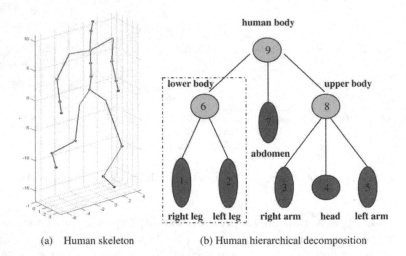

(a)   Human skeleton   (b) Human hierarchical decomposition

Fig. 8. (a) Example of a typical human skeleton used for recognition. (b) Example of a typical hierarchy of human body parts in a tree structure as in [22] ©2010 Elsevier.

nized solely from the joint positions. This concept has been extensively explored ever since. In contrast to the depth maps-based methods, the majority of the skeleton-based methods model temporal dynamics explicitly. One main reason is the natural correspondence of skeletons across time, while this is difficult to establish for general visual and depth data. There are mainly three ways to obtain skeletons: active motion capture (MoCap) systems, monocular or multi-view color images and single view depth maps [24,25]. One difference worth mentioning is the degree of embedded noise. Overall the MoCap data is the cleanest compared to the other two. A multi-view setup is usually adopted for color images, and therefore produces more stable skeleton estimations than those from monocular depth maps. Early methods were mostly tested on MoCap data and skeletons from multi-view image data; while more recent work operates more on noisy skeleton data from monocular depth maps, mainly due to its simple setup. In the following, we first discuss sequential approaches, followed by space time volume approaches.

2.3.1   Skeleton-Based Sequential Approaches

Though we discuss mainly recent research in this study, the seminal work by Campbell and Bobick [26] is still worth mentioning. They represent human actions as curves in low-dimensional phase spaces obtained via projection of 3d joint trajectories. The phase space is defined with each axis being an independent parameter of the body, for example ankle-ankle, or its first derivative. A static pose is interpreted as a point in the phase space, while an action forms a curve. Multiple 2d subspaces are chosen via supervised learning paradigm and the action curves are projected onto these spaces as the action feature. A given actions is projected as a set of points and recognized by verifying whether they are on certain action curves. However, due to their cubic polynomial fitting of the projected curves, only simple movements can be recognized. In particular, they succeeded in recognizing various ballet dance moves. Notice that dynamics are not explicitly considered for their recognition, though such information is embedded in the curve representation. Due to the phase space representation, their method is both view invariant and scale invariant.

Similar to the idea of 2d subspace selection above, Lv et al. [27] designed a set of (spatially) local features based on single joints or combinations of small sets of joints. Their observations suggest that using solely the full pose vector might cause loss of some relevant information and reduce the discriminative power. They consider three types of motions that involve motions of different primary body parts: {*leg+torso, arm, head*}. In the end, they construct a 141 dimensional feature vector from seven types of features including the full pose vector. The skeleton is pre-normalized to avoid dependence on initial body orientation and body size variations. An HMM is built for each feature and action class to model the temporal dynamics. A key novelty of their method is to treat each of the HMM models as a weak classifier and combine them with the multi-class AdaBoost classifier [28] to significantly increase the discriminative power. Besides, they propose a method using dynamic programming to extract from a continuous video the segment that involves an activity considered. They tested their method on two datasets: a set of 1979 MoCap sequences with 243,407 frames in total, collected from the internet, and a set of annotated motion sequences [29]. For the first dataset, they achieved recognition rates of {92.3%, 94.7%, 97.2%} for the three classes of actions separately when half of the data was used as training data, and {88.1%, 91.9%, 94.9%} when the training data was reduced to 1/3. Noticeably, a 30% gain was reached via the use of AdaBoost in this test. A recognition rate of 89.7% was achieved for the second dataset, which is segmented by their proposed method and thus more difficult. Overall their method has achieved promising results with the small classes of actions considered. However, in reality many human actions involve motions of the entire body, such as dancing, and it is not clear how well this method can be generalized to deal with such complex actions.

The recent work by Xia et al. [21] proposed a feature called Histogram of 3d Joint Locations (HOJ3D) that essentially encodes spatial occupancy information relative to the skeleton root, i.e. hip center. Towards this end, they define a modified spherical coordinate system on the hip center and partition the 3d space into n bins, as shown in Figure 9 (a) and (b) respectively. Radial distance is not considered in this spherical coordinate system to make it scale-invariant. Different from other methods that also utilize spatial occupancy information that make binary decision, such as [14] and [9], they perform a probabilistic voting to determine the fractional occupancy, as demonstrated in Figure 9(c). In order to extract dominant features, Linear Discriminant Analysis is applied to reduce the dimensionality from n to (#Class−1). Vector Quantization is performed via K-means to discretize the continuous vectors obtained from the previous step, and discrete HMM is adopted to model the dynamics and recognize actions.

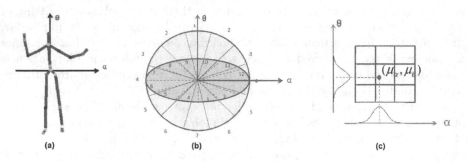

Fig. 9. Reference coordinates of HOJ3D (a) and spherical coordinate system for joint location binning used in [21]. (c) The probabilistic voting for spatial occupancy via a Gaussian weighting function in [21]. ©2012 IEEE.

They tested their approach on both their own dataset and the MSR Action3D dataset [8]. Experiments on the MSR Action3D Dataset [8] showed that their method outperformed [8]. However, the heavy reliance on the hip joint might potentially jeopardize their recognition accuracy, due to the noise embedded in the estimated hip joint location. Currently the estimation of this joint with [25] is not very reliable, especially when the subject is not facing towards the camera.

The above-mentioned methods are mostly limited to single human actions, due to lack of a model of the motion hierarchy. By contrast, Koppula et al. [30,31] explicitly consider human-object interactions. They aimed at joint activity and object affordance labeling from RGBD videos as illustrated in Figure 10. They defined an MRF over the spatio-temporal sequence with two kinds of nodes, namely objects nodes and sub-activity nodes, and edges representing the relationships between object affordances, their relations with sub-activities, and their evolution over time. The explicit modeling of the motion hierarchy enables this method to handle complex activities that involve human-object interactions. Features are defined for both classes of nodes. The object node feature is a vector representing the object's location in the scene and how it changes within the temporal segment including the transformation matrix and displacement of the corresponding points from the SIFT tracker. The sub-activity node feature map gives a vector of features computed using the human skeleton information obtained from a skeleton tracker on RGBD video. By defining the feature vectors, they then train a multi-class SVM classifier on the training data. Given the model parameters, the inference problem is to find the best labeling for the input video. Its equivalent formulation has a linear relaxation which can be solved efficiently using a graph-cut method. Evaluations are conducted based on the Cornell 60 dataset [32] and a new dataset acquired by the authors, named Cornell 120.

Similar to the work of Koppula et al. [30,31], Sung et al. [34,35] also explicitly model the activity hierarchy, however, with a two-layer Maximum Entropy Markov Model (MEMM) [36]. The lower layer nodes of the MEMM represent sub-activities such as "lifting left hand", while higher level nodes represent more

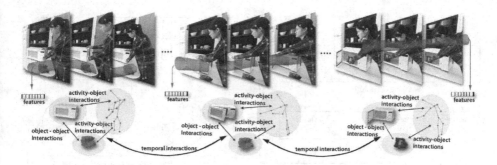

Fig. 10. The MRF graph of [33]. Different types of nodes and relationships modeled in part of the *cleaning objects* activity comprising three sub-activities: reaching, opening and scrubbing. ©2012 IEEE.

general and complex activities such as "pouring water". The features used in their work consist of four components. The first one are body pose features based on joint orientations that are transformed to the local coordinate system of torso to remove view dependency. The angles are represented as quaternions to avoid the well-known gimbal lock phenomenon when using Euler angles. Besides, the angle between each foot and the torso is explicitly emphasized to tell apart sitting poses from standing poses. The second component consists of the positions of the hands relative to the torso and the head, due to the discriminative power of hand positions. The third considers the motion of joints with a temporally sliding window. Besides these skeleton features, they incorporate image and point cloud features as the last component. Specifically, Histogram of Oriented Gradients (HOG) [37] descriptors are used on both RGB and depth data. A key component of their model is dynamic association of the sub-activities with the higher-level activities. In general, they do not assume that the input videos are segmented. Instead, they use GMM to group the training data into clusters that represent sub-activities and utilize the proposed probabilistic model to infer an optimal association of these two layers on-the-fly. Experiments are conducted based on the dataset acquired by the authors.

The work by Wang et al. [9] also utilizes both skeleton and point cloud information. The key idea is that some actions differ mainly due to the objects in interactions, while skeleton information is not sufficient in such cases. Towards this end, they introduced a novel actionlet ensemble model to represent each action and capture the intra-class variance via occupancy information, as illustrated in Figure 11. In terms of skeleton information, one important observation made by them is that the pairwise relative positions of the joints are more discriminative than the joint positions themselves. Interactions between humans and environmental objects are characterized by Local Occupancy Patterns (LOP) at each joint. The LOP features are computed based on the 3d point cloud around a particular joint. The local space of each joint is discretized using a spatial grid as shown in Figure 11. Moreover, they concatenate both feature vectors and apply Short Fourier Transform to obtain the coefficients as

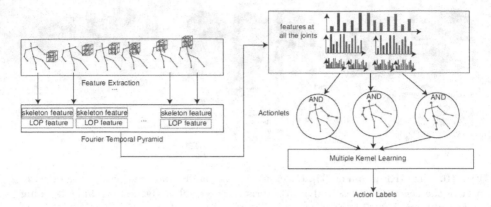

Fig. 11. The actionlet framework proposed by Wang et al. [9] ©2012 IEEE

(a) joint distance   (b) plane   (c) normal plane   (d) velocity   (e) normal velocity

Fig. 12. Relational pose features [38]. (a) Euclidean distance between two joints (red). (b) Distance between a joint (red) and a plane (green) defined by three joints. (c) Distance between a joint (red) and a plane (green) defined by one joint and the normal direction of two joints (black). (d) Velocity of a joint (red) in the direction of two joints (black). (e) Velocity of a joint in normal direction of the plane.

the Fourier Temporal Pyramid features at each joint. The Fourier Temporal Pyramid is insensitive to temporal misalignment and robust to noise, and also can characterize the temporal structure of the actions. An *actionlet* is defined as a conjunctive structure on the base features (Fourier Pyramid features). They learn the discriminative actionlet by iteratively optimizing parameters through a generic SVM solver and obtain an SVM model defining a joint feature map on the data and labels as a linear output function. Once they have training pairs, they employed a mining algorithm to output a discriminative actionlet pool which contains the actionlets meeting the criteria: having a large confidence and a small ambiguity. They evaluated their method using CMU MoCap dataset, MSR Action3D Dataset [8] and a new dataset named MSR Daily Activity 3D. Experiments demonstrated the superior performance of their method compared to other state-of-the-art methods.

A more general approach has been proposed by Yao et al. [38] where skeleton motion is encoded by relational pose features [39], as shown in Figure 12. These features describe geometric relations between specific joints in a single pose or

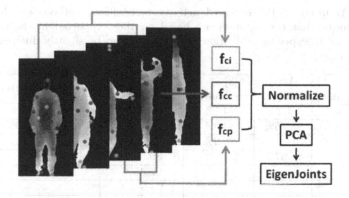

Fig. 13. The EigenJoints features developed by Yang et al. [33] ©2012 IEEE

a short sequence of poses. For action recognition, a Hough forest [40] has been used. Furthermore, a system for coupling the closely intertwined tasks of action recognition and pose estimation is presented. Experiments on a multi-view kitchen dataset [41] indicate that the quality of estimated poses with an average error between 42mm-70mm is sufficient for reliable action recognition.

Similar to the depth maps based category, the sequential methods usually require a larger set of training data. However, the explicit modeling of motion dynamics provide the potential to capture complex and general activities. A major difference is that the dynamics are well defined due to exact semantic definition of joints.

2.3.2   Skeleton-Based Space Time Volume Approaches

The space time volume approaches using skeleton information usually extract global features from the joints, sometimes combined with point cloud data. This line of research is relatively new and only a few methods lie in this category.

Yang et al. [33] developed the EigenJoints features from RGBD sequences as shown in Figure 13. The features include posture features f_{cc}, motion features f_{cp} and offset features f_{ci}. The posture and motion features encode spatial and temporal configuration with pair-wise joint differences in single frames and between consecutive frames, respectively. The offset features represent the difference of a pose with respect to the initial pose with the assumption that the initial pose is generally neutral. They normalize the three channels and apply PCA to reduce redundancy and noise to obtain the EigenJoints descriptor. For classification, they adopt a Naive-Bayes-Nearest-Neighbor (NBNN) classifier due to its simplicity. The video-to-class NN search is accelerated using a KD-tree. Their evaluation on the MSR Action3D dataset [8] demonstrated the effectiveness of their approach. One limitation of their method is the assumption about the initial pose. It is not clear how this assumption affects the recognition accuracy in a more general context.

Table 2. Accuracy of the reviewed activity recognition methods on the popular datasets. Notice that the numbers are based on those reported in the corresponding papers and the specific evaluation methodology can be slightly different even for the same dataset.

| | MSR Action 3D [8] | | | Gesture3D [10] | MSR Daily Activity 3D [9] |
	$\frac{1}{3}$ training	$\frac{2}{3}$ training	cross subject		
[8]	91.36%	94.2%	74.7%	-	-
[13]	96.8%	98.25%	84.8%	-	-
[14]	-	-	86.2%	88.5%	-
[15]	95.83%	97.37%	91.63%	89.20%	-
[11]	-	-	88.89%	92.45%	80%
[16]	-	-	-	-	-
[18]	-	-	-	-	-
[19]	95.8%	97.78%	91.63%	-	-
[26]	-	-	-	-	-
[27]	-	-	-	-	-
[21]	96.2%	97.15%	78.97%	-	-
[30,31]	-	-	-	-	-
[34,35]	-	-	-	-	-
[9]	-	-	88.2%	-	85.75%
[38]	-	-	-	-	-
[33]	95.8%	97.77%	82.33%	-	-

2.4 Summary

A summary of the methods reviewed above, both depth maps-based and skeleton-based, are presented in Table 3. Since all the reviewed methods are capable of dealing with both gestures and actions, only the capability of handling interactions is enumerated. The accuracy of the reviewed methods on the popular datasets are summarized in Table 2. Originally, Wang et al [8] performed three set of tests on the MSR Action 3D Dataset. The first two use one third and two thirds of the data for training, respectively, while the last one was designed for a cross-subject test. This evaluation method is adopted by most of the works that follow, as can be seen in the table. As the MSR Daily Activity Dataset is relatively new, not many methods were evaluated on it. The methods that were not evaluated on these datasets generally performed evaluations on other datasets that are not listed here.

In conclusion, with the excellent opportunities provided by the low-cost depth sensors for activity recognition, promising results have been achieved as evidenced in recent research work. The unique characteristics of the depth sensor data inspire the researchers to investigate effective and efficient approaches for this task, partly based on the traditional work on regular visual data. One line of ongoing research attempts to design more discriminative and meanwhile compact feature vectors from depth and skeleton data to describe human activities. Another possible direction is to extend the current methods to deal with more complicated activities, such as interactions or group activities. In this case, existing works that operate on regular visual data might provide some good insights [4].

Table 3. Summary of methods for action recognition based on data from depth sensors. Here "Seq" refers to "Sequential", "STV" refers to "Space Time Volume" and "Skel" means "Skeleton".

	Taxonomy	Features	Representation	Classifier	View-invariant	Scale-invariant	Interactions
[8]	Depth+STV	Bag of 3d points	2d Projection	Action graph	yes	yes	no
[13]	Depth+STV	STOP	PCA	Action graph	yes	yes	no
[14]	Depth+STV	ROP	Sparse Coding	SVM	yes	yes	no
[15]	Depth+STV	DMM + HOG		SVM	no	yes	no
[11]	Depth+STV	HON4D	Histogram	SVM	yes	yes	no
[16]	Depth+STV	4d Local Spatio-Temporal Features	PCA	Latent Dirichlet Allocation	no	no	yes
[18]	Depth+STV	SIFT-like	PCA + Bag of Words	SVM	no	no	yes
[19]	Depth+Seq	Depth silhouettes + $\mathcal{R}$ Transform		HMM	no	yes	no
[26]	Skel+Seq	3d joint trajectories	Projection in phase spaces	Similar to NN	yes	yes	no
[27]	Skel+Seq	Poses of single and multiple joints		HMM + AdaBoost	yes	yes	no
[21]	Skel+Seq	HOJ3D	Linear Discriminant Analysis	HMM	yes	yes	no
[30,31]	Skel+Seq	Object and Pose features		Multi-class SVM	no	no	yes
[34,35]	Skel+Seq	Pose features + HOG		MEMM	yes	yes	no
[9]	Skel+Seq	LOP	Actionlet	SVM	yes	yes	yes
[38]	Skel+Seq	Relational Pose Features		Hough Forest	yes	yes	no
[33]	Skel+STV	EigenJoints	PCA	NBNN	yes	yes	no

3   Face Motion

Human motion analysis is not restricted to full body motion, but can also be applied to body parts like the face or the hands. In this section, we give an overview of different approaches that capture head or facial motion at different levels of details; see Figures 14, 18 and 19. The lowest level estimates the head pose only, i.e., location and orientation of the head. Approaches for head pose estimation are discussed in Section 3.1. Facial feature points or low-resolution shape models provide more information and are often extracted for applications like face recognition, speech recognition or analysis of facial expressions. While Section 3.2 discusses works for extracting facial feature points, Section 3.3 discusses methods that aim at capturing all details of facial motion. The latter is mainly used in the context of facial animations. Parts of this section appeared in [42].

3.1   Head Pose Estimation

With application ranging from face recognition to driver drowsiness detection, automatic head pose estimation is an important problem. Since the survey [43] gives already an excellent overview of approaches until the year 2007, we focus on more recent approaches for head pose estimation that appeared in 2007 or later. Although the focus is head pose estimation from depth data, we give a broader view that also includes methods that estimate the head pose from RGB data like images or videos. Methods based on 2d images can be subdivided into appearance-based and feature-based approaches, depending on whether they analyze the face as a whole or instead rely on the localization of some specific facial features for head pose estimation.

3.1.1   RGB Appearance-Based Methods

Appearance-based methods usually discretize the head pose space and learn separate detectors for subsets of poses [44,45]. Chen et al. [46] and Balasubramanian et al. [47] present head pose estimation systems with a specific focus on the mapping from the high-dimensional space of facial appearance to the lower-dimensional manifold of head poses. The latter work considers face images with varying poses as lying on a smooth low-dimensional manifold in a high-dimensional feature space. The proposed Biased Manifold Embedding uses the pose angle information of the face images to compute a biased neighborhood of each point in the feature space, prior to determining the low-dimensional embedding. In the same vein, Osadchy et al. [48] instead use a convolutional network to learn the mapping, achieving real-time performance for the face detection problem, while also providing an estimate of the head pose. A very popular family of methods use statistical models of the face shape and appearance, like Active Appearance Models (AAMs) [49], multi-view AAMs [50] and 3d Morphable Models [51,52]. Such methods, however, focus more on tracking facial features rather than estimating the head pose. In this context, the authors of [53] coupled an Active Appearance Model with the POSIT algorithm for head pose tracking.

3.1.2   RGB Feature-Based Methods

Feature-based methods rely on some specific facial features to be visible, and therefore are sensitive to occlusions and to large head rotations. Vatahska et al. [54] use a face detector to roughly classify the pose as frontal, left, or right profile. After this, they detect the eyes and nose tip using AdaBoost classifiers. Finally, the detections are fed into a neural network which estimates the head orientation. Similarly, Whitehill et al. [55] present a discriminative approach to frame-by-frame head pose estimation. Their algorithm relies on the detection of the nose tip and both eyes, thereby limiting the recognizable poses to the ones where both eyes are visible. Morency et al. [56] propose a probabilistic framework called Generalized Adaptive View-based Appearance Model integrating frame-by-frame head pose estimation, differential registration and keyframe tracking.

3.1.3   Head Pose Estimation from Depth or 3D

In general, approaches relying solely on 2d images are sensitive to illumination changes and lack of distinctive features. Moreover, the annotation of head poses from 2d images is intrinsically problematic. Since 3d sensing devices have become available, computer vision researchers have started to leverage the additional depth information for solving some of the inherent limitations of image-based methods. Some of the recent works thus use depth as primary cue [57] or in addition to 2d images [58,59,60].

Seemann et al. [60] presented a neural network-based system fusing skin color histograms and depth information. It tracks at 10 fps but requires the face to be detected in a frontal pose in the first frame of the sequence. The approach in [61] uses head pose estimation only as a pre-processing step to face recognition, and the low reported average errors are only calculated on faces of subjects that belong to the training set. Still in a tracking framework, Morency et al. [59] use instead intensity and depth input images to build a prior model of the face using 3d view-based eigenspaces. Then, they use this model to compute the absolute difference in pose for each new frame. The pose range is limited and manual cropping is necessary. In [58], a 3d face model is aligned to an RGB-depth input stream for tracking features across frames, taking into account the very noisy nature of depth measurements coming from commercial sensors.

Considering instead pure detectors on a frame-by-frame basis, Lu and Jain [62] create hypotheses for the nose position in range images based on directional maxima. For verification, they compute the nose profile using PCA and a curvature-based shape index. Breitenstein et al. [57] presented a real-time system working on range scans provided by the scanner of [63]. Their system can handle large pose variations, facial expressions and partial occlusions, as long as the nose remains visible. Their method relies on several candidate nose positions, suggested by a geometric descriptor. Such hypotheses are all evaluated in parallel on a GPU, which compares them to renderings of a generic template with different orientations. Finally the orientation which minimizes a predefined cost function is selected. Breitenstein et al. also collected a dataset of over 10k annotated range scans of heads. The subjects, both male and female, with and without glasses, were recorded using the scanner of [63] while turning their heads around, trying to span all possible yaw and pitch rotation angles they could. The scans were semi-automatically annotated by a template-based tracking approach for head pose estimation [64] as illustrated in Figure 14. The tracker requires a user-specific head model that has

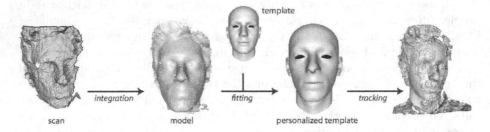

Fig. 14. Head pose tracking with a head template [64]. A user turns the head in front of the depth sensor, the scans are integrated into a point cloud model [69] and a generic template is fit to it using graph-based non-rigid ICP [70]. The personalized template is used for rigid tracking.

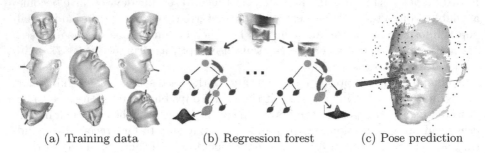

   (a) Training data   (b) Regression forest   (c) Pose prediction

Fig. 15. Head pose estimation with regression forests [66]. (a) A head model is used to generate a large set of training data. (b) Based on the training data, a forest of regression trees is trained. Each tree takes a depth patch as input and regresses the pose parameters. (c) The regressed values of each patch can be considered as votes for the pose parameters. The final estimate is obtained by mean-shift.

been acquired before recording the dataset. The same authors also extended their system to use lower quality depth images from a stereo system [65].

While GPUs allow the evaluation of many hypotheses in real-time, they are not available for embedded systems where power consumption matters. In order to achieve real-time performance without the need of a GPU and to be robust to occlusions, a random forests framework for head pose estimation from depth data has been employed in [66]. The approach is illustrated in Figure 15. In [67], the approach has been further extended to handle noisy sensor data and a dataset with annotated head pose has been collected. The dataset comprises 24 sequences of 20 different subjects (14 men and 6 women, 4 subjects with glasses) that move their heads while sitting about 1 meter away from a Kinect sensor. Some examples of the dataset are shown in Figure 16. The biggest advantage of depth data for head pose estimation in comparison to 2d data is the simplicity of generating an abundance of training data with perfect ground truth. In [66], depth images of head poses are synthetically generated by rendering the 3d morphable model of [68].

Fig. 16. Database for benchmarking head pose estimation from depth data [67]. The green cylinder represents the estimated head pose, while the red one encodes the ground truth.

3.2 Facial Feature Detection

3.2.1 Facial Feature Detection from 2D Data

Facial feature detection from standard images is a well studied problem, often performed as preprocessing for face recognition. Previous contributions can be classified into two categories, depending on whether they use global or local features. Holistic methods, e.g., Active Appearance Models [49,71,72], use the entire facial texture to fit a generative model to a test image. As discussed in Section 3.1, they can also be used for head pose estimation. They are usually affected by lighting changes and a bias towards the average face. The complexity of the modeling is an additional issue. Moreover, these methods perform poorly on unseen identities [73] and cannot handle low-resolution images well.

In recent years, there has been a shift towards methods based on independent local feature detectors [74,75,76,77]. These detectors are discriminative models of image patches centered around facial landmarks. To improve accuracy and reduce the influence of inaccurate detections and false positives, global models of the facial features configuration like pictorial structures [78,79] or Active Shape Models [80] can be used.

3.2.2 Facial Feature Detection from 3D Data

Similar to the 2d case, methods focusing on facial feature localization from range data can be subdivided into categories using global or local information. Among the former class, the authors of [81] deform a bi-linear face model to match a scan of an unseen face in different expressions. Yet, the paper's focus is not on the localization of facial feature points and real-time performance is not achieved. Also Kakadiaris et al. [82] non-rigidly align an annotated model to face meshes. However, constraints need to be imposed on the initial face orientation. Using high quality range scans, Weise et al. [83] presented a real-time system that is capable of tracking facial motion in detail, but requires personalized templates. The same approach has been extended to robustly track head pose and facial deformations using RGB-depth streams provided by commercial sensors like the Kinect [64].

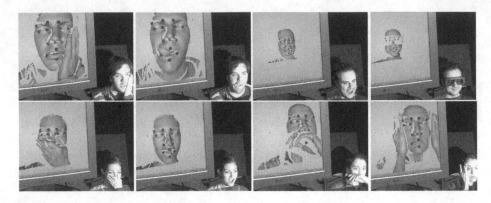

Fig. 17. Real-time facial feature localization using depth from a structured light system as input [42]

Most works that try to directly localize specific feature points from 3d data take advantage of surface curvatures. For example, the authors of [84,85,86] all use curvature to roughly localize the inner corners of the eyes. Such an approach is very sensitive to missing depth data, particularly for the regions around the inner eye corners that are frequently occluded by shadows. Also, Mehryar et al. [87] use surface curvatures by first extracting ridge and valley points, which are then clustered. The clusters are refined using a geometric model imposing a set of distance and angle constraints on the arrangement of candidate landmarks. Colbry et al. [88] use curvature in conjunction with the Shape Index proposed by [89] to locate facial feature points from range scans of faces. The reported execution time of this anchor point detector is 15 seconds per frame. Wang et al. [90] use point signatures [91] and Gabor filters to detect some facial feature points from 3d and 2d data. The method needs all desired landmarks to be visible, thus restricting the range of head poses while being sensitive to occlusions. Yu et al. [92] use genetic algorithms to combine several weak classifiers into a 3d facial landmark detector. Fanelli et al. [42] proposed a real-time system that relies on random forests for localizing fiducials. The system is shown in Figure 17. Ju et al. [93] detect the nose tip and the eyes using binary neural networks, and propose a 3d shape descriptor invariant to pose and expression.

The authors of [94] propose a 3d Statistical Facial Feature Model (SFAM), which models both the global variations in the morphology of the face and the local structures around the landmarks. The low reported errors for the localization of 15 points in scans of neutral faces come at the expense of processing time: over 10 minutes are needed to process one facial scan. In [95], fitting the proposed PCA shape model containing only the upper facial features, i.e., without the mouth, takes on average 2 minutes per face.

For evaluating facial feature detectors on depth data, there are two datasets available. *BU3DFE* [97] contains 100 subjects (56 females and 44 males) posing six basic expressions plus neutral in front of a 3d face scanner. Each of the six prototypic expressions (happiness, disgust, fear, angry, surprise and sadness)

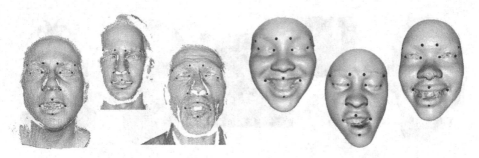

Fig. 18. Successfully localized facial features using the approach [42] on some test scans from the $B3D(AC)^2$ database [96] (left) and the $BU3DFE$ dataset [97] (right)

includes four levels of intensity, i.e., there are 25 static 3d expression models for each subject, resulting in a total of 2500 faces. Each face is annotated with 83 facial points. $B3D(AC)^2$ [96] comprises over 120k depth images and includes 14 subjects, 8 females and 6 males, repeating sentences from 40 movie sequences, both in a neutral and in an induced emotional state.

3.3 Facial Performance Capture

Facial performance capture goes beyond simple shape models or feature point detection and aims at capturing the full geometry of the face, mainly for facial animations. A typical application is performance-based facial animation where the non-rigid surface of the face is tracked and the motion is transferred to a virtual face [98,99]. Most of the work has focused so far on the acquisition of high-quality data using structured light systems [100,101,102,103,104] or passive multi-camera systems [105,106,101,107] in controlled setups. These methods propose different acquisition setups that are optimized for acquisition time, acquisition accuracy, or budget.

There are a few works that go beyond capturing facial motion in studio environments. The approach [108] uses a time-of-flight camera to estimate a few basic facial action units based on the Facial Action Coding System (FACS). The method fits a high-resolution statistical 3d expression morph model to the noisy depth data by an iterative closest point algorithm and regresses the action units from the fitted model. The method [83] achieves real-time performance-based facial animation by generating a user-specific facial expression model offline. During tracking the PCA components of the expression model are estimated and transferred to a PCA model of a target face in real-time. In [64], a robust method based on user-specific blendshapes has been proposed for real-time facial performance capture and animation. In contrast to most other works for facial animation, the approach also works with noisy depth data. The approach is illustrated in Figure 19.

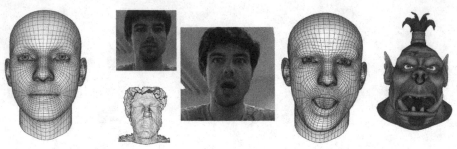

(a) Model generation   (b) Real-time capture and facial animation

Fig. 19. (a) Data from a depth sensor is used to build a user-specific blendshape model. (b) Having build the model, the motion can be transferred to a virtual head in real-time. ©2013 Faceshift AG http://www.faceshift.com.

3.4 Summary

Capturing facial motion from depth data has progressed fast in the last years and several real-time systems for different applications have been developed. While for some applications head pose estimation might be sufficient, more details like facial feature points, facial action units, or full geometry can be captured. Interestingly, the richer output does not necessarily require much higher computational cost, still allowing real-time performance, but it requires more effort for acquiring training data or an additional offline acquisition process, e.g., to acquire a user-specific model. While the discussed methods already perform well in terms of runtime and accuracy, there is further room for improving the accuracy without compromising runtime. For evaluation, several datasets have been released as shown in Table 4. Although each dataset has been recorded for a specific task like head pose estimation [57,42], facial expression recognition [97,109,110], face recognition [111,112,113], or audiovisual speech recognition [96], they can be also used for benchmarking methods for other tasks. Current datasets and methods assume that the head is clearly visible, the handling of crowded scenes for instance with many faces has not been addressed so far.

4   Hand Motion

Capturing the motion of hands shares many similarities with full body pose estimation. However, hands impose some additional challenges like uniform skin color, very large pose variations and severe occlusions that are even difficult to resolve from depth data. Since hands interact with other hands or objects nearly all the time, capturing hand motion is still a very challenging task. Parts of this section appeared in [114].

4.1   Hand Pose Estimation

In the survey [115], various methods for hand pose estimation have been reviewed in the context of human-computer interaction. We also follow the taxonomy used

Table 4. Datasets for evaluating depth-based approaches for head pose estimation and facial feature detection

Dataset	Annotation	Data	Subjects
ETH Face Pose Range Image [57]	head pose	10k depth	20
Biwi Kinect Head Pose [42]	head pose	15k RGBD	20
Binghamton 3D Facial Expression [97]	6 facial expressions, 3 facial points	3k 3d models	100
Bosphorus Database [109]	24 facial points, FACS	5k 3d models	105
3D Dynamic Facial Expression [110]	6 facial expressions, 83 facial points	60k 3d models	101
Texas 3D Face Recognition [111]	25 facial points	1k RGBD	105
Biwi 3D Audiovisual Corpus [96]	face model, emotions, segmented speech	120k RGBD	14
UMB 3D Face [112]	7 facial points	1k RGBD	143
EURECOM Kinect Face [113]	6 facial points	1k RGBD	52

in [115] that splits the approaches in discriminative methods that use classification or regression to estimate the hand pose from image data and generative methods that use a hand model to recover the hand pose.

The model-based approaches mainly differ in the used cues and techniques for solving the problem. The most commonly used image features are silhouettes and edges, but also other cues like shading, color, or optical flow have been used [115]. For instance, edges, optical flow and shading information have been combined in [116] for articulated hand tracking. In [117], a method based on texture and shading has been proposed. A very important cue is depth [118,119] that has been recently revisited in the context of depth sensors [120].

In order to recover the hand pose based on some cues, several techniques have been proposed. One of the first methods for 3d hand pose estimation used local optimization [121], which is still a very popular method due to its efficiency, but it also requires a careful design of the objective function to avoid that the method gets stuck in local minima [114,117]. Other methods rely on filtering techniques like Kalman filter [122] or particle filter [123]. While particle filtering and local stochastic optimization have been combined in [119] to improve the performance of filtering techniques in the high-dimensional space of hand poses, [124,125] proposed to reduce the pose space by using linear subspaces. The methods, however, considered only very few hand poses. Other methods rely on belief propagation [126,127] or particle swarm optimization [128].

Depending on the method, the used hand models also differ as shown in Figure 20. The highest accuracy is achieved with user-specific hand models, e.g., [114,130]. These models need to be acquired offline, similar to user-specific head models, but anatomical properties like fix limb length are retained during tracking. More flexible are graphical models that connect limbs modeled by shape primitives and use often Gaussian distributions to model the allowed distance of two limbs, e.g., [126,127]. For each limb a likelihood is computed and the best hand configuration is inferred from the graphical model connecting the

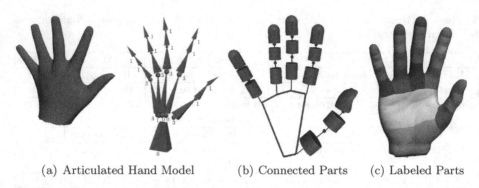

(a) Articulated Hand Model   (b) Connected Parts   (c) Labeled Parts

Fig. 20. Different models for hand pose estimation: (a) Detailed 3d mesh with underlying skeleton [114] (b) Connected body parts [127] (c) Labeled surface for training a body part detector [129]

limbs. A hand model based on a self-organizing map [131] is discussed in the chapter *Gesture Interfaces with Depth Sensors*.

Discriminative approaches like [132,133,134] do not require an explicit hand model, but learn a mapping from image features to hand poses from a large set of training data. Although these methods process the frames independently, temporal consistency can be enforced [135,136,137]. While discriminative methods can recover from errors, the accuracy and type of hand poses that can be handled depends on the training data. Discriminative approaches that process the full hand are therefore not suitable for applications that require accurate hand poses of a-priori unknown actions. However, instead of learning a mapping for the full hand, also a mapping only for body parts can be learned [129] as shown in Figure 20(c). Breaking the hand into parts has the advantage that a larger variation of poses can be handled. Similar approaches have been successfully applied to human pose [3] or head pose estimation [66].

Recently, the focus has been on hand motion capture in the context of interactions. [127] has considered hand tracking from depth data in the context of object manipulation. While the objects were originally treated as occluders, [139] proposed to learn an object dependent hand pose prior to assist tracking. The method assumes that object manipulations of similar objects have been previously observed for training and exploits contact points and geometry of the objects. Such dependencies can also be used to create hand animations [140,141] as shown in Figure 21. In the context of object grasping, a database of 10 000 hand poses with and without grasped objects has been created to recover the hand pose from images using nearest neighbor search [136]. Recently, it has been proposed to track the manipulated object and the hand at the same time to constrain the search space using collision constraints [142]. The object is assumed to be a shape primitive like a cylinder, ellipsoid or box whose parameters are estimated. In [130], particle swarm optimization (PSO) has been applied to hand tracking of two interacting hands from depth data.

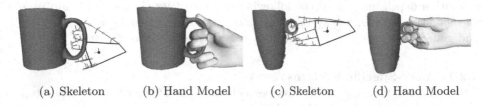

| (a) Skeleton | (b) Hand Model | (c) Skeleton | (d) Hand Model |

Fig. 21. The relations between hands and object classes can be modeled to synthesize hand poses or hand-object animations [138].

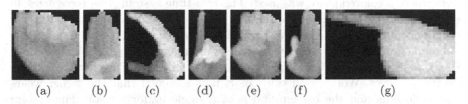

| (a) | (b) | (c) | (d) | (e) | (f) | (g) |

Fig. 22. Alphabet *(A-G)* of the American sign language captured with a ToF camera

Instead of using off-the-shelf depth sensors, some approaches have focused on the sensor design in the context of human-computer interaction (HCI) applications. For instance, Leap Motion[1] developed a controller that allows to capture the motion of finger tips with high accuracy. While the volume that can be captured by the controller is very small, a wrist-worn sensor for hand pose estimation has been proposed in [143]. In [144], RGBD data is used to improve a marker-based system. A more detailed overview of approaches for HCI, including commercial systems, is given in the chapter *Gesture Interfaces with Depth Sensors*.

4.2   Hand Gesture Recognition

Even if the resolution of the hands is too small to estimate the full articulated hand, the gesture of the hand can still be estimated given a suitable training set. In this section, we give an overview of different methods for recognizing hand gestures, in particular letters of a sign language, as shown in Figure 22. Parts of this section appeared in [140].

Recognizing signs of visual-gestural languages like the American sign language (ASL) is a very active field [145,146,147,148,149,150,151]. For instance, the Sign-Speak project [152] aims at developing vision-based technology for translating continuous sign language to text. It is also related to gesture recognition from depth data and optional color data [153,154,155,156,157,158,159,160,161,162], which is discussed in the chapter *Gesture Interfaces with Depth Sensors*. While for gesture recognition usually only a small set of distinctive gestures are used, the letters of a sign language are pre-defined and not very distinctive in low

---

[1] http://www.leapmotion.com

resolution depth images. In the following, we structure the methods into user-specific systems, i.e., the systems are trained and designed for a specific user, and general systems, i.e., the user does not provide any training data:

4.2.1 User-Specific Systems

Polish finger alphabet symbols have been classified in [163] with an off-line setup. The input for each of the considered 23 gestures consisted of a gray-scale image at a relatively high resolution and depth data acquired by a stereo setup. In [164], a real-time recognition system has been developed for Spanish sign language letters where a colored glove was used. The real-time system [165] recognizes 46 gestures including symbols of the ASL. It assumes constant lighting conditions for training and testing and uses a wristband and special background for accurate hand segmentation. More recently, British sign language finger spelling has been investigated in [166] where the specialty is that both hands are involved in the 26 static gestures. Working on skin color, it is assumed that the signer wears suitable clothing and the background is of a single uniform color. The system recognizes also spelled words contained in a pre- defined lexicon.

4.2.2 General Systems

Using a stereo camera to acquire 3d and color data, Takimoto et al. [160] proposed a method for recognizing 41 Japanese sign language characters. Data was acquired from 20 test subjects and the achieved classifier runtime is about 3 frames per second. Although the approach does not require special background or lighting conditions, segmenting the hand, which is a challenging task by itself, is greatly simplified by the use of a black wristband. Colored gloves have been used in [167] for recognizing 23 symbols of the Irish sign language in real-time. A method for recognizing the ASL finger alphabet off-line has been proposed in [168]. Input data was acquired in front of a white background and the hand bounding box was defined for each image manually. A similar setup has been used in [169]. In [140], a method based on average neighborhood margin maximization has been proposed that recognizes the ASL finger alphabet from low-resolution depth data in real-time.

The methods are summarized in Table 5.

4.3 Summary

In contrast to activity recognition and facial motion capture, there is a lack of publicly available datasets for benchmarking and comparing methods for hand pose estimation. Even for RGB data, there are very few datasets that provide ground-truth data [170]. While many depth datasets have been used for hand gesture recognition or recognizing finger alphabet symbols, there is no dataset available that has been consistently used. As shown in Table 5, many methods use a different number of gestures or recording setups. In order to evaluate the progress in this area, publicly available datasets with ground-truth data are needed.

Table 5. Overview of methods for recognizing hand gestures

Method	# of Gest.	Setup	Depth	Resolution	Markers	Real-time
[165]	46	user-specific	no	320x240	wristband	yes
[159]	11	user-specific	yes	160x120		yes
[163]	23	user-specific	yes	320x240 768x576(gray)	black long sleeve	no
[164]	19	user-specific	no		colored glove	yes
[162]	6	user-specific	yes	176x144 640x480(rgb)		yes
[140]	26	user-specific	yes	176x144		yes
[157]	12	general	yes	160x120		yes
[158]	6	general	yes	176x144		yes
[156]	5	general	yes	176x144		yes
[160]	41	general	yes	320x240 1280x960(rgb)	wristband	no
[167]	23	general	no		color glove	yes
[168]	26	general	no		bounding box	no
[169]	26	general	no		bounding box	no
[140]	26	general	yes	176x144		yes

5   Conclusion

Over the last years, a significant progress has been made in the field of human motion analysis from depth data. The success is attested by commercial systems that estimate full body poses for computer games, hand poses for gesture interfaces, or capture detailed head motions for facial animations. It is expected that more approaches in the field will make the transition from the lab to a business. The main advantages of developing applications for depth sensors compared to purely 2d color sensors are (i) the better robustness to lighting conditions, at least in indoor environments, (ii) the resolved scale-distance ambiguity of 2d sensors, making it easier to develop real-time algorithms, (iii) the possibility to synthesize an abundance of training data. Nevertheless, there are still many research challenges that need to be addressed and that cannot be resolved by improving only the data quality provided by the sensors. So far, the most successful approaches for capturing full body motion or specific body parts like hands or the head assume that the subjects are within a specific distance range to the sensor. Dealing with a larger range of distances, however, requires to smoothly blend between analyzing full body motion and the motion of body parts. If the person is far away from the sensor, full body motion can be better analyzed than facial motion. As soon as the person gets closer to the sensor, only parts of the person remain visible and motion analysis is limited to the upper body, hands, or the face. For some applications, even all aspects of human body language need to be taken into account to understand the intend of the user. In sign languages, for instance, it is not only hand gestures that matter, but also the motion of the arms, facial expressions and the movements of the lips. Bringing all these components of motion analysis together, which have been mainly addressed independently, is a big challenge for the future. Another challenge is motion analysis in the context of crowded scenes and interactions. While first approaches address the problem of human-human or human-object interactions, more work needs to be done in this area to achieve performances that are good enough for real-world applications.

References

1. Klette, R., Tee, G.: Understanding human motion: A historic review. In: Rosenhahn, B., Klette, R., Metaxas, D. (eds.) Human Motion. Computational Imaging and Vision, vol. 36, pp. 1–22. Springer, Netherlands (2008)
2. Aggarwal, J.: Motion analysis: Past, present and future. In: Bhanu, B., Ravishankar, C.V., Roy-Chowdhury, A.K., Aghajan, H., Terzopoulos, D. (eds.) Distributed Video Sensor Networks, pp. 27–39. Springer, London (2011)
3. Shotton, J., Fitzgibbon, A., Cook, M., Sharp, T., Finocchio, M., Moore, R., Kipman, A., Blake, A.: Real-time human pose recognition in parts from single depth images. In: IEEE Conference on Computer Vision and Pattern Recognition (2011)
4. Aggarwal, J., Ryoo, M.: Human activity analysis: A review. ACM Computing Surveys 43(2), 16:1–16:43 (2011)
5. Mitra, S., Acharya, T.: Gesture recognition: A survey. IEEE Transactions on Systems, Man, and Cybernetics, Part C: Applications and Reviews 37(3), 311–324 (2007)
6. Moeslund, T.B., Hilton, A., Krüger, V.: A survey of advances in vision-based human motion capture and analysis. Computer Vision and Image Understanding 104(2), 90–126 (2006)
7. Poppe, R.: A survey on vision-based human action recognition. Image and Vision Computing 28(6), 976–990 (2010)
8. Li, W., Zhang, Z., Liu, Z.: Action recognition based on a bag of 3d points. In: Workshop on Human Activity Understanding from 3D Data, pp. 9–14 (2010)
9. Wang, J., Liu, Z., Wu, Y., Yuan, J.: Mining actionlet ensemble for action recognition with depth cameras. In: IEEE Conference on Computer Vision and Pattern Recognition, pp. 1290–1297 (2012)
10. Kurakin, A., Zhang, Z., Liu, Z.: A real time system for dynamic hand gesture recognition with a depth sensor. In: 2012 Proceedings of the 20th European Signal Processing Conference (EUSIPCO), pp. 1975–1979 (2012)
11. Oreifej, O., Liu, Z.: Hon4d: Histogram of oriented 4d normals for activity recognition from depth sequences. In: IEEE Conference on Computer Vision and Pattern Recognition (2013)
12. Li, W., Zhang, Z., Liu, Z.: Expandable data-driven graphical modeling of human actions based on salient postures. IEEE Transactions on Circuits and Systems for Video Technology 18(11), 1499–1510 (2008)
13. Vieira, A.W., Nascimento, E.R., Oliveira, G.L., Liu, Z., Campos, M.F.M.: STOP: Space-time occupancy patterns for 3D action recognition from depth map sequences. In: Alvarez, L., Mejail, M., Gomez, L., Jacobo, J. (eds.) CIARP 2012. LNCS, vol. 7441, pp. 252–259. Springer, Heidelberg (2012)
14. Wang, J., Liu, Z., Chorowski, J., Chen, Z., Wu, Y.: Robust 3D action recognition with random occupancy patterns. In: Fitzgibbon, A., Lazebnik, S., Perona, P., Sato, Y., Schmid, C. (eds.) ECCV 2012, Part II. LNCS, vol. 7573, pp. 872–885. Springer, Heidelberg (2012)

15. Yang, X., Zhang, C., Tian, Y.: Recognizing actions using depth motion maps-based histograms of oriented gradients. In: ACM International Conference on Multimedia, pp. 1057–1060 (2012)
16. Zhang, H., Parker, L.: 4-dimensional local spatio-temporal features for human activity recognition. In: International Conference on Intelligent Robots and Systems, pp. 2044–2049 (2011)
17. Griffiths, T.L., Steyvers, M.: Finding scientific topics. Proceedings of the National Academy of Sciences of the United States of America 101(suppl. 1), 5228–5235 (2004)
18. Lei, J., Ren, X., Fox, D.: Fine-grained kitchen activity recognition using rgb-d. In: ACM Conference on Ubiquitous Computing (2012)
19. Jalal, A., Uddin, M.Z., Kim, J.T., Kim, T.S.: Recognition of human home activities via depth silhouettes and transformation for smart homes. Indoor and Built Environment 21(1), 184–190 (2011)
20. Wang, Y., Huang, K., Tan, T.: Human activity recognition based on r transform. In: IEEE Conference on Computer Vision and Pattern Recognition, pp. 1–8 (2007)
21. Xia, L., Chen, C.C., Aggarwal, J.: View invariant human action recognition using histograms of 3d joints. In: Workshop on Human Activity Understanding from 3D Data, pp. 20–27 (2012)
22. Han, L., Wu, X., Liang, W., Hou, G., Jia, Y.: Discriminative human action recognition in the learned hierarchical manifold space. Image and Vision Computing 28(5), 836–849 (2010)
23. Johansson, G.: Visual motion perception. Scientific American (1975)
24. Ye, M., Wang, X., Yang, R., Ren, L., Pollefeys, M.: Accurate 3d pose estimation from a single depth image. In: IEEE International Conference on Computer Vision, pp. 731–738 (2011)
25. Criminisi, A., Shotton, J., Robertson, D., Konukoglu, E.: Regression forests for efficient anatomy detection and localization in CT studies. In: Menze, B., Langs, G., Tu, Z., Criminisi, A. (eds.) MICCAI 2010. LNCS, vol. 6533, pp. 106–117. Springer, Heidelberg (2011)
26. Campbell, L., Bobick, A.: Recognition of human body motion using phase space constraints. In: IEEE International Conference on Computer Vision, pp. 624–630 (1995)
27. Lv, F., Nevatia, R.: Recognition and segmentation of 3-D human action using HMM and multi-class adaBoost. In: Leonardis, A., Bischof, H., Pinz, A. (eds.) ECCV 2006. LNCS, vol. 3954, pp. 359–372. Springer, Heidelberg (2006)
28. Freund, Y., Schapire, R.E.: A decision-theoretic generalization of on-line learning and an application to boosting. Journal of Computer and System Sciences 55(1), 119–139 (1997)
29. Lee, M.W., Nevatia, R.: Dynamic human pose estimation using markov chain monte carlo approach. In: IEEE Workshops on Application of Computer Vision, pp. 168–175 (2005)
30. Koppula, H.S., Gupta, R., Saxena, A.: Human activity learning using object affordances from rgb-d videos. CoRR abs/1208.0967 (2012)
31. Koppula, H.S., Gupta, R., Saxena, A.: Learning human activities and object affordances from rgb-d videos. CoRR abs/1210.1207 (2012)
32. Lai, K., Bo, L., Ren, X., Fox, D.: Sparse distance learning for object recognition combining rgb and depth information. In: International Conferences on Robotics and Automation, pp. 4007–4013 (2011)

33. Yang, X., Tian, Y.: Eigenjoints-based action recognition using naive-bayes-nearest-neighbor. In: Workshop on Human Activity Understanding from 3D Data, pp. 14–19 (2012)
34. Sung, J., Ponce, C., Selman, B., Saxena, A.: Human activity detection from rgbd images. In: Plan, Activity, and Intent Recognition (2011)
35. Sung, J., Ponce, C., Selman, B., Saxena, A.: Unstructured human activity detection from rgbd images. In: IEEE International Conference on Robotics and Automation, pp. 842–849 (2012)
36. McCallum, A., Freitag, D., Pereira, F.C.N.: Maximum entropy markov models for information extraction and segmentation. In: International Conference on Machine Learning, pp. 591–598 (2000)
37. Dalal, N., Triggs, B.: Histograms of oriented gradients for human detection. In: IEEE Conference on Computer Vision and Pattern Recognition, pp. 886–893 (2005)
38. Yao, A., Gall, J., Van Gool, L.: Coupled action recognition and pose estimation from multiple views. International Journal of Computer Vision 100(1), 16–37 (2012)
39. Müller, M., Röder, T., Clausen, M.: Efficient content-based retrieval of motion capture data. ACM Transactions on Graphics 24, 677–685 (2005)
40. Gall, J., Yao, A., Razavi, N., Van Gool, L., Lempitsky, V.: Hough forests for object detection, tracking, and action recognition. IEEE Transactions on Pattern Analysis and Machine Intelligence (2011)
41. Tenorth, M., Bandouch, J., Beetz, M.: The TUM kitchen data set of everyday manipulation activities for motion tracking and action recognition. In: IEEE Workshop on Tracking Humans for the Evaluation of their Motion in Image Sequences (2009)
42. Fanelli, G., Dantone, M., Gall, J., Fossati, A., Van Gool, L.: Random forests for real time 3d face analysis. International Journal of Computer Vision 101(3), 437–458 (2013)
43. Murphy-Chutorian, E., Trivedi, M.: Head pose estimation in computer vision: A survey. Transactions on Pattern Analysis and Machine Intelligence 31(4), 607–626 (2009)
44. Jones, M., Viola, P.: Fast multi-view face detection. Technical Report TR2003-096, Mitsubishi Electric Research Laboratories (2003)
45. Huang, C., Ding, X., Fang, C.: Head pose estimation based on random forests for multiclass classification. In: International Conference on Pattern Recognition (2010)
46. Chen, L., Zhang, L., Hu, Y., Li, M., Zhang, H.: Head pose estimation using fisher manifold learning. In: Analysis and Modeling of Faces and Gestures (2003)
47. Balasubramanian, V.N., Ye, J., Panchanathan, S.: Biased manifold embedding: A framework for person-independent head pose estimation. In: IEEE Conference on Computer Vision and Pattern Recognition (2007)
48. Osadchy, M., Miller, M.L., LeCun, Y.: Synergistic face detection and pose estimation with energy-based models. In: Neural Information Processing Systems (2005)
49. Cootes, T.F., Edwards, G.J., Taylor, C.J.: Active appearance models. IEEE Transactions on Pattern Analysis and Machine Intelligence 23, 681–685 (2001)
50. Ramnath, K., Koterba, S., Xiao, J., Hu, C., Matthews, I., Baker, S., Cohn, J., Kanade, T.: Multi-view aam fitting and construction. International Journal of Computer Vision 76(2), 183–204 (2008)

51. Blanz, V., Vetter, T.: A morphable model for the synthesis of 3d faces. In: ACM International Conference on Computer Graphics and Interactive Techniques, pp. 187–194 (1999)

52. Storer, M., Urschler, M., Bischof, H.: 3d-mam: 3d morphable appearance model for efficient fine head pose estimation from still images. In: Workshop on Subspace Methods (2009)

53. Martins, P., Batista, J.: Accurate single view model-based head pose estimation. In: Automatic Face and Gesture Recognition (2008)

54. Vatahska, T., Bennewitz, M., Behnke, S.: Feature-based head pose estimation from images. In: International Conference on Humanoid Robots (2007)

55. Whitehill, J., Movellan, J.R.: A discriminative approach to frame-by-frame head pose tracking. In: Automatic Face and Gesture Recognition (2008)

56. Morency, L.P., Whitehill, J., Movellan, J.R.: Generalized adaptive view-based appearance model: Integrated framework for monocular head pose estimation. In: Automatic Face and Gesture Recognition (2008)

57. Breitenstein, M.D., Kuettel, D., Weise, T., Van Gool, L., Pfister, H.: Real-time face pose estimation from single range images. In: IEEE Conference on Computer Vision and Pattern Recognition (2008)

58. Cai, Q., Gallup, D., Zhang, C., Zhang, Z.: 3D deformable face tracking with a commodity depth camera. In: Daniilidis, K., Maragos, P., Paragios, N. (eds.) ECCV 2010, Part III. LNCS, vol. 6313, pp. 229–242. Springer, Heidelberg (2010)

59. Morency, L.P., Sundberg, P., Darrell, T.: Pose estimation using 3d view-based eigenspaces. In: Automatic Face and Gesture Recognition (2003)

60. Seemann, E., Nickel, K., Stiefelhagen, R.: Head pose estimation using stereo vision for human-robot interaction. In: Automatic Face and Gesture Recognition (2004)

61. Mian, A., Bennamoun, M., Owens, R.: Automatic 3d face detection, normalization and recognition. In: 3D Data Processing, Visualization, and Transmission (2006)

62. Lu, X., Jain, A.K.: Automatic feature extraction for multiview 3d face recognition. In: Automatic Face and Gesture Recognition (2006)

63. Weise, T., Leibe, B., Van Gool, L.: Fast 3d scanning with automatic motion compensation. In: IEEE Conference on Computer Vision and Pattern Recognition (2007)

64. Weise, T., Bouaziz, S., Li, H., Pauly, M.: Realtime performance-based facial animation. ACM Transactions on Graphics 30(4) (2011)

65. Breitenstein, M.D., Jensen, J., Høilund, C., Moeslund, T.B., Van Gool, L.: Head pose estimation from passive stereo images. In: Salberg, A.-B., Hardeberg, J.Y., Jenssen, R. (eds.) SCIA 2009. LNCS, vol. 5575, pp. 219–228. Springer, Heidelberg (2009)

66. Fanelli, G., Gall, J., Van Gool, L.: Real time head pose estimation with random regression forests. In: IEEE Conference on Computer Vision and Pattern Recognition (2011)

67. Fanelli, G., Weise, T., Gall, J., Van Gool, L.: Real time head pose estimation from consumer depth cameras. In: Mester, R., Felsberg, M. (eds.) DAGM 2011. LNCS, vol. 6835, pp. 101–110. Springer, Heidelberg (2011)

68. Paysan, P., Knothe, R., Amberg, B., Romdhani, S., Vetter, T.: A 3d face model for pose and illumination invariant face recognition. In: Advanced Video and Signal based Surveillance (2009)

69. Weise, T., Wismer, T., Leibe, B., Van Gool, L.: In-hand scanning with online loop closure. In: 3-D Digital Imaging and Modeling (2009)

70. Li, H., Adams, B., Guibas, L.J., Pauly, M.: Robust single-view geometry and motion reconstruction. ACM Transactions on Graphics 28(5) (2009)

71. Cootes, T.F., Wheeler, G.V., Walker, K.N., Taylor, C.J.: View-based active appearance models. Image and Vision Computing 20(9-10), 657–664 (2002)
72. Matthews, I., Baker, S.: Active appearance models revisited. International Journal of Computer Vision 60(2), 135–164 (2003)
73. Gross, R., Matthews, I., Baker, S.: Generic vs. person specific active appearance models. Image and Vision Computing 23(12), 1080–2093 (2005)
74. Valstar, M., Martinez, B., Binefa, X., Pantic, M.: Facial point detection using boosted regression and graph models. In: IEEE Conference on Computer Vision and Pattern Recognition (2010)
75. Amberg, B., Vetter, T.: Optimal landmark detection using shape models and branch and bound slides. In: IEEE International Conference on Computer Vision (2011)
76. Belhumeur, P.N., Jacobs, D.W., Kriegman, D.J., Kumar, N.: Localizing parts of faces using a consensus of exemplars. In: IEEE Conference on Computer Vision and Pattern Recognition (2011)
77. Dantone, M., Gall, J., Fanelli, G., Van Gool, L.: Real-time facial feature detection using conditional regression forests. In: IEEE Conference on Computer Vision and Pattern Recognition (2012)
78. Felzenszwalb, P.F., Huttenlocher, D.P.: Pictorial structures for object recognition. International Journal of Computer Vision 61(1), 55–79 (2005)
79. Everingham, M., Sivic, J., Zisserman, A.: Hello! my name is... buffy - automatic naming of characters in tv video. In: British Machine Vision Conference (2006)
80. Cristinacce, D., Cootes, T.: Automatic feature localisation with constrained local models. Journal of Pattern Recognition 41(10), 3054–3067 (2008)
81. Mpiperis, I., Malassiotis, S., Strintzis, M.: Bilinear models for 3-d face and facial expression recognition. IEEE Transactions on Information Forensics and Security 3(3), 498–511 (2008)
82. Kakadiaris, I.A., Passalis, G., Toderici, G., Murtuza, M.N., Lu, Y., Karampatziakis, N., Theoharis, T.: Three-dimensional face recognition in the presence of facial expressions: An annotated deformable model approach. IEEE Transactions on Pattern Analysis and Machine Intelligence 29(4), 640–649 (2007)
83. Weise, T., Li, H., Van Gool, L., Pauly, M.: Face/off: live facial puppetry. In: Symposium on Computer Animation, pp. 7–16 (2009)
84. Sun, Y., Yin, L.: Automatic pose estimation of 3d facial models. In: International Conference on Pattern Recognition (2008)
85. Segundo, M., Silva, L., Bellon, O., Queirolo, C.: Automatic face segmentation and facial landmark detection in range images. IEEE Transactions on Systems, Man, and Cybernetics, Part B: Cybernetics 40(5), 1319–1330 (2010)
86. Chang, K.I., Bowyer, K.W., Flynn, P.J.: Multiple nose region matching for 3d face recognition under varying facial expression. IEEE Transactions on Pattern Analysis and Machine Intelligence 28(10), 1695–1700 (2006)
87. Mehryar, S., Martin, K., Plataniotis, K., Stergiopoulos, S.: Automatic landmark detection for 3d face image processing. In: Evolutionary Computation (2010)
88. Colbry, D., Stockman, G., Jain, A.: Detection of anchor points for 3d face verification. In: IEEE Conference on Computer Vision and Pattern Recognition (2005)
89. Dorai, C., Jain, A.K.: COSMOS - A Representation Scheme for 3D Free-Form Objects. IEEE Transactions on Pattern Analysis and Machine Intelligence 19(10), 1115–1130 (1997)
90. Wang, Y., Chua, C., Ho, Y.: Facial feature detection and face recognition from 2d and 3d images. Pattern Recognition Letters 10(23), 1191–1202 (2002)

91. Chua, C.S., Jarvis, R.: Point signatures: A new representation for 3d object recognition. International Journal of Computer Vision 25, 63–85 (1997)
92. Yu, T.H., Moon, Y.S.: A novel genetic algorithm for 3d facial landmark localization. In: Biometrics: Theory, Applications and Systems (2008)
93. Ju, Q., O'keefe, S., Austin, J.: Binary neural network based 3d facial feature localization. In: International Joint Conference on Neural Networks (2009)
94. Zhao, X., Dellandréa, E., Chen, L., Kakadiaris, I.: Accurate landmarking of three-dimensional facial data in the presence of facial expressions and occlusions using a three-dimensional statistical facial feature model. IEEE Transactions on Systems, Man, and Cybernetics, Part B: Cybernetics 41(5), 1417–1428 (2011)
95. Nair, P., Cavallaro, A.: 3-d face detection, landmark localization, and registration using a point distribution model. IEEE Transactions on Multimedia 11(4), 611–623 (2009)
96. Fanelli, G., Gall, J., Romsdorfer, H., Weise, T., Van Gool, L.: A 3-d audio-visual corpus of affective communication. IEEE Transactions on Multimedia 12(6), 591–598 (2010)
97. Yin, L., Wei, X., Sun, Y., Wang, J., Rosato, M.J.: A 3d facial expression database for facial behavior research. In: International Conference on Automatic Face and Gesture Recognition (2006)
98. Lewis, J.P., Pighin, F.: Background mathematics. In: ACM SIGGRAPH Courses (2006)
99. Alexander, O., Rogers, M., Lambeth, W., Chiang, M., Debevec, P.: The digital emily project: photoreal facial modeling and animation. In: ACM SIGGRAPH Courses (2009)
100. Zhang, S., Huang, P.: High-resolution, real-time 3d shape acquisition. In: Workshop on Real-time 3D Sensors and Their Use (2004)
101. Zhang, L., Snavely, N., Curless, B., Seitz, S.M.: Spacetime faces: high resolution capture for modeling and animation. ACM Transactions on Graphics 23(3), 548–558 (2004)
102. Borshukov, G., Piponi, D., Larsen, O., Lewis, J.P., Tempelaar-Lietz, C.: Universal capture - image-based facial animation for "the matrix reloaded". In: ACM SIGGRAPH Courses (2005)
103. Ma, W.C., Hawkins, T., Peers, P., Chabert, C.F., Weiss, M., Debevec, P.: Rapid acquisition of specular and diffuse normal maps from polarized spherical gradient illumination. In: Eurographics Conference on Rendering Techniques, pp. 183–194 (2007)
104. Wilson, C.A., Ghosh, A., Peers, P., Chiang, J.Y., Busch, J., Debevec, P.: Temporal upsampling of performance geometry using photometric alignment. ACM Transactions on Graphics 29(2) (2010)
105. Beeler, T., Bickel, B., Beardsley, P., Sumner, B., Gross, M.: High-quality single-shot capture of facial geometry. ACM Transactions on Graphics 29 (2010)
106. Bradley, D., Heidrich, W., Popa, T., Sheffer, A.: High resolution passive facial performance capture. ACM Transactions on Graphics 29(4) (2010)
107. Furukawa, Y., Ponce, J.: Dense 3d motion capture from synchronized video streams. In: IEEE Conference on Computer Vision and Pattern Recognition (2008)
108. Breidt, M., Buelthoff, H., Curio, C.: Robust semantic analysis by synthesis of 3d facial motion. In: Automatic Face and Gesture Recognition (2011)

109. Savran, A., Celiktutan, O., Akyol, A., Trojanová, J., Dibeklioglu, H., Esenlik, S., Bozkurt, N., Demirkir, C., Akagunduz, E., Caliskan, K., Alyuz, N., Sankur, B., Ulusoy, I., Akarun, L., Sezgin, T.M.: 3d face recognition performance under adversarial conditions. In: Workshop on Multimodal Interfaces, pp. 87–102 (2007)
110. Yin, L., Chen, X., Sun, Y., Worm, T., Reale, M.: A high-resolution 3d dynamic facial expression database. In: Automatic Face and Gesture Recognition (2008)
111. Gupta, S., Markey, M., Bovik, A.: Anthropometric 3d face recognition. International Journal of Computer Vision 90(3), 331–349 (2010)
112. Colombo, A., Cusano, C., Schettini, R.: Umb-db: A database of partially occluded 3d faces. In: Workshop on Benchmarking Facial Image Analysis Technologies, pp. 2113–2119 (2011)
113. Huynh, T., Min, R., Dugelay, J.-L.: An efficient LBP-based descriptor for facial depth images applied to gender recognition using RGB-D face data. In: Park, J.-I., Kim, J. (eds.) ACCV Workshops 2012, Part I. LNCS, vol. 7728, pp. 133–145. Springer, Heidelberg (2013)
114. Ballan, L., Taneja, A., Gall, J., Van Gool, L., Pollefeys, M.: Motion capture of hands in action using discriminative salient points. In: Fitzgibbon, A., Lazebnik, S., Perona, P., Sato, Y., Schmid, C. (eds.) ECCV 2012, Part VI. LNCS, vol. 7577, pp. 640–653. Springer, Heidelberg (2012)
115. Erol, A., Bebis, G., Nicolescu, M., Boyle, R.D., Twombly, X.: Vision-based hand pose estimation: A review. Computer Vision and Image Understanding 108(1-2), 52–73 (2007)
116. Lu, S., Metaxas, D., Samaras, D., Oliensis, J.: Using multiple cues for hand tracking and model refinement. In: IEEE Conference on Computer Vision and Pattern Recognition (2003)
117. de La Gorce, M., Fleet, D.J., Paragios, N.: Model-based 3d hand pose estimation from monocular video. IEEE Transactions on Pattern Analysis and Machine Intelligence 33(9), 1793–1805 (2011)
118. Delamarre, Q., Faugeras, O.D.: 3d articulated models and multiview tracking with physical forces. Computer Vision and Image Understanding 81(3), 328–357 (2001)
119. Bray, M., Koller-Meier, E., Van Gool, L.: Smart particle filtering for high-dimensional tracking. Computer Vision and Image Understanding 106(1), 116–129 (2007)
120. Oikonomidis, I., Kyriazis, N., Argyros, A.: Efficient model-based 3d tracking of hand articulations using kinect. In: British Machine Vision Conference (2011)
121. Rehg, J.M., Kanade, T.: Visual tracking of high dof articulated structures: an application to human hand tracking. In: Eklundh, J.-O. (ed.) ECCV 1994. LNCS, vol. 801, pp. 35–46. Springer, Heidelberg (1994)
122. Stenger, B., Mendonca, P., Cipolla, R.: Model-based 3D tracking of an articulated hand. In: IEEE Conference on Computer Vision and Pattern Recognition, pp. 310–315 (2001)
123. MacCormick, J., Isard, M.: Partitioned sampling, articulated objects, and interface-quality hand tracking. In: Vernon, D. (ed.) ECCV 2000. LNCS, vol. 1843, pp. 3–19. Springer, Heidelberg (2000)
124. Heap, T., Hogg, D.: Towards 3d hand tracking using a deformable model. In: International Conference on Automatic Face and Gesture Recognition (1996)
125. Wu, Y., Lin, J., Huang, T.: Capturing natural hand articulation. In: IEEE International Conference on Computer Vision, pp. 426–432 (2001)

126. Sudderth, E., Mandel, M., Freeman, W., Willsky, A.: Visual Hand Tracking Using Nonparametric Belief Propagation. In: Workshop on Generative Model Based Vision, pp. 189–189 (2004)
127. Hamer, H., Schindler, K., Koller-Meier, E., Van Gool, L.: Tracking a hand manipulating an object. In: IEEE International Conference on Computer Vision, pp. 1475–1482 (2009)
128. Oikonomidis, I., Kyriazis, N., Argyros, A.A.: Markerless and efficient 26-DOF hand pose recovery. In: Kimmel, R., Klette, R., Sugimoto, A. (eds.) ACCV 2010, Part III. LNCS, vol. 6494, pp. 744–757. Springer, Heidelberg (2011)
129. Keskin, C., Kra, F., Kara, Y., Akarun, L.: Real time hand pose estimation using depth sensors. In: Fossati, A., Gall, J., Grabner, H., Ren, X., Konolige, K. (eds.) Consumer Depth Cameras for Computer Vision. Advances in Computer Vision and Pattern Recognition, pp. 119–137. Springer, London (2013)
130. Oikonomidis, I., Kyriazis, N., Argyros, A.A.: Tracking the articulated motion of two strongly interacting hands. In: IEEE Conference on Computer Vision and Pattern Recognition (2012)
131. State, A., Coleca, F., Barth, E., Martinetz, T.: Hand tracking with an extended self-organizing map. In: Estevez, P.A., Principe, J.C., Zegers, P. (eds.) Advances in Self-Organizing Maps. AISC, vol. 198, pp. 115–124. Springer, Heidelberg (2013)
132. Rosales, R., Athitsos, V., Sigal, L., Sclaroff, S.: 3d hand pose reconstruction using specialized mappings. In: IEEE International Conference on Computer Vision, pp. 378–387 (2001)
133. Athitsos, V., Sclaroff, S.: Estimating 3d hand pose from a cluttered image. In: IEEE Conference on Computer Vision and Pattern Recognition, pp. 432–439 (2003)
134. de Campos, T., Murray, D.: Regression-based hand pose estimation from multiple cameras. In: IEEE Conference on Computer Vision and Pattern Recognition, pp. 782–789 (2006)
135. Stenger, B., Thayananthan, A., Torr, P.: Model-based hand tracking using a hierarchical bayesian filter. IEEE Transactions on Pattern Analysis and Machine Intelligence 28(9), 1372–1384 (2006)
136. Romero, J., Kjellström, H., Kragic, D.: Hands in action: Real-time 3d reconstruction of hands in interaction with objects. In: International Conferences on Robotics and Automation, pp. 458–463 (2010)
137. Lee, C.S., Chun, S.Y., Park, S.W.: Articulated hand configuration and rotation estimation using extended torus manifold embedding. In: International Conference on Pattern Recognition, pp. 441–444 (2012)
138. Hamer, H., Gall, J., Urtasun, R., Van Gool, L.: Data-driven animation of hand-object interactions. In: International Conference on Automatic Face and Gesture Recognition, pp. 360–367 (2011)
139. Hamer, H., Gall, J., Weise, T., Van Gool, L.: An object-dependent hand pose prior from sparse training data. In: IEEE Conference on Computer Vision and Pattern Recognition, pp. 671–678 (2010)
140. Uebersax, D., Gall, J., den Bergh, M.V., Van Gool, L.: Real-time sign language letter and word recognition from depth data. In: IEEE Workshop on Human Computer Interaction: Real-Time Vision Aspects of Natural User Interfaces (2011)
141. Ye, Y., Liu, C.K.: Synthesis of detailed hand manipulations using contact sampling. ACM Transactions on Graphics 31(4), 41 (2012)
142. Oikonomidis, I., Kyriazis, N., Argyros, A.: Full dof tracking of a hand interacting with an object by modeling occlusions and physical constraints. In: IEEE International Conference on Computer Vision (2011)

143. Kim, D., Hilliges, O., Izadi, S., Butler, A.D., Chen, J., Oikonomidis, I., Olivier, P.: Digits: Freehand 3d interactions anywhere using a wrist-worn gloveless sensor. In: ACM Symposium on User Interface Software and Technology, pp. 167–176 (2012)

144. Zhao, W., Chai, J., Xu, Y.Q.: Combining marker-based mocap and rgb-d camera for acquiring high-fidelity hand motion data. In: Symposium on Computer Animation, pp. 33–42 (2012)

145. Starner, T., Weaver, J., Pentland, A.: Real-time american sign language recognition using desk and wearable computer based video. IEEE Transactions on Pattern Analysis and Machine Intelligence 20(12), 1371–1375 (1998)

146. Derpanis, K.G., Wildes, R.P., Tsotsos, J.K.: Hand gesture recognition within a linguistics-based framework. In: Pajdla, T., Matas, J(G.) (eds.) ECCV 2004. LNCS, vol. 3021, pp. 282–296. Springer, Heidelberg (2004)

147. Ong, S., Ranganath, S.: Automatic sign language analysis: A survey and the future beyond lexical meaning. IEEE Transactions on Pattern Analysis and Machine Intelligence 27(6), 873–891 (2005)

148. Pei, T., Starner, T., Hamilton, H., Essa, I., Rehg, J.: Learnung the basic units in american sign language using discriminative segmental feature selection. In: IEEE International Conference on Acoustics, Speech and Signal Processing, pp. 4757–4760 (2009)

149. Yang, H.D., Sclaroff, S., Lee, S.W.: Sign language spotting with a threshold model based on conditional random fields. IEEE Transactions on Pattern Analysis and Machine Intelligence 31(7), 1264–1277 (2009)

150. Theodorakis, S., Pitsikalis, V., Maragos, P.: Model-level data-driven sub-units for signs in videos of continuous sign language. In: IEEE International Conference on Acoustics, Speech and Signal Processing, pp. 2262–2265 (2010)

151. Zafrulla, Z., Brashear, H., Hamilton, H., Starner, T.: A novel approach to american sign language (asl) phrase verification using reversed signing. In: IEEE Workshop on CVPR for Human Communicative Behavior Analysis, pp. 48–55 (2010)

152. Dreuw, P., Ney, H., Martinez, G., Crasborn, O., Piater, J., Moya, J.M., Wheatley, M.: The signspeak project - bridging the gap between signers and speakers. In: International Conference on Language Resources and Evaluation (2010)

153. Liu, X., Fujimura, K.: Hand gesture recognition using depth data. In: International Conference on Automatic Face and Gesture Recognition (2004)

154. Mo, Z., Neumann, U.: Real-time hand pose recognition using low-resolution depth images. In: IEEE Conference on Computer Vision and Pattern Recognition, pp. 1499–1505 (2006)

155. Breuer, P., Eckes, C., Müller, S.: Hand gesture recognition with a novel IR time-of-flight range camera–A pilot study. In: Gagalowicz, A., Philips, W. (eds.) MIRAGE 2007. LNCS, vol. 4418, pp. 247–260. Springer, Heidelberg (2007)

156. Soutschek, S., Penne, J., Hornegger, J., Kornhuber, J.: 3-d gesture-based scene navigation in medical imaging applications using time-of-flight cameras. In: Workshop on Time of Flight Camera based Computer Vision (2008)

157. Kollorz, E., Penne, J., Hornegger, J., Barke, A.: Gesture recognition with a time-of-flight camera. International Journal of Intelligent Systems Technologies and Applications 5, 334–343 (2008)

158. Penne, J., Soutschek, S., Fedorowicz, L., Hornegger, J.: Robust real-time 3d time-of-flight based gesture navigation. In: International Conference on Automatic Face and Gesture Recognition (2008)

159. Li, Z., Jarvis, R.: Real time hand gesture recognition using a range camera. In: Australasian Conference on Robotics and Automation (2009)

160. Takimoto, H., Yoshimori, S., Mitsukura, Y., Fukumi, M.: Classification of hand postures based on 3d vision model for human-robot interaction. In: International Symposium on Robot and Human Interactive Communication, pp. 292–297 (2010)
161. Lahamy, H., Litchi, D.: Real-time hand gesture recognition using range cameras. In: Canadian Geomatics Conference (2010)
162. Van den Bergh, M., Van Gool, L.: Combining rgb and tof cameras for real-time 3d hand gesture interaction. In: IEEE Workshop on Applications of Computer Vision (2011)
163. Marnik, J.: The polish finger alphabet hand postures recognition using elastic graph matching. In: Kurzynski, M., Puchala, E., Wozniak, M., Zolnierek, A. (eds.) Computer Recognition Systems 2. ASC, vol. 45, pp. 454–461. Springer, Heidelberg (2007)
164. Incertis, I., Garcia-Bermejo, J., Casanova, E.: Hand gesture recognition for deaf people interfacing. In: International Conference on Pattern Recognition, pp. 100–103 (2006)
165. Lockton, R., Fitzgibbon, A.W.: Real-time gesture recognition using deterministic boosting. In: British Machine Vision Conference (2002)
166. Liwicki, S., Everingham, M.: Automatic recognition of fingerspelled words in british sign language. In: IEEE Workshop on CVPR for Human Communicative Behavior Analysis (2009)
167. Kelly, D., Mc Donald, J., Markham, C.: A person independent system for recognition of hand postures used in sign language. Pattern Recognition Letters 31, 1359–1368 (2010)
168. Amin, M., Yan, H.: Sign language finger alphabet recognition from gabor-pca representation of hand gestures. In: Machine Learning and Cybernetics (2007)
169. Munib, Q., Habeeb, M., Takruri, B., Al-Malik, H.: American sign language (asl) recognition based on hough transform and neural networks. Expert Systems with Applications 32(1), 24–37 (2007)
170. Tzionas, D., Gall, J.: A comparison of directional distances for hand pose estimation. In: Weickert, J., Hein, M., Schiele, B. (eds.) GCPR 2013. LNCS, vol. 8142, pp. 131–141. Springer, Heidelberg (2013)

Full-Body Human Motion Capture
from Monocular Depth Images

Thomas Helten[1], Andreas Baak[1], Meinard Müller[2], and Christian Theobalt[1]

[1] MPI Informatik, Campus E1.4, 66123 Saarbrücken, Germany
{thelten,abaak,theobalt}@mpi-inf.mpg.de
[2] International Audio Laboratories, Am Wolfsmantel 33, 91058 Erlangen, Germany
meinard.mueller@audiolabs-erlangen.de

Abstract. Optical capturing of human body motion has many practical applications, ranging from motion analysis in sports and medicine, over ergonomy research, up to computer animation in game and movie production. Unfortunately, many existing approaches require expensive multi-camera systems and controlled studios for recording, and expect the person to wear special marker suits. Furthermore, marker-less approaches demand dense camera arrays and indoor recording. These requirements and the high acquisition cost of the equipment makes it applicable only to a small number of people. This has changed in recent years, when the availability of inexpensive depth sensors, such as time-of-flight cameras or the Microsoft Kinect has spawned new research on tracking human motions from monocular depth images. These approaches have the potential to make motion capture accessible to much larger user groups. However, despite significant progress over the last years, there are still unsolved challenges that limit applicability of depth-based monocular full body motion capture. Algorithms are challenged by very noisy sensor data, (self) occlusions, or other ambiguities implied by the limited information that a depth sensor can extract of the scene. In this article, we give an overview on the state-of-the-art in full body human motion capture using depth cameras. Especially, we elaborate on the challenges current algorithms face and discuss possible solutions. Furthermore, we investigate how the integration of additional sensor modalities may help to resolve some of the ambiguities and improve tracking results.

1 Introduction

The recording and analysis of full-body human motion data constitutes an important strand of research in computer vision, computer graphics and many related fields of visual computing. Full body human motion capture has many applications in divers areas, ranging from character animation for movie and game productions, sports sciences, and human computer interaction. Unfortunately, the methods for measuring human skeletal motion that were available until recently impose stark constraints on applicability and can lead to high acquisition cost. Most applications in the movie and game industry, medical research and rehabilitation, as well as sports sciences are often based on optical marker-based

M. Grzegorzek et al. (Eds.): Time-of-Flight and Depth Imaging, LNCS 8200, pp. 188–206, 2013.

Fig. 1. (a) Input color images for a typical markerless multi-camera motion capture approach. **(b)** Input depth image for a typical depth tracking approach.

or marker-less approaches, see [1] for an overview. These approaches often need multi-view input images, recorded in controlled environments using expensive and calibrated recording equipment, see also Fig. 1a. These requirements render them unaffordable for many users, or even completely unsuitable, such as in home user applications.

In the recent years, depth sensing devices such as time-of-flight (ToF) cameras or the Microsoft Kinect have triggered a new strand of research, where human motion data is inferred from so called 2.5D depth maps. Such cameras are easy to set-up and are inexpensive compared to the systems required by the approaches above. The provided data is especially appealing for tracking because of two reasons. Firstly, it is more resilient to challenging surface and appearance properties of objects and in most cases independent from controlled lighting conditions. Secondly, the provided depth maps enable easier background subtraction and provide rich geometric information even when using only a single camera, see also Fig. 1b. In consequence, several algorithms were introduced recently that can capture full body human skeletal poses from a single depth camera view. While they do not yet reach the same level of accuracy as classical multi-camera-based approaches, many of them perform in real-time and have paved the trail for some new interaction applications in home user environments.

However, despite the advances in this field, there are still many fundamental algorithmic obstacles to overcome in order to bridge the immense quality and robustness gap between depth-camera based tracking and earlier multi-camera approaches. Current algorithms are challenged by the non-trivial noise characteristics of depth cameras. Understanding and characterizing this noise (see also chapter "Denoising Strategies for Time-of-Flight Data") and properly accommodating for it (see also chapter "Stabilization of 3D Position Measurement") in the pose estimation methods is thus a key requirement. Another set of challenges originates from the fact that depth images are very sparse. While already with multiple available camera views the process of inferring pose from images is highly ambiguous, this problem is even more difficult in monocular pose reconstruction. Algorithms are challenged by occlusions resulting in missing information. Another example is the fact that the orientation of rotationally symmetric body parts, such as arms and legs, is ambiguous in the depth data.

In this article, we want to give an overview on the current state-of-the art in human pose estimation from depth images, see Sect. 2. We will review the advantages and disadvantages of the main categories of algorithmic strategies for monocular pose estimation from depth, which includes generative and discriminative strategies. We will also put a focus on the basic principle of so-called hybrid trackers that combine these two tracking recipes. Based on this review of state-of-the-art, we will elaborate on primary algorithmic limitations and challenges that current methods have to overcome, and present ideas and an outlook to possible ways of achieving this, see Sect. 3. In particular, we will use the example approach presented by Baak *et al.* [2] as instructional example, see Sect. 3.4.

2   State-of-the-Art

Nowadays, most commercial solutions to full-body human motion capture employ techniques that are invasive to the scene. Some approaches are based on mechanical or electronic exoskeletons, or other external sensors placed on the body. But the most widely used techniques require the person to wear special suits with retro-reflective markers whose motion is picked up by a multi-camera system to compute the skeletal motion of the person [3]. Due to the complex apparatus, these approaches are expensive, need a lot of preparation time, and are restricted to controlled recording environments which constrains their application to specialized professional users. To overcome this limitation, researchers in computer vision and computer graphics started to develop marker-less skeletal pose estimation algorithms. They can capture skeletal motion from multi-view video of a moving person, without needing markers in the scene. An extensive overview of these methods is beyond the scope of this chapter, and a review can be found in [4], but the main concepts are as follows. Most approaches use some form of 3D kinematic skeleton model augmented by shape primitives, such as cylinders [5], a surface mesh [6,7,8], or probabilistic density representations attached to the human body [9]. Optimal skeletal pose parameters are often found by minimizing an error metric that assesses the similarity of the projected model to the multi-view image data using features. Local optimization approaches are widely used due to their high efficiency, but they are challenged by the highly multimodal nature of the model-to-image similarity function [9,8]. Global pose optimization methods can overcome some of these limitations, however at the price of needing much longer computation times [10,6]. Some approaches aim to combine the efficiency of local methods with the reliability of global methods by adaptively switching between them [6]. Even though marker-less approaches succeed with a slightly simpler setup, many limitations remain: computation time often precludes real-time processing, recording is still limited to controlled settings, and people are still expected to wear relatively tight clothing. Furthermore, marker-less motion capture methods deliver merely skeletal motion parameters.

In contrast, marker-less performance capture methods go one step further and reconstruct deforming surface geometry from multi-view video in addition to skeletal motion. Some methods estimate the dynamic scene geometry using variants of shape-from-silhouette methods or combinations of shape-from-silhouette and stereo[11,12,13,14], but in such approaches establishing space-time coherence is difficult. Template-based methods deform a shape template to match the deformable surface in the real scene, which implicitly establishes temporal coherence [15,16], also in scenes with ten persons. All the developments explained so far aim towards the goal of high-quality reconstruction, even if that necessitates complex and controlled indoor setup. In contrast, depth-based tracking of full-body human motion focuses on using inexpensive recording equipment that is easy to setup and to use in home user applications. As a consequence, depth based have to deal with various challenges that marker-less tracking approaches do not face. Commercial systems that make use of this kind of motion tracking can be found e. g. in the Microsoft Kinect for XBox[1], the SoftKinetic IISU Middleware[2] for pose and gesture recognition, as well as the SilverFit[3] system for rehabilitation support. So far, several depth-based tracking methods have been published that can be classified into three basic types: Generative approaches, discriminative approaches and hybrid approaches. In this chapter, we give a general overview over full-body tracking approaches. We refer to the chapter "A Survey on Human Motion Analysis from Depth Data" for activity recognition and body part motion in general. Furthermore, we refer to the chapter "Gesture Interfaces with Depth Sensors" for the specific case of hand and arm motion tracking. The later chapter also discusses a special kind of generative tracking approach which makes use of so-called self-organizing maps (SOM).

2.1 Generative Approaches

Generative approaches use parametrized body models that are fit into the depth data using optimization schemes. In particular, the optimization process maximizes a model-to-image consistency measure. This measure is hard to optimize due to the inherent ambiguity in the model-to-data projection. In particular, when using monocular video cameras, this ambiguity precludes efficient and reliable inference of a usable range of 3D body poses. Depth data reduce this ambiguity problem but it is still one of the main algorithmic challenges to make generative methods succeed.

A first approach for obtaining pose and surface of articulated rigid objects from ToF depth images was presented in [17]. Under the assumption that the movement of the tracked object is small w. r. t. the capture speed of the depth camera, the authors track individual bones from a manually pre-labeled depth image using an iterative closest point (ICP) approach. In each frame, previously unlabeled depth pixels are assigned to the bone that best explains the unlabeled depth pixel. However, this approach was not real-time capable, running at around 0.5 frames per second (FPS). Another approach [18] that is specialized on human motion, generates point correspondences for an ICP based optimization from both 3D and 2D input. An example for 2D input could be a body part

---

[1] http://www.xbox.com/Kinect
[2] http://www.softkinetic.com
[3] http://www.silverfit.nl/en.html

Fig. 2. First five geodesic extrema (white spheres) computed for several poses. These five extrema typically correspond to the four end-effectors (two hands, two feet) and the head of the person.

or feature detector working on 2D color images. All 3D points that could be projected onto the 2D feature point now define a ray in 3D space. The closest point of this ray to the model is used to generate a traditional 3D point constraint. The authors report a performance of 25 fps with this method, but the approach is limited to simple non-occluded poses since otherwise the tracker would converge to an erroneous pose minimum from which it cannot recover. Another early approach for real time capable depth-based motion tracking from monocular views was presented in [19]. Here, the authors describe a general pipeline for obtaining pose parameters of humans from a stream of depth images that are then used to drive the motion of a virtual character in *e. g.* video games. To further increase the performance of generative approaches [20] proposed porting the computational intense local optimization to the graphics processor. However, all these approaches tend to fail irrecoverably when the optimization is stuck in a local minimum. This problem also exists in other vision-based approaches and was *e. g.* discussed in [21]. In general, these tracking errors occur due to the ambiguous model-to-data mapping in many poses, as well as fast scene motion. While the latter problem can be remedied by increasing the frame rate, the former was addressed by more elaborated formulations of the energy function. One option was lately presented in [22], where the authors proposed a modified energy function that incorporates empty space information, as well as inter-penetration constraints. A completely different approach was shown in [23]. Here, multiple depth cameras were used for pose estimation which reduces the occlusion problem and enabled capturing the motion of multiple person using high resolution body models. The approach is not real-time capable, though. With all these depth-based methods, real-time pose estimation is still a challenge, tracking may drift, and with exception to [23], the employed shape models are rather coarse which impairs pose estimation accuracy.

2.2   Discriminative Approaches

On the other hand, discriminative approaches focus on detecting certain features in the depth data—such as joint locations—and later combine these independent cues to form a body pose hypothesis. These feature are often learned for a pre-defined set of poses. For this reason, discriminative methods are not dependent on a numerical optimization procedure, and can infer pose also without temporal context and continuity. One algorithm for detecting human body parts in depth images was presented in [24]. Here, the authors use so-called geodesic extrema calculated by iteratively using Dijkstra's algorithm on a graph deduced by connecting all depth pixels in the 2.5D depth data into a map. The assumption here is that geodesic extrema generally align with salient points of the human body, such as the head, the hands, or the feet, see also Fig. 2. To label the retrieved geodesic extrema according to the corresponding body part, the authors employ local shape descriptors on normalized depth image patches centered at the geodesic extrema's positions. Another body part detection approached is pursued in [25], where the authors deduce landmark positions from the depth image and include regularizing information from previous frames. These positions are then used in a kinematic self retargeting framework to estimate the pose parameters of the person. In contrast, the approach described in [26] uses regression forest learned on simple pair-wise depth features to do a pixel-wise classification of the input depth image into body parts. To obtain a working regression forest for joint classification that works under a large range of poses, though, the authors had to train the classifier on approx. 500 000 synthetically generated and labeled depth images. For each body part, joint positions are then inferred by applying a mean shift-based mode finding approach on the pixels assigned to that body part, see also Fig. 3a. Using also regression forests for body part detection, [27] determine the joint positions by letting each depth pixel vote for the joint positions of several joints. After excluding votes from too distant depth pixels and applying a density estimator on the remaining votes, even the probable positions of non-visible joints can be estimated, see also Fig. 3b. Finally, [28] generate correspondences between body parts and a pose and size parametrized human model, which they also achieve by using depth features and regression forests. The parameters of this model are then found using a one shot optimization scheme, *i. e.* without iteratively recomputing the established correspondences. Discriminative approaches show impressive tracking results, where some discriminative methods even succeed in detecting joint information also in non-frontal occluded poses. However, since they often detect features in every depth frame independently, discriminative approaches tend to yield temporally unstable pose estimations results. Furthermore, for many learning-based methods, the effort to train classifiers can be significant.

2.3 Hybrid Approaches

Combining the ideas of generative and discriminative approaches, hybrid approaches try to harness the advantages from both tracker types. On the one hand, hybrid trackers inherit the stability and temporal coherence of pose estimation results common to generative trackers. On the other hand, they show the robustness of pose inference even in partly occluded poses that characterizes discriminative approaches. A first method, in the domain of 3D surface

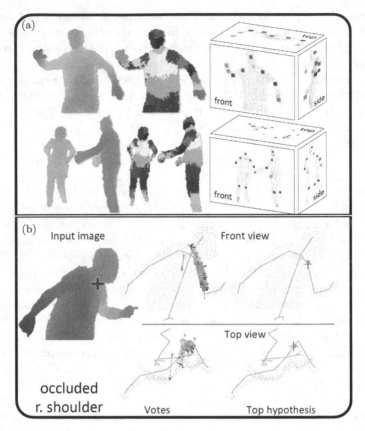

Fig. 3. Regression-forest-based discriminative trackers. The images were taken from the respective papers. (a) Body part and joint detection as presented in [26]. (b) Voting approach for occluded joints as described in [27].

reconstruction, was presented in [29]. Here, the discriminative tracker is used for initializing the surface model, while the generative tracker enforces the observance of distance constraints. The authors also sketched, how their approach can be applied to human pose reconstruction. At the same time, the first method with specialization to human pose estimation was presented in [30]. This work combines the geodesic extrema-based body part recognition presented in [24] with a generative pose optimization scheme based on articulated ICP. Furthermore, the authors introduce a dataset comprising of calibrated ToF depth images and ground-truth marker positions that serves as common benchmark for future work in that field. The works by Baak *et al.* [2] and Ye *et al.* [31] also use a discriminative tracker to initialize a generative pose estimation algorithm. In detail, the approach presented in [31] uses a database consisting of 19 300 poses. For each of these poses, four synthesized depth images were rendered from different views. Using a principal axis based normalization, the point clouds are indexed using their coefficients in a PCA subspace. Here, the normalization of

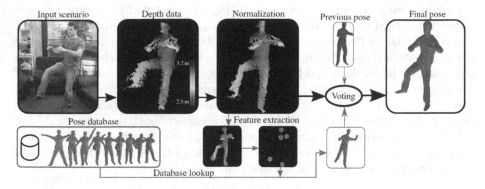

Fig. 4. Schematic overview of a hybrid depth tracker as suggested by Baak et al. [2]

the point cloud in combination with the rendering from four different views is used to retrieve poses from the database independent from the orientation $w.\ r.\ t.$ the depth camera. Note that by storing four different views in the database, the index size is increased to 77 200, while still only 19 300 poses are contained in the database. During tracking, the input point cloud is normalized in the same way, its PCA-coefficients are calculated and used for retrieving a similar point cloud in the database. Finally, they refine the retrieved pose using the Coherent Drift Point algorithm presented in [32]. This approach shows good pose estimation results on the benchmark dataset introduced in [30]. However, their approach does not run in real time—inferring the pose in one frame takes between 60 s and 150 s.

In contrast, the approach showcased in [2] uses a modified iterated version of Dijkstra's algorithm to calculate geodesic extrema similar to the approach in [24]. The stacked positions of the first five geodesic extrema, which often co-align with the head, hands and feet, serve as index into a pose database consisting of 50 000 poses. The suitability of such an approach has been previously discussed in [33], where the authors used the stacked positions of the body's extremities (head, hands, and feet) to index a database containing high dimensional motion data. As index structure the authors employed a kd-tree facilitating fast nearest neighbor searches. To be invariant to certain orientation variations of the person, Baak *et al.* normalize the query and the database poses based on information deduced from the depth point cloud. The incorporated generative tracker is a standard ICP approach that builds correspondences between preselected points from the parametrized human model and points in the depth point cloud. In each frame, they conduct two local optimizations, one initialized using the pose from the previous frame and one using the retrieved pose from the pose database. Using a late fusion step they decide based on a sparse Hausdorff-like distance function which pose obtained from the two local optimizations best describes the observed depth image. This pose is then used as final pose hypothesis, see Fig. 4 for an overview of their approach. While not showing as good results as the approach presented in [31], their tracker runs much faster at around $50 - 60$ frames per second, enabling very responsive tracking. Another real-time approach was recently proposed by e. g. [34]. Here, the authors use a discriminative body-part detector similar to [26] to augment a generative tracker. In particular, they use the pose obtained from the discriminative tracker only for initialization at the beginning of the tracking and for reinitializing the generative tracker in cases of tracking errors. For detecting wrongly tracked frames, they measure how well their body model with the current pose parameters explains the observed point cloud. Hybrid approaches, harnessing the advantages of both tracking worlds, are able to show superior performance compared too purely discriminative or generative approaches. However, even the current state-of-the-art hybrid trackers still have limitations, which we will elaborate on in the following.

3   Open Challenges and Possible Solutions

While providing good overall tracking results, hybrid approaches still suffer from the noisy character and the sparsity of the depth data and are prone to ambiguities originating from occlusions. In this section, we will discuss the various challenges current approaches still face, elaborate on the reasons, and give an outlook how these problems could be approached. For the special case of denoising depth data we refer to the chapter "Denoising Strategies for Time-of-Flight Data".

3.1   Accuracy of the Body Model

Most trackers use an underlying model of the human body. Such models vary drastically ranging from simple representations as graphs [17,25,26,27,28,29,31], over articulated rigid bodies [18,20,22,34] to complex triangle meshes driven by underlying skeletons using skinning approaches [2,23,30]. Here, the complexity of the model mainly depends on the intended application. While some approaches are only interested in tracking specific feature points of the body such as the positions of the extremities [24] or joint positions [26], other approaches try to capture pose parameters such as joint angles [2,22,28,30,31,34], or even the complete surface of the person including cloth wrinkles and folds [23]. Another requirement for a detailed surface model may be the energy function used in generative or hybrid approaches. In particular, ICP-based trackers benefit from an accurate surface model to build meaningful correspondences between the model and the point cloud during optimization. In order to circumvent the problem of obtaining an accurate model of each individual person, some approaches use a fixed body model and scale the input data instead [2]. However, this approach fails for persons with very different body proportions.

In general, the model of the tracked person is often assumed to be created in a pre-processing step using manual modeling or special equipment as full-body laser scanners. While this is a viable way in movie and game productions or in most scientific settings, in home user scenarios it is not feasible. To this end, most algorithms applied in home user scenarios, such as [26] use a different

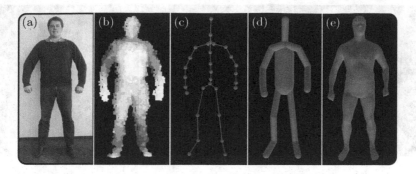

Fig. 5. (a) Body shape of a person to be tracked. **(b)** Depth image of shape. **(c)** Graph model. **(d)** Model based on articulated cylinders and spheres . **(e)** High resolution surface model.

approach. In a pre-processing step the authors use a large number of body models of different sizes and proportions to learn a decision-forest-based classifier that is able to label depth pixels according to the body part they belong to. As a consequence, this classifier becomes invariant to the size of the person and its proportions. During the actual tracking, the learned classifier can be used without obtaining an actual body model of the tracked person. Based on the labeled depth pixel the authors employ a heuristic to deduce the most probable joint position. This approach runs in real-time and works for many tracking applications.

However, for some augmented reality applications the reconstruction quality obtained from simple graphical body models may not be sufficient enough. A popular example is virtual try-on, where the person can wear a piece of virtual apparel that plausibly interacts with the person's body motion. Here, an accurate reconstruction of the person's body surface is beneficial in order to ensure believable visual quality or to give good indication whether the cloth actually fits. One possible approach would be to infer a high resolution body model from depth data in a pre-processing step and then use this model for tracking, visualization or physical simulations of objects in the augmented scene. Recently, one approach [35] has addressed this issue. Here, the authors fit a pose and shape parametrized model into the depth point clouds using an ICP-based approach. The point clouds were obtained from four sequentially captured depth images showing the person from the front, the back and two sides. However, the fact that the person had to reproduce the same pose in all four images and the optimization's runtime of about one hour makes this approach not applicable in home user scenarios. For an explanation how to obtain a pose and shape parametrized model, we refer to [36,37].

3.2 Rotational Ambiguities

Another inherent challenge to all depth-based trackers are rotational ambiguities. Depth data contains rich information about the relative location of objects

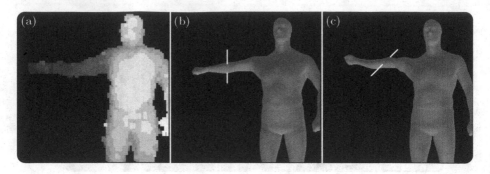

Fig. 6. Rotational ambiguities of depth data. **(a)** Input depth image. **(b)** One typical output from a generative pose estimation procedure. Note that the axis of the elbow joint is vertical. **(c)** Another possible output, the axis of the elbow joint is now horizontal.

which enables easy background subtraction compared to vision based approaches on intensity images. However, depth images reveal only little information about the surface structure and no color information at all. This makes it hard to determine the correct orientation of rotational symmetric objects, such as the body extremities. Since most depth trackers only depend on very simplistic underlying body models with isotropic extremities [18,20,22,34] or even graphs [17,25,26,27,28,29,31] that do not have any volume at all, they can simply ignore the aforementioned problem. However, these trackers also do not provide any pose information about the twist of the arms or the legs. In contrast, trackers that use complex triangle meshes for defining the body's surface [2,23,30] should not ignore rotational ambiguities. In particular, for these approaches the used generative tracker might come to different results depending on its initialization. An example can be seen in Fig. 6. Here, the depth image shown in Fig. 6a reveals only little information on how the arm is oriented. Two possible solutions of a generative tracker are depicted in in Fig. 6b&c. The difference between both solutions lies in the twist of the arm. While in Fig. 6b the axis of the right elbow joint is oriented vertically, it is oriented horizontally in Fig. 6c. In this example, the latter would semantically be the correct pose estimation result. At first glance this might not have huge impact on the overall performance of the tracker. However, a tracking error might serve as initialization for the next frame. Lets consider the scenario that the tracked person bends her arm with the forearm pointing upwards. While this is a straight-forward task for the generative tracker initialized with the pose shown in Fig. 6c, a local optimization starting with the pose shown in Fig. 6b is more likely to get stuck in a local minimum. Unfortunately, none of the presented trackers employs methods to prevent this. While pure generative trackers are likely to fail in such situations and may not be able to proceed, discriminative trackers completely avoid this issue by tracking each frame independently and not relying on local optimization. In contrast, hybrid approaches, such as presented in [2,34], detect the failure of their generative tracker and reinitialize it using pose estimations of their discriminative tracker.

Similar challenges are also faced in other tracking fields as *e. g.* marker-less motion capture. Here, so called silhouetted-based trackers that estimate the pose of the person from multiple, binary (foreground vs. background) images, suffer from the same challenge being unable to determine the correct orientation of the person's extremities. One approach to tackle this was presented in [7], where the authors included information from another sensor modality to correctly detect the orientation of the extremities independent from ambiguous optical information. In particular, their approach relies on orientation data obtained from five inertial sensors attached to the lower legs, forearms and the trunk of the person. By including the measured orientations into the energy function of their generative approach, tracking errors in rotationally symmetric limbs could be avoided.

3.3 Occlusions

The third and by far greatest challenge for today's depth trackers are occlusions. Occlusions stem from the fundamental principle how depth images (and other optical data) is obtained. Light is reflected by some object and detected by some light sensitive sensor inside the camera. If light from an object, *e. g.* a body part, cannot reach the sensor of the camera because another object in between, the object is occluded. As a consequence, one cannot obtain any usable information about the occluded object. Present depth trackers deal with occlusions in various ways. Some trackers simply avoid this by requiring the tracked person to strike only poses where all body parts are clearly visible to the depth camera [2,30,34]. Such trackers often show undefined behavior if the requirements are not met, see Fig. 7 for some representative failure cases. Some discriminative trackers allow for non frontal poses but do not give any pose hypothesis for non-visible parts [25,26,28,34]. In contrast, the approach presented in [27] uses a regression forest-based approach to learn the relative joint positions for a depth pixel based on depth values in its neighborhood. Calculating the density mean on a set of votes yields a hypothesis even for occluded joints. As most learning based approaches, this approach shows good results on poses close to the one used for learning and vice versa. In a pure generative setting, the approach proposed in [22] includes two additional constraints into the energy function to produce plausible results for occluded body parts. The first constraint prevents body parts from entering empty space, *i. e.* parts in the depth image where no foreground pixels were detected. The second constraint prevents body parts from inter-penetrating. However, without an actual measurement it is impossible to deduce the correct pose for occluded body parts.

We see two ways that could help tracking in difficult scenes. Firstly, occlusions could be reduced by dynamically moving the cameras during the recording of the scene. Secondly, occlusions could be handled by adding another input modality that does not depend on visual cues. As for the first approach, the authors in [23] make use of three Kinect depth cameras that are carried by operators around a scene. At a given frame, the depth input of the three Kinects is then fused into one point cloud representation of the whole scene. Using a generative

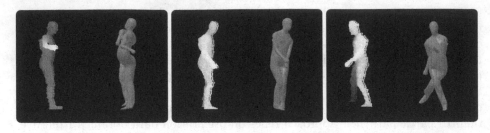

Fig. 7. Illustration of typical tracking artifacts in the case of non-frontal poses and occlusions. Many trackers require the tracked person to face the depth camera and have all arms and legs clearly visible. If those requirements are not met, this results in strong tracking artifacts. These example images where generated using the approach presented in [2].

tracking approach, the poses of the persons are tracked by fitting a rigged surface mesh into the point cloud. While this approach shows good results even for multiple persons in close contact, the runtime of the approach is not real-time and the use of multiple Kinect cameras is not feasible in home user scenarios. Furthermore, the use of several Kinect cameras simultaneously bears its own challenge since these cameras, in contrast to color cameras, interfere with each other's measurement. In order to reduce the interference of multiple Kinects, the authors of [38,39] applied vibration patterns to each camera. These vibrations have the effect that the point pattern projected by one Kinect looks blurred when seen from a different Kinect. In contrast, the pattern does not look blurred for the Kinect it is projected from, since its projector is moved in the same way its camera is. A similar effect is achieved in the approach presented in [23], since the three Kinects are not installed on tripods but hand-held by the camera operators. However, even when using multiple depth cameras, occlusions are difficult to prevent in many tracking scenarios.

As for the second approach, the fusion of different sensor modalities has become a successful approach for dealing with challenging tasks, in other research fields. An approach combining two complementary sensor types for full body human tracking in large areas was presented in [40]. Here, densely placed inertial sensors, one placed on every limb of the body, provide an occlusion independent estimation of the persons body configuration using measured global orientations. Since inertial sensors cannot measure their position, this information is provided by an optical system mounted to a robot accompanying the tracked person. Unfortunately, their approach does not include the rich optical information for supporting the tracking of the persons body configuration. Their approach rather solves two independent sub task, determining the local body configuration and estimating the global position of the person.

At this point, we want to take a second look on the approach presented in [7], which we also discussed in Sect. 3.2. In this approach, the main intention of using inertial sensors in a classical marker-less tracking framework was to prevent erroneous tracking that stems from the ambiguous representation of body

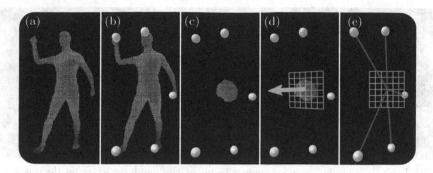

Fig. 8. Normalization of the query pose as presented in [2]. **(a)** Input point cloud of the tracked person. **(b)** Detected end effector positions. **(c)** Segmentation of the torso using mean-shift approach. **(d)** Plane fitted into torso points. The normal of the plane determines the front direction. **(e)** Normalized (front direction pointing towards camera) end effector positions as used for querying.

extremities in silhouette images. Another interesting side-effect is that the inertial sensors provide information about the limb orientations even in situations when the limbs are not visible to the camera. While in the presented scenario this effect was not important because multiple cameras enabled an almost occlusion free observation of the tracked person, this effect might be very important in monocular tracking approaches. In particular, many current depth-based trackers would benefit from additional information that does not depend on visual cues. In the following, we will take a state-of-the-art depth tracker and explain in detail how inertial information could be included to increase the performance in challenging tracking situations.

3.4 Improvement of a Hybrid Tracking Approach

The hybrid depth tracker presented by Baak *et al.* [2] states a typical example for combining a generative (local optimization) approach with a discriminative (DB lookup) approach. While their real-time tracking approach shows good performance on fast and dynamic motions, the tracker requires the person to face the camera during tracking. Furthermore, if body parts are occluded, the tracker might produce erroneous tracking results, see also Fig. 7. In this section, we elaborate on some of the limitations of this approach and discuss modifications to enhance its tracking performance. Furthermore, we will show that including additional complementary sensor information, such as provided by inertial sensors, may support the tracking in challenging tracking situations.

The requirement for frontal poses stems from design decisions made by the authors. In particular, the authors employ a database with normalized poses that serve as initialization to the generative tracker. As query to the database, the authors employ so called geodesic extrema, inspired by [24], computed on the depth point cloud that often co-align with salient features of the persons body such as the head, hands and feet. The normalization of the database was chosen

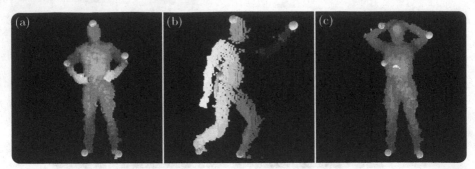

Fig. 9. Typical tracking situations when some of the geodesic extrema do not align with the hand, feet and head

to enable a densely sampled pose space while not requiring to sample the same pose in various global orientations. To this end, their database only contains poses, where the person is facing the camera frontally. As a consequence, also the query to the database needs to be normalized in the same way. By fitting a plane into a subset of depth pixels representing the torso of the person, the authors compute a front direction that serves as basis for the normalization, see also Fig. 8. Note that this way of normalization only works for near frontal poses and it is prone to noise and limbs occluding the torso. In order to pursue a normalization also in poses with occlusions, an additional inertial sensor could be leveraged to obtain a stable estimation of the person's front direction. This approach works for arbitrary rotations and is independent of optical clues that are prone to occlusions. This would already stabilize the lookup of poses from the database in cases when the geodesic extrema are calculated correctly.

However, there will be many occasions remaining where the query to the database, the geodesic extrema, cannot be calculated correctly. Some of these occasions with or without occlusions are shown in Fig. 9. The question is, whether it is possible to obtain poses from a database based on sparse features that are independent to occlusions. In computer animation this question is related to the data-driven reconstruction of human motions from sparse control signals. Many papers have come up that are inspired by an approach using sparse optical features presented in [41]. In particular, the two approaches [42,43] based on sparse inertial sensors data are interesting in our context since they do not rely on optical but inertial cues. In particular, the authors use the readings from inexpensive accelerometers fixed to the body to retrieve poses from a database. Unfortunately, the authors state, that using accelerometer data to obtain poses from the database is challenging because of the noisy characteristics of the data and the lack of discrimination of certain motions. This fact was further examined in [44], where the authors concluded that features based on orientations are better suited to describe full-body human motions than features based on accelerations. To conclude, a sparse set of inertial sensors could also be used to obtain a pose prior from a pose database when using *e. g.* orientation-based features are used for indexing. Such additional sensors could be easily added to the extremities of the person using straps.

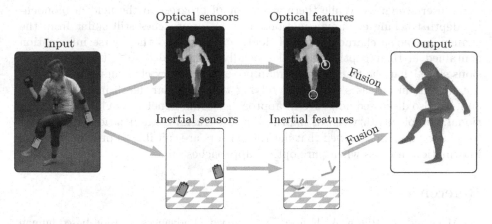

Fig. 10. Sketch of a fusion approach that uses optical depth data and inertial data to generate a single combined pose hypothesis.

Inertial data could also be used to support generative trackers. The idea is, to include information about the limbs orientations directly during the generative tracker's optimization. In contrast to the approach presented in [40], we propose not to solve two independent problems but building a combined energy function that incorporates visual and inertial constraints. In particular, optical cues might add positional constraints, while inertial sensors contribute with rotational constraints, see also Fig. 10. This would help to prevent tracking errors in a similar fashion as described in [7]. Furthermore, the inertial sensors would provide information about limbs even when they are not visible to the depth camera. This concept is modular in a way that one could selectively add inertial sensors to those parts of the body that need highly accurate tracking and do not attach sensors to body parts one does not need as accurate tracking. Overall, this enables selective tracking accuracy that can be adopted to the need of specific applications. Please note that the additional information needed to resolve rotational ambiguities might also be obtained from other sensor modalities such as RGB-input from a color camera. In particular, one could use feature tracking-based or optical-flow-based cues to stabilize tracking, see also [45].

4   Conclusion

In this chapter, we showed how recent depth cameras can be employed for tracking full-body human motion. Based on the unique properties of the provided depth data, such as easy background subtraction and geometric information, monocular tracking approaches become feasible that are not possible with traditional marker-less techniques. Furthermore, being much cheaper and easier to setup than systems used by traditional vision-based approaches, depth cameras, such as the Microsoft Kinect, have enabled applications even in uncontrolled home user scenarios. While there was a lot of progress in the field of monocular depth tracking of human motions, current approaches still suffer from the challenging noise characteristics of depth cameras and the sparse information contained in their depth images. Especially rotational ambiguities and occlusions show, that the tracking of human poses is still very challenging and maybe not feasible in all cases when only relying to monocular depth images. To this end, we also discussed how current approaches could benefit from including additional, complementary sensor information for tracking stabilization. Here, work from other domains showed that inertial sensors are suitable to provide valuable information in cases when pure optical approaches fail.

References

1. Moeslund, T., Hilton, A., Krüger, V.: A survey of advances in vision-based human motion capture and analysis. CVIU 104(2), 90–126 (2006)
2. Baak, A., Müller, M., Bharaj, G., Seidel, H.P., Theobalt, C.: A data-driven approach for real-time full body pose reconstruction from a depth camera. In: ICCV (2011)
3. Menache, A.: Understanding Motion Capture for Computer Animation and Video Games, 1st edn. Morgan Kaufmann Publishers Inc., San Francisco (1999)
4. Poppe, R.: A survey on vision-based human action recognition. Image and Vision Computing 28(6), 976–990 (2010)
5. Bregler, C., Malik, J., Pullen, K.: Twist based acquisition and tracking of animal and human kinematics. IJCV 56(3), 179–194 (2004)
6. Gall, J., Stoll, C., de Aguiar, E., Theobalt, C., Rosenhahn, B., Seidel, H.P.: Motion capture using joint skeleton tracking and surface estimation. In: CVPR, pp. 1746–1753 (2009)
7. Pons-Moll, G., Baak, A., Helten, T., Müller, M., Seidel, H.P., Rosenhahn, B.: Multisensor-fusion for 3d full-body human motion capture. In: CVPR, pp. 663–670 (2010)
8. Liu, Y., Stoll, C., Gall, J., Seidel, H.P., Theobalt, C.: Markerless motion capture of interacting characters using multi-view image segmentation. In: CVPR, pp. 1249–1256 (2011)
9. Stoll, C., Hasler, N., Gall, J., Seidel, H.P., Theobalt, C.: Fast articulated motion tracking using a sums of gaussians body model. In: ICCV, pp. 951–958 (2011)
10. Deutscher, J., Blake, A., Reid, I.: Articulated body motion capture by annealed particle filtering. In: CVPR, vol. 2, pp. 126–133 (2000)
11. Starck, J., Hilton, A.: Spherical matching for temporal correspondence of non-rigid surfaces. In: ICCV, pp. 1387–1394 (2005)
12. Starck, J., Hilton, A.: Correspondence labelling for wide-timeframe free-form surface matching. In: ICCV, pp. 1–8 (2007)
13. Starck, J., Hilton, A.: Surface capture for performance-based animation. IEEE Computer Graphics and Applications 27(3), 21–31 (2007)
14. Matusik, W., Buehler, C., Raskar, R., Gortler, S., McMillan, L.: Image-based visual hulls. In: SIGGRAPH 2000, pp. 369–374 (2000)
15. de Aguiar, E., Stoll, C., Theobalt, C., Naveed, A., Seidel, H.P., Thrun, S.: Performance capture from sparse multi-view video. TOG 27, 1–10 (2008)
16. Vlasic, D., Baran, I., Matusik, W., Popović, J.: Articulated mesh animation from multi-view silhouettes. TOG (2008)

17. Pekelny, Y., Gotsman, C.: Articulated object reconstruction and markerless motion capture from depth video. CGF 27(2), 399–408 (2008)
18. Knoop, S., Vacek, S., Dillmann, R.: Fusion of 2D and 3D sensor data for articulated body tracking. Robotics and Autonomous Systems 57(3), 321–329 (2009)
19. Bleiweiss, A., Kutliroff, E., Eilat, G.: Markerless motion capture using a single depth sensor. In: SIGGRAPH ASIA Sketches (2009)
20. Friborg, R.M., Hauberg, S., Erleben, K.: GPU accelerated likelihoods for stereo-based articulated tracking. In: Kutulakos, K.N. (ed.) ECCV 2010 Workshops, Part II. LNCS, vol. 6554, pp. 359–371. Springer, Heidelberg (2012)
21. Demirdjian, D., Taycher, L., Shakhnarovich, G., Graumanand, K., Darrell, T.: Avoiding the streetlight effect: Tracking by exploring likelihood modes. In: ICCV, vol. 1, pp. 357–364 (2005)
22. Ganapathi, V., Plagemann, C., Koller, D., Thrun, S.: Real-time human pose tracking from range data. In: Fitzgibbon, A., Lazebnik, S., Perona, P., Sato, Y., Schmid, C. (eds.) ECCV 2012, Part VI. LNCS, vol. 7577, pp. 738–751. Springer, Heidelberg (2012)
23. Ye, G., Liu, Y., Hasler, N., Ji, X., Dai, Q., Theobalt, C.: Performance capture of interacting characters with handheld kinects. In: Fitzgibbon, A., Lazebnik, S., Perona, P., Sato, Y., Schmid, C. (eds.) ECCV 2012, Part II. LNCS, vol. 7573, pp. 828–841. Springer, Heidelberg (2012)
24. Plagemann, C., Ganapathi, V., Koller, D., Thrun, S.: Realtime identification and localization of body parts from depth images. In: ICRA, Anchorage, Alaska, USA (2010)
25. Zhu, Y., Dariush, B., Fujimura, K.: Kinematic self retargeting: A framework for human pose estimation. CVIU 114(12), 1362–1375 (2010), Special issue on Time-of-Flight Camera Based Computer Vision
26. Shotton, J., Fitzgibbon, A., Cook, M., Sharp, T., Finocchio, M., Moore, R., Kipman, A., Blake, A.: Real-time human pose recognition in parts from a single depth image. In: CVPR (2011)
27. Girshick, R., Shotton, J., Kohli, P., Criminisi, A., Fitzgibbon, A.: Efficient regression of general-activity human poses from depth images. In: ICCV, pp. 415–422 (2011)
28. Taylor, J., Shotton, J., Sharp, T., Fitzgibbon, A.W.: The Vitruvian manifold: Inferring dense correspondences for one-shot human pose estimation. In: CVPR (2012)
29. Salzmann, M., Urtasun, R.: Combining discriminative and generative methods for 3D deformable surface and articulated pose reconstruction. In: CVPR (2010)
30. Ganapathi, V., Plagemann, C., Thrun, S., Koller, D.: Real time motion capture using a single time-of-flight camera. In: CVPR (2010)
31. Ye, M., Wang, X., Yang, R., Ren, L., Pollefeys, M.: Accurate 3d pose estimation from a single depth image. In: ICCV, pp. 731–738 (2011)
32. Liao, M., Zhang, Q., Wang, H., Yang, R., Gong, M.: Modeling deformable objects from a single depth camera. In: ICCV, pp. 167–174 (2009)
33. Krüger, B., Tautges, J., Weber, A., Zinke, A.: Fast local and global similarity searches in large motion capture databases. In: Symposium on Computer Animation, pp. 1–10 (2010)
34. Wei, X., Zhang, P., Chai, J.: Accurate realtime full-body motion capture using a single depth camera. TOG 31(6), 188:1–188:12 (2012)
35. Weiss, A., Hirshberg, D., Black, M.: Home 3D body scans from noisy image and range data. In: ICCV (2011)
36. Anguelov, D., Srinivasan, P., Koller, D., Thrun, S., Rodgers, J., Davis, J.: Scape: Shape completion and animation of people. ACM TOG 24, 408–416 (2005)

37. Hasler, N., Stoll, C., Sunkel, M., Rosenhahn, B., Seidel, H.P.: A statistical model of human pose and body shape. CGF 2(28) (March 2009)
38. Maimone, A., Fuchs, H.: Reducing interference between multiple structured light depth sensors using motion. In: 2012 IEEE Virtual Reality Short Papers and Posters (VRW), pp. 51–54 (2012)
39. Butler, A., Izadi, S., Hilliges, O., Molyneaux, D., Hodges, S., Kim, D.: Shake'n'sense: Reducing interference for overlapping structured light depth cameras. In: Proceedings of the SIGCHI Conference on Human Factors in Computing Systems, CHI 2012, pp. 1933–1936 (2012)
40. Ziegler, J., Kretzschmar, H., Stachniss, C., Grisetti, G., Burgard, W.: Accurate human motion capture in large areas by combining IMU- and laser-based people tracking. In: IROS, pp. 86–91 (2011)
41. Chai, J., Hodgins, J.K.: Performance animation from low-dimensional control signals. TOG 24(3), 686–696 (2005)
42. Slyper, R., Hodgins, J.K.: Action capture with accelerometers. In: Symposium on Computer Animation, pp. 193–199 (2008)
43. Tautges, J., Zinke, A., Krüger, B., Baumann, J., Weber, A., Helten, T., Müller, M., Seidel, H.P., Eberhardt, B.: Motion reconstruction using sparse accelerometer data. TOG 30(3), 18 (2011)
44. Helten, T., Müller, M., Tautges, J., Weber, A., Seidel, H.-P.: Towards cross-modal comparison of human motion data. In: Mester, R., Felsberg, M. (eds.) DAGM 2011. LNCS, vol. 6835, pp. 61–70. Springer, Heidelberg (2011)
45. Brox, T., Rosenhahn, B., Gall, J., Cremers, D.: Combined region- and motion-based 3d tracking of rigid and articulated objects. IEEE Transactions on Pattern Analysis and Machine Intelligence 32(3), 402–415 (2010)

Gesture Interfaces with Depth Sensors

Foti Coleca[1,2], Thomas Martinetz[1], and Erhardt Barth[1]

[1] Institute for Neuro- and Bioinformatics, University of Lübeck,
160 Ratzeburger Allee, 23562, Lübeck, Germany
{coleca,martinetz,barth}@inb.uni-luebeck.de
[2] gestigon GmbH, Maria-Goeppert Straße 1, 23562 Lübeck, Germany

Abstract. Computers and other electronic devices shrink and the need for a human interface remains. This generates a tremendous interest in alternative interfaces such as touch-less gesture interfaces, which can create a large, generic interface with a small piece of hardware. However, the acceptance of novel interfaces is hard to predict and may challenge the required computer-vision algorithms in terms of robustness, latency, precision, and the complexity of the problems involved.

In this article, we provide an overview of current gesture interfaces that are based on depth sensors. The focus is on the algorithms and systems that operate in the near range and can recognize hand gestures of increasing complexity, from simple wipes to the tracking of a full hand-skeleton.

1 Introduction

In this chapter we focus on gestural interfaces, specifically close-range applications using a depth camera.

Gesture interfaces are different from the input devices currently in use, and for them to be successful, they must be designed from the ground up, with natural human interaction in mind. For this purpose, we first present a gesture taxonomy.

In Section 2 we show how depth cameras affected the field of gesture interaction and algorithmic approaches to hand pose estimation. We then guide the reader through the state of the art. Thereby, related hardware issues are presented only briefly, the focus being the algorithmic approaches. While the main discussion is about solutions which use depth sensors, we also give a brief overview of methods that are using 2D cameras.

The next section is dedicated to identifying remaining challenges, from hardware shortcomings to environment and ergonomic limitations, also proposing solutions to some of these limitations.

Section 4 follows recent developments in hardware, commercial solutions, as well as our own work in the field. We first give an overview on pose estimation using self-organizing maps and then present a few recent extensions.

Finally, Section 5 provides some example applications of gestural interfaces, showing the wide variety of fields that can benefit from this technology.

M. Grzegorzek et al. (Eds.): Time-of-Flight and Depth Imaging, LNCS 8200, pp. 207–227, 2013.
© Springer-Verlag Berlin Heidelberg 2013

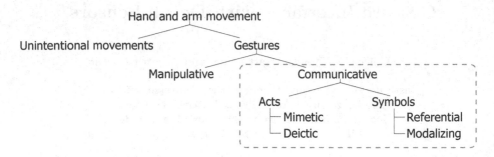

Fig. 1. Hand and arm movement types, as shown in [1]. Communicative gestures are the main focus of touch-less gestural interfaces.

1.1 Gesture Taxonomies

Humans use gestures in everyday life to communicate and interact with the environment. It is not obvious what gestures are and how they can be used to build a better interface. As a brief introduction to the topic, we summarize, in Fig. 1, the hand and arm movement taxonomy:

Unintentional movements are movements unrelated to, and not serving a meaningful communication purpose. These are dependent entirely on the context of the situation, as the same gesture that can be used to communicate something in a certain situation might be completely unintentional in another.

Gestures are hand and arm movements done with the specific intention of communication. Gestures specifically made during verbal communication between humans are known as *gesticulations*. They are first separated by their physicality, as *manipulative* and *communicative* gestures.

Manipulative gestures are used to physically act upon objects in an environment, and depend on the type of action being done on the objects themselves. In the context of human-computer interaction, these are found in interfaces where a direct physical contact is required to use them (e.g. touch-based interfaces).

Communicative gestures have a communicational purpose and are used together with, or instead of, natural speech. Communicative gestures are the focus of touch-less gestural interfaces. Depending on the situation, any part of the body can be used to generate them. They can bring a richer means of interaction, at the cost of being harder to detect and classify.

Acts relate directly to the intended interpretation, are transparent, and can be understood without prior learning. They can either be *mimetic* imitating actions or objects or *deictic*, pointing gestures, which are further split into *specific*, *generic*, and *metonymic* (when pointing at an object to signify some entity related to it). Deictic gestures are useful in simple interfaces, as pointing is a natural way of communicating intention. Example applications are controlling a slideshow [2] or even robots [3].

Symbols are motion short-hand that cannot be used without prior learning. They can vary greatly between cultures and are deeply rooted in the human interpersonal communication. Symbols are useful for gesture interfaces as humans are adept at learning novel ones, which can be created specifically to control said interface. The two categories of symbols are *referential* and *modalizing*. The former refer to iconic gestures linked directly to meanings (e.g. the thumbs-up gesture, rubbing fingers and thumb together to symbolize money), while the latter are used to change the meaning (mode) of communication, (eg. shrugging shoulders to indicate uncertainty, which would not be apparent if one would only read a transcript of the conversation).

2 State of the Art

2.1 Time-of-Flight Sensors and Alternative Hardware

Time-of-flight (ToF) sensors have led to the first compact 3D cameras that could deliver depth maps at video rate [4]. Early work with 3D cameras was based on either the Swissranger cameras [5,6,7,8,9,10], the PMD sensors [11,12] or the Canesta cameras [13], which were all using the same principle of light modulation and phase measurement. Alternatively, some authors were using the 3DV Zcam [14], which used pulses, and was one of the early compact 3D devices, but was not widely available. With the introduction of the low-cost Microsoft Kinect, the field has expanded quickly [15,16,17,18,19,20,21,22]. Limitations of ToF cameras and open issues are discussed in Section 3.1 as well as in Chapters 1 and 2 of this book.

With stereo-based approaches it is difficult to obtain a dense range map. This issue is hard to overcome because stereo disparities can only be estimated at those locations which have a distinct image structure, and it is known that such image patches are rare in natural images [23]. A further limitation is size, because miniaturization is limited by the need to have a sufficient baseline. We have performed extensive tests with different stereo cameras and different illumination settings, and have always obtained range maps that cannot properly resolve the fingers of a hand.

3D cameras that use structured light also require a baseline and two optical systems, for the camera and the projector. Moreover, insensitivity to ambient light is more difficult to achieve. Limitations are discussed in Section 3.1.

2.2 Algorithmic Approaches

Gesture interfaces can range from simple motion detection to complex, pose-driven gesture recognition. In this section, we will focus on hand-pose estimation for gesture recognition. Although there exist a variety of methods to capture the pose of the hand, most can be categorized using combinations of the following dichotomies (Fig. 2):

Partial methods estimate the locations of specific features of the hand. These include approaches from simple geometry and motion parameter extraction of the hand image such as blob tracking and averaging (hand center) to fingertip detection and tracking.

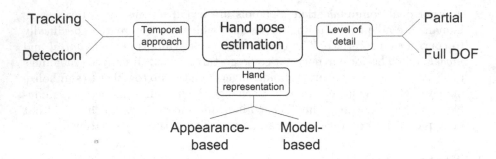

Fig. 2. Pose estimation dichotomies

Full DOF (degree-of-freedom) methods attempt to extract all the kinematic parameters of the hand pose such as fingertips, joint positions, hand orientation, finger angles etc. This is usually done with a full hand skeleton, via a model-based approach.

Appearance-based approaches try to infer gestures directly from the appearance of the hand. These methods are used frequently with 2D cameras, as they are based on a series of 2D views of the 3D object.

Model-based methods estimate the hand position and the specific angles of the joints using a model or skeleton. The model can vary greatly in complexity, from using simple geometric primitives to model a hand skeleton, to accurate computer renderings of hand meshes. Usually these methods attempt to recover the full degree of freedom of the hand.

Tracking approaches use the previous discovered parameters of the hand pose to predict the new ones. This approach is used extensively in methods that need to search over a large state space for the parameters which best match the current hand configuration (i.e. model-based approaches). Using prior information, the search can be restricted only to the most probable hand configurations.

Detection methods disregard temporal information and attempt a single-shot pose estimation. This is sometimes preferred, as the hand and fingers are capable of rapid motion, making time coherence assumptions useless [24].

Methods are often combined to balance their strengths and weaknesses. For example if only tracking is used the tracker may drift away, and when only detection is used, the hand pose can be unstable.

Hand pose estimation is a particularly difficult problem, which poses a number of challenges:

Size : compared to the human body (also used in gesture interfaces), the hand is significantly smaller, with, complex articulated fingers, which are easily affected by segmentation errors [20].

High dimensionality : human hand models used for pose estimation usually have around 26 degrees of freedom [24], the state space being very large.

Skin : The hand is chromatically uniform, which poses a problem for finger detection using color, especially in complex poses. The skin color is also heavily dependent on scene illumination, if skin segmentation is used for hand detection.

Severe self-occlusions : Due to the complexity of the hand, fingers often occlude each other while gesturing. Trying to bypass this problem by forcing the user into non-self-occluding poses (such as an keeping the hand parallel to the interface) makes for an unnatural interface experience and should therefore be avoided.

Performance : Real-world interfaces need short response times in order to be usable. With the ever-increasing computing power available and the introduction of 3D cameras, which simplify tasks like scene segmentation, real-time performance is no longer an unattainable goal.

2.2.1 Using 2D Cameras

The progress made in the early day of gesture interfaces and the limitations of the early approaches are comprehensively reviewed in [1]. The authors conclude that "Although the current progress is encouraging, further theoretical as well as computational advances are needed before gestures can be widely used for HCI" (Human-Computer Interaction). The review emphasizes the popular distinction between model-based and appearance-based approaches and separates between volumetric and skeletal hand models. Regarding applications, a distinction is made between manipulative and communicative gestures. We may conclude that many of the conceptual issues had been clarified early but still, we had to wait for many years until a more mature sensing technology and a few new algorithmic ideas have brought the field much closer to real applications.

Due to limitations of the computing hardware and the lack of depth sensors, early approaches often relied on detecting the hands using a color skin model [25]. Only a few approaches have been developed into systems that would work reliably under a variety of conditions, as for instance [25]. Here, 2D-color-blobs associated with the hands and the head are tracked based on a Maximum A Posteriori Probability approach. In [26] hidden Markov models (HMM) were used for the recognition of 18 different Tai Chi gestures. Different features extracted from a stereo-camera system that could track the head and the hands were evaluated; typical recognition rates were around 90 percent correct. Using more than two RGB cameras can enhance the performance of 2D-camera based hand-pose estimation. This approach is used in [27] with no less than 8 cameras, which allows for the pose capture of two strongly interacting hands and an additional object. These methods usually aggravate the problem of computational overload, which can be then dealt with by using GPUs instead of CPUs [28].

2.2.2 Using 3D Cameras

The approach for body-skeleton tracking developed by Shotton et al. [29] was extended to the hand pose in [15]. The authors claim real-time performance but do not show hand poses for real-life data. Another popular approach is to detect fingertips and use the positions directly as input to the gesture interface [11,30]. In one of the first approaches that used depth data for hand pose estimation [31], the authors employed an active, structured-light stereo system to detect the fingertips with a combination of skin segmentation and 3D principal curvature analysis. The detected fingertips and hand position and orientation were subsequently used for a coarse model of the hand, achieving real-time detection of static or dynamic gestures. A model-based approach is used also in [32], where the hand direction is first coarsely estimated using principal component analysis (PCA), after which a model fitting is able to estimate 7 degrees of freedom of the hand.

When moving from RGB cameras to 3D cameras, the issue of choosing appropriate representations or features had to be readdressed [4,5,14,33]. Even when using standard methods such as the PCA on 3D data, the interpretation of the main axes may differ in 3D [14].

Segmenting objects by their distance from the camera is often a better way of recognizing the hand compared to color segmentation, for example, by assuming it to be the *closest object* to the camera [34], especially in cases where multiple people are in the frame or there is a partial hand-face occlusion [35]. Still, some approaches [35,36] use skin color for hand detection, mainly for enhancing depth-based segmentation. While the authors of [35] do not report a significant increase in performance, there are certain situations where a combination of skin and depth for hand segmentation may be useful, for instance the former example would be enhanced by assuming the hand to be the *closest skin colored object*, which would exclude other objects close to the camera, such as a keyboard. It would also provide a better hand segmentation for users that wear long-sleeved shirts and salvage cases where depth segmentation is prone to errors, such as the hand being too close to another object.

When using ToF sensors, quite a few authors have stressed the importance of fusing the 2D and 3D data (the intensity and the range maps) [5,7,8,9,10,37,38]. In [38], for example, the recognition rates for a set of simple arm gestures were between 78% and 88% correct when using only the 3D data, while with the fused 3D and 2D data the rates improved the rates to between 90% and 95%. The authors of [38], also argue for representations of gestures as a sequence of discrete primitives as opposed to recognizing gestures through a trajectory based approach. Their approach is further developed in [10] by including optical flow for better motion estimation. Another approach is [21], which uses two Kinects and two RGB cameras to capture a wider 3D scene, which improves the robustness of hand tracking, while the high definition web cams determine the hand pose. As well as fusing data from depth and RGB images, the authors of [36] use angular data from an inertial measurement unit to normalize and orient the hand upwards for pose estimation.

Hand pose estimation for sign language recognition is also a very active field. The authors of [39] use a combination of three letter classifiers to detect words from sequences of hand gestures. As a novel feature, the letter classifiers are improved by updating the training samples when a word is detected with high confidence. For an extended overview of sign language recognition systems we direct the reader to Chapter 4.2 of this book.

The bag of visual-and-depth-words approach is used in [40] in conjunction with a concatenated Viewpoint Feature Histogram (VFH) and Camera Roll Histogram (CRH) feature vector. Spatio-temporal pyramids are used to fuse geometrical and temporal information. With the addition of late fusion of the RGB (Histogram of Oriented Gradients, Histogram of Optical Flow) and depth (VFH-CRH) descriptors, the mean Levenshtein distance between the recognized sequence of gestures and the ground truth is improved from 0.30 to 0.26.

The authors of [17] achieve a 87% hand gesture recognition accuracy with a multi-step approach, finding hand-sized blobs, performing scale and rotation normalization, then extracting four feature descriptors and classifying gestures using an action graph as an alternative to HMMs. In [18], a 26 DOF hand model is matched to the hand pose using particle swarm optimization. The GPU is then used to accelerate the implementation to near real-time frame rates (15 Hz). Model-based pose detection is also used in [19]: a one-shot pose estimation is done using a hand pose database consisting of 20 prototype models (poses) rendered from 86 different viewpoints. The images from the database are compared to the actual segmented hand pose by means of a weighted depth matching and chamfer distance similarity measure. In tests, the authors discovered that anthropometric features varied greatly between users' hands and that the real-world 3D data could not be aligned perfectly to the generated poses. They obtain a recognition rate of 76% for a 1–64 pixels error between the winner pose and the real-world 3D pose. The authors of [20] achieve a recognition rate of 90% and a runtime of 0.5 s per pose, with a method based on Earth-Mover's distance. This method is also robust to finger-melding poses, when two fingers are close enough, or partially occluding each other, to be considered to be part of the same blob. Alternative approaches use the full-body tracking of the OpenNI framework to help in hand detection [21] or provide a basis for full-body gesture detection [22].

Only few approaches deal with the simultaneous tracking of body and hands [41,42]. While in [41] the authors have shown how gesture recognition can be improved by tracking both the body and the hands, the only reference to simultaneous and real-time extraction of hand and body skeletons we are aware of is [42].

3   Main Remaining Challenges

3.1   Shortcomings of Current 3D Cameras

ToF Sensors

Low resolution is common in ToF cameras compared to regular RGB ones. While the resolution is sufficient for tracking two hands at a particular distance, the flexible tracking of hands at various distance ranges would require higher resolution. Alternatively, in such cases, the interface might be reduced only to simple gesture recognition via blob tracking, as the fingers might not be clear enough.

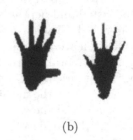

(a)   (b)

Fig. 3. (a) Frame from a near-range ToF camera (PMD CamBoard Micro): note the large amount of noise in the background and near the edges of objects. (b) Motion artifacts: the moving hand (right) has thinner fingers than the static hand (left).

Working range is limited by the range ambiguities inherent to the ToF principle and also by the illumination they use. This is not necessarily an issue for near-range gestural interfaces, although they tend to have more noise due to the lower level of active illumination (Fig. 3a).

Motion artifacts may lead to erroneous values at the borders of the measured objects. This issue is more prominent for hand gestures, as panning the hand can lead to loss of data around the fingers, effectively making them thinner and therefore harder to track (Fig. 3b).

Systematic distance errors, multiple reflections and **flying pixels** may also affect ToF-based gesture interfaces. We refer to [4] and Chapters 1, 2 where various solutions to these problems are discussed.

Structured Light Sensors (PrimeSense Technology)

Low resolution may not be apparent as the device has an output resolution of 640x480. From measurements on the Microsoft Kinect (Fig. 4b), the spatial localization of an edge is approximately 2 pixels off in either direction perpendicular to the edge, which indicates that the effective lateral resolution of the sensor is about 4 times lower in x and y directions.

Working range is limited by design, as the sensor was built to work best at medium range and indoors. At close range (less than 40cm) the sensor fails to produce any data (Fig. 4a). Although there are devices that improve close range output ("near mode" for the Kinect for Windows and the PrimeSense Carmine short range sensor), they are still limited to around 40cm.

Missing data occurs maily due to the baseline between the sensor and the illuminating laser, resulting in shadows around the outside of object borders. Data can also be missing in regions where the diffraction pattern has hot spots (more obvious at close range). Also, where the sensor does not have enough information from the pattern to make a depth measurement, small patches of missing data can occur (Fig. 4a).

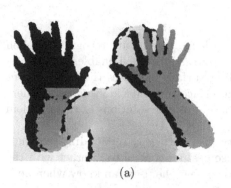
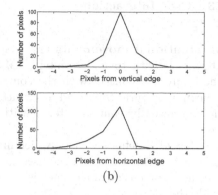

(a)   (b)

Fig. 4. (a) Kinect sensor artifacts: missing data (black) due to shadowing and near range (right hand) and hot spots (left hand). (b) Vertical (top) and horizontal (bottom) edge fidelity denote reduced lateral resolution. The graphs represent the position deviation of the edges of a rectangular object placed at 100 cm from the Kinect sensor. The deviation is calculated by counting erroneous pixels that correspond to the background inside the object boundary and vice-versa over a strip of the edge. Similar results have been found by [43].

Environment Limitations

One must also consider the limitations of cameras that require active lighting before using them in environments with substantial infrared light. Typical scenarios are outdoors in full sun, in cars near the dashboard, or in rooms that use high powered incandescent lighting. A different set of limitations is created by scenarios which require the cameras to be behind a transparent cover, such as digital signage or window-shopping entertainment: while the sensors themselves are not affected by a transparent surface, reflexions from the active lighting can cause sensor saturation with loss of information in those regions.

3.2   Latency and Real-Time Performance

Although approaches like the ones to be presented in Section 4 can run in real time on rather modest hardware, future requirements will aim at further reducing cost and size. The complexity of hardware and algorithms must be therefore further reduced.

For most applications, a tight coupling between the hands and the application is essential. Current solutions all provide a more or less squashy and wobbly interaction due to both the latencies of the sensor readout and of the middleware. In addition to reduced latencies, more realistic and predictive models are needed.

Moreover, since the hand can move very fast, with speeds of up to $5\,\mathrm{ms}^{-1}$ for translation and $300°\mathrm{s}^{-1}$ for wrist rotation [24], higher framerates may be required.

3.3   User Interaction

Unintentional movements are a big challenge for gesture recognition when interacting with touch-less interfaces. In contrast to touch-enabled interfaces, where physical contact with the controlling surface indicates the user's intent to begin a gestural command, touch-less interfaces must decide when and where the user actually wants to interact with them. Possible solutions to this problem are:

Active area defines a region which limits the interface to a bounding rectangle (2D) or box (3D) in which the user can use gesture control to interact with the interface. Some type of feedback is needed so that the user can know when he is inside the active area.

Modal interfaces become active when a "clutch" action is performed by the user. This can be anything from giving a vocal command or using a very obvious and unique gesture such as waving, opening the hand to show all five fingers or making a gesture with his other hand. After this action is performed, the interface is active, and the user can interact with it by performing other gestures. Deactivating the interface can be done automatically, e.g. after the user finishes the current gesture, after a preset idle time, or by moving the hand outside the active area of the interface (in conjunction with the previous strategy).

Dwell time is usually implemented for emulating virtual buttons: in order to interact with the interface, the user must perform a gesture for a certain amount of time. For example, to press a button, the user must point to it, and then keep his hand inside the button perimeter for a preset time. This is usually done in conjunction with visual or auditory feedback (a timer, change of color or short sound) to announce to the user that if he keeps doing the gesture the corresponding action will be performed.

Preset idle pose is a variation of the modal interface: instead of switching to the active state after the specific gesture has been performed, here the interface is in a neutral state while a certain gesture is performed, becoming active when the gesture is changed. This is implemented usually to force users in a particular pose to better suit the application purpose. For example, if accuracy is needed for a particular interface, the user could be forced to keep his thumb and index fingers in an "L" shape, with the rest of the fingers being curled. The application can then track the index finger as a cursor and use the thumb moving towards the hand as an indication of interface activation, with the benefit of stability while gesturing (the index finger does not move much when adducting the thumb).

Multi-modal interaction presents the user with other forms of input that can be used to gain attention of the gesture recognition system: a vocal command, head and gaze tracking, or even pushing a button (where extreme robustness is required, for instance in medical applications) can be used to activate the interface.

Ergonomic limitations can become an issue with touch-less interfaces that force the user in unnatural poses. Humans prefer having their hands supported by the work surface, while the work is done with wrist and elbow movements. In the case of interacting with interfaces by the means of pointing gestures, fatigue and sore-ness quickly set in if the hand is held in an unsupported position for too long.

Possible solutions to this problem include not being limited to hand-only or pointing gestures for interface control, or requiring the use of hand gestures only for a short time. Cubic-foot applications should not have this issue, as users can support their elbows on the desktop or their body. The main takeaway from this limitation is that interfaces should be designed from the ground up, with human biomechanics in mind.

3.4 Novel Gesture Interfaces and Standards

There is a growing agreement that touch-less gesture interfaces should not be designed as computer-mouse replacements. Instead, the whole interface needs to be re-designed in order to enable the potential of such novel interfaces. In order to be accepted, these novel interfaces must be standardized in the sense that similar actions should be triggered by similar gestures across different applications.

3.5 Multi-modal Interfaces

Examples of alternatives to gesture interfaces are speech recognition and gaze tracking. All these modalities have their strengths and weaknesses and one future challenge will be to fuse them. For example, gaze is much faster for pointing but can hardly produce any semantics, which could be done by speech and/or gestures. The recognition of emotions and the integration of wearable sensors could be further extensions.

4 Selected Recent Developments

4.1 3D Cameras

Currently ToF cameras are becoming much smaller and also cheaper. The Cre-ative Interactive Gesture Camera Developer Kit, for example, costs US$150, while solutions based on PrimeSense technology are more expensive (US$200 and US$250 for the PrimeSense Carmine sensor and Microsoft Kinect for Win-dows sensor respectively). Similarly, ToF modules for automotive and consumer applications are expected to be targeted at prices well below US$100. The pace at which ToF cameras have been shrinking is impressive and it certainly facilitates the development of near-range gesture interfaces.

Light-field cameras are another interesting option since they neither require a baseline nor active illumination. We have tested Raytrix[1] light field cameras with the algorithms presented in the next section and found that they provide more robust hand-skeleton tracking than standard stereo systems.

---

[1] www.raytrix.de

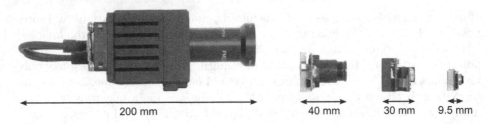

Fig. 5. Various ToF cameras, from left to right: PMD CamCube, PMD CamBoard Micro, PMD CamBoard Nano, and the most recent PMD CamBoard Pico. Other manufacturers have completed a similar miniaturization process (e.g. SoftKinetic).

4.2   Commercial Solutions

There are a number of commercial solutions for desktop PCs which provide a framework for body tracking and gesture recognition, such as the Omek Beckon[2], the SoftKinetic iisu SDK[3] and the Microsoft Kinect for Windows[4].

Probably the most widely known body tracking solution is the Microsoft Kinect for Xbox360. It employs machine learning algorithms to estimate the user's body posture [29], which is then used as input for interactive games on the console. However, extensions to hand gestures have only been recently introduced for the Kinect for Windows, but hand skeleton tracking is still not available.

Regarding hand gesture recognition, a recent collaboration between Intel, Creative and SoftKinetic released the Creative Interactive Gesture Camera Developer Kit[5]. It is a near-range time-of-flight camera that allows tracking of the user's hand up to one meter. While the accompanying software solution does not fully model the hand in 3 dimensions, it does provide the extended fingertips' position and various anatomical landmarks (palm, elbow).

The Leap Motion[6] device promises to allow full 3D tracking of the user's fingers, provided they keep their hands over the device's field of view. The device itself is a small box that needs to be placed on the user's desktop and facing upward. At the time of this writing, the device has not been released yet. Finally, there have been some attempts to use mobile devices to track the user's hand or face and respond to simple gestures.

Another solution for hand and finger detection is provided by Metrilus[7]. Their algorithms include finger tracking, pointing, swipes, and direction evaluation.

For full hand skeleton tracking, 3Gear Systems[8] proposes a desktop solution which involves a PrimeSense[9] Carmine short range sensor mounted above the

---

[2] www.omekinteractive.com

[3] www.softkinetic.com

[4] www.microsoft.com/en-us/kinectforwindows

[5] www.click.intel.com/intelsdk/

[6] www.leapmotion.com

[7] http://www.metrilus.de/

[8] www.threegear.com

[9] www.primesense.com

user's desk. The system provides hand pose estimation and gesture recognition with the added step of first calibrating the model with the user's hands.

Omek Interactive's Grasp solution promises full hand skeleton tracking, although it is not currently available for review.

An alternative solution for hand skeleton tracking, which is of low complexity and requires no calibration, has been developed by gestigon[10], and it is based on the approach presented in the next section.

4.3   Hand and Body Tracking Using Self Organizing Maps

In this section we will present some of our own recent developments, showing how self-organizing maps (SOM) can be used for hand and full body tracking. We use a range camera for data acquisition and apply a SOM-learning process for each frame in order to capture the pose. While the standard SOM algorithm [6] and some extensions [44] have been proposed before, we will introduce further constraints and a performance analysis on an embedded system. Details on the embedded system implementation are given in [45].

4.3.1   The SOM Tracking Algorithm

SOMs are a well-established method for topology-preserving data transformations and have been used for gesture recognition based on 2D appearance models, for which the SOM can help to find the low-dimensional space of hand-pose transformations [46]. Similarly, in [47] SOMs are used as an intermediate stage to cluster hand trajectories before feeding them into an HMM for gesture recognition. These uses of SOMs, however, are completely different from our approach, which we will describe next.

The node-based SOM tracking algorithm proposed by [6,42] (which we will refer from now on as the Standard SOM Algorithm) takes a different approach, by modeling the hand as a SOM topology. The process starts with the initialization of the network weights in the shape of the hand topology (Fig. 6c) in the center of the hand point cloud, followed by the iteration of two steps: the competition and the update of the weights. At every iteration, a sample point from the dataset is randomly chosen. First, during the competition phase, a winner node (i.e. the weight with the minimum Euclidean distance to the sample point) is computed.

Next, the update phase aims at decreasing the distance between the two points by moving the winner-node weight towards the sample point by a fraction ϵ of the distance between them. The standard SOM algorithm then also applies a neighborhood update, in the sense that not only the winner-node weight is updated, but also the weights of the neighbor-nodes, with a smaller learning rate.

These steps are repeated for hundreds or thousands of iterations. This makes the skeleton graph fit to the point cloud and stay within its confines.

---

[10] www.gestigon.com

4.3.2   Topology Expansion

We expand the 44-node upper body topology presented in [6,42] (Fig. 6a) to two topologies, one representing the whole body (Fig. 6b), and the other representing the human hand (Fig. 6c). The models were chosen so they mimic the anatomical landmarks of their real-world counterparts — limbs and joints for the body and phalanges and interphalangeal joints for the hand. The rigid bodies (torso and palm) are modeled as a mesh. Both produce good qualitative results in our implementation.

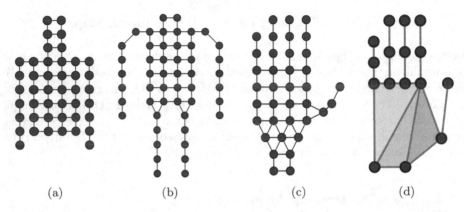

(a)   (b)   (c)   (d)

Fig. 6. SOM topologies: (a) The upper body topology proposed in [6]; (b), (c) Expanded topologies for the whole body and the hand; (d) The extended SOM hand topology for segments and planes

4.3.3   The Extended SOM

Our proposed algorithm extends the competition and the update step to 1D and 2D network segments. The 1D-segments are the lines between pairs of connected nodes, and the 2D-segments are the triangles determined by triples of connected nodes. 1D-segments allow to represent the fingers more accurately, and the 2D-segments model the palm of the hand. We now have not only elements of dimension zero (nodes) like in the standard case described in the last section, but also elements of dimension one and two for representing the data distribution. The new topology can be seen in Fig. 6d.

This approach is motivated by the fact that a hand-like topology involves a difficult separation between the nodes corresponding to different fingers. A node that belongs to one finger can easily be attracted by another finger, given the topological closeness. This may lead to an erroneous tracking of the hand and destroy the topological relations. With these 1D and 2D segments we can represent fingers and parts of the palm more accurately and expect the self-organizing maps to be less prone to this type of errors.

4.3.4   Performance Analysis

Because the algorithms have low computational complexity, they can be implemented on low power devices, such as embedded systems. We implemented both the standard SOM algorithm and the extended version on a PandaBoard ES, which is the next iteration of the popular Pandaboard platform. It is powered by a Texas Instruments OMAP4460 system-on-chip (SoC), which is used in a number of mobile devices available on the market such as the Samsung Galaxy Nexus. The board features a 1.2 GHz dual-core Cortex-A9 ARM CPU, a PowerVR SGX 540 graphics processing unit, 1 GB DDR2 SDRAM, two USB 2.0 ports, Ethernet connection and various other peripherals.

After implementing the standard SOM for the hand and whole-body skeleton, we have obtained the results shown in Figure 7. We have been able to successfully reach our target of real-time performance, at 30 frames per second (FPS).

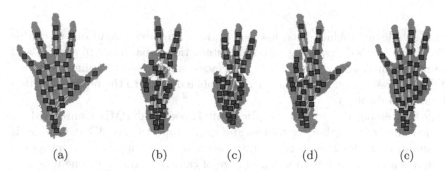

(a)   (b)   (c)   (d)   (c)

Fig. 7. The Standard SOM Algorithm results for various hand poses [45]

It can be seen that the hand tracker is able to cope with missing data (Fig. 7b,c as white areas on the palm), the skeleton's topology remaining stable, the fingers being retracted in the palm. This is considered to be correct behavior, as the fingers will be reported as "bent" to a subsequent gesture recognition algorithm.

The results for the extended SOM for hand tracking can be seen below. Although the competition and update phases are more complex than those of the standard SOM, the algorithm still runs in real time (30 FPS) with the same number of iterations, as the new topology has less than half the nodes of the old one (16 vs. 37). In figure 8 we show five hand poses taken directly from the real-time video on the embedded platform. The qualitative performance is similar to the one of the node-only SOM implementation. The topology converges correctly on the straightened as well as the bent fingers.

In figures 8d and e, hand poses in which the fingers are held together are shown. The fingers remain in the correct places and do not retract into the palm — the new segment-plane updates solve the problem of the previous SOM implementation that appeared when data points were too close to each other and the nodes from one finger wandered into the space of other fingers. This allows for a more robust representation of the hand gestures, as melded fingers (that could come from out-of-plane hand rotations or hands which are too far away for the camera to distinguish between fingers) are no longer a problem.

The computational efficiency of the method makes it ideal for implementations on a low-powered systems such as embedded devices. The algorithm could be

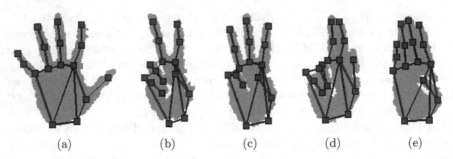

(a)   (b)   (c)   (d)   (e)

Fig. 8. The extended SOM results for various hand poses

used in such devices, which need low-power, low-complexity solutions to enable gesture technologies — granting extended interaction capabilities to current and future mobile interfaces. Natural user interfaces can be used to enhance the usability of devices ranging from the current mobile devices to the next generation head-mounted displays.

From the testing done with the Microsoft Kinect and PMD CamBoard we concluded that our method is robust and can adapt to any 3D data that is being supplied, as long as it is accurate enough, meaning that the proposed algorithm is able to work with a wide range of cameras. Another benefit is that the self-organizing map approach can easily be applied to any deformable object that needs to be tracked by simply changing the network topology (e.g. torso, full body, pets etc.). This presents a definite advantage over methods that use machine learning to recognize objects, as the self-organizing map algorithm need not be trained in advance.

However, the SOM approach has its limitations: it requires hand segmentation and adequate initialization. Also, since only a topology is being defined, it is not obvious how geometrical constraints can be applied.

5   Example Applications

5.1   Consumer

Cubic Foot applications have been pioneered by Intel in an attempt to make ultrabooks more interesting. The idea is to use the 3D volume spanned by the opened notebook for gesture-based interaction (i.e. the "cubic foot"). Currently, the hand gestures are all based on fingertips, not a full hand skeleton. However, this initiative has contributed to the ongoing miniaturization of ToF cameras and it seems that ToF sensors may win the race for the smallest sensor for gesture interfaces, although some promising alternatives such as the Leap Motion device exist.

Gaming applications have always been big adopters of alternative input interfaces. One of the first commercial touch-less controllers designed for games was the Sony EyeToy, a QVGA resolution webcam that could be used in low-light environments. Released in 2003, it leveraged the PlayStation 2 powerful video processor to let users interact with games using their whole body as the input device. Other gesture interfaces followed: the Nintendo Wii console along with the Wii Remote as a motion sensing device in 2006, EyeToy's successor, the PlayStation Eye and its accompanying motion sensing controller, the PlayStation Move in 2010, and soon after, the Microsoft Kinect for XBOX360, a definitive boost to gesture control interfaces.

Mobile and Embedded Control is another range of applications that could benefit from gesture control. Almost every commercial gesture control framework on the market today is aimed at desktop PCs, due to the computing power required by the algorithms they use. As mobile platforms shrink in size, gestural interfaces will start to become a viable alternative to touch-based interaction [45]. Gesture control could be a potent interface with which the user could control device parameters of mobile applications or other personal devices such as cameras. Being able to control appliances such as TVs from a distance without the need for a remote control is starting to become a feature in the new range of consumer devices, although only for high-end models, due to the limitations described above.

5.2 Automotive

Automotive suppliers aim at (i) replacing the growing number of buttons and joysticks in the car by a generic virtual interface and (ii) creating new forms of interaction. This will, however, be a gradual development starting with simple gestures that control harmless functions. Due to the extreme variations in ambient light and high demands on reliability and robustness, this application field has its own challenges.

5.3 Medical

The prototypical medical application is that of using gestures during surgery to access medical records or to control equipment in a sterile environment. The obvious benefit is the lack of physical contact between the operator and the device. Moreover, surgeons prefer not having to put down their tools in order to be able to press buttons or touchscreens. We refer to Chapter 4.1 for a review of such applications.

5.4 Digital Signage

As gesture control is a highly user-interactive experience, gesture driven signage will certainly see emergence in the future, with some companies specializing in gesture marketing (e.g. GestureTek [11] and ZiiCON [12]). Possible applications in this area include virtual tours, information kiosks, gaming, art installations, even

---

[11] www.gesturetek.com

[12] www.ziicon.com

interactive window-shopping which could, for instance, take the user's clothing dimensions automatically or target marketing based on one's actions. Because the system is tracking the user at all times for gesture input, features such as customizing an ad for the tracked person could be used to grab attention and increase the impact of the signage.

5.5 Sign Language

This is an application that many consider to be obvious and useful [15,16]. From our own experience and extensive discussions with German associations, however, the interpretation of hand gestures is not sufficient for communication because facial expressions are essential for those who "speak" and read sign language. While the extraction of a hand skeleton can provide a good basis for sign recognition, the problem of recognizing facial expressions has to be solved in addition. For an overview of gestural language recognition please refer to Chapter 4.2 of this book.

6 Summary

Gesture interfaces promise to change the way we interact with devices. To fully exploit this potential, however, one needs to rethink the human-machine interface and adapt it to the new technological opportunities. An essential component of such gesture interfaces is hand pose estimation which, as shown in Section 2.2, remains a challenging problem although a number of promising approaches and commercial solutions exist.

One approach to alleviate some of these issues is using a depth sensor. This increases robustness to lighting conditions and gives the possibility of discriminating objects based on their depth, making segmentation a more straightforward process. Depth sensors have led to considerable progress in the field and are now becoming small and low-cost devices, which, however, still need to overcome certain limitations that we have underlined in Section 3.1.

A further limiting factor is the complexity of the algorithms needed to estimate the many degrees of freedom that a gesturing hand can have. This is particularly true for approaches that operate with a full geometrical model of the hand. As an alternative, approaches that only define the topology have lower complexity but may sometimes fail to precisely extract the correct pose and may therefore require additional constraints.

Currently, although commercial solutions exist, they are limited to specific use-cases, such as desktop or cubic foot interaction. We have also presented our own work in the field, which is based on self-organizing maps for hand pose estimation. The method has the benefit of tracking and estimating the hand skeleton in a single stage, with significant performance gains.

Finally, we have presented several commercial application domains in which gesture control can be used in order to build a better interface. As gestures are often used in human communication, is seems natural to extend them to human-machine interaction for more intuitive interfaces.

References

1. Pavlovic, V., Sharma, R., Huang, T.: Visual interpretation of hand gestures for human-computer interaction: A review. IEEE Transactions on Pattern Analysis and Machine Intelligence 19(7), 677–695 (1997)
2. Haker, M., Böhme, M., Martinetz, T., Barth, E.: Deictic gestures with a time-of-flight camera. In: Kopp, S., Wachsmuth, I. (eds.) GW 2009. LNCS, vol. 5934, pp. 110–121. Springer, Heidelberg (2010)
3. Droeschel, D., Stuckler, J., Behnke, S.: Learning to interpret pointing gestures with a time-of-flight camera. In: 2011 6th ACM/IEEE International Conference on Human-Robot Interaction (HRI), pp. 481–488 (2011)
4. Kolb, A., Barth, E., Koch, R., Larsen, R.: Time-of-flight cameras in computer graphics. Computer Graphics Forum 29(1), 141–159 (2010)
5. Böhme, M., Haker, M., Martinetz, T., Barth, E.: A facial feature tracker for human-computer interaction based on 3D Time-of-Flight cameras. International Journal of Intelligent Systems Technologies and Applications 5(3/4), 264–273 (2008)
6. Haker, M., Böhme, M., Martinetz, T., Barth, E.: Self-organizing maps for pose estimation with a time-of-flight camera. In: Kolb, A., Koch, R. (eds.) Dyn3D 2009. LNCS, vol. 5742, pp. 142–153. Springer, Heidelberg (2009)
7. Böhme, M., Haker, M., Martinetz, T., Barth, E.: Head tracking with combined face and nose detection. In: Proceedings of the IEEE International Symposium on Signals, Circuits & Systems (ISSCS), Iaşi, Romania (2009)
8. Böhme, M., Haker, M., Riemer, K., Martinetz, T., Barth, E.: Face detection using a time-of-flight camera. In: Kolb, A., Koch, R. (eds.) Dyn3D 2009. LNCS, vol. 5742, pp. 167–176. Springer, Heidelberg (2009)
9. Böhme, M., Haker, M., Martinetz, T., Barth, E.: Shading constraint improves accuracy of time-of-flight measurements. Computer Vision and Image Understanding 114, 1329–1335 (2010)
10. Holte, M., Moeslund, T., Fihl, P.: View-invariant gesture recognition using 3D optical flow and harmonic motion context. Computer Vision and Image Understanding 114(12), 1353–1361 (2010), Special issue on Time-of-Flight Camera Based Computer Vision
11. Haubner, N., Schwanecke, U., Dorner, R., Lehmann, S., Luderschmidt, J.: Recognition of dynamic hand gestures with time-of-flight cameras. In: Dörner, R., Krömker, D. (eds.) Self Integrating Systems for Better Living Environments: First Workshop, Sensyble. Number 1, pp. 7–13 (2010)
12. Kollorz, E., Penne, J., Hornegger, J., Barke, A.: Gesture recognition with a time-of-flight camera. Int. J. Intell. Syst. Technol. Appl. 5(3/4), 334–343 (2008)
13. Mo, Z., Neumann, U.: Real-time hand pose recognition using low-resolution depth images. In: IEEE Computer Society Conference on Computer Vision and Pattern Recognition, vol. 2, pp. 1499–1505 (2006)
14. Suryanarayan, P., Subramanian, A., Mandalapu, D.: Dynamic hand pose recognition using depth data. In: 2010 20th International Conference on Pattern Recognition (ICPR), pp. 3105–3108 (August 2010)
15. Keskin, C., Kirac, F., Kara, Y., Akarun, L.: Randomized decision forests for static and dynamic hand shape classification. In: 2012 IEEE Computer Society Conference on Computer Vision and Pattern Recognition Workshops (CVPRW), pp. 31–36 (2012)
16. Keskin, C., Kirac, F., Kara, Y., Akarun, L.: Real time hand pose estimation using depth sensors. In: Fossati, A., Gall, J., Grabner, H., Ren, X., Konolige, K. (eds.) Consumer Depth Cameras for Computer Vision. Advances in Computer Vision and Pattern Recognition, pp. 119–137. Springer, London (2013)

17. Kurakin, A., Zhang, Z., Liu, Z.: A real time system for dynamic hand gesture recognition with a depth sensor. In: 2012 Proceedings of the 20th European Signal Processing Conference (EUSIPCO), pp. 1975–1979 (2012)
18. Oikonomidis, I., Kyriazis, N., Argyros, A.A.: Efficient model-based 3D tracking of hand articulations using kinect. In: British Machine Vision Conference, Dundee, UK, vol. 2 (2011)
19. Doliotis, P., Athitsos, V., Kosmopoulos, D., Perantonis, S.: Hand shape and 3D pose estimation using depth data from a single cluttered frame. In: Bebis, G., Boyle, R., Parvin, B., Koracin, D., Fowlkes, C., Wang, S., Choi, M.-H., Mantler, S., Schulze, J., Acevedo, D., Mueller, K., Papka, M. (eds.) ISVC 2012, Part I. LNCS, vol. 7431, pp. 148–158. Springer, Heidelberg (2012)
20. Ren, Z., Yuan, J., Zhang, Z.: Robust hand gesture recognition based on finger-earth mover's distance with a commodity depth camera. In: Proceedings of the 19th ACM International Conference on Multimedia (MM 2011), pp. 1093–1096. ACM, New York (2011)
21. Caputo, M., Denker, K., Dums, B., Umlauf, G.: 3D hand gesture recognition based on sensor fusion of commodity hardware. In: Reiterer, H., Deussen, O. (eds.) Mensch & Computer 2012: Interaktiv Informiert Allgegenwärtig und Allumfassend!?, München (Oldenbourg Verlag), pp. 293–302 (2012)
22. Reyes, M., Dominguez, G., Escalera, S.: Feature weighting in dynamic time warping for gesture recognition in depth data. In: 2011 IEEE International Conference on Computer Vision Workshops (ICCV Workshops), pp. 1182–1188 (2011)
23. Zetzsche, C., Barth, E., Wegmann, B.: The importance of intrinsically two-dimensional image features in biological vision and picture coding. In: Watson, A.B. (ed.) Digital Images and Human Vision, pp. 109–138. MIT Press (October 1993)
24. Erol, A., Bebis, G., Nicolescu, M., Boyle, R.D., Twombly, X.: Vision-based hand pose estimation: A review. Computer Vision and Image Understanding 108(12), 52–73 (2007), Special Issue on Vision for Human-Computer Interaction
25. Wren, C., Azarbayejani, A., Darrell, T., Pentland, A.: Pfinder: Real-time tracking of the human body. IEEE Transactions on Pattern Analysis and Machine Intelligence 19(7), 780–785 (1997)
26. Campbell, L., Becker, D., Azarbayejani, A., Bobick, A., Pentland, A.: Invariant features for 3-D gesture recognition. In: Proceedings of the Second International Conference on Automatic Face and Gesture Recognition, pp. 157–162 (1996)
27. Ballan, L., Taneja, A., Gall, J., Van Gool, L., Pollefeys, M.: Motion capture of hands in action using discriminative salient points. In: Fitzgibbon, A., Lazebnik, S., Perona, P., Sato, Y., Schmid, C. (eds.) ECCV 2012, Part VI. LNCS, vol. 7577, pp. 640–653. Springer, Heidelberg (2012)
28. Oikonomidis, I., Kyriazis, N., Argyros, A.A.: Markerless and efficient 26-DOF hand pose recovery. In: Kimmel, R., Klette, R., Sugimoto, A. (eds.) ACCV 2010, Part III. LNCS, vol. 6494, pp. 744–757. Springer, Heidelberg (2011)
29. Shotton, J., Sharp, T., Kipman, A., Fitzgibbon, A., Finocchio, M., Blake, A., Cook, M., Moore, R.: Real-time human pose recognition in parts from single depth images. Commun. ACM 56(1), 116–124 (2013)
30. Lahamy, H., Litchi, D.: Real-time hand gesture recognition using range cameras. In: Canadian Geomatics Conference (CGC), vol. 10 (2010)
31. Malassiotis, S., Tsalakanidou, F., Mavridis, N., Giagourta, V., Grammalidis, N., Strintzis, M.: A face and gesture recognition system based on an active stereo sensor. In: Proceedings of the 2001 International Conference on Image Processing, vol. 3, pp. 955–958 (2001)

32. Breuer, P., Eckes, C., Müller, S.: Hand gesture recognition with a novel IR time-of-flight range camera–A pilot study. In: Gagalowicz, A., Philips, W. (eds.) MIRAGE 2007. LNCS, vol. 4418, pp. 247–260. Springer, Heidelberg (2007)

33. Zhu, X., Wong, K.Y.K.: Single-frame hand gesture recognition using color and depth kernel descriptors. In: 2012 21st International Conference on Pattern Recognition (ICPR), pp. 2989–2992 (November 2012)

34. Liu, X., Fujimura, K.: Hand gesture recognition using depth data. In: Proceedings of the Sixth IEEE International Conference on Automatic Face and Gesture Recognition, pp. 529–534 (2004)

35. Van den Bergh, M., Van Gool, L.: Combining RGB and ToF cameras for real-time 3D hand gesture interaction. In: IEEE Workshop on Applications of Computer Vision (WACV), pp. 66–72 (2011)

36. Trindade, P., Lobo, J., Barreto, J.: Hand gesture recognition using color and depth images enhanced with hand angular pose data. In: 2012 IEEE Conference on Multisensor Fusion and Integration for Intelligent Systems (MFI), pp. 71–76 (2012)

37. Ghobadi, S., Loepprich, O., Hartmann, K., Loffeld, O.: Hand segmentation using 2D/3D images. In: Cree, M.J. (ed.) IVCNZ 2007 Conference, University of Waikato, pp. 64–69 (2007)

38. Holte, M., Moeslund, T., Fihl, P.: Fusion of range and intensity information for view invariant gesture recognition. In: IEEE Computer Society Conference on Computer Vision and Pattern Recognition Workshops (CVPRW 2008), pp. 1–7 (2008)

39. Uebersax, D., Gall, J., Van den Bergh, M., Van Gool, L.: Real-time sign language letter and word recognition from depth data. In: 2011 IEEE International Conference on Computer Vision Workshops (ICCV Workshops), pp. 383–390 (2011)

40. Hernandez-Vela, A., Bautista, M., Perez-Sala, X., Ponce, V., Baro, X., Pujol, O., Angulo, C., Escalera, S.: BoVDW: Bag-of-visual-and-depth-words for gesture recognition. In: 2012 21st International Conference on Pattern Recognition (ICPR), pp. 449–452 (2012)

41. Song, Y., Demirdjian, D., Davis, R.: Multi-signal gesture recognition using temporal smoothing hidden conditional random fields. In: 2011 IEEE International Conference on Automatic Face Gesture Recognition and Workshops (FG 2011), pp. 388–393 (2011)

42. Haker, M., Barth, E., Martinetz, T.: Method for the real-time-capable, computer-assisted analysis of an image sequence containing a variable pose, International patent WO/2010/130245 (filed: May 6, 2010)

43. Andersen, M.R., Jensen, T., Lisouski, P., Mortensen, A.K., Hansen, M.K., Gregersen, T., Ahrendt, P.: Kinect depth sensor evaluation for computer vision applications. Technical report ECE-TR-6, Department of Engineering Electrical and Computer Engineering, Aarhus University (2012)

44. State, A., Coleca, F., Barth, E., Martinetz, T.: Hand tracking with an extended self-organizing map. In: Estevez, P.A., Principe, J.C., Zegers, P. (eds.) Advances in Self-Organizing Maps. AISC, vol. 198, pp. 115–124. Springer, Heidelberg (2013)

45. Coleca, F., Klement, S., Martinetz, T., Barth, E.: Real-time skeleton tracking for embedded systems. In: Proceedings of Multimedia Content and Mobile Devices SPIE Conference, vol. 8667 (2013)

46. Guan, H., Feris, R., Turk, M.: The isometric self-organizing map for 3D hand pose estimation. In: 7th International Conference on Automatic Face and Gesture Recognition (FGR 2006), pp. 263–268 (2006)

47. Caridakis, G., Karpouzis, K., Drosopoulos, A., Kollias, S.: Somm: Self organizing markov map for gesture recognition. Pattern Recognition Letters 31(1), 52–59 (2010)

Real-Time Range Imaging
in Health Care: A Survey

Sebastian Bauer[1], Alexander Seitel[2,3], Hannes Hofmann[4], Tobias Blum[5],
Jakob Wasza[1], Michael Balda[4], Hans-Peter Meinzer[3], Nassir Navab[5],
Joachim Hornegger[1], and Lena Maier-Hein[2,3]

[1] Pattern Recognition Lab, Friedrich-Alexander-Universität Erlangen-Nürnberg,
Erlangen, Germany
sebastian.bauer@cs.fau.de
[2] Junior group: Computer-assisted Interventions
[3] Division of Medical and Biological Informatics,
German Cancer Research Center (DKFZ), Heidelberg, Germany
l.maier-hein@dkfz-heidelberg.de
[4] Metrilus GmbH, Erlangen, Germany
michael.balda@metrilus.de
[5] Computer Aided Medical Procedures & Augmented Reality (CAMP),
Technische Universität München, Munich, Germany
blum@in.tum.de

Abstract. The recent availability of dynamic, dense, and low-cost range
imaging has gained widespread interest in health care. It opens up new
opportunities and has an increasing impact on both research and commercial activities. This chapter presents a state-of-the-art survey on the
integration of modern range imaging sensors into medical applications.
The scope is to identify promising applications and methods, and to
provide an overview of recent developments in this rapidly evolving domain. The survey covers a broad range of topics, including guidance in
computer-assisted interventions, operation room monitoring and workflow analysis, touch-less interaction and on-patient visualization, as well
as prevention and support in elderly care and rehabilitation. We put em-
phasis on dynamic and interactive tasks where real-time and dense 3-D
imaging forms the key aspect. While considering different range imaging
modalities that fulfill these requirements, we particularly investigate the
impact of Time-of-Flight imaging in this domain. Eventually, we discuss
practical demands and limitations, and open research issues and challenges that are of fundamental importance for the progression of the field.

1 Introduction

Computer assistance became increasingly important in health care over the last
decades. Applications include computer-aided diagnosis, therapy support, virtual and augmented reality for intervention support and training, as well as
systems to assist handicapped and elderly people. One of the key tasks for efficient computer-assistance in health care is a robust localization and tracking

M. Grzegorzek et al. (Eds.): Time-of-Flight and Depth Imaging, LNCS 8200, pp. 228–254, 2013.
© Springer-Verlag Berlin Heidelberg 2013

of the objects (operation situs, instruments) and persons (patient, physician, clinical staff) involved in the specific medical procedure. So far, this is typically performed using either (1) optical or electromagnetic tracking technologies that require markers to be attached to the target, or (2) by means of intra-operative radiographic imaging that implies a substantial radiation exposure to the patient and/or the physician. Marker-based approaches often complicate the clinical workflow and are thus not widely accepted in clinical routine.

In recent years, range imaging (RI) based techniques for marker-less, radiation-free localization have experienced a remarkable development with the availability of dynamic, dense and low-cost RI devices such as Time-of-Flight (ToF) cameras and Microsoft Kinect. Indeed, these modalities have been applied for numerous applications in the clinical environment, beyond marker-less localization. The scope of this state-of-the-art survey is to give a comprehensive overview of the use of range imaging devices in the context of health care, with a focus on dynamic tasks that require real-time and non-scanning 3-D perception. To our knowledge, it is the first review to address the fast growing number of research activities in this area.

The remainder of this chapter is organized as follows. The main part of the survey divides into four fields of application: guidance in computer-assisted interventions (Sect. 2), monitoring for operation room safety and workflow analysis (Sect. 3), touch-less interaction and on-patient visualization (Sect. 4), and diagnosis, prevention and support in screening, elderly care, rehabilitation and assistance for handicapped people (Sect. 5). In addition, we outline opportunities and limitations of different range imaging modalities, practical issues and dedicated software frameworks with a focus on the specific demands in medical applications (Sect. 6). Eventually, we conclude with a discussion (Sect. 7) where we summarize the most substantial challenges that must be tackled to increase the range of potential applications in the particular field of health care, and identify future research directions.

2 Guidance in Computer-Assisted Interventions

Guidance in computer-assisted interventions (CAI) is typically provided by establishing the spatial relationship between anatomical structures (acquired with some imaging modality prior to the intervention) and the medical instruments used during the intervention. This requires a registration of pre-operative patient-specific models to intra-operatively acquired data. One of the main challenges in this context is the fast, accurate, and robust acquisition of the patient anatomy during the intervention. Many CAI applications rely on modalities with limited imaging quality, such as ultrasound (US), or expensive and impracticable acquisition procedures, such as magnetic resonance imaging (MRI), or utilize custom designed markers that can be localized with optical or magnetic tracking systems. In contrast, real-time RI holds a simple, marker-less and non-ionizing alternative in interventional imaging. CAIs based on range imaging typically follow a generic workflow:

Treatment Planning: Prior to intervention, the patient's anatomy is acquired using standard medical imaging modalities such as computed tomography (CT) or MRI. Commonly, a treatment plan is derived from this data to be applied during intervention. Depending on the application, a simultaneous capture of range imaging data may be required during this planning stage.

Interventional Imaging: During the intervention, real-time RI allows for a continuous, marker-less and non-radiographic monitoring of the external body surface or the operation situs.

Surface Registration: To transfer the treatment plan to the patient, the acquired RI surface is typically registered to a reference shape being extracted from the planning data before the intervention. This may involve the determination of the patient's orientation and pose, as well as non-rigid deformations induced by respiration, cardiac motion or interventional tissue manipulation. As this chapter is not intended to review surface registration techniques, we refer to dedicated surveys for more information [1,2,3,4,5].

Guidance: The application of the treatment plan to the patient is accomplished by some sort of guidance that supports the physician during the intervention, e.g. by means of augmented reality (AR) visualization.

Below, we summarize applications and methods that have been proposed in the context of RI-based CAI for diagnostic and interventional imaging (Sect. 2.1), radiation therapy (Sect. 2.2), tomographic reconstruction (Sect. 2.3), open and percutaneous interventions (Sect. 2.4), and 3-D endoscopy for minimally-invasive procedures (Sect. 2.5).

2.1   Patient Setup in Diagnostic and Interventional Imaging

In the past decade, substantial progress has been made in improving the image acquisition process in CT and MRI. However, optimizing the pre-imaging workflow has been considered only lately. In clinical practice, patient setup and scanner initialization including patient positioning, table adjustment, and the input of patient-specific parameters into the scanner software are performed manually, being both tedious and time consuming [6,7]. The automation of these steps would reduce both the examination time and the workload for clinical staff, thereby relieving the health care system. In CT imaging, the initial patient setup accounts for a substantial share of the entire procedure. To speedup the pre-imaging CT workflow, Schaller et al. proposed a marker-less system based on ToF imaging that identifies the coarse location of anatomical regions for prone and supine patient postures at interactive framerates [6]. The alignment of the pre-defined anatomical target with the scanner isocenter can then be performed in an automatic manner by either positioning the treatment table w.r.t. a non-moving acquisition device (CT/MRI), or by transforming a moving acquisition device (e.g. C-arm CT) to coincide with the target. Note that a calibration between the coordinate systems of the RI camera and the scanner is required for this approach (cf. Sect. 6). Grimm et al. investigated the use of RI in the pre-imaging protocol for MRI [7]. In today's clinical routine, first, the

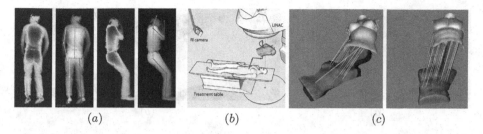

(a)   (b)   (c)

Fig. 1. (a) Estimating the body pose of a reclined patient on ToF data, for supine (left) and lateral left postures (right) [7]. The skeleton of the estimated pose is overlaid, with the right and left extremities labeled in red and yellow, respectively. (b) Patient setup in RT, where the intra-fractional patient surface acquired with an RI camera is registered to a reference shape extracted from planning data (depicted in gray). The aligning transformation (in blue) is then applied to the treatment table. (c) Feature-based multi-modal surface registration between Microsoft Kinect (bottom) and CT data (top). [8]. The colored lines indicate the established point correspondences.

patient orientation (head/feet first), posture (prone, supine, lateral left, right) and additional biometric information (body height, weight) must be specified by hand. Second, the radiologist manually defines the region of interest on the patient's body, typically using laser cross-hairs. To automate these tasks, Grimm et al. proposed a ToF-based system to detect both patient orientation and posture. In addition, using a model-based optimization framework, the articulated body pose of the reclined patient is estimated (Fig. 1a). This allows for a computerized localization of the scanning target, automating the pre-imaging workflow. Natural limitations involve the presence of blankets or additional equipment occluding the external patient surface, such as optional body coils in MR. In these cases, the localization must be performed prior to equipment placement.

2.2 Positioning and Motion Management in Radiation Therapy

The automation of patient setup is of particular interest for repeat treatments such as in fractionated radiation therapy (RT), where the tumor is irradiated in a sequence of treatment sessions. Reproducible patient setup constitutes a key component for accurate dose delivery. Prior to each fraction, the target location known from tomographic planning data must be accurately aligned w.r.t. the isocenter of the treatment system (Fig. 1b). Conventionally, this alignment is performed in a two-step procedure, comprising (1) manual coarse patient setup using laser cross-hairs and skin markers, and (2) position verification and refinement using radiographic imaging. Over the past years, systems for non-radiographic patient setup and monitoring in RT have been proposed using different RI technologies, including active stereo vision [9], ToF imaging [10], structured light [8,11,12], and light sectioning [13,14]. These systems estimate the rigid transformation that aligns the intra-fractionally acquired external body surface of the patient with a given reference shape extracted from tomographic

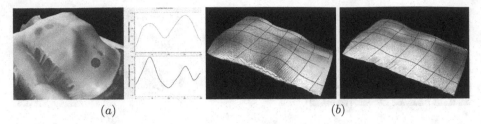

Fig. 2. (*a*) 1-D respiration surrogates extracted from Microsoft Kinect data, differentiating between thoracic (in green) and abdominal (in blue) motion. The target region (left) is set individually for each patient. (*b*) Dense surface deformation tracking [18] from sparse RI measurements (depicted in blue), using prior shape information from planning data (in gray). The magnitude of the local displacements is color-coded.

planning data. This transformation can then be transferred to the treatment table control for automatic positioning. The focus of early solutions was on setup verification, restricting the automatic patient alignment to a fine-scale positioning and thus still requiring a manual setup initialization [9,13]. The first ToF-based systems for automatic patient setup in RT were proposed by Schaller et al. [15] and Placht et al. [10]. However, these systems rely on rigid surface registration techniques and thus do not account for deformations induced by respiratory motion. To cope with this issue, Wasza et al. proposed a system for motion-compensated positioning based on patient-specific 4-D shape priors [11]. As the underlying iterative closest point (ICP) algorithm [16,17] for these surface registration techniques is susceptible to local minima, the methods are restricted to resolving small initial misalignments. Targeting fully-automatic patient setup, Bauer et al. and Placht et al. proposed feature-based approaches that are capable to cope with gross initial misalignments [8,10]. Both rely on matching feature descriptors that encode the local surface topography. Point correspondences between the intra-fractional patient shape and a given reference then yield the aligning transformation (Fig. 1c). More specifically, Placht et al. presented a mono-modal ToF-based solution where the intra-fractional patient shape is aligned to an RI reference shape acquired prior to the first fraction [10]. Bauer et al. proposed a multi-modal surface registration scheme that enables a direct alignment of intra-fractional structured light data (Microsoft Kinect) to a reference shape extracted from pre-fractional tomographic planning data [8]. Both studies indicate the feasibility of the approach, yet being restricted to phantom experiments.

Real-time monitoring of the patient body holds great potential for the management of respiratory motion, being a rapidly evolving field in modern medicine. Motion management is of particular interest in image-guided RT for abdominal and thoracic targets where motion induces a substantial source of error. Accounting for potential targeting errors and to assure adequate dosimetric coverage of the tumor-bearing tissue, large safety margins are typically applied. However, this comes at the cost of irradiating surrounding radio-sensitive structures. To reduce tolerances between the planned and actually delivered dose distribution, a multitude of techniques for respiratory motion management have been developed over the past decades [19,20]. Early strategies in RI-based motion tracking were restricted to low-dimensional respiration surrogates (cf. Fig. 2a). Schaller et al. presented a ToF-based system to acquire a low-dimensional respiratory signal [21]. Lately, similar systems using Microsoft Kinect have been presented by Xia et al. and Alnowami et al. [22,23]. In contrast, recent RT motion tracking solutions target dense surface deformation tracking that better reflect the complexity of respiratory motion [24,25]. In combination with 4-D CT or MRI planning data, they can be used to establish patient-specific motion models [26] that correlate external body deformation with internal tumor motion. These models can then be applied for non-radiographic motion-compensated dose delivery. First approaches to reconstructing dense non-rigid torso deformations induced by respiratory motion were proposed only recently, (Fig. 2b). Bauer et al. developed a joint variational formulation that simultaneously solves the intertwined tasks of denoising ToF data and its registration to a reference surface [27]. Schaerer et al. studied the application of a non-rigid extension of the ICP algorithm with a commercially available stereo vision based RT solution [28]. Further promising approaches for dense surface deformation tracking include sparse-to-dense shape registration based on a grid-type triangulation sensor [18], and photometry-driven surface registration [29]. Let us further remark that the analysis of dense displacement fields also allows for an automatic distinction between abdominal and thoracic respiration [30].

2.3 Motion Compensation in Tomographic Reconstruction

Beyond the discussed applications in RT, dense surface deformation tracking could also help reducing motion artifacts in tomographic reconstruction. Gianoli et al. proposed the use of marker-based surface tracking to extract a multidimensional respiration surrogate for reducing artifacts in retrospective 4-D CT image sorting [31]. The experiments revealed that using multiple surrogates reduced uncertainties in breathing phase identification compared to conventional methods based on a mono-dimensional surrogate, cf. Sect. 2.2. In addition, RI-based body surface tracking is of particular interest for motion compensation in nuclear medical imaging such as positron emission tomography (PET) and single-photon emission computed tomography (SPECT) [32]. Based on previous concepts for motion compensation in PET/SPECT using marker-based tracking [33,34,35], dense and real-time RI has been attracting interest in this field lately [36,37] Open issues in this context such as the calibration and synchronization to the scanner are discussed in Sect. 6.

2.4 Guidance for Open and Percutaneous Interventions

Guidance systems for open and percutaneous interventions require additional intra-operative imaging modalities to relate the present patient anatomy to the pre-operatively acquired planning data. Current systems use either radiographic

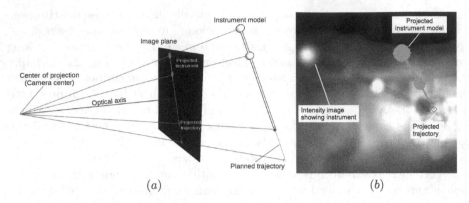

(a) (b)

Fig. 3. Marker-less navigation concept for percutaneous needle insertions [41]. (a) Projection of the virtual needle model into the image plane of the RI camera. (b) AR view of the intensity image with projected final instrument position.

imaging modalities or rely on tracking techniques that require additional markers to be attached to the instrument and the patient. To date, many of those systems have not become widely accepted in clinical routine because their benefit to the patient could not exceed the problems arising from the additional hardware complexity, radiation exposure and higher costs. Real-time RI constitutes an alternative for marker-less intra-operative acquisition of the operation area. In recent years, a variety of applications emerged that utilize range imaging cameras for intra-operative guidance, navigation and AR. One of the first approaches to assist open surgeries with marker-less guidance was presented by Cash et al. [38,39]. They proposed a system for image-guided liver surgery based on a laser range scanner and presented a method for recovering soft-tissue deformations using incomplete surface data [40]. Although this concept was presented using a laser scanner for surface acquisition, it can be seen as the starting point for following research on the application of RI technologies in open surgery.

Mersmann et al. [42] investigated the suitability of ToF cameras as intra-operative modality for surface acquisition by comparing ToF and CT surfaces of explanted human and porcine organs. Furthermore, they investigated the use of ToF cameras as a marker-less inside-out tracking device for AR visualization during image-guided procedures as opposed to the marker-based variant presented in [43]. Dos Santos [44] presented a surface matching approach that allows for non-rigid intra-operative registration of ToF data.

Wang et al [45] proposed a needle tracking algorithm that is able to track standard biopsy needles within the field of view of the Microsoft Kinect camera without needing to attach any additional markers. Due to their thinness, biopsy needles can hardly be reconstructed in the depth map. Instead, the idea is to use the Kinect device as a stereo camera with the infrared and the RGB sensor forming the stereo pair. Based on the needle being detected in both images separately, its 3-D pose can be estimated in four degrees of freedom. In a first evaluation the feasibility of the approach was shown. Navigated needle insertions have also been realized using range imaging techniques. Nicolau et al. [46] were one of the first groups to use a custom-made structured light camera system to assist percutaneous needle insertions. Having a video projector integrated into their structured light system, they were also able to project an AR view of internal organs directly onto the patient's surface. Seitel et al. [41] proposed another marker-less navigation approach for percutaneous needle insertions. Its main idea is to use an RI camera as a single modality for patient localization and instrument guidance. For guidance of the instrument, its virtual model is projected onto the image plane of the intensity/RGB image of the RI camera to provide guidance information during navigation, see Fig. 3. The accuracy of the presented approaches may not yet be sufficient for clinical use, however, along with a prospective increase in depth resolution, the integration of motion compensation methods and deformation models they hold great potential for future clinical applicability.

2.5 3-D Endoscopy for Minimally Invasive Procedures

While open surgery involves cutting the skin and dividing the underlying tissues to gain direct access to the surgical target, minimally-invasive surgery (MIS) is performed through small incisions in the skin in order to reduce surgical trauma. Laparoscopic surgery refers to MIS performed in the abdominal or pelvic cavities. As no direct view on the surgical target is possible, an endoscopic camera is used to provide a 2-D view of the anatomical structures as well as the instruments applied. Due to the limited field of view, the difficult hand-eye coordination as well as the loss of depth perception and tactile feedback, laparoscopic interventions generally require a lot of skill and experience to be performed successfully. Hence, computer-assisted laparoscopy is subject of ongoing research. One of the main difficulties to be addressed is again the acquisition of the 3-D structure of the patient anatomy in an accurate, fast and robust manner during the procedure (cf. Sect. 2.4). Optical techniques for laparoscopic 3-D surface reconstruction can roughly be divided into two categories [47]. Passive methods, such as stereoscopy [48]), shape-from-shading [49], shape-from-motion (SfM) [50], and simultaneous localization and mapping (SLAM) [51] need only endoscopic RGB images as input. Active methods, such as structured light [52,53] and ToF require controlled light to be projected into the environment. For a comprehensive review of these different techniques in the context of MIS we refer to Maier-Hein et al. [54]. In this chapter, we review recent advances related to ToF endoscopy.

While all the passive and active methods enumerated above have already been successfully applied in various fields, anatomic reconstruction for MIS poses several specific challenges: Firstly, the methods must be able to cope with a dynamic environment. Furthermore, human tissue often tends to be of homogeneous texture, making automatic feature detection and matching, required by most passive methods, difficult. Finally, miniaturization is necessary in order to build small devices that fit into the ports used in laparoscopic interventions. Behind this background, ToF imaging is a very interesting alternative for 3-D surface reconstruction in laparoscopic surgery, because it is real-time compatible, does not rely on salient features and does not require a baseline.

The first ToF-based endoscope was proposed by Penne et al. [55]. The authors combined a commercial ToF camera featuring a lateral resolution of 64×48 px with a rigid standard endoscope optics. The standard illumination units of the ToF camera were replaced by a fiber-coupled high-power laser diode connected to the illumination fiber bundle of the endoscope. In a subsequent study, a higher resolution ToF camera featuring a lateral resolution of 204×204 px was used in a similar setup [56]. Recently, the company Richard Wolf GmbH (Knittlingen, Germany) introduced their first prototypical ToF endoscope. It features both a white light source as well as a ToF illumination unit and simultaneously generates range images (64×48 px), corresponding gray-scale amplitude images and standard definition RGB images (640×480 px) at a framerate of ∼30 Hz. One application being addressed with these initial prototypes was laparoscopic instrument localization [57]. Furthermore, first approaches to the fusion of endoscopic ToF and SfM [58] as well as SLAM [59] have been proposed.

In the context of endoscopy, the major advantages of ToF compared to other reconstruction techniques are the registered depth and intensity data at high framerates and the compact design without scanning component or baseline. However, the reconstruction accuracy of the first prototypical ToF endoscopes is not yet sufficient for clinical application, cf. Sect. 6.1. Still, due to the continuous technological advances related to ToF as well as the growing number of applications in various areas, ToF measurement precision and accuracy can be expected to increase further, thus making ToF endoscopy a new technique with high potential for computer-assisted endoscopy. Applications besides intraoperative registration for AR guidance are instrument tracking, collision avoidance in robotic-assisted MIS, and quantitative metric measurements.

3   Monitoring for OR Safety and Workflow Analysis

Monitoring the working area of operating rooms (OR) or intensive care units using a multi-camera setup of conventional cameras or RI cameras has attracted increasing attention lately [60,61]. The reason for this interest is twofold. First, it can help improve both medical staff and patient safety by monitoring human-robot interaction (Sect. 3.1). Second, it holds great potential to analyze and optimize the efficiency of clinical workflows (Sect. 3.2).

3.1   Room Monitoring for Safety in Robot-Assisted Interventions

Collision avoidance in interventional environments is an emerging topic with the increased use of robotics in the OR. Real-time range imaging holds potential to ensure safe workspace sharing in this context. Let us point out the requirements for an RI-based collision avoidance system. First, it needs to have a low latency to cope with the dynamics of the scene. The particular demands in terms of latency and framerate can be derived from the given maximum velocity of the moving components in the scene. Second, as the scene of an OR during intervention is usually rather complex, occlusion will occur. Multiple cameras can be used to resolve the occlusion problem and provide additional redundancy in the data. However, note that RI technologies such as ToF or structured light suffer from signal interference that has to be coped with (cf. Sect. 6). Another open topic is the optimal placement of cameras in a multi-camera setup to ensure sufficient coverage of the monitored workspace. On the other hand, one wants to use as few cameras as possible, because of interference, the amount of data to be processed, and the cost of the system. The overall system accuracy is limited by the individual sensor accuracy and the accuracy of the calibration of the sensors to each other. Since the moving components usually cannot be stopped instantaneously, a safety margin of the collision area in the centimeter range is mandatory. Consequently, the accuracy demands in human-robot collision avoidance scenarios are in that range as well.

The aim of the EU projects SAFROS [62] and ACTIVE [63] is to address the described problems. For instance, Mönnich et al. and Nicolai et al. proposed an OR supervision system based on multiple RI cameras [64,65]. In particular, they used seven ToF cameras in order to monitor the scene from different perspectives. Based on extrinsic camera calibration, the system enables a volumetric reconstruction of the OR workspace.

3.2 Monitoring, Analysis, and Modeling of Workflows

Another research direction where RI cameras are of great interest is the modeling, recognition, analysis and interpretation of workflows and activities during surgery. A computer system that is able to understand activities inside the OR has several potential applications such as context-aware guidance and provision of user interfaces, relevance based visualization, monitoring of the operation for unexpected events, automatic documentation, or prediction of the remaining duration of a surgery. Most work in this area is based on the concept of recording several medical procedures and generating a statistical model of the workflow. Later, during a running medical procedure, intra-operative data from RI cameras is compared to this statistical model [66].

One example of using range images for workflow recognition has been shown by Padoy et al., using a real-time 3-D reconstruction of a simulated OR that was obtained from a multi-camera system [67]. Based on the 3-D reconstruction, the motion flow of staff and objects inside the OR was computed and a statistical model was generated. This model allows detection of surgical phases during a running surgery. Lea et al. used a single RI camera to detect medical staff in a pediatric intensive care unit [68]. They extracted features such as position, orientation and interaction between persons from the range images. Based on these features they recognized different actions during the intervention. There are also related applications that do not require a temporal workflow model. For instance, Ladikos et al. [69] used a real-time 3-D reconstruction of an OR to analyze radiation exposure during interventions. They recognize the position of OR staff with respect to an X-ray device and can model the radiation exposure over the course of an intervention. Compared to standard radiation counters the advantage of such a system is that the radiation exposure for each part of the body is simulated. For inexperienced OR staff it is also very interesting that after the intervention it can be visualized when and where the radiation exposure occurred to increase the awareness of the dangers of radiation.

4 Touch-Less Interaction and Visualization

Real-time range imaging also holds potential for touch-less interaction in sterile environments (Sect. 4.1) and for on-patient visualization of medical data (Sect. 4.2). In this section, we summarize the developments in these two emerging fields of application.

4.1 Touch-Less Interaction in Sterile Environments

The recent advent of touch-less real-time user-machine interaction that came along with the introduction of low-cost RI sensors has also evoked interest in the medical domain. In particular, gesture control holds potential in areas such as interventional radiology, neurosurgery or navigated surgery where volumetric scans such as CT or MRI are commonly used for intra-operative guidance. There are two main arguments for using touch-less interaction in medical interventions. First, the surgeon has to remain sterile. This limits the usability of mouse and keyboard. Second, operating rooms are typically packed. Therefore, workstations allowing access to medical images usually require the surgeon to move away from the patient. Today, the surgeon commonly delegates the interaction with computers to nurses. However, this often leads to misunderstandings and delays, in particular for complex tasks. In general, there are different alternative solutions to range imaging for touch-less interaction such as data gloves, accelerometers, optical or magnetic tracking systems and hand recognition in color cameras. However, these solutions either require hardware or markers to be worn by the user, or are less robust. In the last decade, several systems for touch-less interaction using stereo cameras [70], ToF imaging [71] and recently Microsoft Kinect [72,73,74,75,76,77] have been proposed. A commercially available system using infrared stereo cameras to access patient records in the OR is offered by Karl Storz GmbH, Tuttlingen, Germany [78]. For a more general overview on RI-based gesture recognition we refer to Chap. *Gesture Interfaces with Depth Sensors.*

As gesture-based interaction is not an established input method such as keyboards or touch-screens, finding appropriate interaction metaphors is still a topic of ongoing research. Existing prototypes use different concepts such as mapping the hand position to the position of the mouse pointer and using clicking gestures [70,72]. Other systems analyze gestures of the fingers [71,73], the hands [73,75,74,76,79] or analyze the hand position w.r.t. the body [76]. Most existing research prototypes allow navigation through either 2-D or 3-D image data. For 2-D images, the selection of slices, zoom and changing brightness and contrast are common operations that have been implemented. For 3-D image viewing,

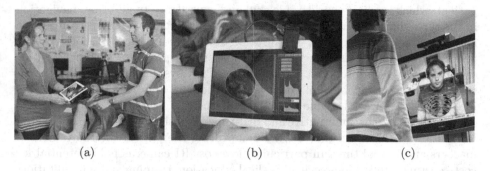

(a)   (b)   (c)

Fig. 4. Concept of on-patient visualization. (a,b) The pose of the display and thus the viewing direction of the user is continuously computed based on surface data captured with a range imaging device [83], © DKFZ, Tobias Schwerdt. (c) AR overlay of anatomical information in a magic mirror for education of anatomy [84].

rotation and translation are common operations. Another functionality that has been implemented is the measurement of the size of a structure [71]. Additional functions that have been tested in some prototypes are control of OR parameters such as turning on or off the light [70,79]. One common problem of gesture-based user interfaces is to differentiate between intended and unintended gestures. Different methods to address this issue have been proposed, such as using a specific interaction zone [70,73] or distance [72], using certain gestures [71], using voice recognition to activate gesture recognition [76,79] or analyzing the pose of the user with respect to the display [74].

To evaluate the use of touch-less interactions for medical applications several studies have been conducted, involving participants without medical background [71,75,77], medical doctors in a simulated setup [76,77] and medical doctors in real surgeries [80]. All studies reported results in favor of touch-less interaction. Most systems are still prototypes and research on using gesture-based interaction in real medical interventions has rarely been addressed. Nevertheless, gesture-based interaction holds great potential as there is an increasing need for user interfaces to operate computer-based systems in the OR and gesture-based user interfaces have substantial advantages over traditional interfaces.

4.2   On-patient Visualization of Medical Data

The visualization of anatomical data for the purpose of disease diagnosis, surgical planning, or orientation during interventional radiology and surgery is an integral part of modern health care. However, only few medical imaging modalities are capable of providing real-time images of the patient's anatomy. A common procedure therefore involves the acquisition of static 3-D image data, e.g. by means of CT or MRI scanners, and subsequent manipulation and visualization of the acquired data on a workstation. However, in such conventional techniques it is usually the task of the physician to mentally transfer the 3-D virtual image to the patient, which requires considerable skill and experience. In addition, navigation in the three-dimensional data set may be rather cumbersome. To overcome these issues, methods for on-patient visualization during medical interventions via AR, using head-mounted displays [81] or intra-operative projector systems [82], for example, have been proposed. However, these AR systems are typically expensive, require the attachment of markers to the patient, or are difficult to integrate into the medical workflow due to bulky equipment.

A novel alternative for intuitive and real-time on-patient visualization of anatomical data are RI devices that allow for capturing the patient anatomy without markers and in real-time. In particular, low-cost RI cameras hold potential for cost-sensitive applications such as medical education, training and rehabilitation. One promising application involves tracking the pose of a person in order to visualize subsurface anatomical detail via AR, as suggested by Maier-Hein et al. [83] and Blum et al. [84]. Maier-Hein et al. [83] proposed mounting a ToF camera to a portable display or tablet for on-patient visualization of medical images, as shown in Fig. 4a,b. The basic idea is to compute the pose of the mobile display relative to previously acquired 3-D tomographic data set by means of surface registration (cf. Sect. 2). Estimating the pose of the camera and thus the viewing direction of the physician allows for visualization of internal anatomical structures on the portable display as illustrated in Fig. 4b. In addition, navigation through medical imaging data becomes more intuitive because it is performed directly at the object of interest. As the quality of visualization depends on the accuracy of surface registration, the authors proposed an anisotropic ICP variant [85,86] that accounts for the resolution and precision of RI devices in different directions. A trimmed version of the algorithm, which allows for aligning partially overlapping surfaces, has been also applied in this context [87].

Blum et al. [84] presented a system that involves tracking of a person in front of a large screen that serves as a kind of mirror (cf. Fig.4c). Registration of the person's body surface, captured with an RI device, with a virtual patient model allows for AR visualization of subsurface anatomical detail in the mirror. The system can be applied for education purposes as it provides an intuitive visualization of anatomical information. It can be further used to support patient-doctor communication, based on the visualization of patient-specific data. Note that instead of surface registration between the medical data and the RI-based shape of the user, full-body motion capture methods (cf. Chaps. *Full-Body Human Motion Capture from Monocular Depth Images* and *A Survey on Human Motion Analysis from Depth Data*) may be applied.

5   Diagnosis, Prevention and Support

In this section, we summarize the developments in diverse fields of applications. More specifically, we review the use of real-time range imaging in elderly care (Sect. 5.1), early diagnosis and screening (Sect. 5.2), rehabilitation (Sect. 5.3), and support for handicapped people (Sect. 5.4).

5.1   Activity Assessment in Elderly Care

In-home activity assessment in elderly care is a rapidly evolving field. The need for care facilities and the associated costs for the health insurance system can be alleviated by low-cost systems that allow older adults to continue life in independent settings. These systems focus on monitoring the health status, sharing information about presence and daily activities, and providing on-line assistance and coaching. Low-cost range imaging holds great potential in this context. For instance, recognition of early indicators of functional decline such as deviations in gait using RI-based pose estimation [88] can help preventing accidents, automatic detection of abnormal events such as falls [89] can improve the respond time in emergency situations, and retrospective data analysis can help understand the mechanisms that led to an event. In elderly care, both static installations [90,91,92,93] and mobile robotic platforms [94,95,96] that incorporate dense and real-time range imaging have been proposed. Most systems that rely on human pose analysis exploit the mass-market proven skeletal tracking that ships with Microsoft Kinect [97]. ToF-based pose estimation has been rarely considered [98,99].

5.2   Early Diagnosis and Screening

The detection of abnormal behavior based on range imaging technologies also holds potential for early diagnosis and screening, for different groups of patients. Information about daily lifestyle and deviations from the normal can help in early diagnosis or progression analysis for cognitive impaired people such as Alzheimer's [100] or Parkinson's disease patients [88]. Low-cost RI devices further open the possibility of large-scale screening of at-risk groups. For instance, in developmental disorders such as autism and schizophrenia, observing behavioral precursors in early childhood using 3-D perception for activity recognition [101,102] can allow for early intervention and thus improve patient outcomes. In sleep monitoring, range imaging is gaining interest for non-contact measurement of sleep conditions or diagnosis of sleep apnea, for instance using ToF [103] or structured light [104] range imaging.

5.3   Treatment Support in Rehabilitation

RI sensors have also attracted interest in the field of physical therapy. The basic idea of using *serious games* in rehabilitation is to increase motivation and engagement of the patient, thus improving exercise performance, perseverance and rehabilitation outcomes [105]. RI-based games are of particular interest, as the embedded sensors simultaneously allow for a quantitative assessment of performance. Hence, the rehabilitation progress can be tracked and analyzed to modify the therapy, if necessary. Furthermore, the workload of professional therapists is reduced. Low-cost RI systems have lately been considered for tele-rehabilitation techniques [106,107] that are beneficial for translating skills learned in therapy to everyday life. Tele-rehabilitation systems allow the therapist to monitor the patient during exercising at home, track their activity and progress, and provide feedback. Recently, RI-based rehabilitation systems for physically disabled patients [108,109,110,111], chronic pain patients [112] and patients after neurological injuries [113,114] have been proposed. The vast majority of approaches in the field of serious games builds on Microsoft Kinect, being inherently embedded in an off-the-shelf gaming console.

5.4   Aids for Handicapped People

Recently, first approaches towards the use of assistive technologies to support handicapped people were proposed [115]. The integration of an RI device into an augmented blindman's cane or head-mounted systems could aid visually impaired people in navigation by identifying and describing surroundings beyond the limited sensing range of a physical cane [116,117,118,119]. For instance, Gassert et al. [117] described the augmentation of a white cane with a ToF sensor. Low-cost range imaging has been also proposed for autonomous transportation vehicles that follow handicapped people using 3-D perception [120].

6   Practical Issues

Medical applications impose several practical demands on RI cameras, including real-time capability and a high degree of absolute accuracy, reliability, and robustness. However, RI data are typically prone to inaccuracies due to technological limitations. In this section, we identify issues that are specific for applications in health care (Sect. 6.1). Dedicated software frameworks for RI processing that explicitly address medical applications are briefly outlined in Sect. 6.2.

6.1   Issues and Limitations

First and foremost, the enhancement of RI measurement data in terms of denoising and correction of modality-specific systematic errors – such as intensity- or temperature-related distance errors, motion artifacts, and outliers at depth discontinuities in ToF imaging – assumes a critical role in the processing pipeline. In theory, some of these systematic errors could be compensated for by a calibration procedure performed once before clinical use. For ToF-based systems, a practical approach would further assume a constant temperature after a warm-up period and a fixed integration time that must be chosen in an application-specific manner. However, even though progress has been made in understanding the underlying technological issues, a robust and holistic calibration and correction of systematic errors is still an open field of research. This particularly applies for the young discipline of ToF imaging, for a comprehensive treatment we refer to Chap. *Technical Foundation and Calibration Methods for Time-of-Flight Cameras.* Here, the focus is on practical aspects that are specific for medical applications. Thus we conclude that the quality of RI data is a limiting factor concerning the spectrum of medical applications that can be potentially addressed. Indeed, the achievable degree of accuracy of today's RI cameras hinders a more widespread usage.

The acquisition of RI data in a medical context poses several challenges. The systems typically face a dynamic and often unpredictable environment, and occlusions that result from clinical staff or interventional devices such as linear accelerators or C-arm CT systems that may temporally obstruct the field of view of the RI camera (cf. Sect. 2). Yet, even in a static scenario with known acquisition geometry, small reconstruction frustums, shallow acquisition angles or a large working distance may deteriorate the quality of RI data or invoke self-occlusions. Applications where the patient is partially covered by a blanket or equipment are even more challenging or impossible to address with RI.

For many clinical scenarios, using a multi-camera acquisition setup can help to improve the scene coverage in both dynamic and static environments (cf. Sect. 3). However, this typically entails substantial efforts w.r.t. robust and recurrent intrinsic and extrinsic calibration, potentially introducing an additional error source. Furthermore, available RI technologies such as ToF or structured light are known to suffer from issues due to signal interference. For ToF imaging, several techniques to suppress interference have been investigated, such as modulation frequency or code division multiplexing (see [121] for an overview). For structured light, the usage of different light frequencies for the pattern can be used. Maimone et al. [122] have proposed a multiple Kinect system that involves vibrating the Kinects at distinct frequencies. If the cameras support a framerate that is substantially higher than the overall required framerate, temporal multiplexing with an external trigger may be used. In addition to mutual signal interference in a multi-camera setup, the influence of the infrared part of ambient or high-intensity surgical lighting on RI reconstruction robustness and accuracy should be investigated.

Besides acquisition constraints in a medical environment, surface and tissue properties of the observed object assume a decisive role. In particular for ToF-based open surgery (Sect. 2.4) and endoscopic procedures (Sect. 2.5), translucent and glossy organ surfaces impair RI measurements. For instance, specular highlights may cause invalid depth measurements due to sensor saturation. Furthermore, reflective or absorbing tissues and fluids such as blood [123] may lead to multi-path or sub-surface penetration, signal attenuation and scattering issues with ToF imaging [124,125,126] that might impair both absolute accuracy and signal-to-noise ratio. These are critical issues to be addressed in future work. Note that similar effects occur with applications that involve range imaging of the external body surface. In this context, different skin types may influence the range measurements.

Another important issue for the application of RI technologies in health care concerns a proper integration into clinical routine. The need for a warm-up period for ToF devices, frequent re-calibration procedures for multi-camera setups, or frequent re-calibration between the sensor and scanner coordinate systems might be problematic for certain clinical workflows. For patient setup and monitoring solutions, system calibration w.r.t. a treatment couch coordinate system has been shown to be manageable. For instance, the VisionRT system being a widely established range imaging system in RT relies on a calibration with a dedicated pattern [127]. In contrast, for calibrating the RI coordinate system w.r.t. imaging modalities such as CT, MRI, US, PET or SPECT, the design of customized calibration patterns may be necessary. This also applies for the joint application of RI-based and conventional tracking solutions using optical or electromagnetic markers. In addition, let us stress that the accuracy of system calibration w.r.t. different modalities and coordinate systems highly depends on the accuracy and reliability of the RI measurement data itself.

For RI-based guidance in computer-assisted intervention, an open field of research beyond calibration concerns the relation of the measured external topography to the internal structures given from tomographic data (CT/MR). In clinical practice, the external shape acquired with an RI system during intervention typically does not coincide with the shape extracted from tomographic planning data due to non-rigid deformations that occur due to body twist and bend, respiration, cardiac motion, or tissue manipulation. Promising future directions involve the use of generic or patient-specific models that correlate external motion to internal motion based on dynamic 4-D CT/MR data [24,25]. Only little research has investigated the use of biomechanical models propagating surface deformations to the internal structures known from a static tomographic scan.

Range imaging systems that are intended to be used in surgical and endoscopic interventions need to be compact. This implies several restrictions for the different range imaging principles, such as miniaturized illumination units for ToF sensors in general, sufficient light transmission for 3-D ToF endoscopy and a small baseline for structured light sensors. In the context of endoscopic applications in MIS, errors caused by background illumination can be neglected due to the controlled environment. On the other hand, working in a cavity of reflecting tissue poses challenges regarding multi-path reflexions. Furthermore, it is a great challenge to transmit enough light to the tissue, which leads to a low signal-to-noise ratio in endoscopic ToF images and hence a decreased measurement accuracy in camera direction compared to standard ToF cameras. It is theoretically possible to increase measurement accuracy by operating the ToF device with a higher modulation frequency [128]. Due to the small working volume in laparoscopic interventions, the reduced ambiguity range would be acceptable.

In conclusion, we stress that the integration of range imaging systems into clinical routine is restricted due to the lack of certified standard hardware or the early prototype stage of dedicated devices such as in 3-D endoscopy. This hinders experimental studies involving patients and, thus, most research on surgical and endoscopic applications relies on synthetic phantom or animal studies.

6.2   Software Frameworks

Two open-source frameworks have addressed range imaging in medical applications so far: MITK-ToF [129] as an integration into the well-known *Medical Imaging Interaction Toolkit* (MITK) [130] and the *Range Imaging Toolkit* (RITK) [131]. Both frameworks build upon the *Insight Segmentation and Registration Toolkit* (ITK) [132], which is considered as de-factor standard in open-source medical image processing. Whereas the focus of MITK-ToF is more on the medical integration and interaction with other modules, RITK has a strong focus on hardware accelerated multi-view range data streaming to satisfy real-time demands in clinical practice, e.g. using general purpose computing on graphics processing units (GPGPU). As a general RI framework, the *Point Cloud Library* [133] has become popular in the computer vision community.

7   Discussion

In this chapter we have given an overview of the application of range imaging in different fields of health care. While some are merely in a proof of concept state and still require basic research to be done, others are already close to being employed in commercial products. Most often, RI is used for localization and tracking of objects and persons in 3-D workspace. Commercially available systems that solve these tasks utilize marker-based solutions or radiographic imaging. However, attaching markers is time-consuming and complicates the workflow. Radiation on the other hand is harmful to both the patient and medical staff. The main advantages of RI cameras are that they operate touch-less (sterile), marker-free (no setup required), fast (real-time), and dense (non-scanning).

Range imaging can help improve health care in many areas. Outside a clinical environment, even at home, body tracking and pose detection can support prevention, rehabilitation, and remote diagnosis. Location and pose information is also required for automatic patient positioning. When tracked over time, information about non-rigid surface deformations can be used to compensate for patient motion, e.g. in tomographic reconstruction, or radiation therapy. With additional instrument tracking, guidance is viable. Robust localization and 3-D surface information is also the basis for AR applications that hold potential in interventional navigation as well as human-doctor communication. Touch-less gesture recognition promises to solve the problem of sterile human-machine-interaction in the OR. The technology is mature, however, its widespread acceptance is hampered by the lack of a common, intuitive set of gestures. Finally, 3-D endoscopy and room supervision are areas where range imaging creates new types of data. Both hold great potential, but still require considerable research.

Future research on real-time RI in health care should cover three areas. First, there are several open research questions which have to be tackled. Since the underlying technologies are relatively new and still immature to some degree, available RI cameras have shortcomings, which have to be resolved (e.g. systematic errors, low spatial resolution). Further, the registration of RI measurements to data acquired with conventional medical imaging modalities is important. Other open questions regard the adequacy of the acquired data, e.g. whether external surface information is sufficient for tracking internal structures, or whether the achievable absolute accuracy is acceptable for a given application. Second, everyday issues of current applications and prototypes must be solved. This involves their integration into clinical scenarios and workflows, including e.g. multi-camera setups, calibration and synchronization to a scanner or treatment system, and real-time implementation of algorithms. Third, medical certification for RI devices and related clinical applications is another fundamental requirement for the progression of the field. Once these issues have been solved and range imaging technology has been established in daily health care routine, it will lead to new, more efficient and safe workflows.

References

1. Wolf, I., Vetter, M., Wegner, I., Böttger, T., Nolden, M., Schöbinger, M., Hastenteufel, M., Kunert, T., Meinzer, H.P.: The medical imaging interaction toolkit. Med. Image Anal. 9, 594–604 (2005)
2. Salvi, J., Matabosch, C., Fofi, D., Forest, J.: A review of recent range image registration methods with accuracy evaluation. Image Vis. Comput. 25(5), 578–596 (2007)
3. van Kaick, O., Zhang, H., Hamarneh, G., Cohen-Or, D.: A survey on shape correspondence. Computer Graphics Forum 30(6), 1681–1707 (2011)
4. Heimann, T., Meinzer, H.P.: Statistical shape models for 3D medical image segmentation: A review. Med. Image Anal. 13(4), 543–563 (2009)
5. Sotiras, A., Christos, D., Paragios, N.: Deformable medical image registration: A survey. Research Report RR-7919, INRIA (2012)
6. Schaller, C., Rohkohl, C., Penne, J., Stürmer, M., Hornegger, J.: Inverse C-arm positioning for interventional procedures using real-time body part detection. In: Yang, G.-Z., Hawkes, D., Rueckert, D., Noble, A., Taylor, C. (eds.) MICCAI 2009, Part I. LNCS, vol. 5761, pp. 549–556. Springer, Heidelberg (2009)
7. Grimm, R., Bauer, S., Sukkau, J., Hornegger, J., Greiner, G.: Markerless estimation of patient orientation, posture and pose using range and pressure imaging. Int. J. Comput. Assist. Radiol. Surg. 7(6), 921–929 (2012)
8. Bauer, S., Wasza, J., Haase, S., Marosi, N., Hornegger, J.: Multi-modal surface registration for markerless initial patient setup in radiation therapy using Microsoft's Kinect sensor. In: ICCV Workshop on Consumer Depth Cameras for Computer Vision, pp. 1175–1181. IEEE (2011)
9. Schöffel, P.J., Harms, W., Sroka-Perez, G., Schlegel, W., Karger, C.P.: Accuracy of a commercial optical 3D surface imaging system for realignment of patients for radiotherapy of the thorax. Phys. Med. Biol. 52(13), 3949–3963 (2007)
10. Placht, S., Stancanello, J., Schaller, C., Balda, M., Angelopoulou, E.: Fast time-of-flight camera based surface registration for radiotherapy patient positioning. Med. Phys. 39(1), 4–17 (2012)
11. Wasza, J., Bauer, S., Hornegger, J.: Real-time motion compensated patient positioning and non-rigid deformation estimation using 4-D shape priors. In: Ayache, N., Delingette, H., Golland, P., Mori, K. (eds.) MICCAI 2012, Part II. LNCS, vol. 7511, pp. 576–583. Springer, Heidelberg (2012)
12. Lindl, B.L., Müller, R.G., Lang, S., Lablanca, M.D.H., Klöck, S.: Topos: A new topometric patient positioning and tracking system for radiation therapy based on structured white light. Med. Phys. 40(4), 042701 (2013)
13. Brahme, A., Nyman, P., Skatt, B.: 4D laser camera for accurate patient positioning, collision avoidance, image fusion and adaptive approaches during diagnostic and therapeutic procedures. Med. Phys. 35(5), 1670–1681 (2008)
14. Ettl, S., Fouladi-Movahed, S., Bauer, S., Arold, O., Willomitzer, F., Huber, F., Rampp, S., Stefan, H., Hornegger, J., Häusler, G.: Medical applications enabled by a motion-robust optical 3D sensor. In: DGaO Conference (2012)

15. Schaller, C., Adelt, A., Penne, J., Hornegger, J.: Time-of-flight sensor for patient positioning. In: Samei, E., Hsieh, J. (eds.) SPIE Medical Imaging, vol. 7258, p. 726110 (2009)
16. Besl, J., McKay, N.: A method for registration of 3-D shapes. IEEE Trans. Pattern Anal. Mach. Intell. 14(2), 239–256 (1992)
17. Chen, Y., Medioni, G.: Object modelling by registration of multiple range images. Image Vis. Comput. 10(3), 145–155 (1992)
18. Bauer, S., Berkels, B., Ettl, S., Arold, O., Hornegger, J., Rumpf, M.: Marker-less reconstruction of dense 4-D surface motion fields using active laser triangulation for respiratory motion management. In: Ayache, N., Delingette, H., Golland, P., Mori, K. (eds.) MICCAI 2012, Part I. LNCS, vol. 7510, pp. 414–421. Springer, Heidelberg (2012)
19. Keall, P.J., Mageras, G.S., Balter, J.M., Emery, R.S., Forster, K.M., Jiang, S.B., Kapatoes, J.M., Low, D.A., Murphy, M.J., Murray, B.R., Ramsey, C.R., Herk, M.B.V., Vedam, S.S., Wong, J.W., Yorke, E.: The management of respiratory motion in radiation oncology report of AAPM task group 76. Med. Phys. 33(10), 3874–3900 (2006)
20. Verellen, D., Depuydt, T., Gevaert, T., Linthout, N., Tournel, K., Duchateau, M., Reynders, T., Storme, G., Ridder, M.D.: Gating and tracking, 4D in thoracic tumours. Cancer Radiother. 14(67), 446–454 (2010)
21. Schaller, C., Penne, J., Hornegger, J.: Time-of-Flight Sensor for Respiratory Motion Gating. Med. Phys. 35(7), 3090–3093 (2008)
22. Xia, J., Siochi, R.A.: A real-time respiratory motion monitoring system using kinect: Proof of concept. Med. Phys. 39(5), 2682–2685 (2012)
23. Alnowami, M., Alnwaimi, B., Tahavori, F., Copland, M., Wells, K.: A quantitative assessment of using the kinect for Xbox360 for respiratory surface motion tracking. In: SPIE Medical Imaging, pp. 83161T-10 (2012)
24. Yan, H., Yin, F.F., Zhu, G.P., Ajlouni, M., Kim, J.H.: The correlation evaluation of a tumor tracking system using multiple external markers. Med. Phys. 33(11), 4073–4084 (2006)
25. Fayad, H., Pan, T., Clement, J.F., Visvikis, D.: Correlation of respiratory motion between external patient surface and internal anatomical landmarks. Med. Phys. 38(6), 3157–3164 (2011)
26. McClelland, J., Hawkes, D., Schaeffter, T., King, A.: Respiratory motion models: A review. Med. Image Anal. 17(1), 19–42 (2013)
27. Bauer, S., Berkels, B., Hornegger, J., Rumpf, M.: Joint ToF image denoising and registration with a ct surface in radiation therapy. In: Bruckstein, A.M., ter Haar Romeny, B.M., Bronstein, A.M., Bronstein, M.M. (eds.) SSVM 2011. LNCS, vol. 6667, pp. 98–109. Springer, Heidelberg (2012)
28. Schaerer, J., Fassi, A., Riboldi, M., Cerveri, P., Baroni, G., Sarrut, D.: Multi-dimensional respiratory motion tracking from markerless optical surface imaging based on deformable mesh registration. Phys. Med. Biol. 57(2), 357–373 (2012)
29. Bauer, S., Wasza, J., Hornegger, J.: Photometric estimation of 3D surface motion fields for respiration management. In: Tolxdorff, T., Deserno, T.M., Handels, H., Meinzer, H.P. (eds.) Bildverarbeitung für die Medizin, pp. 105–110. Springer (2012)
30. Wasza, J., Bauer, S., Haase, S., Hornegger, J.: Sparse principal axes statistical surface deformation models for respiration analysis and classification. In: Tolxdorff, T., Deserno, T.M., Handels, H., Meinzer, H.P. (eds.) Bildverarbeitung für die Medizin, pp. 316–321. Springer (2012)

31. Gianoli, C., Riboldi, M., Spadea, M.F., Travaini, L.L., Ferrari, M., Mei, R., Orecchia, R., Baroni, G.: A multiple points method for 4D CT image sorting. Med. Phys. 38(2), 656–667 (2011)

32. Bettinardi, V., Bernardi, E.D., Presotto, L., Gilardi, M.: Motion-tracking hardware and advanced applications in PET and PET/CT. PET Clinics 8(1), 11–28 (2013)

33. Alnowami, M.R., Lewis, E., Guy, M., Wells, K.: An observation model for motion correction in nuclear medicine. In: SPIE Medical Imaging, pp. 76232F–9 (2010)

34. Bruyant, P., Gennert, M.A., Speckert, G., Beach, R., Morgenstern, J., Kumar, N., Nadella, S., King, M.: A robust visual tracking system for patient motion detection in SPECT: Hardware solutions. IEEE Trans. Nucl. Sci. 52(5), 1288–1294

35. McNamara, J.E., Pretorius, P.H., Johnson, K., Mukherjee, J.M., Dey, J., Gennert, M.A., King, M.A.: A flexible multicamera visual-tracking system for detecting and correcting motion-induced artifacts in cardiac SPECT slices. Med. Phys. 36(5), 1913–1923 (2009)

36. Olesen, O.V., Jorgensen, M.R., Paulsen, R.R., Hojgaard, L., Roed, B., Larsen, R.: Structured light 3D tracking system for measuring motions in PET brain imaging. In: SPIE Medical Imaging, pp. 76250X–11 (2010)

37. Noonan, P., Howard, J., Tout, D., Armstrong, I., Williams, H., Cootes, T., Hallett, W., Hinz, R.: Accurate markerless respiratory tracking for gated whole body PET using the Microsoft Kinect. In: IEEE NSS-MIC (2012)

38. Cash, D.M., Sinha, T.K., Chapman, W.C., Terawaki, H., Dawant, B.M., Galloway, R.L., Miga, M.I.: Incorporation of a laser range scanner into image-guided liver surgery: Surface acquisition, registration, and tracking. Med. Phys. 30(7), 1671–1682 (2003)

39. Cash, D.M., Miga, M.I., Glasgow, S.C., Dawant, B.M., Clements, L.W., Cao, Z., Galloway, R.L., Chapman, W.C.: Concepts and preliminary data toward the realization of image-guided liver surgery. J. Gastrointest. Surg. 11, 844–859 (2007)

40. Cash, D.M., Miga, M.I., Sinha, T.K., Galloway, R.L., Chapman, W.C.: Compensating for intraoperative soft-tissue deformations using incomplete surface data and finite elements. IEEE Trans. Med. Imaging 24(11), 1479–1491 (2005)

41. Seitel, A.: Markerless Navigation For Percutaneus Needle Insertions. PhD thesis, Universität Heidelberg (2012)

42. Mersmann, S., Müller, M., Seitel, A., Arnegger, F., Tetzlaff, R., Dinkel, J., Baumhauer, M., Schmied, B., Meinzer, H.P., Maier-Hein, L.: Time-of-flight camera technology for augmented reality in computer-assisted interventions. In: Wong, K.H., Holmes, D.R. (eds.) SPIE Medical Imaging, p. 79642C (2011)

43. Baumhauer, M., Simpfendörfer, T., Stich, B.M., Teber, D., Gutt, C., Rassweiler, J., Meinzer, H.P., Wolf, I.: Soft tissue navigation for laparoscopic partial nephrectomy. Int. J. Comput. Assist. Radiol. Surg. 3, 307–314 (2008)

44. dos Santos, T.R.: Muti-Modal Partial Surface Matching For Intraoperative Registration. PhD thesis, Universität Heidelberg (2012)

45. Wang, X.L., Stolka, P.J., Boctor, E., Hager, G., Choti, M.: The Kinect as an interventional tracking system. In: SPIE Medical Imaging, pp. 83160U–6 (2012)

46. Nicolau, S., Brenot, J., Goffin, L., Graebling, P., Soler, L., Marescaux, J.: A structured light system to guide percutaneous punctures in interventional radiology. In: SPIE Medical Imaging, p. 700016 (2008)

47. Mirota, D.J., Ishii, M., Hager, G.D.: Vision-based navigation in image-guided interventions. Annu. Rev. Biomed. Eng. 13(13), 297–319 (2011)

48. Stoyanov, D., Mylonas, G.P., Deligianni, F., Darzi, A., Yang, G.Z.: Soft-tissue motion tracking and structure estimation for robotic assisted MIS procedures. In: Duncan, J.S., Gerig, G. (eds.) MICCAI 2005. LNCS, vol. 3750, pp. 139–146. Springer, Heidelberg (2005)

49. Collins, T., Bartoli, A.: Towards live monocular 3D laparoscopy using shading and specularity information. In: Abolmaesumi, P., Joskowicz, L., Navab, N., Jannin, P. (eds.) IPCAI 2012. LNCS, vol. 7330, pp. 11–21. Springer, Heidelberg (2012)

50. Malti, A., Bartoli, A., Collins, T.: Template-based conformal shape-from-motion-and-shading for laparoscopy. In: Abolmaesumi, P., Joskowicz, L., Navab, N., Jannin, P. (eds.) IPCAI 2012. LNCS, vol. 7330, pp. 1–10. Springer, Heidelberg (2012)

51. Mountney, P., Stoyanov, D., Yang, G.Z.: Three-dimensional tissue deformation recovery and tracking. IEEE Signal Proc. Mag. 27, 14–24 (2010)

52. Clancy, N.T., Stoyanov, D., Yang, G.Z., Elson, D.S.: An endoscopic structured lighting probe using spectral encoding. In: SPIE Novel Biophotonic Techniques and Applications, vol. 8090 (2011)

53. Schmalz, C., Forster, F., Schick, A., Angelopoulou, E.: An endoscopic 3D scanner based on structured light. Med. Image Anal. 16(5), 1063–1072 (2012)

54. Maier-Hein, L., Mountney, P., Bartoli, A., Elhawary, H., Elson, D., Groch, A., Kolb, A., Rodrigues, M., Sorger, J., Speidel, S., Stoyanov, D.: Optical techniques for 3D surface reconstruction in computer-assisted laparoscopic surgery. Med. Image Anal. (in press, 2013)

55. Penne, J., Höller, K., Stürmer, M., Schrauder, T., Schneider, A., Engelbrecht, R., Feußner, H., Schmauss, B., Hornegger, J.: Time-of-flight 3-D endoscopy. In: Yang, G.-Z., Hawkes, D., Rueckert, D., Noble, A., Taylor, C. (eds.) MICCAI 2009, Part I. LNCS, vol. 5761, pp. 467–474. Springer, Heidelberg (2009)

56. Groch, A., Seitel, A., Hempel, S., Speidel, S., Engelbrecht, R., Penne, J., Höller, K., Röhl, S., Yung, K., Bodenstedt, S., Pflaum, F., dos Santos, T., Mersmann, S., Meinzer, H.P., Hornegger, J., Maier-Hein, L.: 3D surface reconstruction for laparoscopic computer-assisted interventions: Comparison of state of the art methods. In: SPIE Medical Imaging, vol. 796415 (2011)

57. Haase, S., Wasza, J., Kilgus, T., Hornegger, J.: Laparoscopic instrument localization using a 3-D Time-of-Flight/RGB endoscope. In: Workshop on the Applications of Computer Vision, pp. 449–454. IEEE (2013)

58. Groch, A., Haase, S., Wagner, M., Kilgus, T., Kenngott, H., Schlemmer, H.P., Hornegger, J., Meinzer, H.P., Maier-Hein, L.: A probabilistic approach to fusion of Time-of-Flight and multiple view based 3D surface reconstruction for laparoscopic interventions. Int. J. Comput. Assist. Radiol. Surg. 7, S397–S398 (2012)

59. Kolb, C., Groch, A., Seitel, A., Kilgus, T., Haase, S., Bendl, R., Meinzer, H.P., Hornegger, J., Maier-Hein, L.: Simultaneous localization and soft-tissue shape recovery with a time of flight endoscope for computer-assisted surgery. Int. J. Comput. Assist. Radiol. Surg. (in press, 2013)

60. Ladikos, A., Benhimane, S., Navab, N.: Real-time 3D reconstruction for collision avoidance in interventional environments. In: Metaxas, D., Axel, L., Fichtinger, G., Székely, G. (eds.) MICCAI 2008, Part II. LNCS, vol. 5242, pp. 526–534. Springer, Heidelberg (2008)

61. Navab, N., Holzer, S.: Real-time 3D reconstruction: Applications to collision detection and surgical workflow monitoring. In: IROS Workshop on Methods for Safer Surgical Robotics Procedures (2011)

62. SAFROS project, http://www.safros.eu/

63. ACTIVE project, http://www.active-fp7.eu/

64. Mönnich, H., Nicolai, P., Raczkowsky, J., Wörn, H.: A semi-autonomous robotic teleoperation surgery setup with multi 3D camera supervision. Int. J. Comput. Assist. Radiol. Surg., 132–133 (2011)
65. Nicolai, P., Raczkowsky, J.: Operation room supervision for safe robotic surgery with a multi 3D-camera setup. In: IROS Workshop on Methods for Safer Surgical Robotics Procedures (2011)
66. Katic, D., Wekerle, A.L., Gärtner, F., Kenngott, H., Müller-Stich, B.P., Dillmann, R., Speidel, S.: Ontology-based prediction of surgical events in laparoscopic surgery. In: SPIE Medical Imaging, pp. 86711A–7 (2013)
67. Padoy, N., Mateus, D., Weinland, D., Berger, M.O., Navab, N.: Workflow monitoring based on 3D motion features. In: ICCV Workshop on Video-oriented Object and Event Classification, pp. 585–592. IEEE (2009)
68. Lea, C.S., Fackler, J.C., Hager, G.D., Taylor, R.H.: Towards automated activity recognition in an intensive care unit. In: MICCAI Workshop on Modeling and Monitoring of Computer Assisted Interventions, pp. 19–28 (2012)
69. Ladikos, A., Cagniart, C., Ghotbi, R., Reiser, M., Navab, N.: Estimating radiation exposure in interventional environments. In: Jiang, T., Navab, N., Pluim, J.P.W., Viergever, M.A. (eds.) MICCAI 2010, Part III. LNCS, vol. 6363, pp. 237–244. Springer, Heidelberg (2010)
70. Gratzel, C., Fong, T., Grange, S., Baur, C.: A non-contact mouse for surgeon-computer interaction. Technology and Health Care – European Society for Engineering and Medicine 12(3), 245–258 (2004)
71. Soutschek, S., Penne, J., Hornegger, J., Kornhuber, J.: 3-D gesture-based scene navigation in medical imaging applications using Time-Of-Flight cameras. In: CVPR Workshop on Time of Flight Camera based Computer Vision, pp. 1–6. IEEE (2008)
72. Ruppert, G., Reis, L., Amorim, P., de Moraes, T., da Silva, J.: Touchless gesture user interface for interactive image visualization in urological surgery. World J. Urol. 30, 1–5 (2012)
73. Gallo, L., Placitelli, A.P., Ciampi, M.: Controller-free exploration of medical image data: Experiencing the Kinect. In: International Symposium on Computer-Based Medical Systems, pp. 1–6. IEEE (2011)
74. Jacob, M., Cange, C., Packer, R., Wachs, J.P.: Intention, context and gesture recognition for sterile MRI navigation in the operating room. In: Alvarez, L., Mejail, M., Gomez, L., Jacobo, J. (eds.) CIARP 2012. LNCS, vol. 7441, pp. 220–227. Springer, Heidelberg (2012)
75. Kirmizibayrak, C., Radeva, N., Wakid, M., Philbeck, J., Sibert, J., Hahn, J.: Evaluation of gesture based interfaces for medical volume visualization tasks. In: International Conference on Virtual Reality Continuum and Its Applications in Industry, pp. 69–74. ACM (2011)
76. Ebert, L., Hatch, G., Ampanozi, G., Thali, M., Ross, S.: You can't touch this: Touch-free navigation through radiological images. Surg. Innov. 19(3), 301–307 (2012)
77. Bigdelou, A., Stauder, R., Benz, T., Okur, A., Blum, T., Ghotbi, R., Navab, N.: HCI design in the OR: A gesturing case-study. In: MICCAI Workshop on Modeling and Monitoring of Computer Assisted Interventions, Springer, pp. 10–18. Springer (2012)
78. Karl Storz GmbH, Tuttlingen, Germany, http://www.mi-report.com
79. Bigdelou, A., Benz, T., Schwarz, L., Navab, N.: Simultaneous categorical and spatio-temporal 3D gestures using Kinect. In: Symposium on 3D User Interfaces, pp. 53–60. IEEE (2012)

80. Dressler, C., Neumuth, T., Fischer, M., Abri, O., Strauss, G.: Intraoperative Bedienung einer elektronischen Patientenakte durch den Operateur. HNO 59(9), 900–907 (2011)

81. Navab, N., Traub, J., Sielhorst, T., Feuerstein, M., Bichlmeier, C.: Action- and workflow-driven augmented reality for computer-aided medical procedures. IEEE Comput. Graph. Appl. 27(5), 10–14 (2007)

82. Sugimoto, M., Yasuda, H., Koda, K., Suzuki, M., Yamazaki, M., Tezuka, T., Kosugi, C., Higuchi, R., Watayo, Y., Yagawa, Y., Uemura, S., Tsuchiya, H., Azuma, T.: Image overlay navigation by markerless surface registration in gastrointestinal, hepatobiliary and pancreatic surgery. J. Hepatobiliary Pancreat Sci. 17(5), 629–636 (2010)

83. Maier-Hein, L., Franz, A.M., Fangerau, M., Schmidt, M., Seitel, A., Mersmann, S., Kilgus, T., Groch, A., Yung, K., dos Santos, T.R., Meinzer, H.P.: Towards mobile augmented reality for on-patient visualization of medical images. In: Bildverarbeitung für die Medizin, pp. 389–393. Springer (2011)

84. Blum, T., Kleeberger, V., Bichlmeier, C., Navab, N.: mirracle: An augmented reality magic mirror system for anatomy education. In: Virtual Reality, pp. 115–116. IEEE (2012)

85. Maier-Hein, L., Schmidt, M., Franz, A., dos Santos, T., Scitel, A., Jähne, B., Fitzpatrick, J., Meinzer, H.: Accounting for anisotropic noise in fine registration of time-of-flight range data with high-resolution surface data. In: Jiang, T., Navab, N., Pluim, J.P.W., Viergever, M.A. (eds.) MICCAI 2010, Part I. LNCS, vol. 6361, pp. 251–258. Springer, Heidelberg (2010)

86. Maier-Hein, L., Franz, A., dos Santos, T., Schmidt, M., Fangerau, M., Meinzer, H.P., Fitzpatrick, J.M.: Convergent iterative closest-point algorithm to accomodate anisotropic and inhomogenous localization error. IEEE Trans. Pattern Anal. Mach. Intell. 34(8), 1520–1532 (2012)

87. Kilgus, T., Franz, A.M., Seitel, A., März, K., Bartha, L., Fangerau, M., Mersmann, S., Groch, A., Meinzer, H.P., Maier-Hein, L.: Registration of partially overlapping surfaces for range image based augmented reality on mobile devices. In: SPIE Medical Imaging, p. 83160T (2012)

88. Gabel, M., Gilad-Bachrach, R., Renshaw, E., Schuster, A.: Full body gait analysis with Kinect. In: International Conference of Engineering in Medicine and Biology Society, pp. 1964–1967. IEEE (2012)

89. Parra-Dominguez, G., Taati, B., Mihailidis, A.: 3D human motion analysis to detect abnormal events on stairs. In: International Conference on 3D Imaging, Modeling, Processing, Visualization and Transmission, pp. 97–103 (2012)

90. Garcia, J.A., Navarro, K.F., Schoene, D., Smith, S.T., Pisan, Y.: Exergames for the elderly: towards an embedded Kinect-based clinical test of falls risk. Studies in Health Technology and Informatics. In: Health Informatics: Building a Healthcare Future Through Trusted Information, pp. 51–57. IOS (2012)

91. Parajuli, M., Tran, D., Ma, W., Sharma, D.: Senior health monitoring using Kinect. In: International Conference on Communications and Electronics, pp. 309–312 (2012)

92. Stone, E., Skubic, M.: Evaluation of an inexpensive depth camera for in-home gait assessment. J. Ambient Intell. Smart Environ. 3(4), 349–361 (2011)

93. Stone, E., Skubic, M.: Passive in-home measurement of stride-to-stride gait variability comparing vision and Kinect sensing. In: International Conference of Engineering in Medicine and Biology Society, pp. 6491–6494 (2011)

94. Gross, H., Schroeter, C., Mueller, S., Volkhardt, M., Einhorn, E., Bley, A., Martin, C., Langner, T., Merten, M.: Progress in developing a socially assistive mobile home robot companion for the elderly with mild cognitive impairment. In: IEEE/RSJ IROS, pp. 2430–2437 (2011)

95. Lowet, D., Isken, M., Lee, W., van Heesch, F., Eertink, E.: Robotic telepresence for 24/07 remote assistance to elderly at home, workshop on social robotic telepresence. In: International Symposium on Robot and Human Interactive Communication. IEEE (2012)

96. Woo, J., Wada, K., Kubota, N.: Robot partner system for elderly people care by using sensor network. In: International Conference on Biomedical Robotics and Biomechatronics, IEEE, RAS, EMBS, pp. 1329–1334 (2012)

97. Shotton, J., Girshick, R., Fitzgibbon, A., Sharp, T., Cook, M., Finocchio, M., Moore, R., Kohli, P., Criminisi, A., Kipman, A., Blake, A.: Efficient human pose estimation from single depth images. IEEE Trans. Pattern Anal. Mach. Intell. 99 (2012) (PrePrints)

98. Ganapathi, V., Plagemann, C., Koller, D., Thrun, S.: Real time motion capture using a single Time-of-Flight camera. In: CVPR, pp. 755–762. IEEE (2010)

99. Schwarz, L., Mkhitaryan, A., Mateus, D., Navab, N.: Estimating human 3D pose from Time-of-Flight images based on geodesic distances and optical flow. In: International Conference on Automatic Face Gesture Recognition and Workshops, pp. 700–706. IEEE (2011)

100. Coronato, A., Gallo, L.: Towards abnormal behavior detection of cognitive impaired people. In: International Conference on Pervasive Computing and Communications Workshops, pp. 859–864. IEEE (2012)

101. Sivalingam, R., Cherian, A., Fasching, J., Walczak, N., Bird, N.D., Morellas, V., Murphy, B., Cullen, K., Lim, K., Sapiro, G., Papanikolopoulos, N.: A multi-sensor visual tracking system for behavior monitoring of at-risk children. In: ICRA, pp. 1345–1350 (2012)

102. Walczak, N., Fasching, J., Toczyski, W.D., Sivalingam, R., Bird, N.D., Cullen, K., Morellas, V., Murphy, B., Sapiro, G., Papanikolopoulos, N.: A nonintrusive system for behavioral analysis of children using multiple RGB+depth sensors. In: Workshop on the Applications of Computer Vision, pp. 217–222 (2012)

103. Falie, D., Ichim, M., David, L.: Respiratory motion visualization and the sleep apnea diagnosis with the time of flight (ToF) camera. In: International Conference on Visualization, Imaging and Simulation, WSEAS, pp. 179–184 (2008)

104. Yu, M.C., Wu, H., Liou, J.L., Lee, M.S., Hung, Y.P.: Breath and position monitoring during sleeping with a depth camera. In: HEALTHINF, pp. 12–22 (2012)

105. Smith, S.T., Schoene, D.: The use of exercise-based videogames for training and rehabilitation of physical function in older adults: current practice and guidelines for future research. Aging Health 8(3), 243–252 (2012)

106. Virtualware Group, Basauri, Spain, http://virtualrehab.info/en/

107. Jintronix, Inc., Montreal, QC, Canada, http://www.jintronix.com/

108. Chang, Y.J., Chen, S.F., Huang, J.D.: A Kinect-based system for physical rehabilitation: A pilot study for young adults with motor disabilities. Research in Developmental Disabilities 32(6), 2566–2570 (2011)

109. da Gama, A., Chaves, T., Figueiredo, L., Teichrieb, V.: Improving motor rehabilitation process through a natural interaction based system using Kinect sensor. In: IEEE Symposium on 3D User Interfaces, pp. 145–146 (2012)

110. Huang, J.D.: Kinerehab: A Kinect-based system for physical rehabilitation: a pilot study for young adults with motor disabilities. In: International ACM SIGACCESS Conference on Computers and Accessibility, pp. 319–320. ASSETS (2011)

111. Soutschek, S., Maier, A., Bauer, S., Kugler, P., Bebenek, M., Steckmann, S., von Stengel, S., Kemmler, W., Hornegger, J., Kornhuber, J.: Measurement of angles in Time-of-Flight data for the automatic supervision of training exercises. In: IEEE Conference on Pervasive Computing Technologies for Healthcare, pp. 1–4 (2010)
112. Schoenauer, C., Pintaric, T., Kaufmann, H., Jansen Kosterink, S., Vollenbroek-Hutten, M.: Chronic pain rehabilitation with a serious game using multimodal input. In: International Conference on Virtual Rehabilitation, pp. 1–8 (2011)
113. Chang, C.Y., Lange, B., Zhang, M., Koenig, S., Requejo, P., Somboon, N., Sawchuk, A.A., Rizzo, A.A.: Towards pervasive physical rehabilitation using Microsoft Kinect. In: International Conference on Pervasive Computing Technologies for Healthcare, pp. 159–162 (2012)
114. Lange, B., Chang, C.Y., Suma, E., Newman, B., Rizzo, A., Bolas, M.: Development and evaluation of low cost game-based balance rehabilitation tool using the Microsoft Kinect sensor. In: International Conference of Engineering in Medicine and Biology Society, pp. 1831–1834. IEEE (2011)
115. Hersh, M., Johnson, M., Keating, D.: Assistive Technology for Visually Impaired and Blind People. Springer (2007)
116. Gallo, S., Chapuis, D., Santos-Carreras, L., Kim, Y., Retornaz, P., Bleuler, H., Gassert, R.: Augmented white cane with multimodal haptic feedback. In: International Conference on Biomedical Robotics and Biomechatronics, IEEE, RAS, EMBS, pp. 149–155 (2010)
117. Gassert, R., Kim, Y., Oggier, T., Riesch, M., Deschler, M., Prott, C., Schneller, S., Hayward, V.: White cane with integrated electronic travel aid using 3D TOF sensor, Patent WO 2012/040703 (2012)
118. Katz, B., Kammoun, S., Parseihian, G., Gutierrez, O., Brilhault, A., Auvray, M., Truillet, P., Denis, M., Thorpe, S., Jouffrais, C.: Navig: Augmented reality guidance system for the visually impaired. Virtual Reality 16, 253–269 (2012)
119. Ong, S.K., Zhang, J., Nee, A.Y.C.: Assistive obstacle detection and navigation devices for vision-impaired users. Disability and Rehabilitation: Assistive Technology (2013) (Epub ahead of print)
120. IS2you, Santa Maria, Portugal, http://www.is2you.eu/eng/products.html
121. Buttgen, B.: Extending Time-of-Flight optical 3D-imaging to extreme operating conditions. PhD thesis, Universite de Neuchatel (2007)
122. Maimone, A., Fuchs, H.: Reducing interference between multiple structured light depth sensors using motion. In: IEEE Virtual Reality, pp. 51–54 (2012)
123. Roggan, A., Friebel, M., Dörschel, K., Hahn, A., Müller, G.: Optical properties of circulating human blood in the wavelength range 400-2500 nm. J. Biomed. Opt. 4(1), 36–46 (1999)
124. Fuchs, S.: Multipath interference compensation in time-of-flight camera images. In: ICPR, pp. 3583–3586 (2010)
125. Dorrington, A.A., Godbaz, J.P., Cree, M.J., Payne, A.D., Streeter, L.V.: Separating true range measurements from multi-path and scattering interference in commercial range cameras. In: SPIE Electronic Imaging, pp. 786404–786410 (2011)
126. Wu, D., O'Toole, M., Velten, A., Agrawal, A., Raskar, R.: Decomposing global light transport using time of flight imaging. In: CVPR, pp. 366–373. IEEE (2012)
127. Bert, C., Metheany, K.G., Doppke, K., Chen, G.T.Y.: A phantom evaluation of a stereo-vision surface imaging system for radiotherapy patient setup. Med. Phys. 32(9), 2753–2762 (2005)
128. Lange, R.: 3D Time-of-Flight Distance Measurement with Custom Solid-State Image Sensors in CMOS/CCD-Technology. PhD thesis, University of Siegen (2000)

129. Seitel, A., Yung, K., Mersmann, S., Kilgus, T., Groch, A., Santos, T., Franz, A., Nolden, M., Meinzer, H.P., Maier-Hein, L.: MITK-ToF - range data within MITK. Int. J. Comput. Assist. Radiol. Surg. 7, 87–96 (2012)
130. Wolf, I., Vetter, M., Wegner, I., Böttger, T., Nolden, M., Schöbinger, M., Hastenteufel, M., Kunert, T., Meinzer, H.P.: The medical imaging interaction toolkit. Med. Image Anal. 9, 594–604 (2005)
131. Wasza, J., Bauer, S., Haase, S., Schmid, M., Reichert, S., Hornegger, J.: RITK: The range imaging toolkit - a framework for 3-D range image stream processing. In: Eisert, P., Hornegger, J., Polthier, K. (eds.) International Workshop on Vision, Modeling and Visualization, pp. 57–64 (2011)
132. Ibanez, L., Schroeder, W., Ng, L., Cates, J.: The ITK Software Guide, 2nd edn. Kitware, Inc. (2005)
133. Rusu, R.B., Cousins, S.: 3D is here: Point cloud library (PCL). In: ICRA, pp. 1–4 (2011)

Part IV

Proceedings of the Workshop on Imaging New Modalities

A State of the Art Report on Kinect Sensor Setups in Computer Vision

Kai Berger[1], Stephan Meister[2], Rahul Nair[2], and Daniel Kondermann[2]

[1] OeRC Oxford, University of Oxford
`firstname.lastname@oerc.ox.ac.uk`
[2] Heidelberg Collaboratory for Image Processing, University of Heidelberg
`firstname.lastname@iwr.uni-heidelberg.de`

Abstract. During the last three years after the launch of the Microsoft Kinect® in the end-consumer market we have become witnesses of a small revolution in computer vision research towards the use of a standardized consumer-grade RGBD sensor for scene content retrieval. Beside classical localization and motion capturing tasks the Kinect has successfully been employed for the reconstruction of opaque and transparent objects. This report gives a comprehensive overview over the main publications using the Microsoft Kinect out of its original context as a decision-forest based motion-capturing tool.

1 Introduction

In early March 2010 Microsoft released a press text [54] that it would work together with PrimeSense, a Tel-Aviv based chip supplier, on a "groundbreaking optical-sensing and recognition technology to aid gesture control platforms." for the upcoming holidays. The goal of the project, internally known as "Project Natal" was to develop a new controller-free entertainment environment. Microsoft anticipated a paradigm shift on how people would interact with consumer-grade electronic devices.

The device itself was presented to a public audience at the E3 game convention. The device was launched in North America on November 4, 2010 and in Europe on November 10, 2010. By the beginning of 2012, 24 million units were sold. On February 1, 2012, Microsoft released the Kinect® for Windows SDK [53] and it is believed that more than 300 companies are working on apps that employ the Microsoft Kinect. In November 2010, Adafruit Industries funded an open-source driver development for Kinect. Although Microsoft initially disapproved their approach, they later clarified their position claiming that the USB connection was left open by design. Adafruit recognized Hèctor Martìn's work on a Linux driver that allows the use of both the RGB camera and depth sensitivity functions of the device. It is publicly available for download under the name *libfreenect* [62]. It is estimated that the OpenKinect community consists of roughly 2000 members who are contributing their time and code to the project. The code contributed to OpenKinect is made available under an Apache 2.0 or optional GPL2 license. Another open source API is provided via the OpenNI

M. Grzegorzek et al. (Eds.): Time-of-Flight and Depth Imaging, LNCS 8200, pp. 257–272, 2013.

framework of the OpenNI Organization [63] in which PrimeSense is a major contributor. In the middle of May 2013 Microsoft released a technical demo of the successor, Microsoft Kinect 2.0, which is based on Time-Of-Flight imaging. Both the availability of a consumer-grade RGBD sensor at a competitive price and the Open Source project that allowed to easily read out the essential streams from the sensor, quickly sparked an interest in the research community.

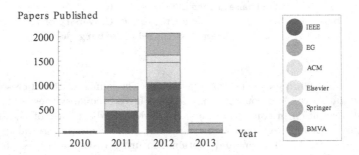

Fig. 1. The impact of the Microsoft Kinect in the computer vision field is significant: over the last three years, over 3000 papers related to the Microsoft Kinect have been published in renowned journals and proceedings (e.g., IEEE Explore, Digital Library of Eurographics, Proceedings of the ACM, Elsevier). Keywords associated with the Kinect include simultaneous localization and mapping, object reconstruction, multiple Kinect, interference mitigation, transparency and calibration.

Over the last three years a significant part of the published papers has been devoted to the use of the Kinect in a scientific context, Fig. 1. Over 3000 papers have been published in renowned journals and proceedings, e.g., Elsevier (208 papers), Eurographics (36 papers), ACM (651 papers), Springer (746 papers) or IEEE Explore (1518 papers), which publishes CVPR and ICCV proceedings among others. Of these, 276 papers refer to simultaneous localization and mapping problems and 227 are related to object reconstruction. Another 17 articles recognize the challenge that transparency, e.g. from a glass object, would pose on a sensor like the Kinect and proposed algorithms to reconstruct such transparent objects from depth streams from the Kinect. Finally, 47 papers address new ways to calibrate the Kinect. Further details about the deployment of a single Microsoft Kinect in academic context can be found in the manuscript submitted by Han et al. [27].

We recognize that there are still new ambitious research projects incorporating the Microsoft Kinect, e.g. the project Kinect@Home [2]. There, the user can help robotics and computer vision researchers around the world by scanning their office/living room environment with the Kinect. In return the user is delivered a 3D model of the very room.

The remainder of this state-of-the-art report is structured as follows: after reviewing the sensor itself in Section 2, we will introduce papers related to its use as a simultaneous localization and mapping tool in Section 3. Afterwards, we will expand on motion capturing scenarios in which the Kinect has been employed, e.g. hand tracking, Section 4. Then, we will have a look into the research field that incorporates the Kinect as a tool to reconstruct non-opaque objects and motion, Section 5. In Section 6 we will present methods to improve or denoise Kinect depth maps while focusing on sensor fusion approaches. Finally, we will conclude and give an outlook, Section 7.

2   The Kinect 1.0 Sensor

The Microsoft Kinect is the first structured light sensor available for the consumer market. Designed as a motion sensing input device for the gaming console Microsoft XBox 360® the Kinect is intended to be used for gaming purposes. A typical usage environment can be seen in Figure 2(Left). With the Kinect it is possible for the XBox 360 to track movements of multiple players in a game. Its pattern emission technique was invented by PrimeSense and licensed by Microsoft for use in the Project Natal. The project OpenKinect provided the open source library libfreenect that enables PCs to use the Kinect as an input device via USB 2.0. This enabled users to experiment with an easy to access realtime capable depth tracking system. Compared to state-of-the-art depth capturing systems, e.g. time-of-flight (ToF) cameras, the system costs were negligible. With the success of the Kinect, other company's devices licensing the same technique from PrimeSense did appear. Asus introduced two devices called Xtion and Xtion LIVE with the underlying technique being the same as in the Kinect.

The coded light approach employed for the depth mapping is a simple and effective way to acquire depth data of a scene. A light, here an IR laser, projects a unique pattern onto the surface of the scene (see Figure 2(Center) for an example). This projection is recorded by a camera which is capable of capturing in the spectrum in which the pattern is emitted. Then, an integrated circuit computes the disparity for subpatterns by comparing them to their default positions at a given distance. For the disparity values the distance in meters for each pixel in the depth image can be computed. The structured light or active stereo approach is well known and has long been used by structured light scanners e.g. in the form of gray-codes for high precision depth measurements. The special pattern of the

Fig. 2. Typically, the Microsoft Kinect would be found in the living room of a Microsoft Xbox user. **Left:** typical usage scene, **Center:** infrared pattern, **Right:** colorcoded depth map.

light used in the Kinect is particulary suited for fast disparity estimation using block-matching and has been introduced by PrimeSense. In so far the Kinect suffers from the same depth estimation problems as other active or also passive stereo systems, mainly inaccurate depth at occlusion boundaries and problems with reflecting or transparent surfaces. A colorcoded representation of the depth values can be seen in Figure 2(Right).

3   SLAM and 3D Reconstruction

3D reconstruction and simultaneous localization and mapping (SLAM) are two closely connected fields of application which both can benefit from accurate depth data. Both can rely on either monoscopic reconstruction methods without prior depth information, sparse 3D data e.g. from laser rangefinders or dense depth maps e.g. from stereoscopic systems. Although systems utilizing only depth data or only visual data have been in use for decades, the integration of RGBD to make the systems more robust is a relatively new development. Apart from algorithms which were specifically designed for the Kinect we will also cover those that combine RGB and depth data in new ways and those which were inspired by these works even if they are not specifically limited to the Kinect.

A first step in both algorithm classes is the estimation of camera movement between consecutive frames. As shown by Handa et al. [28] tracking does generally benefit from high-frame rates alongside high resolution and low SNR. The Kinect sensor fills a niche in that it can supply dense depth maps in realtime. Examples for odometry algorithms which use depth data were presented by Kerl [41] or Steinbrücker [75]. Additionally, it has been shown by Newman and Ho [58] that visual features can effectively be used to solve the loop-closing problem in SLAM applications. The simultaneous availability of RGB and depth data can in this context be further exploited to calculate a dense scene flow [23]. Specific calibration considerations are discussed in [73] or [33]. Currently, there is no known SLAM system that uses multiple Kinects, although motion tracking with stationary cameras was demonstrated e.g. by Faion et al. [19] or Schönauer and Kaufmann [71].

One of the first methods to utilize the Kinect in a SLAM system is the framework presented by Henry et al. [30][31]. Here, features extracted from the RGB images are used for the initial camera pose estimation which is then refined by applying an iterative closest point algorithm (ICP) on the depth data. Hu et al. [34] use a similar approach but fall back to pure RGB based pose estimation if the depth features are insufficient, thereby adding the advantages of depth maps without inheriting their problems. Another approach was presented by Endres et al. [18] who also extract RGB features but then reproject these features into 3d to perform pose estimation in a closed form. All these algorithms can be used for online processing but unlike most recent developments which utilize GPU computation they are not real-time capable. Additionally, they do not always produce dense 3d representations like the following reconstruction algorithms as this is generally not necessary for localization tasks.

Accurate 3d reconstruction was until now a slow and expensive process as it was mostly based on laser or structured light scanners. The KinectFusion algorithm which was first introduced by Newcombe, Izadi et al. [57][38] and its subsequent improvements [66][32][83] represent a new direction in algorithm development as it is fast and depends only on commodity hardware. It creates an implicit voxel representation of a scene from the depth data using truncated signed distances functions. Each new view from the camera is registered using an Iterative Closest Point (ICP) algorithm. In that regard it behaves similar to other SLAM algorithms but the in-memory voxel representation allows for highly parallelized processing using GPUs. By providing a realtime 3D reconstruction method in the low to medium accuracy range (mm to cm regarding depth) it makes 3D scanning affordable for a wide field of potential users.

An analysis of the KinectFusion reconstruction performance has been performed by Meister et al. [52]. They compared the 3D meshes created by the KinectFusion system with high accuracy scans from LiDAR or structured light scanners to provide definite accuracy measures for mesh surfaces and derived values. The results suggest that the method is suitable even for applications where one would suspect an accuracy as high as possible to be mandatory. The geometric errors of 3D meshes created by KinectFusion can range from 10mm for small scenes (less than 1 m across, see Figure 3 for an example) to 80mm for room sized scenes. This may be too large for industrial inspection purposes but perfectly reasonable for the creation of synthetic test sequences for low-level image processing tasks, such as stereo matching or optical flow evaluation.

Despite it's impressive impact on both research and application alike the algorithm should not be considered a full SLAM solution. It's biggest drawbacks are the limited scan volume ($\approx 100 - 200m^3$ depending on graphics memory), the tendency to loose camera tracking in regions with few geometry features and the lack of explicit loop-closure handling. Some direct modifications of the algorithm try to alleviate these problems. Moving Volume Kinect by Roth et

Fig. 3. Ground truth mesh, Kinect fusion mesh and euclidean surface error for scanned object from [52]

al. [66] allows the camera to leave the initial bounding volume but the basic limits for the 3d model still apply. Others like Kinfu Large Scale [32] or [87] use more memory efficient data structures to represent the volume data, e.g. by using octrees. Kintinuous by Whelan et al. [83] continuously converts the volume data to point clouds for processing in main memory. This effectively removes any hard size limitations for the mapping volume. Whelan et al. also combined their system with the odometry estimation by Steinbrücker to make it more robust in case of missing geometric features [82]. This method is so far the only KinectFusion inspired algorithm that integrates RGB data. Bylow et al. [11] directly use the signed distance function of the voxel representation instead of ICP to estimate the camera movement more exactly. Keller et al. [40] drop the voxel representation altogether and use point-based fusion instead. Their approach handles the Kinect specific depth noise better and can handle dynamic scene content.

Other recent works try to combine SLAM with real-time capabilities and dense 3d reconstruction. Examples include the works by Lee et al. [44] who directly create a polygon representation from the acquired depth data or Henry et al. [29] who combine volumetric fusion with large-scale models. Finally, Stückler et al. [76] [77] use a different method based on a surfel representation of the environment. The camera pose estimation is also different in that it is estimated by a likelihood optimization approach on the surfel distribution. These recent developments suggest that the distinction between SLAM and 3D reconstruction may disappear in the near future as both algorithm types profit from improvements made to each other.

4 Motion Capturing Setups

Shotton et al. [72] introduced the Kinect and its underlying algorithm as a tool to capture the human pose from monocular depth images. Quickly thereafter, monocular motion capturing has gotten into the focus of the research community [22,65,60], with the Microsoft Kinect being the device to generate datasets and benchmarks. What can be done with this research has been shown by Chen et al. [13]. Besides the tracking of limbs and joints quickly other research fields in monocular depth processing have emerged.

One interesting research direction for example is to use the Microsoft Kinect as a hand-tracking device. Oikonomidis [61] presents an approach based on particle swarms to discriminate between the palm and single fingers. Frati and his colleagues [21] assume the hand to always be closest to the camera and calculate convexity defects from the bounding box of the hand with the help of OpenCV while Reheja and his colleagues first detect the palm with a circular filter and then remove it to arrive at the shapes of individual fingertips in the depth image [64]. An interesting approach has been proposed by Van den Bergh et al. [6], who estimate the orientation of the hand from the orientation of the forearm in the depth image. The posture itself is estimated by employing an Average Neighborhood Margin Maximization (ANMM) algorithm [80].

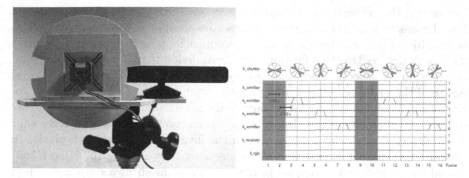

Fig. 4. An approach to incorporate multiple Kinects nondestructively in a motion capturing setup: An externally synced rolling shutter assigns one Kinect a unique time slot so that three other Kinects can capture as well. Such setups enable the capturing of obstructed motions or of motions with the actor not facing a camera. Red dots represent the emitters (projectors) while green dots represent receivers (cameras). Reproduced from [70].

With the Microsoft Kinect it is also possible to capture facial movements. Zollhofer et al. [89] showed how to fit deformable facial meshes to depth data captured from human faces by relying on feature points (eyes, nose) in the depth data. Leyvand et al. also examine the face recognition of identical twins given depth and motion data from the Microsoft Kinect [46].

In 2011, Berger and his colleagues showed, that it is also possible to employ multiple Microsoft Kinects in one scene for motion capturing research [5]. Their incentive was to enable the capturing of partially obstructed poses, e.g. from persons facing away from the camera or in small rooms. Using a specifically tailored external hardware shutter [70] they were able to reduce the sensor noise introduced from neighboring Kinects, Fig. 4. Their approach relied on synchronized rolling shutters for up to four devices. This idea was quickly adopted and further developed by Maimone and Fuchs [50] in a shake and sense approach: each Kinect sensor would slightly rotate around its up vector introducing scene motion to the imaged scene except for its own projected pattern which always moves accordingly. Thus, the accuracy of the depth image generated from its own pattern would increase due to blurred out sensor noise from other Kinects. The motion would be accounted for from the Kinect's inertial sensor data. This approach was further refined by Butler and his colleagues [10] who basically hot-melt glued a motor to each device to introduce arbitrary motion.

5   Opaque and Transparent Reconstruction

With the availability of accurate depth data, the complete 3D reconstruction of objects with the consumer-grade Kinect became a popular research branch. For example, Tam and his colleagues [78] register point clouds captured with the Kinect to each other.

However, the reconstruction need not necessarily be restricted to opaque objects. Lysenkov and his colleagues [48] describe an approach to recognize transparent objects, e.g. a water glass, and to recognize its pose from the input images of a Kinect device. Due to reflection and transmission the IR pattern shone onto the transparent objects is not usable for depth estimation. Consequently, pixel regions of the projected object in the depth image obtain invalid values, e.g. appear black. They use a key observation: Transparent and opaque objects create surface and silhouette edges. Image edgels corresponding to a silhouette edge can be detected at the boundary between the invalid and valid depth pixels. To recognize transparent objects one can reconstruct it by moving the Kinect 360° around the object or by comparing it to a similar mesh in a database. They, however, decide to register it beforehand by powdering it and thus making it temporarily opaque. The silhouettes of the registered object are then used for training. During the test phase later, they compare the silhouette edges created by invalid pixels in the depth images with the silhouettes in the database using Procrustes Analysis as proposed by [51]. When a non-powdering approach is pursued, the authors stress that it is important to provide additional calibration information [47] for the Kinect in order to reconstruct its location to the transparent object, whose only viable information are the silhouette edges retrieved from the depth images. Another approach to reconstruct transparent objects with the Kinect is to incorporate the RGB-sensor. Chiu et al. [15] propose to calibrate the RGB-camera with the IR-camera to arrive at a multi-modal stereo image (i.e., depth, and the stereo from disparity between the RGB- and IR-camera).

When the object to be reconstructed becomes time-varying, it is impossible to powder and capture it beforehand. In their work, Berger et al. [4] examined the possibilities to reconstruct transparent gas flows using the Kinect. They ruled out seeding particles and decided to follow a Background-oriented Schlieren approach. The projected IR-pattern of each Kinect is hereby used as the background pattern. The silhouette boundaries would become visible in the depth sensor by the index gradient between the flowing gas, there propane, and its surrounding medium (air). As propane obtains a refractive index of roughly 1.34 the difference to the surrounding air would be sufficiently high enough to introduce noticeable pixel deviations at a distance of $3m$ between scene walls and the Kinect camera. They concluded, that, when they would place three Kinects in an half-arc around the flowing gas and projection walls at a fixed distance opposite to it, they could detect difference in the depth images that would suffice for silhouettes. Using the silhouettes of each Kinect they could enclose the gas volume in the reconstructed visual hull for each frame. The silhouette generation relied on fitting polynomials from left and right in each image [1,4]. In further research they concluded that it is also viable to directly use the deviations in the IR-images for the silhouette reconstruction, by relying on a sparse spot-based optical flow algorithm [69].

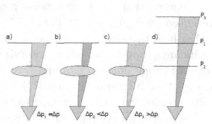

Fig. 5. The reconstruction of non-opaque motion. Three Kinects are placed in a circular half-arc around propane gas flow, projection walls opposite to each Kinect. As the Kinects do not interfere destructively with each other, meaningful information can be retrieved for each sensor. The refractive index gradient present in the scene would result in detectable depth deviations in each Kinect's depth image stream. Reproduced from [4]

6   Enhancing Depth Data

Although the Kinect delivers RGBD data of a sufficient quality for many applications, it is far from perfect. For example, as the projector is located to the right of the cameras, no depth data can be obtained in areas to the left of occlusion boundaries due to shadowing. If the depth map is then additionally registered to the RGB image, further information is lost. Other effects which are present throughout the image are errors due to the sparsity of the point pattern, the block size used for matching and the unknown smoothing that may additionally be applied to the raw data. Most of these errors can best be observed at depth edges. They lead to inaccurate depth boundaries, blobbing artifacts and a reduced effective lateral resolution. Also like every other active depth imaging technique the Kinect relies on the reflected light being of sufficient intensity. This is not the case with dark IR absorbing surfaces that may additionally lie at an angle to the camera or when strong IR light sources such as direct sun light are present in the scene [55].

The question remains whether there is a real need for better quality or higher resolution depth data. ICP [7][86] which is at the core of many pose and 3d reconstruction algorithms using Kinect, will produce better results given better input data. Also, accurate silhouette information is a strong cue used for 3d reconstruction [43].Some applications even depend on good initial depth data. As an example the visual effects industry frequently requires dynamic scene geometry at resolutions ranging from Full HD to 4K [39]. Current depth cameras meet the dynamic imaging requirement but fail to provide the necessary lateral resolution. In the following we will review the various lines of research dealing with the enhancement of depth images. Often, the papers presented deal with Time of Flight data instead of Kinect. Many of these algorithms work on the depth images and thus can be directly applied to Kinect data. Others also take into account the noise characteristics of Time of Flight sensors which are generally quite different from those of the Kinect. Here, the noise model used must be replaced with the Kinect noise model such es the empirical model recently presented by Nguyen et al. [59].

Depth data denoising as a subdiscipline of image denoising has progressed significantly and many edge preserving denoising techniques can be applied directly to range images. Examples would be diffusion based filters [81], non local means [9] or bilateral filtering [79]. Unlike RGB images, depth images are generally considered to be comparitively smooth with few distinct edges [35][84]. This property allows for a much stronger regularization than would be possible in RGB images. Lenzen et al. [45] apply an adaptive first and second order total variation approach to regularize depth data while retaining edges and slopes. Schoner et al. [68] apply a clustering approach to identify regions with similar properties. Aodha et al. [49] learn the relation between noisy input images and filtered output using decision tree ensembles [8].

As mentioned above, Kinect depth data contains many invalid pixels. To alleviate this problem, hole filling strategies which are related to image inpainting can be employed. Danciu et al. presented a single-frame method based on morphological filters [17]. Other Methods additionally use temporal information to make the inpainting more robust. Xu et al. first detect moving objects to improve edge stability before filling in holes [85], while Camplani and Salgado use bilateral filtering in combination with a temporal consistency constraint [12].

A different method to enhance Kinect data is to apply a sensor fusion approach by adding additional depth imaging modalities to create superresolution depth images. The sensor fusion methods can be differentiated by the employed camera setup. As strategies for using multiple Kinects have been discussed in Section 5 we will therefore limit ourselves to approaches using one or two additional RGB cameras. As the Kinect sensor itself includes a RGB camera and an IR camera, it can be used directly for RGBD fusion. Often though, an external RGB camera with a higher resolution is used for the fusion approach. After aligning the RGB and IR camera employing standard camera calibration techniques the main assumption is that depth edges often coincide with RGB edges. Chen et al. [14] for example employ cross bilateral filtering to smooth the resulting depth maps. Huhle et al. propose a graphical model with data terms based on RGB and depth gradient strength in [36] and in [37] adapted non local means filtering to encompass the additional data. Chiu et al. [15] on the other hand use the cross modal stereo information between the IR and the RGB sensor directly.

Most works which combine depth cameras with a regular passive stereo setup have been done with ToF imagers but as already mentioned the methods can be adapted to Kinect most of the time. One exception it the recently presented method by Somanath et al. [74] which uses a kinect to improve stereo depth estimates in ambiguous or low-textured regions. These methods use the range imaging data to initialize stereo matching and impose constraints on the search range depending on the depth budget and stereo noise model. Local methods

[42],[24],[3],[26],[16],[56] combine the stereo and the range imaging data term on a per pixel level. Gudmundsson et al.[24] apply a hierarchical stereo matching algorithm directly on the remapped depth data without considering uncertainties. Kuhnert et al.[42] and Hahne et al.[26] compute binary confidences in the depth image and let stereo refine the result in regions with low confidence. Nair et al.[56] and Dal Mutto et al. [16] locally combine confidences from both stereo and the depth image into the the the stereo matching framework. Global methods [20],[56],[88],[25] additionally apply spatial regularization techniques to propagate more information to regions with low stereo or depth image confidence. Inference of the global energy is then done using different optimization methods such as graph cuts[25], semi global optimization[20], MAP-MRF [88] or by minimizing the total variation[56],[67].

7   Conclusion

This state of the art report has reviewed the Kinect as a consumer-grade motion capturing toolkit and recognized its impact in the computer vision community. The output of the Kinect, depth-, RGB- and IR-images at realtime framerate enabled researchers to use the device in various scenarios. Simultaneous localization and mapping (SLAM) in the context of robotics and object reconstruction showed that the Kinect sensor fills a niche in that it can supply dense depth maps in realtime. Out of its intended context the Kinect was employed to track gestures and recognize faces. In small room environments it was shown that multiple Kinect sensors could capture motion without interfering destructively with each other thus enabling the capturing of obstructed motions or the motions of actors facing away from one camera. Recently, it was examined if non-opaque objects can be reconstructed as well. By relying on silhouette edges present in the depth images, e.g. around invalid depth pixel, the question could be answered positively for glass objects and gas flows. We conclude that this capturing has made an impact to the community that is unprecedented and sparked very creative research ideas. Additionally many advancements in the field of sensor fusion or depth map denoising e.g. from time-of-flight imaging can be applied to the Kinect camera to improve its accuracy.

Although now, 3 years later, a new generation of consumer-grade motion capturing devices is ready to be deployed and to challenge the position of the Microsoft Kinect. We believe that the impact of the Kinect and similar devices will continue to increase in the next years and that it will become the standard prototyping-research tool on every desktop in the vision community.

Acknowledgements. This work has been partially funded by the Intel Visual Computing Institute, Saarbrücken (IVCI) as part of the Project "Algorithms for Low Cost Depth Imaging" and the Engineering and Physical Sciences Research Council (EPSRC) grant on Video Visualization. Kinect and Xbox 360 are registered trademarks of Microsoft Corporation. This is an independent publication and is not affiliated with, nor has it been authorized, sponsored, or otherwise approved by Microsoft Corporation.

References

1. Albers, M., Berger, B.K., Magnor, E.P.D.I.M.: The capturing of turbulent gas flows using multiple kinects. Bachelor thesis, Technical University Braunschweig (2012)
2. Aydemir, A., Henell, D., Jensfelt, P., Shilkrot, R.: Kinect@ home: Crowdsourcing a large 3d dataset of real environments. In: 2012 AAAI Spring Symposium Series (2012)
3. Bartczak, B., Koch, R.: Dense depth maps from low resolution time-of-flight depth and high resolution color views. In: Bebis, G., et al. (eds.) ISVC 2009, Part II. LNCS, vol. 5876, pp. 228–239. Springer, Heidelberg (2009)
4. Berger, K., Ruhl, K., Albers, M., Schroder, Y., Scholz, A., Kokemuller, J., Guthe, S., Magnor, M.: The capturing of turbulent gas flows using multiple kinects. In: 2011 IEEE International Conference on Computer Vision Workshops (ICCV Workshops), pp. 1108–1113. IEEE (2011)
5. Berger, K., Ruhl, K., Brümmer, C., Schröder, Y., Scholz, A., Magnor, M.: Markerless motion capture using multiple color-depth sensors. In: Proc. Vision, Modeling and Visualization (VMV), vol. 2011, p. 3 (2011)
6. Van den Bergh, M., Carton, D., De Nijs, R., Mitsou, N., Landsiedel, C., Kuehnlenz, K., Wollherr, D., Van Gool, L., Buss, M.: Real-time 3D hand gesture interaction with a robot for understanding directions from humans. In: 2011 IEEE RO-MAN, pp. 357–362. IEEE (2011)
7. Besl, P.J., McKay, N.D.: A method for registration of 3-d shapes. IEEE Transactions on Pattern Analysis and Machine Intelligence 14(2), 239–256 (1992)
8. Breiman, L.: Random forests. Machine learning 45(1), 5–32 (2001)
9. Buades, A., Coll, B., Morel, J.M.: A non-local algorithm for image denoising. In: IEEE Computer Society Conference on Computer Vision and Pattern Recognition (CVPR 2005), vol. 2, pp. 60–65. IEEE (2005)
10. Butler, D.A., Izadi, S., Hilliges, O., Molyneaux, D., Hodges, S., Kim, D.: Shake'n'sense: Reducing interference for overlapping structured light depth cameras. In: Proceedings of the 2012 ACM Annual Conference on Human Factors in Computing Systems, pp. 1933–1936. ACM (2012)
11. Bylow, E., Sturm, J., Kerl, C., Kahl, F., Cremers, D.: Real-time camera tracking and 3d reconstruction using signed distance functions. In: Robotics: Science and Systems Conference (RSS) (2013)
12. Camplani, M., Salgado, L.: Efficient spatio-temporal hole filling strategy for kinect depth maps. In: International Society for Optics and Photonics, IS&T/SPIE Electronic Imaging, p. 82900E (2012)
13. Chen, J., Izadi, S., Fitzgibbon, A.: Kinêtre: Animating the world with the human body. In: Proceedings of the 25th Annual ACM Symposium on User Interface Software and Technology, pp. 435–444. ACM (2012)
14. Chen, L., Lin, H., Li, S.: Depth image enhancement for kinect using region growing and bilateral filter. In: 2012 21st International Conference on Pattern Recognition (ICPR), pp. 3070–3073. IEEE (2012)
15. Chiu, W.C., Blanke, U., Fritz, M.: Improving the kinect by cross-modal stereo. In: 22nd British Machine Vision Conference (BMVC) (2011)
16. Dal Mutto, C., Zanuttigh, P., Cortelazzo, G.M.: A probabilistic approach to tof and stereo data fusion. In: 3DPVT, Paris, France (May 2010)
17. Danciu, G., Banu, S.M., Caliman, A.: Shadow removal in depth images morphology-based for kinect cameras. In: 2012 16th International Conference on System Theory, Control and Computing (ICSTCC), pp. 1–6. IEEE (2012)

18. Endres, F., Hess, J., Engelhard, N., Sturm, J., Cremers, D., Burgard, W.: An evaluation of the rgb-d slam system. In: IEEE International Conference on Robotics and Automation (ICRA), pp. 1691–1696. IEEE (2012)
19. Faion, F., Friedberger, S., Zea, A., Hanebeck, U.D.: Intelligent sensor-scheduling for multi-kinect-tracking. In: Proc. IEEE/RSJ Int. Conf. on Intelligent Robots and Systems (IROS) (2012)
20. Fischer, J., Arbeiter, G., Verl, A.: Combination of time-of-flight depth and stereo using semiglobal optimization. In: Int. Conf. on Robotics and Automation (ICRA), pp. 3548–3553. IEEE (2011)
21. Frati, V., Prattichizzo, D.: Using kinect for hand tracking and rendering in wearable haptics. In: 2011 IEEE World Haptics Conference (WHC), pp. 317–321. IEEE (2011)
22. Girshick, R., Shotton, J., Kohli, P., Criminisi, A., Fitzgibbon, A.: Efficient regression of general-activity human poses from depth images. In: 2011 IEEE International Conference on Computer Vision (ICCV), pp. 415–422. IEEE (2011)
23. Gottfried, J.-M., Fehr, J., Garbe, C.: Computing range flow from multi-modal kinect data. Advances in Visual Computing, 758–767 (2011)
24. Gudmundsson, S.A., Aanaes, H., Larsen, R.: Fusion of stereo vision and time-of-flight imaging for improved 3D estimation. IJISTA 5(3), 425–433 (2008)
25. Hahne, U., Alexa, M.: Combining time-of-flight depth and stereo images without accurate extrinsic calibration. IJISTA 5(3), 325–333 (2008)
26. Hahne, U., Alexa, M.: Depth imaging by combining time-of-flight and on-demand stereo. In: Kolb, A., Koch, R. (eds.) Dyn3D 2009. LNCS, vol. 5742, pp. 70–83. Springer, Heidelberg (2009)
27. Han, J., Shao, L., Xu, D., Shotton, J.: Enhanced computer vision with microsoft kinect sensor: A review. IEEE Transactions on Cybernetics (2013)
28. Handa, A., Newcombe, R.A., Angeli, A., Davison, A.J.: Real-Time camera tracking: when is high frame-rate best? In: Fitzgibbon, A., Lazebnik, S., Perona, P., Sato, Y., Schmid, C. (eds.) ECCV 2012, Part VII. LNCS, vol. 7578, pp. 222–235. Springer, Heidelberg (2012),
    http://link.springer.com/chapter/10.1007/978-3-642-33786-4_17
29. Henry, P., Fox, D., Bhowmik, A., Mongia, R.: Patch Volumes: Segmentation-based Consistens Mapping with RGB-D Cameras. In: International Conference on 3D Vision 2013 (3DV) (2013)
30. Henry, P., Krainin, M., Herbst, E., Ren, X., Fox, D.: Rgb-d mapping: Using depth cameras for dense 3d modeling of indoor environments. In: The 12th International Symposium on Experimental Robotics (ISER), vol. 20, pp. 22–25 (2010)
31. Henry, P., Krainin, M., Herbst, E., Ren, X., Fox, D.: Rgb-d mapping: Using kinect-style depth cameras for dense 3d modeling of indoor environments. The International Journal of Robotics Research 31(5), 647–663 (2012)
32. Heredia, F., Favier, R.: Point cloud library developers blog, kinfu large scale (June 18, 2012), http://www.pointclouds.org/blog/srcs/
33. Daniel Herrera, C., Kannala, J., Heikkilä, J.: Accurate and practical calibration of a depth and color camera pair. In: Real, P., Diaz-Pernil, D., Molina-Abril, H., Berciano, A., Kropatsch, W. (eds.) CAIP 2011, Part II. LNCS, vol. 6855, pp. 437–445. Springer, Heidelberg (2011)
34. Hu, G., Huang, S., Zhao, L., Alempijevic, A., Dissanayake, G.: A robust rgb-d slam algorithm. In: 2012 IEEE/RSJ International Conference on Intelligent Robots and Systems (IROS) (2012)
35. Huang, J., Lee, A.B., Mumford, D.: Statistics of range images. In: Proceedings of the IEEE Conference on Computer Vision and Pattern Recognition, vol. 1, pp. 324–331. IEEE (2000)

36. Huhle, B., Fleck, S., Schilling, A.: Integrating 3D time-of-flight camera data and high resolution images for 3Dtv applications. In: Proc. 3DTV Conf. IEEE (2007)
37. Huhle, B., Schairer, T., Jenke, P., Straßer, W.: Robust non-local denoising of colored depth data. In: IEEE Computer Society Conference on Computer Vision and Pattern Recognition Workshops (CVPRW 2008), pp. 1–7. IEEE (2008)
38. Izadi, S., Newcombe, R.A., Kim, D., Hilliges, O., Molyneaux, D., Hodges, S., Kohli, P., Shotton, J., Davison, A.J., Fitzgibbon, A.: KinectFusion: Real-time dynamic 3D surface reconstruction and interaction. In: ACM SIGGRAPH 2011 Talks, p. 23. ACM (2011)
39. Kate Solomon - techradar.com: Meerkats to go Ultra HD in BBC's first 4K broadcast, http://www.techradar.com/news/tv/television/
meerkats-togo-ultra-hd-in-bbcs-first-4k-broadcast-1127915/
40. Keller, M., Lefloch, D., Lambers, M., Izadi, S., Weyrich, T., Kolb, A.: Real-time 3D Reconstruction in Dynamic Scenes using Point-based Fusion. In: International Conference on 3D Vision 2013 (3DV) (2013)
41. Kerl, C., Sturm, J., Cremers, D.: Robust odometry estimation for rgb-d cameras. In: Proc. of the IEEE Int. Conf. on Robotics and Automation (ICRA) (May 2013)
42. Kuhnert, K., Stommel, M.: Fusion of stereo-camera and pmd-camera data for real-time suited precise 3d environment reconstruction. In: Int. Conf. on Intelligent Robots and Systems, pp. 4780–4785. IEEE (2006)
43. Laurentini, A.: The visual hull concept for silhouette-based image understanding. IEEE Transactions on Pattern Analysis and Machine Intelligence 16(2), 150–162 (1994)
44. Lee, T., Lim, S., Lee, S., An, S., Oh, S.: Indoor mapping using planes extracted from noisy rgb-d sensors. In: 2012 IEEE/RSJ International Conference on Intelligent Robots and Systems (IROS) (2012)
45. Lenzen, F., Schäfer, H., Garbe, C.: Denoising time-of-flight data with adaptive total variation. In: Bebis, G. (ed.) ISVC 2011, Part I. LNCS, vol. 6938, pp. 337–346. Springer, Heidelberg (2011)
46. Leyvand, T., Meekhof, C., Wei, Y.C., Sun, J., Guo, B.: Kinect identity: Technology and experience. Computer 44(4), 94–96 (2011)
47. Lysenkov, I., Eruhimov, V.: Pose refinement of transparent rigid objects with a stereo camera. In: 22th International Conference on Computer Graphics and Vision (GraphiCon 2012) (2012)
48. Lysenkov, I., Eruhimov, V., Bradski, G.: Recognition and pose estimation of rigid transparent objects with a kinect sensor. In: Robotics: Science and Systems VIII, Sydney, Australia (2012)
49. Mac Aodha, O., Campbell, N.D.F., Nair, A., Brostow, G.J.: Patch based synthesis for single depth image super-resolution. In: Fitzgibbon, A., Lazebnik, S., Perona, P., Sato, Y., Schmid, C. (eds.) ECCV 2012, Part III. LNCS, vol. 7574, pp. 71–84. Springer, Heidelberg (2012)
50. Maimone, A., Fuchs, H.: Reducing interference between multiple structured light depth sensors using motion. In: 2012 IEEE Virtual Reality Workshops (VR), pp. 51–54. IEEE (2012)
51. Mardia, K., Dryden, I.: The statistical analysis of shape data. Biometrika 76(2), 271–281 (1989)
52. Meister, S., Izadi, S., Kohli, P., Hämmerle, M., Rother, C., Kondermann, D.: When can we use kinectfusion for ground truth acquisition? In: 2012 IEEE/RSJ International Conference on Intelligent Robots and Systems (IROS). Workshops & Tutorials (2012)
53. Microsoft Corporation: Kinect for windows sdk,
http://www.microsoft.com/enus/kinectforwindows/

54. Microsoft News Center: Microsoft press release (March 2010),
    http://www.microsoft.com/en-us/news/press/2010/mar10/
    03-31PrimeSensePR.aspx
55. Microsoft Xbox support: Room lighting conditions for kinect,
    http://support.xbox.com/en-US/xbox-360/kinect/lighting/
56. Nair, R., Lenzen, F., Meister, S., Schäfer, H., Garbe, C., Kondermann, D.: High ac-
    curacy TOF and stereo sensor fusion at interactive rates. In: Fusiello, A., Murino,
    V., Cucchiara, R. (eds.) ECCV 2012 Ws/Demos, Part II. LNCS, vol. 7584, pp. 1–11.
    Springer, Heidelberg (2012)
57. Newcombe, R.A., Izadi, S., Hilliges, O., Molyneaux, D., Kim, D., Davison, A.J.,
    Kohli, P., Shotton, J., Hodges, S., Fitzgibbon, A.: KinectFusion: Real-time dense
    surface mapping and tracking. In: 2011 10th IEEE International Symposium on
    Mixed and Augmented Reality, vol. 7, pp. 127–136 (2011)
58. Newman, P., Ho, K.: Slam-loop closing with visually salient features. In: Pro-
    ceedings of the 2005 IEEE International Conference on Robotics and Automation
    (ICRA 2005), pp. 635–642. IEEE (2005)
59. Nguyen, C.V., Izadi, S., Lovell, D.: Modeling kinect sensor noise for improved 3D
    reconstruction and tracking. In: Second International Conference on 3D Imaging,
    Modeling, Processing, Visualization and Transmission (3DIMPVT), pp. 524–530.
    IEEE (2012)
60. Nowozin, S., Rother, C., Bagon, S., Sharp, T., Yao, B., Kohli, P.: Decision tree
    fields. In: 2011 IEEE International Conference on Computer Vision (ICCV), pp.
    1668–1675. IEEE (2011)
61. Oikonomidis, I., Kyriazis, N., Argyros, A.: Efficient model-based 3d tracking of
    hand articulations using kinect. BMVC (August 2, 2011)
62. Openkinect Project: libfreenect, http://openkinect.org/
63. OpenNI: Openni framework, http://www.openni.org
64. Raheja, J.L., Chaudhary, A., Singal, K.: Tracking of fingertips and centers of palm
    using kinect. In: 2011 Third International Conference on Computational Intelli-
    gence, Modelling and Simulation (CIMSiM), pp. 248–252. IEEE (2011)
65. Raptis, M., Kirovski, D., Hoppe, H.: Real-time classification of dance gestures from
    skeleton animation. In: Proceedings of the 2011 ACM SIGGRAPH/Eurographics
    Symposium on Computer Animation, pp. 147–156. ACM (2011)
66. Roth, H., Vona, M.: Moving volume kinectfusion. In: British Machine Vision Conf.
    (BMVC), Surrey, UK (2012)
67. Ruhl, K., Klose, F., Lipski, C., Magnor, M.: Integrating approximate depth data
    into dense image correspondence estimation. In: Proceedings of the 9th European
    Conference on Visual Media Production, pp. 26–31. ACM (2012)
68. Schoner, H., Moser, B., Dorrington, A.A., Payne, A.D., Cree, M.J., Heise, B.,
    Bauer, F.: A clustering based denoising technique for range images of time of
    flight cameras. In: 2008 International Conference on Computational Intelligence
    for Modelling Control & Automation, pp. 999–1004. IEEE (2008)
69. Schröder, Y., Berger, K., Magnor, M.: Super resolution for active light sensor en-
    hancement. Bachelor thesis, University of Braunschweig (March 2012)
70. Schröder, Y., Scholz, A., Berger, K., Ruhl, K., Guthe, S., Magnor, M.: Multiple
    kinect studies. Computer Graphics (2011)
71. Schnauer, C., Kaufmann, H.: Wide area motion tracking using consumer hardware.
    In: Proceedings of Workshop on Whole Body Interaction in Games and Enter-
    tainment, Advances in Computer Entertainment Technology (ACE 2011), Lisbon,
    Portugal (2011)

72. Shotton, J., Fitzgibbon, A., Cook, M., Sharp, T., Finocchio, M., Moore, R., Kipman, A., Blake, A.: Real-time human pose recognition in parts from single depth images. In: 2011 IEEE Conference on Computer Vision and Pattern Recognition (CVPR), pp. 1297–1304. IEEE (2011)
73. Smisek, J., Jancosek, M., Pajdla, T.: 3d with kinect. In: 2011 IEEE International Conference on Computer Vision Workshops (ICCV Workshops), pp. 1154–1160. IEEE (2011)
74. Somanath, G., Cohen, S., Price, B., Kambhamettu, C.: Stereo+Kinect for High Resolution Stereo Correspondences. In: International Conference on 3D Vision 2013 (3DV) (2013)
75. Steinbrücker, F., Sturm, J., Cremers, D.: Real-time visual odometry from dense rgb-d images. In: 2011 IEEE International Conference on Computer Vision Workshops (ICCV Workshops), pp. 719–722. IEEE (2011)
76. Stuckler, J., Behnke, S.: Integrating depth and color cues for dense multi-resolution scene mapping using rgb-d cameras. In: 2012 IEEE Conference on Multisensor Fusion and Integration for Intelligent Systems (MFI), pp. 162–167. IEEE (2012)
77. Stückler, J., Behnke, S.: Multi-resolution surfel maps for efficient dense 3D modeling and tracking. Journal of Visual Communication and Image Representation (2013)
78. Tam, G., Cheng, Z.Q., Lai, Y.K., Langbein, F., Liu, Y., Marshall, A., Martin, R., Sun, X.F., Rosin, P.: Registration of 3d point clouds and meshes: A survey from rigid to non-rigid. IEEE Transactions on Visualization and Computer Graphics PP(99), 1 (2012)
79. Tomasi, C., Manduchi, R.: Bilateral filtering for gray and color images. In: Sixth International Conference on Computer Vision, pp. 839–846. IEEE (1998)
80. Wang, F., Zhang, C.: Feature extraction by maximizing the average neighborhood margin. In: IEEE Conference on Computer Vision and Pattern Recognition (CVPR 2007), pp. 1–8. IEEE (2007)
81. Weickert, J.: Anisotropic diffusion in image processing, vol. 1. Teubner Stuttgart (1998)
82. Whelan, T., Johannsson, H., Kaess, M., Leonard, J.J., McDonald, J.: Robust real-time visual odometry for dense rgb-d mapping. In: IEEE Intl. Conf. on Robotics and Automation (ICRA), Karlsruhe, Germany (2013)
83. Whelan, T., Kaess, M., Fallon, M., Johannsson, H., Leonard, J., McDonald, J.: Kintinuous: Spatially extended kinectfusion. Technical Report MIT-CSAIL-TR-2012-020, CSAIL Technical Reports (2012), http://hdl.handle.net/1721.1/71756
84. Woodford, O., Torr, P., Reid, I., Fitzgibbon, A.: Global stereo reconstruction under second-order smoothness priors. IEEE Transactions on Pattern Analysis and Machine Intelligence 31(12), 2115–2128 (2009)
85. Xu, K., Zhou, J., Wang, Z.: A method of hole-filling for the depth map generated by kinect with moving objects detection. In: 2012 IEEE International Symposium on Broadband Multimedia Systems and Broadcasting (BMSB), pp. 1–5. IEEE (2012)
86. Yang, C., Medioni, G.: Object modelling by registration of multiple range images. Image and Vision Computing 10(3), 145–155 (1992)
87. Zeng, M., Zhao, F., Zheng, J., Liu, X.: A memory-efficient kinectFusion using octree. In: Hu, S.-M., Martin, R.R. (eds.) CVM 2012. LNCS, vol. 7633, pp. 234–241. Springer, Heidelberg (2012)
88. Zhu, J., Wang, L., Yang, R., J., Davis, J., et al.: Reliability fusion of time-of-flight depth and stereo for high quality depth maps. TPAMI (99), 1 (2011)
89. Zollhöfer, M., Martinek, M., Greiner, G., Stamminger, M., Süßmuth, J.: Automatic reconstruction of personalized avatars from 3D face scans. Computer Animation and Virtual Worlds 22(2-3), 195–202 (2011)

Real-Time Motion Artifact Compensation for PMD-ToF Images

Thomas Hoegg[1], Damien Lefloch[2], and Andreas Kolb[2]

[1] Christ-Elektronik GmbH, Alpenstr. 34, 87700 Memmingen, Germany
thoegg@christ-elektronik.de
[2] University of Siegen, Hoelderlinstr. 3, 57076 Siegen, Germany
{damien.lefloch,andreas.kolb}@uni-siegen.de

Abstract. Time-of-Flight (ToF) cameras gained a lot of scientific attention and became a vivid field of research in the last years. A still remaining problem of ToF cameras are motion artifacts in dynamic scenes. This paper presents a new preprocessing method for a fast motion artifact compensation. We introduce a flow like algorithm that supports motion estimation, search field reduction and motion field optimization. The main focus lies on real-time processing capabilities. The approach is extensively tested and compared against other motion compensation techniques. For the evaluation, we use quantitative (ground-truth data, statistic error comparison) and qualitative (real environments, visual comparison) test methods. We show, that our proposed algorithm runs in real-time within a GPU based processing hardware (using NVIDIA Cuda) and corrects motion artifacts in a reliable way.

1 Introduction

Time-of-Flight (ToF) sensors as the PMD camera [1] offer an elegant way to measure depth data. They become more and more important for the computer vision and graphics domain and also for industrial applications [2]. Having advantages such as high performance and no mechanical overhead compared to e.g. laser scanners, they also posses many problems, especially in accuracy and noise behavior. Most of these errors can be corrected well by applying good calibration models [3] and pre-filtering (e.g. low-pass filtering). However, artifacts arising from dynamic scenes are still not resolved satisfactorily. Moving objects in scenes result in a blur effect (motion artifacts) in acquired depth images. A fast movement leads to strong artifacts, related to the sensor's working principle which is based on the sequential acquisition of four so-called phase images in order to generate a depth map (see also Sec. 3). Artifacts occur in areas where corresponding phase image values do not align to each other, resulting in a incorrect distance calculation.

In this paper we propose a new algorithm to perform a fast real-time motion compensation with high frame rates (above 50 FPS). We focus on high flexibility to allow the algorithm to be either computed parallelized on a GPU using CUDA [4] or to simply port it to small devices like an FPGA preprocessing platform.

M. Grzegorzek et al. (Eds.): Time-of-Flight and Depth Imaging, LNCS 8200, pp. 273–288, 2013.

To fulfill these requirements, a linear movement with constant motion between the four consecutive phase images is assumed. Hence, the algorithm still allows an arbitrary degree of freedom assuming this linear behavior for each individual pixel (see Sec. 5). Invalid pixels are replaced by corresponding values of the spatial neighborhood. This leads to simpler and faster processing compared to standard methods shown in Sec. 2. For the evaluation, a PMD CamCube 3.0 with a resolution of 200×200 pixel is used. The big advantages of the proposed method are the possibility of an automatic motion detection, a search direction restriction, the repeatability of results in different applications and also the system performance.

The remainder of this paper is organized as follows. Sec. 2 discusses the related work. In Sec. 3 we describe the working principle of PMD cameras. Sec. 4 introduces our proposed algorithm for the motion compensation. In Sec. 5 we show our results. Sec. 6 concludes this paper.

2   Related Work

In the last years, several methods have been proposed to detect and compensate motion artifacts.

Hussmann et al. [5] introduce a motion compensation for linear object motion on a conveyor belt. Areas of motion artifacts are identified using phase image differences. These areas are binarized for each individual difference image using a threshold. The length of motion is determined by processing each line of the binary images and counting the lines with white pixels. Once knowing the length, every phase image is moved accordingly before the distances are calculated. The algorithm is implemented exemplary on an FPGA platform, but it is restricted to a linear motion in a range between $90 - 100cm$ due to the small object size and the camera field of view.

Schmidt [6] proposes a method handling motion artifacts as disturbances in the raw data. Motion artifacts are calculated for each phase image using a temporal derivative. High temporal derivatives of the raw data are then replaced by previously valid values. An advantage compared to Hussmann et al. is the arbitrary degree of freedom. Lee et al. [7] propose a similar approach where they detect motion artifacts by temporal-spatial coherence of neighboring pixels directly on the hardware level.

Another method was proposed by Lindner et al. [8]. This method computes a dense optical flow to compensate spatial shifts between subsequent phase images (three flow calculations). Lefloch et al. [9] proposed a method improving this approach. Necessary computation steps can be reduced to two flow calculations. The missing step is replaced by a polynomial approximation. One big disadvantage is the system performance. The optical flow computation is a very time consuming task and thus is a heavy burden for real-time processing, if further pocessing tasks need to be performed.

Our proposed method uses particular parts from Lindner and Lefloch [8,9] (flow field) and Hussmann [5] (binarization of the motion area). The algorithm restricts the motion to blurred areas only and optimizes the flow field detection.

3   The Time-of-Flight Principle

The following section gives a brief introduction to the functionality of ToF cameras serving as a basis for the method proposed in this paper.

An intensity modulated, incoherent infrared (IR) light is emitted with a modulation frequency f using the cameras' illumination units to determine the phase shift between outgoing and incoming optical signals. Each camera pixel correlates the incoming signal $s(t)$ with the reference signal $r(t)$ to estimate the correlation function. This process is repeated four times for every pixel with different internal phase shift $\tau_i = i \cdot \pi$ in order to sample the correlation function between s and r.

The PMD camera for instance is a two-tap sensor. It allows the acquistion of two corresponding values for the same pixel at the same time, represented in the camera as two phases P_{A_i}, P_{B_i}. In theory, if there is no motion and other influences, the phases are complementary, i.e. measuring phase values at two positions with $180°$ difference: $P_{B_i} = P_{A_{(i+2) \bmod 4}}$. Internally, the phase image is represented by the difference $P_i = P_{A_i} - P_{B_i}$ in order to compensate for hardware inaccuracies. Using the four phase images P_i, the phase shift ϕ, the amplitude A and the intensity I can be calculated:

$$\phi = \arctan 2(P_0 - P_2, P_3 - P_1) \tag{1}$$

$$I = \frac{P_0 + P_1 + P_2 + P_3}{4} \tag{2}$$

$$A = \frac{1}{2} \cdot \sqrt{(P_3 - P_1)^2 + (P_0 - P_2)^2}. \tag{3}$$

The resulting distance D is then received using the angular modulation frequency $\omega = 2\pi f$ and the speed of light $c \approx 3 \cdot 10^8 ms^{-1}$:

$$D = \frac{c}{2\omega}\phi. \tag{4}$$

4   A Method for Fast Linear Motion Compensation

In this section we start with an analysis of the origin of motion artifacts and continue with a detailed description of our proposed method.

4.1   Problem Analysis

ToF-cameras as the PMD camera have the advantage to be able to acquire full distance-/depth-images of the whole scene at a time. This is done using a sequence of four phase images, as described in Sec. 3 and shown in Fig. 1.

One full phase acquisition is split in two parts: acquisition and readout. The acquisition time is equal to the integration time set, the readout time of actual PMD cameras is stated as about $3.5ms$. Ideally all four phase images would simultaneously be recorded. In reality the acquisition is sequentially done

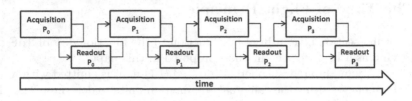

Fig. 1. Schematic view of the acquisition process of a PMD frame using four phase images

(see Fig. 1). Motion artifacts typically arise in areas of unmatching raw phase values due to motion (see. Fig. 2). It mainly occurs at object boundaries and in regions of inhomogeneous reflection. This effect becomes more extensive the faster an object moves, the closer the object is to the camera and the higher the scene is exposed (high integration times) [8].

Fig. 2 shows the default demodulation of a car (left images), moving from right to the left and of a moving hand (right images). In both scenes, the blurred areas are marked red. It can be seen that especially these areas contain many motion artifacts.

Fig. 2. Top: Demodulation of the car's phase image sequence and a corresponding closeup. Bottom: A moving hand scene and a corresponding closeup. Left: Motion areas are marked red. Right: The closeups of the red marked motion areas.

Blurred areas in depth maps lead to incorrect distance computations. The goal of motion compensation approaches is the elimination of these areas to minimize errors. The motion during a single acquisition is not considered here and is nearly negligible for small integration times ($< 1ms$).

4.2   The Motion Compensation Approach

The proposed method works on a per pixel basis allowing arbitrary motion directions. It is divided into several steps, starting with a phase normalization. The normalization is done to compensate the sensor's pixel gains and to equalize the image illumination. This is necessary due to the block-matching like working principle of the approach and to obtain comparable raw values. In a second step the area of motion is estimated to improve the processing time. The motion direction is then determined with a correspondence search in the spatial neighborhood. Once knowing this kind of flow field, the raw values can be corrected. The processing pipeline can be seen in Fig. 3 and will be explained in the following sections.

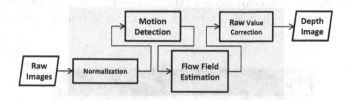

Fig. 3. The motion detection and processing pipeline used for our algorithm

Phase Normalization. According to the behavior and design of PMD cameras, there are several aspects for the pixel correspondence search, which have to be taken care of. One point is the radial light attenuation. Images become darker from the center to the border. Another aspect is the difference in pixel gains, which has to be individually corrected for each sensor and every pixel.

To compensate these two problems, a pixel adjustment is performed using the method proposed by Lindner et al. [8] by applying a pixel-wise intensity correction function

$$f_{P_A}(P_{A_i}) = \tilde{P}_{A_i}, \; f_{P_B}(P_{B_i}) = \tilde{P}_{B_i} \text{ with } i = 0\ldots3 \tag{5}$$

to minimize

$$\sum_{i=0}^{3}(\tilde{P}_{A_i} + \tilde{P}_{B_i}) = h_{\text{ref}}. \tag{6}$$

The brightest pixel in a homogeneous surface is taken and used as reference intensity, the fitting functions are assumed to be logarithmic as $f_X(X_i) = a\sqrt{X_i + b} + cX_i + d$.

Applying these corrections improve the search as shown by Lindner et al.

Motion Detection. Since the motion estimation is a computation intensive task, an important preprocessing step is to detect areas of apparent motions first. Motion can be detected using the changes in the total per-pixel intensity for the subsequent phase images, i.e.

$$P_i^+ = P_{A_i} + P_{B_i} \tag{7}$$

$$M = \sum_{i=1}^{3} |P_i^+ - P_0^+| \tag{8}$$

In a next step, the estimated motion image M is binarized

$$B = M > \theta \tag{9}$$

where B is the binary image and θ a threshold value that is determined experimentally. In our experiments we found that for $\theta = 650$ (about 1% of the maximum of $P_{A_i/B_i} = 65535$) we get reliable results. Fig. 4 shows the motion image and its corresponding binary image. White areas (ones) on the right side indicate unmatching raw values.

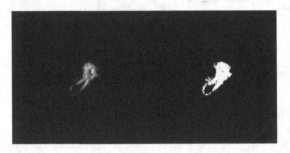

Fig. 4. The moving hand from Fig. 2 with extracted motion artifacts. Left: The motion image M calculated using Eq. 8. Right: The binarized image B thresholded using Eq. 9.

Motion Direction Estimation. Inspired by the idea of the optical flow motion estimation, we propose a simpler way to determine a 2D vector displacement map (U, V) without subpixel precision. Each pixel value represents a unique displacement vector $(u, v)^T$.

Our approach assumes a linear motion between all raw phase images with a constant velocity (see Sec. 5). A pixel-wise motion displacement is estimated for all detected pixels in B. Therefore a motion window around every invalid pixel is defined, which limits the detectable motion around these pixels. The window is assumed to be squared with an odd size between 3 and 11 pixels (**M**otion **W**indow **S**ize, MWS). Vectors from the center (the invalid pixel) to all neighbors are calculated and scaled according to the phase image index. Let (dx, dy) be a single delta for a possible pixel correspondence shift between adjacent phase images, then the respective shifted phase values for the i-th phase image are given as:

$$P_{shifted,i}(x, y) = P_i(x + i \cdot dx, y + i \cdot dy), i \in \{0, 1, 2, 3\} \tag{10}$$

P_i and $P_{shifted,i}$ represent the particular phase image with index i. dx and dy are the applied deltas from the the center (see also Fig. 6) with a maximum value of:

$$dx_{max} = dy_{max} = (MWS - 1)/2 \tag{11}$$

and an odd Motion Window Size (MWS). The maximum euclidean pixel distance l between two corresponding points of phase image P_0 and P_3 is given as:

$$l = 3 \cdot \left\| \overrightarrow{(dx_{max}, dy_{max})} \right\| \tag{12}$$

In compliance with Eq. 12 and some knowledge about the expected motion in a scene, the motion window size can be preset to optimize the system performance. In our examples we set $MWS = 5$, yielding reliable results in most of the situations (see Sec. 5). Fig. 5 shows, how search vectors are defined and introduces the coordinate system exemplarily for a 5×5 motion window.

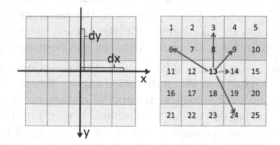

Fig. 5. Left: The coordinate system and an example offset $dx = dy = 2$. Right: The grid cells are numbered in a row-wise order. Index '13' indicates the start position. Five sample vectors are presented here.

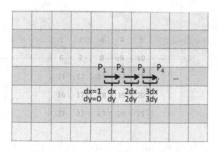

Fig. 6. An example flow for a shift $dx = 1$ and $dy = 0$. This leads to a maximum shift between the four phase images of 3 pixels.

For the estimation of the best corresponding flow, the Sum of Squared Differences (ssd) for all possible flow vectors within the defined motion window is calculated:

$$ssd_{index}(x, y, dx, dy) = \sum_1^3 (P_0(x, y) - P_{shifted,i}(x, y, dx, dy))^2 \tag{13}$$

Accordingly, the best correspondence value has the minimal deviation from the first phase image. So the final flow vector for the currently processed pixel can be expressed as:

$$(u, v)^T = \text{argmin}\,(ssd(x, y, dx, dy)) \qquad (14)$$

The number of possible vectors MWS^2 is leading to a time complexity $T(n) = \mathcal{O}(n^2)$. A quadratic complexity allows only small motion window sizes (about 11×11) to perform the algorithm in real-time. To overcome this problem, the search direction can be restricted to an initial or mean direction from a previous frame.

4.3   Search Space Reduction

An additional performance optimization can be achieved using a search space reduction as can be seen in Fig. 7. Therefore the mean direction angle of a previous frame is used as initial guess for the current motion. The direction angle $\varphi_{(u,v)^T}$ for one pixel is calculated between the positive x-axis $\overrightarrow{x}$ and the corresponding flow vector $\overrightarrow{f(u, v)}$. The mean motion direction angle φ is defined as average of all estimated flow vector direction angles. Assuming a small motion between two consecutive frames, the amount of change of the mean direction angle is small. Now using this assumption, all pixel (x', y') in the search window whose position vector has an angle in the range of $\varphi \pm \rho/2$ ($0° \leq \rho \leq 359°$) are taken into consideration for the motion estimation. The raw phase value correction is then applied to the reduced flow field as described in Sec. 4.5.

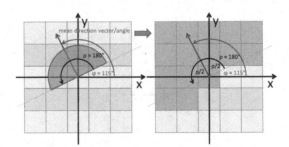

Fig. 7. Left: The mean motion vector (115° in this example) calculated in a previous frame (red arrow) and an exemplary search space reduction to 180°. Right: Valid motion vectors resulting out of the reduction are marked green.

All possible flow direction angles in a motion window can be precalculated. So it is also easy to port this to small platforms as e.g. an FPGA by using lookup-tables.

4.4   Flow Field Optimization

In order to improve the robustness of the approach, a possible optimization is optionally applied taking the spatial neighborhood into account. A median filter is used to filter outliers. Therfore all motion vectors in a neighborhood with size MWS are considered. Median filtering is then performed using the direction angle as defined in Sec. 4.3. The vector length is kept.

4.5   Raw Phase Value Correction

Once the flow field (U, V) is determined, it can be applied to the raw phase values $P_{A_{0-3}}$ and $P_{B_{0-3}}$ according to Eq. 10. Each vector of the flow field is applied to its corresponding raw value. After the data correction has been applied, the depth values can be reconstructed according two the principle described in Sec. 3. The results and evaluation can be seen in Sec. 5.

5   Results

The following subsections give detailed information about the motion compensation results obtained with our proposed method. To perform a comprehensive analysis, the evaluation is split in two parts. In the first part, a quantitative evaluation is done, to allow the comparison of results against ground-truth data. Using artificial scenes gives reproducable and reliable results. In the second part, we do a qualitative evaluation in real scenes. Having the disadvantage that generally no ground-truth models are available, a visual evaluation makes it possible to see if the correction could successfully be applied.

5.1   Quantitative Results

Our method has been tested in a variety of scenes of different complexities (simulated and real environments). A robustness and peformance evaluation can be done using simulated data (see Table 2 and Table 3). Similar to Lefloch et al. [9] we use different data sets generated with a simulator [10]. The statistic evaluations are done with the tool CloudCompare[1]. The first data set is a buddha figure, the second is a dragon. Both figures are used as input for the simulator. An artificial, planar wall is placed in a distance of 4 meters. In front of this wall, in a distance of about 3 meters, the figures are placed. This setup provides reliable ground-truth data. To obtain motion data, we acquire several different images at different camera positions. The camera is transformed between each individual phase acquisition. For the buddha, we use a simple lateral camera translation of 1cm (about $2m/s$ motion speed). In the dragon figure setup, the camera is rotated 1 degree (about $200deg/s$ angular velocity) around the z-axis (line of sight).

---

[1] http://www.danielgm.net/cc/

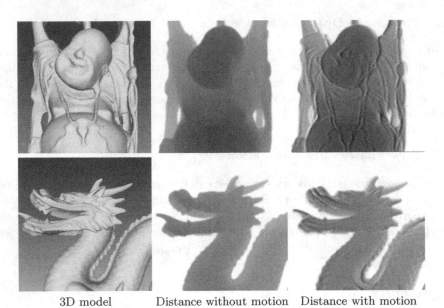

3D model   Distance without motion   Distance with motion

Fig. 8. Two different data sets (buddha (top) and dragon (bottom)) that have been used for the robustness evaluation of our approach; Left: The ground-truth 3D model. Center: The cartesian distance image without any motion. Right: The cartesian distance image with motion.

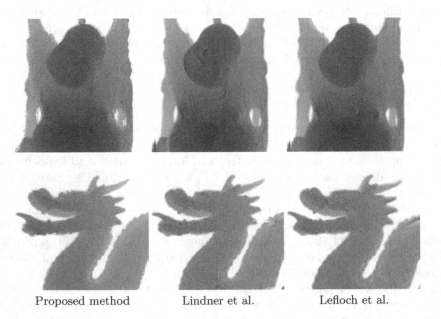

Proposed method   Lindner et al.   Lefloch et al.

Fig. 9. The results of the three evaluated methods. As can be seen, all the methods give good results visually comparing them to the ground-truth distance with no motion shown in Fig. 8.

Using the ground-truth of Fig. 8, we can easily generate comparable results between the different motion compensation approaches (see also Fig. 9).

Table 1 shows a statistic evaluation of the buddha and dragon scene without motion compensation; here, static background pixels are discarded. The dynamic scene is created as previously described.

Table 1. The deviation of the ground-truth depth data (flying pixels included) of the buddha and dragon scene from the underlying meshs. It shows the mean distance error and the deviation for the static and the dynamic scene.

Scenes	Distance errors from Ground-truth (cm)			
	Static (no motion)		Dynamic (with motion)	
	Mean	Sigma	Mean	Sigma
Buddha	0.64	3.12	5.96	9.32
Dragon	1.25	4.62	7.75	14.37

For further evaluation, several different setups are created to verify the quality of the proposed method. The first test shows the behavior of the algorithm with different settings for the Motion Window Size (MWS), neighborhood filtering (NH), motion area estimation (θ) and also search space restriction (ρ) (see Sec. 4.2). Table 2 and Table 3 contain the test results of the different setups and show the detailed behaviour of the proposed algorithm using different parameter sets. Especially the remaining depth error compared to the ground-truth data and the system performance is highlighted. It can be seen that as expected, the best results are given without any limitation and restricition of the search space ($\theta = 0$, $\rho = 0$). The mean error of the buddha motion scene is reduced from $5.96cm$ ($\pm9.32cm$) to $1.14cm$ ($\pm3.02cm$), the dragon scene is corrected from a mean error of $7.75cm$ ($\pm14.37cm$) to $2.07cm$ ($\pm5.65cm$). Furhtermore it can be seen that with an increasing θ the correction performance gets better, but the quality decreases. Another fact that gets visible is, that using the neighborhood flow smoothing also improves the mean error, but with the disadvantage of losing performance: With the same settings and neighborhood filtering we can correct the buddha scene in $16.13ms$, without neighborhood filtering it takes $11.57ms$ only. A similar behavior can be seen for the dragon scene in Table 3. In addition, restricting the algorithm to a maximum direction deviation also improves the correction quality (mean error) and the system performance. This can be achieved by the rejection of a large number of search vectors in the motion window. We reject up to 36% of the possible directions ($MWS = 7$, $\rho = 90°$, 1000000 direction search vectors, rejected directions between 110770 and 716877) in the buddha scene and up to 30% ($MWS = 7$, $\rho = 90°$, 1000000 direction search vectors, rejected directions between 118916 and 583470) in the dragon scene. Please note that the execution time is an average value of 100 measurements. Furthemore it can be seen that the mean motion direction φ most closely approximates the expected linear translation of the buddha scene of 180°.

Additionally we compare our algorithm against the methods proposed by [8] and [9]. Our approach reduces the mean error of the buddha scene to 1.14cm ($\pm 3.02cm$), compared to Lindner 1.13cm ($\pm 4.39cm$) and Lefloch 1.46cm ($\pm 4.40cm$). For the dragon scene, the remaining mean error with our method is 2.07cm ($\pm 5.65cm$), for Lindner 2.26cm ($\pm 7.57cm$) and for Lefloch 3.14cm ($\pm 8.00cm$). The results between the three compared methods are nearly equal, but our method can score with the execution time, which is about half the time of the method from Lefloch et al. and an eight of Lindner et al.

Table 2. The statistic evaluation of the buddha scene and the behavior of the mean error in relation to different parameters. Statistics are shown for different motion windows sizes, neighborhood filtering (NH) on(x) and off(-), binarization thresholds θ and a search space restriction ρ.

Buddha Scene				Distance errors from Ground-truth corrected				
MWS	NH	θ	ρ (°)	**Mean** (cm)	**Sigma** (cm)	φ (°)	Rejected Directions	∅ Time (ms)
5	-	0	-	**1.15**	3.10	-	0	12.58
5	-	650	-	1.70	3.54	-	0	11.57
5	-	3276	-	3.49	4.70	-	0	10.59
5	-	5243	-	4.22	5.18	-	0	10.13
5	x	650	-	1.38	3.05	-	0	16.13
5	-	650	90	1.34	3.33	206.36	118916	**9.79**
5	x	650	90	1.46	3.24	223.98	110770	13.18
5	-	650	180	1.34	3.38	179.21	212408	11.08
5	x	650	180	1.27	3.04	190.33	212408	13.49
7	-	0	-	**1.14**	3.02	-	0	25.04
7	-	650	-	1.16	3.08	-	0	23.54
7	x	650	-	1.34	3.03	-	0	31.86
7	-	650	90	1.35	3.35	174.34	716877	**12.15**
7	x	650	90	1.35	3.13	178.90	716877	21.16
7	-	650	180	1.35	3.37	179.74	477918	15.18
7	x	650	180	1.37	3.04	187.10	477918	23.53
Method Lindner et al.								
-	-	-	-	1.13	4.39	-	-	71.87
Method Lefloch et al.								
-	-	-	-	1.46	4.40	-	-	25.60

The result of our tested setups is a good correction compared to the input mean error that can be seen in Table 1. Furthermore in comparison with Lindner and Lefloch, our method gives slightly better (dragon scene) or nearly equal (buddha scene) results and is also suitable for real-time applications with a framerate of 50–100 FPS allowing additional data processing as requested. Note: Compared to the evaluation of Lefloch et al. [9], we use a smaller clamping distance (3.85m) to remove the wall, explaining the slightly different mean and sigma values. In our opinion a good default parameter set is a threshold $\theta = 650$ and $MWS = 5$. Another helpful setting is a direction restriction to the mean motion direction. The default settings and the search area restriction significantly

Table 3. The statistic evaluation of the dragon scene and the behavior of the mean error in relation to different parameters. Statistics are shown for different motion windows sizes, neighborhood filtering (NH) on(x) and off(-), binarization thresholds θ and a search space restriction ρ.

Dragon Scene				Distance errors from Ground-truth corrected				
MWS	NH	θ	ρ (°)	Mean (cm)	Sigma (cm)	φ (°)	Rejected Directions	$\varnothing$ Time (ms)
5	-	0	-	**2.08**	5.70	-	0	12.09
5	-	650	-	2.09	5.71	-	0	11.97
5	-	3276	-	2.43	6.04	-	0	11.57
5	-	5243	-	2.62	6.01	-	0	10.89
5	x	650	-	2.22	5.51	-	0	14.31
5	-	650	90	2.12	5.49	186.68	259320	**9.40**
5	x	650	90	2.37	5.75	206.36	118916	11.89
5	-	650	180	2.16	5.68	182.36	172880	9.83
5	x	650	180	2.33	5.70	198.20	131326	13.13
7	-	0	-	**2.07**	5.65	-	0	21.44
7	-	650	-	2.07	5.65	-	0	20.55
7	x	650	-	2.35	5.48	-	0	26.45
7	-	650	90	2.44	5.63	210.65	176064	**11.30**
7	x	650	90	2.17	5.66	184.70	583470	17.61
7	-	650	180	2.18	5.77	184.02	388980	14.28
7	x	650	180	2.42	5.64	201.35	206714	20.67
Method Lindner et al.								
-	-	-	-	2.26	7.57	-	-	80.76
Method Lefloch et al.								
-	-	-	-	3.14	8.00	-	-	24.07

optimize the system performance and the motion compensation quality. Our tests were executed on an Intel Core i7-3770K CPU @ 3.50 GHz and an NVIDIA GeForce GTX 680, 2GB graphics card.

5.2 Qualitative Results

This part of the evaluation shows the behavior of real environments and applications. Two different setups are built. Unfortunately, there are no ground-truth values for these real world data sets, therefore they are limited to a visual comparison. The first scene shows a moving hand as can be seen in Fig. 10. The hand is moved very fast from one side to the other. The figure shows how the blurred images are corrected using our proposed method. Furthermore the images also show the motion area and direction restriction ($MWS = 5, \theta = 650, angle = 90°$). It can be seen that the blur is fully corrected.

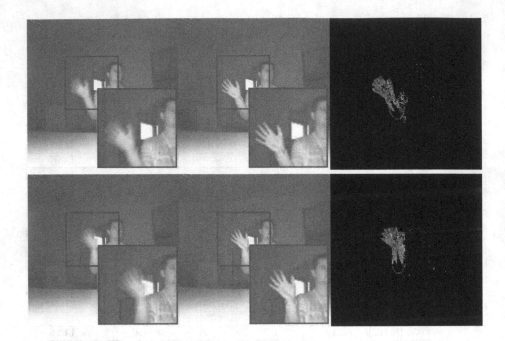

Fig. 10. Hand scene: the left column contains images with motion artifacts, the middle column contains the corresponding motion compensated images using our proposed method and the right column contains the related flow images (red: horizontal motion, green: vertical motion). The mean estimated motion direction for the top row is $\emptyset = 125.08°$, for the bottom row $\emptyset = 91.91°$.

The second evaluated scene contains a car moving lateral in front of the camera. Motion occurs mainly on edges, the mirror and the wheels. The visual determined movement direction is about 270°. The algorithm is parameterized with $MWS = 5, \theta = 650, angle = 90°$. Area, direction and also the correction is successfully applied and leads to the expected results as can be seen in Fig. 11.

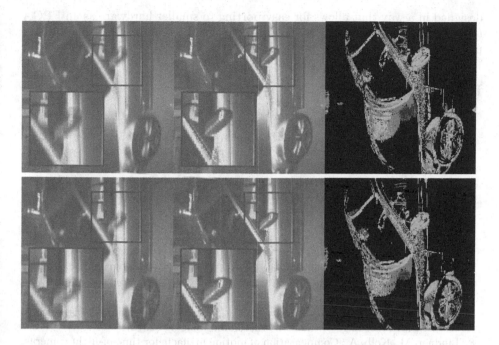

Fig. 11. Car scene: The left column contains images with motion artifacts, the middle column contains the corresponding motion compensated images using our proposed method and the right column contains the related flow images (red: horizontal motion, green: vertical motion). The mean estimated motion direction for the top row is $\emptyset = 228.20°$, for the bottom row $\emptyset = 232.71°$.

6   Conclusion

In this paper we presented a new method for a fast motion artifact compensation for Time-of-Flight cameras. The approach is based on several assumptions such as linear motion between the four consecutive phase images of the PMD camera. Our algorithm uses a thresholding and binarization method to restrict the artifact correction area to spaces where in fact motion occurs. Furthermore we propose an approach to find pixel correspondences in a local neighborhood (motion field estimation), a local search area minimization by tracking the mean motion direction of a previous frame and an optional motion field smoothing. We show that the algorithm gives good results for simulated data (linear and non linear motion) and also for real data. Furthermore we show that we get comparable results in the mean value correction (compared to Lindner et al. [8] and Lefloch et al. [9]) and the algorithm can work in real-time (execution time about 10 ms and a frame rate of up to 100 FPS).

The proposed method still has a high potential to be optimized so that it also supports phase image motion correction. Furhthermore the threshold θ can be automatically adapted via statistics of the observed scene. The algorithm is also designed in a way that allows for easy porting to smaller hardware as an FPGA (no subpixel flow, possibility of lookup-tables for the search area reduction and parallelization).

References

1. pmdtechnologies GmbH (May 2013), http://www.pmdtec.com
2. Prusak, A., Melnychuk, O., Roth, H., Schiller, I.: Pose estimation and map building with a time-of-flight-camera for robot navigation. Int. Journal Intell. Sys. Techn. & App. 5(3), 355–364 (2008)
3. Marvin, L., Ingo, S., Andreas, K., Reinhard, K.: Time-of-flight sensor calibration for accurate range sensing. Comput. Vis. Image Underst. 114(12), 1318–1328 (2010)
4. NVIDIA (May 2013), http://www.nvidia.com
5. Hussmann, S., Hermanski, A., Edeler, T.: Real-time motion artifact suppression in tof camera systems. IEEE Transactions on Instrumentation and Measurement 60(5), 1682–1690 (2011)
6. Schmidt, M.: Analysis, Modeling and Dynamic Optimization of 3D Time-of-Flight Imaging Systems. PhD thesis, IWR, Fakultät für Physik und Astronomie, Univ. Heidelberg (2011)
7. Lee, S., Kang, B., Kim, J.D., Kim, C.Y.: Motion blur-free time-of-flight range sensor. In: Proceedings of the SPIE Electronic Imaging (2012)
8. Lindner, M., Kolb, A.: Compensation of motion artifacts for time-of-flight cameras. In: Kolb, A., Koch, R. (eds.) Dyn3D 2009. LNCS, vol. 5742, pp. 16–27. Springer, Heidelberg (2009)
9. Lefloch, D., Hoegg, T., Kolb, A.: Real-time motion artifacts compensation of tof sensors data on gpu. In: Proceedings of SPIE, vol. 8738 (2013)
10. Keller, M., Kolb, A.: Real-time simulation of time-of-flight sensors. J. Simulation Practice and Theory 17, 967–978 (2009)

Real-Time Image Stabilization for ToF Cameras on Mobile Platforms

Benjamin Langmann, Klaus Hartmann, and Otmar Loffeld

Center for Sensor Systems (ZESS), University of Siegen,
Paul-Bonatz-Str. 9-11, 57068 Siegen, Germany
{langmann,hartmann,loffeld}@zess.uni-siegen.de

Abstract. In recent years, depth cameras gained increasing acceptance in the areas of robotics and autonomous systems. However, on mobile platforms depth measurements with continuous wave amplitude modulation Time-of-Flight cameras suffer from motion artifacts, since multiple acquisitions are required in order to compute one depth map (resulting in longer effective exposure times). Some lenses of different manufacturers include image stabilizers, but they are only able to compensate for small image shifts. Moreover, when performing a phase unwrapping based on the acquisition of multiple depth maps with different modulation frequencies, the motion artifacts are significantly more severe. In this paper, a method to compensate camera motions during the acquisition of a single depth map as well as for multiple depth maps is presented. Image shifts are estimated firstly and after normalization the individual phase images are shifted accordingly. The proposed approach is evaluated on different scenes and it is able to facilitate ToF imaging on mobile platforms.

1 Introduction

Depth imaging devices act as an important sensor in the areas of robotics, autonomous systems and similar research fields. However, as camera motions during an image acquisition result in a blur for color imaging, they result in motion artifacts for depth imaging. These artifacts consist of invalid depth measurements and can in general assume any value. Most Time-of-Flight depth cameras, e.g. based on the Photonic Mixer Device (PMD), utilize multiple images namely phase images to compute one depth map. Motion artifacts are here caused by camera motions during the acquisition of a single phase image and in between the acquisitions of the phase images. The former case can usually be neglected due to the relatively short exposure times which are commonly applied. Since typical acquisition times for all phase images required to obtain one depth map lie between 10 ms and 50 ms, the camera can be subject to significant motion during that time on mobile platforms. Two features in the scene induce motion artifacts for continuous wave amplitude modulation ToF depth cameras. The first one are of course edges, which result in measuring different distances, i.e. phase shifts. Secondly, different reflectivities introduce motion artifacts additionally and the reason for this will be discussed later on.

M. Grzegorzek et al. (Eds.): Time-of-Flight and Depth Imaging, LNCS 8200, pp. 289–301, 2013.
© Springer-Verlag Berlin Heidelberg 2013

An approach to compensate camera motions in between multiple phase images is proposed in this paper. It works by firstly estimating the lateral camera motion in between phase images and then by shifting the phase images accordingly. Several peculiarities of PMD chips have to be considered and will be discussed in the course of this paper. Moreover, when a multi-frequency phase unwrapping approach is applied in order to extend the measurement range, motion artifacts become a severe limitation. Therefore, we extend the proposed image stabilization technique to multiple depth maps.

The paper is structured as follows. The related research is discussed in Section 2 and in Section 3 the hardware used in this paper is presented. Afterwards, the proposed method is presented in Section 4. Experiments to demonstrate the capabilities and limitations of the proposed approach are reviewed in Section 5 and the paper ends with a conclusion in Section 6.

2   Related Work

In [1] Lottner et al. analyze motion artifacts encountered for sufficiently fast motion of objects in the scene when using PMD cameras. Lindner and Kolb introduce in [2] motion compensation based on optical flow for moving objects in videos acquired with PMD cameras. In an industry environment motion compensation is demonstrated by Hussmann et al. in [3] and [4]. They perform the motion compensation on PMD depth maps and the motion is detected by comparison of binary foreground maps. Axial motion of ToF cameras is discussed in [5] using the Windowed Discrete Fourier Transform.

Unlike most previous approaches, the proposed method does not treat motion artifacts like so-called flying pixels and tries to remove them by estimating local motion. These approaches produce visibly nice results but may also result in incorrect contours of objects (since a flying pixel is caused by a mixture of multiple distances). Instead, whole phase images are shifted in relation to each other in order to account for the observed camera motion. This method is computationally inexpensive and does not introduce incorrect measurements. The approach neglects camera rotations around the roll axis, since this kind of rotation typically causes small effects for short acquisition times and since rotating a phase image to compensate it would introduce aliasing.

Phase unwrapping to remove ambiguities in depth measurements is a common task in several research areas, e.g. remote sensing. In the context of depth imaging, a probabilistic approach to remove ambiguities in a single depth image is proposed in [6]. An optimization is performed based on a cost function aiming at the removal of discontinuities. In [7] this method is extended to incorporate multiple measurements with different modulation frequencies and hence different ambiguity ranges. A different approach based on a single depth map is introduced in[8]. The unambiguous depth of an object is inferred here by observing how much infrared light it reflects. The approach does not handle each pixel individually, but finds edges in the depth map in order to account for the different reflectivity of objects, which would otherwise compromise the results.

Phase unwrapping methods are in general not completely stable and a method to obtain smooth results in subsequent phase unwrapped depth maps is described in [9]. Moreover, in [10] phase unwrapping is performed with the help of stereo information.

3   ZESS MultiCam with Medium-Range Lighting

Recently, a new version of the MultiCam (cf. [11]) equipped with Gigabit Ethernet, a 3 megapixel color CMOS chip and the 19k PMD chip of PMD Technologies was developed. Both chips share the same lens utilizing a Bauernfeind prism with an integrated beam splitter. The heart of the camera is a Xilinx FPGA chip and the camera features a C-mount lens adapter. See Fig. 1 for a picture and specifications of the MultiCam.

MultiCam characteristics	
Interface	Gigabit Ethernet
Lens adapter	C-mount
Frame rate	12 fps (up to 80 fps with reduced 2D resolution)
Color chip	Aptina MT9T031
- Resolution	2048 × 1536
- Chip size	6.55 mm × 4.92 mm
PMD chip	PMDTec 19k
- Resolution	160 × 120
- Chip size	7.2 mm × 5.4 mm

Fig. 1. The MultiCam, a 2D/3D monocular camera, and its specifications

We developed a medium-range lighting system, which can be easily scaled up, and it was designed to capture large viewing angles, e.g. 40 degrees. The light is produced by chip LEDs with a maximum continuous optical power of 3.5 Watt, which are available from Osram (SFH-4750). These LEDs have an emission peak at 860 nm, the active area is relatively dense unlike large LED arrays and they feature low and symmetric rise and fall times of only 10 ns. Three prototypes with up to 26 LEDs with 3.5 Watt continuous optical power each are shown in Fig. 2. A collimator with a half angle of 11 degrees is mounted on each LED and the LEDs are adjusted to cover the observed area. With this lighting systems we can capture scenes up to 70 meters for smaller viewing angles and depending on the exposure times possible. The device in Fig. 2(c) is mounted on a rotary table, which was used to simulate camera motions in the experiments.

Measurement results of an outdoor scene are shown in Fig. 3 using only 8 LEDs. The distance to the building is 50 meters. The results demonstrate the capabilities of this approach with weaknesses at small objects and highly structured objects due to the limited lateral resolution of the PMD chip.

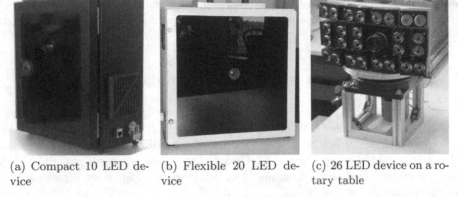

(a) Compact 10 LED de-   (b) Flexible 20 LED de-   (c) 26 LED device on a ro-
vice   vice   tary table

Fig. 2. Three medium-range development prototypes with 10, 20 and 26 LEDs

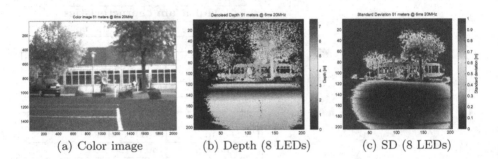

(a) Color image   (b) Depth (8 LEDs)   (c) SD (8 LEDs)

Fig. 3. Measurement results obtained with the medium-range lighting using 8 LEDs. A modulation frequency of 20 MHz and an exposure time of 6 ms were used and the distance to the building is 50 meters.

4   ToF Image Stabilization

Continuous wave amplitude modulation based ToF imaging operates normally by acquiring four images under different phase shift. Motion artifacts in the computed depth map occur obviously when measurement samples of objects with different distances are combined resulting in a so-called mixed phase. However, when working with PMD chips, motion artifacts additionally occur for different intensities, e.g. on a checkerboard. Different effective offsets and gains of both channels of PMD pixels caused by significant variations in the chip will not get canceled out in the four phase algorithm as when all samples originate from one PMD pixel. For details on PMD imaging see [12] or [13].

The proposed acquisition procedure is outlined as follows: Firstly, the phase images are normalized using the calibration method described in Section 4.1. Then the lateral image shifts between the first phase image and all three consecutive phase images, which are caused by rotations around and motions on the pitch and jaw axis of the camera (perspective effects can be neglected), are estimated with the method detailed in Section 4.2. Afterwards, the phase images are shifted and the standard PMD computations to obtain depth, modulation amplitude and grayscale images are performed as described in Section 4.3. Ambiguities of depth measurements in larger scenes can be resolved with the phase unwrapping approach discussed in Section 4.4 while compensating for these camera motions.

4.1   Intensity Calibration for PMD Chips

When camera motions are compensated by combining measurements of different pixels, e.g. by using shifted phase images, pixel values must be comparable. However, this requires an intensity calibration of all PMD pixels to account for the fixed pattern noise. The same calibration is necessary in most applications, in which the grayscale image of a PMD camera is utilized in a given task. In Fig. 4 the raw intensity values for one channel of a phase image are shown. Current PMD imaging chips utilize three AD converters with different effective offsets and gains, which results in vertical lines in addition to pixel variations. In order to perform the normalization, a set of images with different exposure times of a uniformly lit diffuse glass is acquired. The relative offset and gain for both channels of each pixel can be estimated based on these images, which enables an affine normalization of the phase images. The resulting intensity values for one channel are also given in Fig. 4.

The exact calibration procedure is detailed in the following. Let Γ_i for $\Gamma \in [A, B]$ and $i = 1, \ldots, n$ be n phase images for a PMD channel Γ. The index i describes here different acquisitions, since the phase is not of importance now. The pixels of the image are denoted by $\Gamma_i^{(x,y)}$ and let t_i be the associated integration time. Then the average pixel value $\mu_\Gamma^{(x,y)}$ is given by

$$\mu_\Gamma^{(x,y)} = \frac{1}{n} \sum_{i=1}^{n} \Gamma_i^{(x,y)} \ . \tag{1}$$

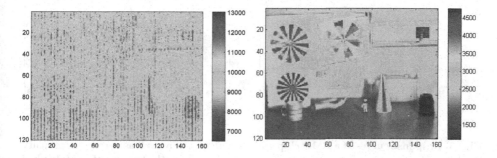

Fig. 4. Affine normalization of a PMD phase image. Left: original phase image for the first PMD channel, right: normalized image.

The affine parameters for each channel $\alpha_\Gamma^{(x,y)}$ and $\beta_\Gamma^{(x,y)}$ are calculated with

$$\tau_i = t_i - \frac{1}{n}\sum_{j=1}^{n} t_j \tag{2}$$

$$\alpha_\Gamma^{(x,y)} = \frac{\sum_{i=1}^{n} \tau_i \cdot \left(\Gamma_i^{(x,y)} - \mu_\Gamma^{(x,y)}\right)}{\sum_{i=1}^{n}\tau_i^2} \tag{3}$$

$$\beta_\Gamma^{(x,y)} = \mu_\Gamma^{(x,y)} - \alpha_\Gamma^{(x,y)} \frac{1}{n}\left(\sum_{j=1}^{n} t_j\right) . \tag{4}$$

Now the normalized pixel value $\hat{\Gamma}^{(x,y)}$ of a PMD channel Γ for an acquired pixel value $\Gamma^{(x,y)}$ can be computed with

$$\mu_\Gamma^\alpha = \frac{1}{|\Gamma|}\sum_{(x,y)\in\Gamma} \alpha_\Gamma^{(x,y)} \tag{5}$$

$$\hat{\Gamma}^{(x,y)} = \left(\Gamma^{(x,y)} - \beta_\Gamma^{(x,y)}\right) \cdot \frac{\mu_\Gamma^\alpha}{\alpha_\Gamma^{(x,y)}} . \tag{6}$$

All recent PMD chips feature a mechanism to remove ambient light (Suppression of Backlight Illumination - SBI), which enables outdoor imaging. However, the SBI obviously also effects the intensity values, which will disturb motion estimates based on these intensity images. In order to characterize this behavior, a dataset consisting of 100 images for integration times between 0.1 ms and 5 ms with a step size of 0.1 ms was acquired. The raw values for both channels A and

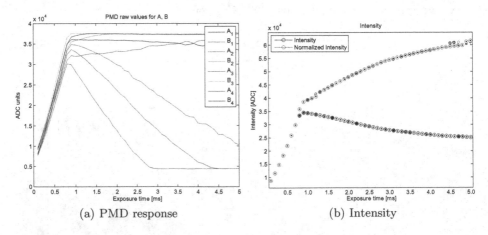

(a) PMD response   (b) Intensity

Fig. 5. Response curves of a PMD chip and the calculated as well as corrected intensity for different exposure times. Shown are the raw values for both channels of a single pixel and four phase offsets in the first graph and the intensity values using the standard formula as well as with SBI correction in the second.

B as well as for the four phase images are displayed for one pixel in Fig. 5(a). One can clearly observe the linear region of the PMD chip up to 0.8 ms. The SBI is active for higher integration times. The PMD chip enters the saturation region for one phase image when applying integration times larger than 2.5 ms. In 5(b) the resulting phase intensity values $I_i^{(x,y)} = A_i^{(x,y)} + B_i^{(x,y)}$ are plotted. In order to obtain increasing intensity values a correction was applied as follows. If the value $\Gamma_i^{(x,y)}$ of one channel $\Gamma \in [A, B]$ of a PMD pixel exceeds a threshold, e.g. $\gamma_{thres} = 36500$, a normalization term of $3 \cdot |A_i^{(x,y)} - B_i^{(x,y)}|$ is added to the phase intensity $I_i^{(x,y)}$. If the intensity response of a PMD chip is known for a given lens, the real intensity can be determined for an exposure time and modulation amplitude.

4.2   Motion Estimation

Vandewalle et al. introduced a method for planar motion estimation based on the Fourier Transformation in [14]. Since fast rotations around the roll axis are rarely observed in typical situations, the method is reduced to lateral image shifts for an increased robustness as well as to avoid aliasing when rotating images.

Let $f(\underline{x})$ be the reference image and $g(\underline{x})$ the actually observed one with $g(\underline{x}) = f(\underline{x} + \Delta\underline{x})$ with Fourier Transformations $F(\xi)$ and $G(\xi)$. Then the following holds

$$G(\xi) = \int g(\underline{x})e^{-i2\pi\xi^T \cdot \underline{x}}d\underline{x} \tag{7}$$

$$= \int f(\underline{x} + \Delta\underline{x})e^{-i2\pi\xi^T \cdot \underline{x}}d\underline{x} \tag{8}$$

$$= \int f(\underline{\hat{x}})e^{-i2\pi\xi^T \cdot (\underline{\hat{x}} - \Delta\underline{x})}d\underline{\hat{x}} \tag{9}$$

$$= e^{i2\pi\xi^T \cdot \Delta\underline{x}} \cdot \int f(\underline{\hat{x}})e^{-i2\pi\xi^T \cdot \underline{\hat{x}}}d\underline{\hat{x}} \tag{10}$$

$$= e^{i2\pi\xi^T \cdot \Delta\underline{x}} \cdot F(\xi) \tag{11}$$

with a substitution $\underline{\hat{x}} = \underline{x} + \Delta\underline{x}$.

Therefore, the phase difference $e^{i2\pi\xi^T \cdot \Delta\underline{x}}$ can be obtained given $F(\xi)$ and $G(\xi)$ with

$$\xi^T \cdot \Delta\underline{x} = \frac{1}{2\pi} \arg\left(\frac{G(\xi)}{F(\xi)}\right) . \tag{12}$$

Instead of computing $\Delta\underline{x}$ with for a single ξ, Vandewalle et al. argue to construct a system of linear equations for a set of frequencies and to use the least squares estimate for $\Delta\underline{x}$ in order to avoid aliasing.

4.3   Intra-frame Motion Compensation

High accuracy motion compensation for dynamic scenes including local and global motion is difficult to perform in real-time, in particular when it serves as a pre-processing step and other image processing tasks are should be processed in parallel. In order to accomplish motion compensation (MC) in real-time, we simplify the task by considering only global motions, neglecting roll and by restricting image shifts to full pixels. Let A_i and B_i with $i = 1, 2, 3, 4$ be the phase images for PMD channel A and B respectively acquired with the i-th phase shift and let $I_i = A_i + B_i$ be the phase intensity image. With the motion estimation method detailed in Section 4.2 the lateral image shifts Δ_i between I_1 and I_i for $i = 2, 3, 4$ can be determined and rounded to the nearest integer. These image shift are applied to the associated phase images (can be replaced with pointer arithmeticians) and the PMD calculations for demodulation are performed.

4.4   Phase Unwrapping

Continuous wave amplitude modulation Time-of-Flight depth measurements do not measure distances directly, but derive the distance from the phase difference between emitted and received light. This means that the distance measured is ambiguous and multiples of the half wavelength $\lambda = \frac{c}{2\nu}$ with c being the speed of light can be added. If the observed scene contains longer distances than λ and if the modulation frequency should not be decreased in order the to maintain the depth resolution, a method to perform a phase unwrapping is required to retrieve correct distances. In the following, a method which combines the depth maps obtained with two different modulation frequencies is presented, which extends the unambiguous range to the lowest common multiple of both half wavelengths. Let $d_1, d_2, \ldots, d_n$ be distances measured with modulation frequencies $\nu_1, \nu_2, \ldots, \nu_n$. Then the most likely absolute distance $\hat{d}_i = d_i + k_i \frac{c}{2\nu_i}$ of all measurements combined can be obtained by minimizing the squared difference of all proposed real distances

$$min_{k_1,\ldots,k_n \in \mathcal{N}_0} \left\{ \sum_{i=1}^{n-1} \sum_{j=i+1}^{n} \left(d_i + k_i \frac{c}{2\nu_i} - d_j - k_j \frac{c}{2\nu_j} \right)^2 \right\} . \qquad (13)$$

The obvious approach is to combine a small frequency (e.g. 1 MHz with an ambiguity range of 150 m) and a larger frequency with a high depth resolution. However, this poses a significant challenge to the lighting devices. In practice, the frequencies must be similar to avoid damages and unstable behavior or low power lighting. If the size of the set is small, e.g. just two, the minimization can be performed by just calculating all possibilities (up to a given maximum distance).

Motion artifacts are even more prominent when phase unwrapping is conducted. However, the motion compensated depth maps acquired with two (or more) modulation frequencies can also be motion compensated (inter-frame MC). The camera motion can then be estimated based on both first phase intensity images I_1 and the depth maps are shifted accordingly. Alternatively, the camera motion can be estimated based on all four pairs of phase intensity images by averaging the image shifts.

5 Experiments

In Fig. 6 an example for the intra-frame MC is given for a test setup acquired with an exposure time of 5 ms, a 50 mm lens and two different modulation frequencies. A motion between phase images of about 1.2 pixels is estimated and subsequent images with different modulation frequencies are shown. The results demonstrate that the motion artifacts can be largely reduced. However, at the edges of objects and high contrast regions some artifacts persist, since only full pixel shift are applied.

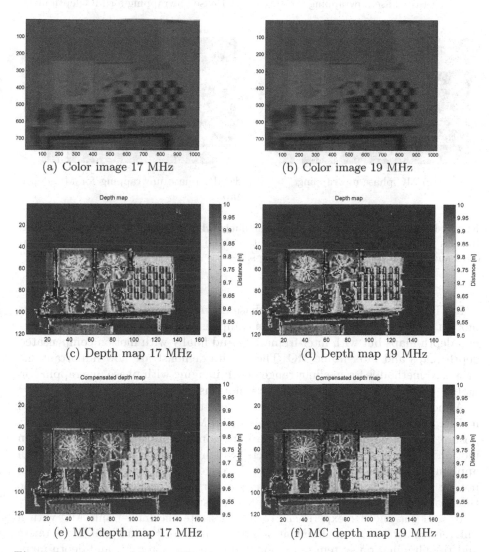

Fig. 6. Results for real-time motion compensation experiment involving a moving camera and two modulation frequencies

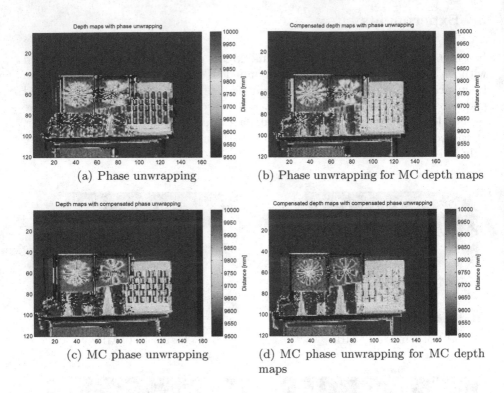

(a) Phase unwrapping

(b) Phase unwrapping for MC depth maps

(c) MC phase unwrapping

(d) MC phase unwrapping for MC depth maps

Fig. 7. Demonstration of severe motion artifacts when performing phase unwrapping. Results for normal and motion compensated (MC) phase unwrapping based on standard and motion compensated depth maps.

In Fig. 7 four cases to perform the phase unwrapping are considered: Without motion compensation, with two motion compensated depth maps, with two normal depth maps but with inter-frame MC and finally with motion compensated depth maps and inter-frame MC. The results demonstrate how important the proposed method is for medium-range depth imaging with phase unwrapping on mobile platforms or when other camera motions occur.

A more realistic experiment to demonstrate the intra-frame MC is displayed in Fig. 8. Here a modulation frequency of 20 MHz, a 8.5 mm lens and an exposure time of 10 ms were used. A fast motion was introduced and results in motion artifacts at the edges of objects, which are successfully removed when applying the MC. Only flying pixels at the edges of objects remain, which cannot be corrected without affecting the contours of objects. However, a simple thresholding with the modulation amplitude usually allow to remove them.

Results for another experiment to demonstrate the inter-frame MC with a different camera, lens and illumination system are depicted in Fig. 9. The camera and the illumination system were mounted on a rotation table and depth maps were acquired with alternating modulation frequencies of 17 and 19 MHz and

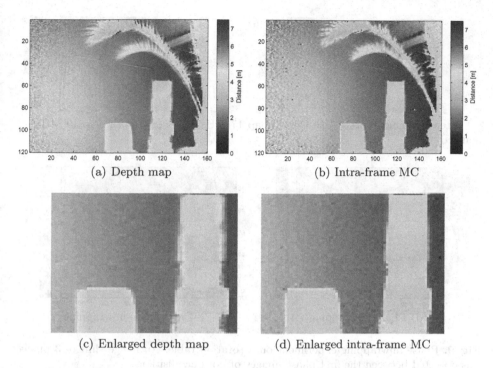

(a) Depth map   (b) Intra-frame MC

(c) Enlarged depth map   (d) Enlarged intra-frame MC

Fig. 8. Experiment to evaluate the intra-frame MC using a single modulation frequency of 20 MHz

an exposure time of 5 ms. The results show how the incorrect estimation of the real distances can be reduced at discontinuities, e.g. at the doors. It should be mentioned here that we observe multi-path reflections on the reflective floor.

The inter-frame is not effective for slow camera motions and short acquisition times. The angular velocity v which results in an image shift of one pixel between the first and the last phase image can serve as a criterion and it is calculated with

$$v = \frac{\alpha_{cam}}{N \cdot t_{acq}} \tag{14}$$

in degrees per second for an opening angle of α_{cam}, N pixels in direction of the rotation and an acquisition time of $t_{acq} = 3 * (t_{exp} + t_{ro})$. Here t_{exp} is the exposure time for a phase image and t_{ro} is the read-out time of the PMD chip. In the experiments we get for a horizontal rotation (yaw axis), the 19k PMD chip and an exposure time of 5 ms a velocity of $14.2°/s$ for a 8.5 mm lens and for a 50 mm lens a critical angular velocity of $2.6°/s$.

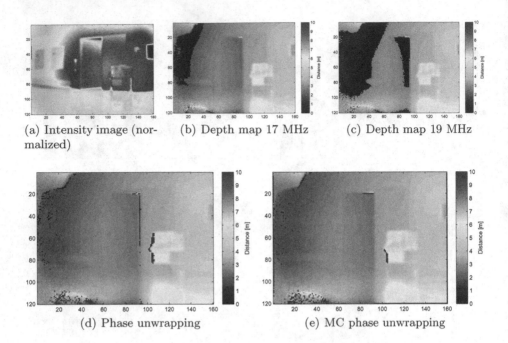

(a) Intensity image (normalized) (b) Depth map 17 MHz (c) Depth map 19 MHz

(d) Phase unwrapping (e) MC phase unwrapping

Fig. 9. Phase unwrapping experiment on a rotation table. An image shift of 3 pixels was detected between the first phase images of both acquisitions.

6   Conclusion

Operating a depth camera on a mobile platform poses challenges in general and for ToF depth cameras motions of the camera during the acquisition on a depth map results in motion artifacts. The longer the acquisition time is, the more severe are the motion artifacts. This is in particular a problem when measuring larger scenes due to required larger exposure times or even when fusing multiple depth maps for phase unwrapping as well as in order to reduce noise. In this paper, real-time methods to reduce these motion artifacts significantly are presented. Based on methods to calibrate the fixed pattern noise and to estimate image shifts, phase images are aligned before processing in order to reduce the motion artifacts originating from global motions in the images. Similarly, multiple depth maps are fused with the proposed approach to obtain depth measurements of larger scenes. The approach was evaluated with several experiments to confirm its capabilities and in order to decide if the methods are required for a given application.

Acknowledgments. This work was funded by the German Research Foundation (DFG) as part of the research training group 1564 "Imaging New Modalities".

References

1. Lottner, O., Sluiter, A., Hartmann, K., Weihs, W.: Movement artefacts in range images of time-of-flight cameras. In: International Symposium on Signals, Circuits and Systems (ISSCS 2007), vol. 1, pp. 1–4 (2007)
2. Lindner, M., Kolb, A.: Compensation of motion artifacts for time-of-flight cameras. In: Kolb, A., Koch, R. (eds.) Dyn3D 2009. LNCS, vol. 5742, pp. 16–27. Springer, Heidelberg (2009)
3. Hussmann, S., Hermanski, A., Edeler, T.: Real-time motion supression in tof range images. In: Proc. IEEE Instrumentation and Measurement Technology Conf. (I2MTC), pp. 697–701 (2010)
4. Hussmann, S., Hermanski, A., Edeler, T.: Real-time motion artifact suppression in tof camera systems. IEEE Trans. Instrum. Meas. 60, 1682–1690 (2011)
5. Drayton, B., Carnegie, D., Dorrington, A.: Phase algorithms for reducing axial motion and linearity error in indirect time of flight cameras. IEEE Sensors Journal PP, 1–1 (2013)
6. Droeschel, D., Holz, D., Behnke, S.: Probabilistic Phase Unwrapping for Time-of-Flight Cameras. In: Proceedings of the Joint Conference of the 41st International Symposium on Robotics (ISR 2010) and the 6th German Conference on Robotics (ROBOTIK 2010), Munich, Germany, pp. 318–324 (2010)
7. Droeschel, D., Holz, D., Behnke, S.: Multi-frequency phase unwrapping for time-of-flight cameras. In: 2010 IEEE/RSJ International Conference on Intelligent Robots and Systems (IROS), pp. 1463–1469 (2010)
8. McClure, S.H., Cree, M.J., Dorrington, A.A., Payne, A.D.: Resolving depth-measurement ambiguity with commercially available range imaging cameras. In: Proc. SPIE, Image Processing: Machine Vision Applications III, vol. 7538, pp. 75380K–75380K-12 (2010)
9. Choi, O., Lee, S., Lim, H.: Interframe consistent multifrequency phase unwrapping for time-of-flight cameras. Optical Engineering 52, 057005 (2013)
10. Choi, O., Lee, S.: Fusion of time-of-flight and stereo for disambiguation of depth measurements. In: Lee, K.M., Matsushita, Y., Rehg, J.M., Hu, Z. (eds.) ACCV 2012, Part IV. LNCS, vol. 7727, pp. 640–653. Springer, Heidelberg (2013)
11. Prasad, T., Hartmann, K., Weihs, W., Ghobadi, S., Sluiter, A.: First steps in enhancing 3d vision technique using 2d/3d sensors. In: Computer Vision Winter Workshop, Telc, Czech Republic, pp. 82–86 (2006)
12. Möller, T., Kraft, H., Frey, J., Albrecht, M., Lange, R.: Robust 3d measurement with pmd sensors. Range Imaging Day, Zürich Section 5 (2005)
13. Lottner, O., Weihs, W., Hartmann, K.: Systematic non-linearity for multiple distributed illumination units for time-of-flight (pmd) cameras. In: 12th WSEAS International Conference on SYSTEMS. Heraklion, Greece, July 22-24 (2008)
14. Vandewalle, P., Suesstrunk, S., Vetterli, M.: A Frequency Domain Approach to Registration of Aliased Images with Application to Super-Resolution. EURASIP Journal on Applied Signal Processing (special issue on Super-resolution) (2006)

On the Calibration of Focused Plenoptic Cameras

Ole Johannsen[1], Christian Heinze[2], Bastian Goldluecke[1],
and Christian Perwaß[2]

[1] Heidelberg Collaboratory for Image Processing, University Heidelberg
[2] Raytrix GmbH, Schauenburgerstr. 116,
24116 Kiel, Germany

Abstract. Plenoptic cameras provide a robust way to capture 3D information with a single shot. This is accomplished by encoding the direction of the incoming rays with a microlens array (MLA) in front of the camera sensor. In the *focused plenoptic camera*, a MLA acts like multiple small cameras that capture the *virtual scene* on the focus plane of a main lens from slightly different angles, which enables algorithmic depth reconstruction. This *virtual depth* is measured on the camera side, and independent of the main lens used. The connection between actual lateral distances and virtual depth, however, does depend on the main lens parameters, and needs to be carefully calibrated. In this paper, we propose an approach to calibrate focused plenoptic cameras, which allows a metric analysis of a given scene. To achieve this, we minimize an energy model based upon the thin lens equation. The model allows to estimate intrinsic and extrinsic parameters and corrects for radial lateral as well as radial depth distortion.

Keywords: focused plenoptic camera, plenoptic 2.0, metric calibration, calibration, depth distortion, Raytrix.

1 Introduction

While normal 2D cameras only record the intensity of light at a certain position on the image sensor, plenoptic cameras capture the complete 4D lightfield on position on the image sensor, plenoptic cameras capture the complete 4D lightfield on the sensor plane. The 4D lightfield is an intensity function that not only depends on the position on the imaging plane, but also the incident direction. This additional information allows an algorithmic 3D reconstruction of the captured scene [19,4,10,11].

The idea of plenoptic cameras originates in the early 20th century. First described using a grid of pinholes inside a camera by Ives in 1903 [6], Lippmann in 1908 proposed the use of microlenses in front of the image plane [8]. Emerging from these concepts, a lot of research on plenoptic cameras has been done, varying from setups with multiple independent cameras over such ones with microlenses in front of

M. Grzegorzek et al. (Eds.): Time-of-Flight and Depth Imaging, LNCS 8200, pp. 302–317, 2013.

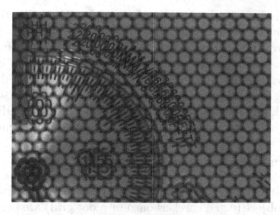

Fig. 1. Detail of a raw image captured by a plenoptic 2.0 camera by Raytrix. Objects closer to the camera are visible in more microlens images. The different types of microlenses can be distinguished in this image by comparing the sharpness of the projections.

an image sensor. Several improvements to the design have been proposed, for example, cameras manufactured by Raytrix[1] employ multiple types of microlenses to accomplish a larger depth of field. Based on the different types of input data, a multitude of different concepts for estimating depth, like EPI stacks [19,18,4,2], focus stacks [10,11], or multiview stereo approaches [7,1] has been introduced.

For any kind of 3D camera, it is of interest to be able to metrically measure the depth and determine the extent of a captured object. Hence, a lot of work has been put into calibrating plenoptic cameras. Vaish et al. [16] and Svoboda et al. [15] work on calibrating plenoptic multi-camera arrays while Dansereau et al. [5] deal with the calibration of unfocused lenslet-based plenoptic cameras like the ones commercially available from Lytro[2].

This paper concentrates on the metric depth reconstruction with *focused* lenslet-based plenoptic cameras or *plenoptic 2.0* cameras [9] as commercially available from Raytrix [12] (see figure 3). The idea of depth reconstruction with a focused plenoptic camera is to find the virtual point an object point is focused on by the main lens. Since points at different distances to the main lens are focused upon different distances behind the main lens, a reconstruction of the original 3D scene is possible.

The location a scene point is projected to on the sensor side of the camera does not only depend on the point's distance to the camera, but also on the focal length and focus distance of the main lens. A metric surveying of objects is impossible without knowing the exact parameters of the camera. Our contribution is to introduce a model of how to estimate those parameters to calibrate a plenoptic 2.0 camera.

The paper is organized as follows. First, a brief introduction to camera models is given and afterwards, the depth estimation algorithm implemented in a

---

[1] see www.raytrix.de

[2] see www.lytro.com

Raytrix camera is described in terms of these models. In section 2.3, distortion models are introduced, which allow for the correction of lens errors. Here we propose a novel type of distortion model, which corrects for distortion in depth dimension. The effect of this type of distortion is that objects located on a plane perpendicular to the optical axis are projected to different virtual depths depending on their position in the frame. Section 3 describes the final calibration model, after which we show results on a number of different camera configurations. Finally, we give an outlook on possible future work.

2 Theoretical Background

The concept behind calibrating a camera lens combination is that multiple images of a known object (e.g. a checkerboard or a dot grid) are taken. The known dimensions of the model and the extracted projections on the sensor are then leveraged to estimate the intrinsic and extrinsic camera parameters. The extrinsic camera parameters describe the position and rotation of the model points in relation to the camera, while the intrinsic camera parameters parametrize the projection through the lens. Additionally, correction parameters like lens distortion must be calculated.

In this chapter, we introduce the theoretical background for these topics. First, a short introduction to camera models is given, which is an important prerequisite to understand depth estimation with a plenoptic camera. Second, we shed some light on lens distortion models and introduce the proposed depth distortion model.

2.1 Camera Models

In order to describe the perspective projections and optical properties of cameras, multiple camera models have been proposed over time. One of the most simple models is the pinhole camera model, which is often used in computer graphics. In this model, points in the object space are projected through the optical center (the pinhole) onto an image plane resulting in a 2D representation of the 3D object space.

While this model is useful for generating 2D images in computer graphics or even for calibrating 2D cameras [20], any depth information is lost by the projection. Hence, a more physically motivated model has to be chosen to describe a plenoptic camera. The thin lens model describes the distance between an object in front of the camera and the virtual point where the light emitted from that object is focused on behind the lens.

Looking at figure 2, one can see rays emerging from the two object points O_1 and O_2. Each ray is bent according to the focal point of the lens and focused upon I_1 and I_2, respectively. The intercept theorem leads to the thin lens equation, which describes the connection between an object at a distance b along the optical axis from the camera, the distance of its focused representation a and the focal length f of the lens as

$$\frac{1}{f} = \frac{1}{a} + \frac{1}{b}. \tag{1}$$

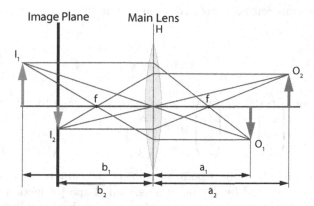

Fig. 2. Thin Lens Camera Model. Object points O_i are projected through the lens and focused to virtual image points I_i behind the lens. If a virtual image point lies upon the image plane, the point is *in focus* and therefore captured sharply, while points away from the focus plane are projected in front or behind the image plane and hence appear blurred. This effect is called depth of field (DOF).

As one can see in figure 2, this model also describes the effect of depth of field (DOF): an object that is at the focus distance of the camera (in this case a_2) is focused precisely onto the image plane resulting in a sharp representation of that point in the image, while an object in front (or behind) that focus plane is focused behind (or in front) of the image plane (O_1 and I_1). Hence, the light of an object point that is out of focus influences a larger area, resulting in a blurred representation of that point.

The thin lens model only holds for lenses whose thickness is negligible in comparison to its focal length. As this must not always be the case, the thin lens model can be extended to the thick lens model. This model includes an offset (the lens thickness) to the model, hence, the thin lens model is a special case of the thick lens model. It can be shown that any combination of lenses – in particular any single lens – can be approximated by the thick lens model, although multiple effects like aberrations or distortion are not included. While with normal camera lenses, the difference between both models is negligible, especially in the field of microscopy the thin lens model can not be used to describe the optics of the lens.

Consequently, the thick lens model would be the perfect model to build the basis for the desired calibration algorithm. Unfortunately, the given information is generally not sufficient to distinguish between the thin lens and the thick lens model, as this requires knowledge of the absolute distance between a point in front and one behind the camera. Hence, the lens thickness is impossible to estimate by only using calibration targets. For this reason, we will use the thin lens model for the remainder of the paper in order to model the main lens.

If the coordinate system is placed with its origin at the intersection of the main lens axis with the lens plane and the z-axis running along the main lens axis, the thin lens projection can be expressed as matrix multiplication in homogeneous coordinates

$$\tilde{i} = Ao, i = \frac{\tilde{i}}{\tilde{i}_4},$$

$$\text{with } i = \begin{pmatrix} i_1 \\ i_2 \\ i_3 \\ 1 \end{pmatrix}, \tilde{i} = \begin{pmatrix} \tilde{i}_1 \\ \tilde{i}_2 \\ \tilde{i}_3 \\ \tilde{i}_4 \end{pmatrix}, o = \begin{pmatrix} o_1 \\ o_2 \\ o_3 \\ 1 \end{pmatrix} \text{ and } A := \begin{pmatrix} 1 & 0 & 0 & 0 \\ 0 & 1 & 0 & 0 \\ 0 & 0 & 1 & 0 \\ 0 & 0 & -\frac{1}{f} & 1 \end{pmatrix}. \quad (2)$$

Above, the point o is the object point in front of the camera, i the virtual point onto which o is projected by the main lens, and A the projection matrix. The multiplication Ao leads to the representation $\tilde{i}$ of i in homogenous coordinates, from which i can easily be recovered.

2.2 Depth Estimation

The image in a plenoptic 2.0 camera is captured through a microlens array, see figure 1. This allows algorithms to estimate the virtual depth of a given scene. As described by the thin lens model, an object point is focused behind the main lens onto a virtual image point. The cone of rays between this virtual point and the lens is split up by the microlenses and focused at different points onto the image plane, see figure 3. As only the position of these projections is of interest, the pinhole model is sufficient to describe the effect of the microlenses.

Looking at just the microlens array, in figure 4 one can see how the projection i_1 and i_2 arise as the projections of the main lens' virtual image point i

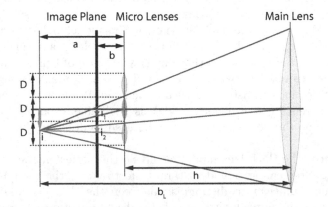

Fig. 3. Schematics of a plenoptic camera. An object point (not shown) is projected through the main lens (right side) onto the virtual image point i. The resulting light cone is split up by the microlenses and focused onto the image plane at i_1 and i_2. Thus, depth estimation can be performed by finding corresponding projections and calculating the parallax.

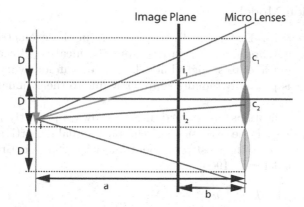

Fig. 4. The Raytrix plenoptic camera estimates depth with correspondence search in the microlens domains. The result of the internal algorithm is a virtual depth $v := a/b$ for each pixel given in multiples of the distance b between microlens array and image plane.

onto the image plane. The depth reconstruction works similar to that in stereo cameras: a pair of microlenses is chosen, corresponding points are identified and triangulated. To identify matching projections in multiple lenses, pixel patches are compared. The usually chosen photoconsistency measure is the sum of absolute differences over small pixel patches along the epipolar lines. For this to work, sufficient object structure and image contrast are needed.

We define the *virtual depth* v of the image point i as the distance between i and the MLA, given in multiples of the distance b between the sensor and the MLA, as returned by the depth estimation algorithm of the Raytrix camera. Thus, $v = \frac{a}{b}$, see figure 3. As one can see in figure 4, the virtual depth can be computed from the detected correspondences using the intercept theorem. Assuming the distance $D = \|c_1 - c_2\|$ between the microlens centers c_1 and c_2 to be known, the intercept theorem leads to

$$v := \frac{a}{b} = \frac{\|i - c_1\|}{\|i_1 - c_1\|} = \frac{D}{\|i_1 - i_2\|}. \tag{3}$$

To calibrate this model, we need to estimate this distance b as well as the distance h between the main lens and the MLA. Knowledge of both allows virtual depths to be transformed to metric distances: $b_L = h + v \cdot b$, which can be projected in front of the camera by the thin lens equation (see eq. 1).

The virtual depth can also be used to reconstruct the refocused image [13]. This refocused image is equivalent to a picture a common 2D camera would have taken. Due to the increasing redundancy for higher virtual depths, the relative resolution decreases. As each point has to be projected at least 4 times – twice for every dimension of the image – for depth estimation to work the resolution of the refocused image is one quarter of the raw image.

2.3   Distortion Models

Lateral Distortion. Distortion describes errors in the geometric projection through a lens. It represents a deviation from the ideal rectilinear projection which maps straight lines to straight lines. Distortion can follow many patterns, but in general it is primarily radially symmetric due to the symmetric design of a lens.

However, in applications the distortion is not always perfectly radially symmetric. Therefore, multiple extensions of the pure radial distortion model have been introduced. One of the most prominent and widely used is Brown's distortion correction model from 1966 [3],

$$
\begin{aligned}
x_u =& (x_d - x_c)(1 + k_1 r^2 + k_2 r^4 + \cdots) \\
& + (p_1(r^2 + 2(x_d - x_c)^2) + 2p_2(x_d - x_c)(y_d - y_c))(1 + p_3 r^2 + \cdots), \\
y_u =& (y_d - y_c)(1 + k_1 r^2 + k_2 r^4 + \cdots) \\
& + (p_2(r^2 + 2(y_d - y_c)^2) + 2p_1(x_d - x_c)(y_d - y_c))(1 + p_3 r^2 + \cdots).
\end{aligned}
\tag{4}
$$

Here the point (x_u, y_u) is the undistorted and (x_d, y_d) the distorted image point. The parameters k_i describe the radial distortion and the parameters p_i the tangential distortion. (x_c, y_c) is an offset as the origin of the distortion is not necessarily the center of the image. The radius r is defined by the Euclidean distance to the origin of distortion $\sqrt{(x_d - x_c)^2 + (y_d - y_c)^2}$.

Brown deducts this formula from the thin prism model, which states that any skew of lenses inside a lens can be obtained by combining a perfect lens which is also perfectly aligned with a thin prism. The distortion model was designed to be an approximation to ray-tracing. In general, the even degrees of the polynomials are predominant. Hence, in most calibration algorithms, only these degrees are taken into account. The distortion model we use includes the coefficients k_1, k_2, p_1, p_2 and p_3.

Distortion in Direction of the Optical Axis. A second kind of distortion is that of distortion in direction of the optical axis which in this paper we term the *depth distortion*. It originates from the Petzval field curvature which describes a slight change of focal length for points at greater distance from the optical axis [14]. This kind of distortion does not effect the position of a point in lateral direction, but the distance it is projected to in depth dimension. Hence, in 2D imaging it would only result in a slight blur at the image corners. But as one can observe in figure 5, the effect leads to a depth distortion for the plenoptic camera. As this kind of distortion behaves similarly to the lateral distortion, we model it with a structurally similar formula depending on the off-center radius r.

Although in this way, this kind of distortion can be easily compensated for, another aspect has to be taken into account as well. The depth distortion changes over the depth range of the camera. Therefore, the distortion does not only depend on the radius but also on the virtual depth. We think the reason for the change in the depth distortion over the depth range is that the main lens is

Fig. 5. Color-coded 3D representation of a plane captured by a Raytrix camera with a standard Nikon AF Nikkor 50mm 1:1.8D lens. The depth distortion bends the plane, with the effect becoming stronger with increasing radius from the center. The difference between the estimated depth at the center and the border is about 0.5 virtual depth units, corresponding to approximately 3mm if reprojected in front of the camera.

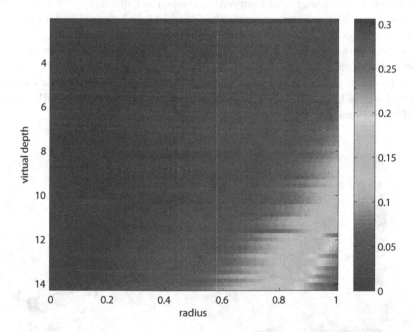

Fig. 6. Depth radial distortion for different virtual depths. The depth distortion increases in magnitude with increasing radius from the image center, but also with increasing virtual depth. The dependence on virtual depth is approximately linear.

optimized in a way that the effect of Petzval field curvature is minimal at the image plane, while the focused plenoptic camera calculates depth *behind* this plane. Hence, the main lens correction is not sufficient in this scenario.

Further experimental analysis of the depth distortion suggests that the distortion changes linearly with the virtual depth. Figure 6 visualises this behavior. Thus, we suggest calculating the depth distortion depending on the radius which is linearly adapted by the virtual depth,

$$r' = r \cdot (s_1 + v_d \cdot s_2) \tag{5}$$

$$v_u = v_d + t_1 r' + t_2 r'^2 +_3 r'^4, \tag{6}$$

where v_u is the undistorted and v_d the distorted virtual depth, respectively, while s_i are the radial and t_i the depth distortion coefficients to be determined during calibration.

3   The Calibration Model

The main idea behind the calibration is to capture a target with a known pattern (in our case a dot pattern with a known grid size – see figure 7(a)). These dots are detected in the image and their virtual depth is calculated. We now need to establish the model parameters such that the detected virtual points are equal to the projection of a model grid with the correct size.

To detect these virtual points first the virtual depth of the given scene and the refocused image have to be calculated as described by Perwaß[13]. The dot pattern has to be detected and positions have to be converted to metric distances. The pixel size is known but due to the different resolution of the depth map and the refocused image it has to be adapted.

(a) Target capture setup   (b) Linear axis used to measure the ground truth

Fig. 7. Experimental setup to (a) capture individual targets and to (b) measure the ground truth depth of a target plane

parameter		model variable	number of unknowns
intrinsic	focal length	f	1
	focus distance	h	1
	distance between MLA and sensor	b	1
	distortion offset	x_c, y_c	2
	lateral distortion	k_i, p_i	5
	depth distortion	s_i, t_i	5
ext.	rotation	R_j	3
	translation	T_j	3
	total		21

Fig. 8. Parameters to be optimized for during calibration

As in 2D calibration approaches, the unknown variables can be divided into two groups: the extrinsic and the intrinsic camera parameters, see figure 8. The former describe the position and rotation of the calibration target (or the camera, depending on the point of view), the latter the characteristics of the modeled plenoptic camera like focal length and the distance between the image plane and the modeled lens. A parameter specific to plenoptic cameras is the distance between the microlens array and the image plane (corresponding to the factor between virtual and metric depth). Due to imperfect lenses, we also have to compensate for distortion. For that, the distortion models previously introduced will be used.

The parameters are estimated by minimizing the residual between the rotated, translated and projected model points (which is equivalent to a rotated and translated camera) and the measured image points. The distortion model is applied to the measured points as they are supposed to rectify images. The residual, which depends on the unknowns summarized in figure 8, is given by

$$R = \sum_{j=1}^{C} \sum_{i=1}^{N_j} (dist(p_{ji}) - \pi_A(T_j R_j m_{ji}))^2, \qquad (7)$$

where C is the number of targets used for calibration, N_j is the number of points found on target j. For each i, j, the vector p_{ji} represents the measured point, m_{ji} the corresponding model point, R_j the rotation matrix of target j and T_j the translation matrix of that target. The projection π_A is computed according to the thin lens camera model and depends on the projection matrix A, i.e. ultimately only on the focal length f, see equation 2. $dist(\cdot)$ represents both the lateral (see section 2.3) as well as the depth distortion (see equation 6).

As can be seen in figure 8, we need 15 parameters to describe the intrinsic characteristics of the camera and 6 for the position of each target. Hence, for C targets, a total of $6C + 15$ parameters are used.

As the overall energy is non-convex and has local minima, for more robust results, the optimization proceeds in several steps. First, only the initial pose is estimated. For this, the parameters for focal length f, focus distance h and multilens array distance b are initialized with their theoretical quantities from the technical specifications of lenses and cameras. As these values are usually close to the final results, this is a good choice to start the optimization with. However, due to small deviations in manufacturing, they might not be exact, and we find that optimization is still required.

Afterwards, all model parameters except for the distortion are estimated. If a good initialization for the distance b between the MLA and the sensor is unknown and therefore might be far off, we suggest an iterative approach to determine this parameter: should the change in b be above a certain threshold after optimizing the whole model for the first time, all parameters except b are reset to the initial values. This is suggested especially for higher focal length as the algorithm might otherwise converge to local optima which are far off.

Finally, the distortion parameters are computed. As the undistorted model already tried to (erroneously) compensate for the distortion, we suggest iterating this part with a linear scaling factor to the lateral distortion, which is gradually phased out during optimization iterations.

For all optimization steps above, the Matlab implementation of the sequential quadratic programming (SQP) algorithm was used, which proved to be sufficiently accurate and efficient. Depending on the number of targets and the number of points on each of these the approximate computation time is between one to fifteen minutes.

4   Results

In order to evaluate the calibration, we use a linear axis as shown in figure 7(b) to generate ground truth data. A target showing a random noise pattern is placed perpendicular to the optical axis of the camera and moved along this axis, and we estimate the virtual depth of the captured scene. Due to possible slight skew of the target and depth distortion, a skewed paraboloid was fitted to the data and only the depth measured at the extrema of the paraboloid – i.e. the center of the distortion – was used for the virtual depth. This paraboloid was also used to estimate the depth distortion for different virtual depths. In addition, the actual real-world distance between the image sensor and the target was measured. This way, it is possible to compare the real distance between camera and object to the one obtained from calibrating the camera system.

To compare this ground truth data with the calibration parameters from the optimization, the estimated distances for various virtual depths were reprojected in front of the camera according to the thin lens model and compared to the measured data. We observe that absolute distances can generally not be estimated, which is the expected behaviour. On the one hand, the relation between the virtual depth and the relative change in metric distances is very similar if focal length, focus distance and distance to the object are increased simultaneously. On the other hand, as the lens thickness is neglected, it is not assured that the model can fit reality. Hence, there is a fixed offset of as much as $20cm$ between the calculated and the measured sensor-target distance. This error does not improve by using more points or targets.

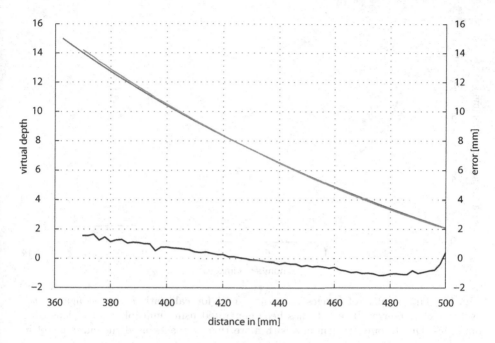

Fig. 9. A comparison shows that the measured ground truth data (green) and the data calculated from the calibration (red) correspond quite well (left axis). The difference between both graphs is plotted in black (right axis). The average relative error is only $0.36mm$, while the absolute error (see text) amounts to $245mm$. Three targets with a total of 2055 points were used for this calibration.

However, if we correct for this fixed offset and only consider the relative differences between the various virtual depths, the results fit reality very well. Figure 9 shows both the measured depth curve (green) and the shifted estimated curve (red). Two kinds of errors can be seen. On the one hand there is some noise present in the ground truth. This is due to measurement errors and the standard deviation of the estimation. On the other hand, systematic errors can be seen: the error is not completely random. This might be due to inaccuracies while identifying the marks on the targets, or because of improperly printed targets – we have experimented with this, and an error of 1-2% in the distance between the spots would explain the difference between the two curves quite closely.

We now discuss to what extend other parameters influence the quality of the calibration. First of all, the number of targets used for the calibration plays an important role. The more targets used, the better and more robust the results, see figure 10. This is not surprising, as more data generally works towards reducing the influence of deviations in measurements on the error. More input data may also be generated by using a finer dot grid on the targets. Experiments show that although the quality of the estimate improves with the number of points per target, the number of targets is generally more important. In general, we suggest using at least 3 targets with a few hundred points each.

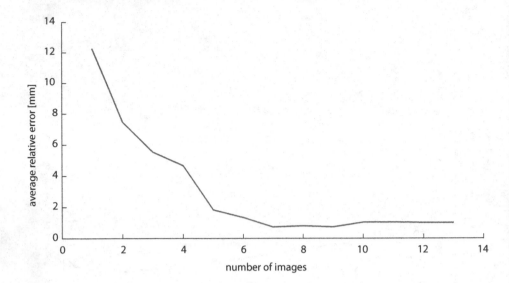

Fig. 10. The number of images of targets used for calibration plotted against the average relative error. The data has been generated using multiple camera lens combinations. Due to only few samples with more than 9 images used the curve is not as monotonous as expected.

We have compared multiple lenses on the same camera, and the results for the distance between the sensor and the MLA are robust, that is this distance is approximately the same for all lenses. Another point that is important for calibrating plenoptic cameras is that the actual focal length and focus distance change for different focal settings of the lens. As one can see in figure 11, the effective focal length of a Zeiss Makro Planar T* 100mm f/2 ZE is between $110mm$ and $130mm$ depending on the focus distance. This corresponds to the observed behaviour when mounted on a DSLR.

Furthermore, one can see that the results for the R29 are better than that of the R5. This is due to several reasons. First, because the R29 creates larger and sharper images as well as has a higher depth resolution. Second, the R5's ground truth data is noisier than that of the R29. Third, the wide angle lenses used with the R5 are more difficult to calibrate.

Figure 12 shows how depth values on a plane are corrected by the depth distortion estimation. While figure 12(a) shows initial erroneous depth estimates in virtual depth for different virtual depths and radii, correcting this data by the introduced distortion model as shown in 12(b) leads to considerably improved results. There is close to no systematic error present. This is particularly remarkable as the correction works on the whole depth range, while the targets used for the calibration only cover part of it.

camera	dot spacing	declared on lens		computed from calibration		difference
		focal length	focus distance	focal length	focus distance	
R5M		25	300	22.60	300.63	4.22
		25	500	24.59	552.55	7.21
		50	500	55.93	607.89	1.25
		50	700	51.29	741.58	7.33
		75	900	79.12	1036.24	3.09
R29M	4	50	440	55.39	444.82	1.81
	16	50	440	56.07	450.45	1.27
		50	500	64.11	491.10	1.60
		100	440	107.35	332.85	2.00
		100	500	131.37	508.46	1.13
	4	100	700	119.50	734.66	1.86
	16	100	700	120.15	741.30	1.90

Fig. 11. Declared versus calculated values depending on focal length and focus distance for different cameras and lenses and spacing of the target dots. If no dot spacing distance is given above, the values were averaged over targets with spacing between $2mm$ and $8mm$. All distances are given in millimeters. In addition, the average relative difference between the ground truth and the projected depth curve is given.

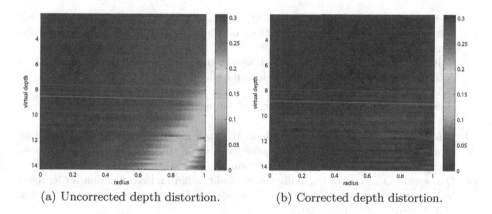

(a) Uncorrected depth distortion.   (b) Corrected depth distortion.

Fig. 12. Depth distortion over different radii and virtual depths. The depth distortion increases with higher virtual depths and radii. The error is given in virtual depth units.

5   Conclusion

We have presented a way to compute a metric calibration for plenoptic 2.0 cameras. Based upon the thin lens equation, a quadratic residual was determined, which can be minimized by standard optimization techniques. In addition, distortion is taken into account. Here, a newly developed model was presented, which corrects for depth distortion over varying virtual depths and radii.

We have tested our method on a number of different camera models available from Raytrix. The results show that although the absolute distance between an object and the camera can not be precisely estimated, the relative distances between the virtual depth levels are calculated correctly. The depth distortion model leads to an accurate correction of the data over the complete depth range, even if calibration targets only cover part of it.

In the future, we plan to extend the presented model. Investigating another lateral distortion model might be interesting, which describes the tangential distortion as a tilt of the main lens. Wang et al. [17] show that in terms of quality, this is equivalent to the standard model. However, due to the information on the tilt of the main lens, the correction of the depth distortion as well as the general depth calibration might be improved.

Another factor which has been neglected are the microlenses itself. First, calibration might improve if done for each type of microlens separately. Second, experiments suggest that distortion within the microlenses influences the depth estimation. Hence, we think that an extension of the model which can correct for the lateral distortion within the microlenses can further improve results.

References

1. Bishop, T., Favaro, P.: The light field camera: Extended depth of field, aliasing, and superresolution. IEEE Transactions on Pattern Analysis and Machine Intelligence 34(5), 972–986 (2012)
2. Bolles, R., Baker, H., Marimont, D.: Epipolar-plane image analysis: An approach to determining structure from motion. International Journal of Computer Vision 1(1), 7–55 (1987)
3. Brown, D.C.: Decentering distortion of lenses. Photometric Engineering 32(3), 444–462 (1966)
4. Criminisi, A., Kang, S., Swaminathan, R., Szeliski, R., Anandan, P.: Extracting layers and analyzing their specular properties using epipolar-plane-image analysis. Computer Vision and Image Understanding 97(1), 51–85 (2005)
5. Dansereau, D., Pizarro, O., Williams, S.: Calibration and rectification for lenselet-based plenoptic cameras. In: Proc. International Conference on Computer Vision and Pattern Recognition (2013)
6. Ives, F.: Parallax stereogram and process of making same (April 1903)
7. Kolmogorov, V., Zabih, R.: Multi-camera scene reconstruction via graph cuts. In: Heyden, A., Sparr, G., Nielsen, M., Johansen, P. (eds.) ECCV 2002, Part III. LNCS, vol. 2352, pp. 82–96. Springer, Heidelberg (2002)
8. Lippmann, G.: Épreuves réversibles donnant la sensation du relief. J. Phys. Theor. Appl. 7(1), 821–825 (1908)
9. Lumsdaine, A., Georgiev, T.: The focused plenoptic camera. In: Proc. IEEE International Conference on Computational Photography, pp. 1–8 (2009)
10. Nayar, S., Nakagawa, Y.: Shape from focus. IEEE Transactions on Pattern Analysis and Machine Intelligence 16(8), 824–831 (1994)
11. Perez, N., Luke, J.: Simultaneous estimation of super-resolved depth and all-in-focus images from a plenoptic camera. In: 3DTV Conference: The True Vision-Capture, Transmission and Display of 3D Video, pp. 1–4. IEEE (2009)

12. Perwass, C., Wietzke, L.: The next generation of photography (2010),
    http://www.raytrix.de
13. Perwass, C., Wietzke, L.: Single lens 3D camera with extended depth-of-field. In:
    Proc. SPIE 8291, Human Vision and Electronic Imaging XVII (2012)
14. Riedl, M.: Optical design fundamentals for infrared systems. SPIE Optical engi-
    neering Press (2001)
15. Svoboda, T., Martinec, D., Pajdla, T.: A convenient multicamera self-calibration
    for virtual environments. Presence: Teleoper. Virtual Environ. 14(4), 407–422
    (2005)
16. Vaish, V., Wilburn, B., Joshi, N., Levoy, M.: Using plane + parallax for calibrating
    dense camera arrays. In: Proc. International Conference on Computer Vision and
    Pattern Recognition (2004)
17. Wang, J., Shi, F., Zhang, J., Liu, Y.: A new calibration model of camera lens
    distortion. Pattern Recognition 41(2), 607–615 (2008)
18. Wanner, S., Fehr, J., Jähne, B.: Generating EPI representations of 4D light fields
    with a single lens focused plenoptic camera. In: Bebis, G. (ed.) ISVC 2011, Part I.
    LNCS, vol. 6938, pp. 90–101. Springer, Heidelberg (2011)
19. Wanner, S., Goldluecke, B.: Globally consistent depth labeling of 4D light fields.
    In: Proc. International Conference on Computer Vision and Pattern Recognition,
    pp. 41–48 (2012)
20. Zhang, Z.: A flexible new technique for camera calibration. IEEE Transactions on
    Pattern Analysis and Machine Intelligence (2000)

Author Index